COURTLY CONTRADICTIONS

Figurae

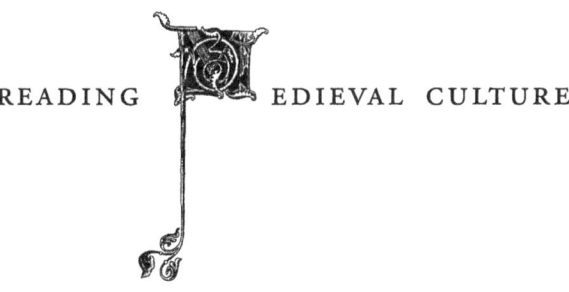

READING MEDIEVAL CULTURE

ADVISORY BOARD

Daniel Boyarin, Kevin Brownlee,
Marina Scordilis Brownlee, Jacqueline Cerquiglini-Toulet,
Rachel Jacoff, Sarah Kay, V. A. Kolve,
Jan-Dirk Müller, Stephen G. Nichols,
Jeffrey Schnapp, Karla Taylor, David Wallace,
Rainer Warning, Michel Zink

COURTLY CONTRADICTIONS

THE EMERGENCE OF THE LITERARY
OBJECT IN THE TWELFTH CENTURY

Sarah Kay

Stanford University Press, Stanford, California 2001

Stanford University Press
Stanford, California

© 2001 by the Board of Trustees of the
Leland Stanford Junior University

Printed in the United States of America
On acid-free, archival-quality paper

Library of Congress Cataloging-in-Publication Data

Kay, Sarah.
   Courtly contradictions : the emergence of the literary object
in the twelfth century / Sarah Kay.
      p.   cm. — (Figurae)
   Includes bibliographical data and index.
   ISBN 0-8047-3079-2 (alk. paper)
   1. Literature, Medieval—History and criticism.
2. Courtly love in literature.   I. Title.
II. Figurae (Stanford, Calif.)
PN682.C6 K39   2001
809'.933543—dc21   2001020685

Original Printing 2001
Last figure below indicates year of this printing:
10   09   08   07   06   05   04   03   02   01

Typeset by James P. Brommer in 11/14 Garamond

FOR COLIN

Preface and acknowledgments

This book contains a variety of material, some of it quite technical and difficult, which will be familiar to some readers but unfamiliar to others. I have tried to explain my own understanding of it as I go along, but inevitably these explanations will seem oversimplified to some while remaining challenging to others. To the first, I can only apologize and suggest they skip the parts they find tiresome. To the second, a few words of reassurance. I have used the Introduction to expound the role and place of contradiction in medieval and psychoanalytical thought. The Introduction, then, contains the intellectual foundations of what follows. However, it contains more information than a reader interested primarily in literary analysis will need in order to understand subsequent chapters. The Introduction is not "introductory" in the sense that you need to understand everything in it before moving on. Indeed, mindful that some readers will want to consult this book selectively, I have sought always to redefine the theoretical framework that is immediately relevant to the discussion in hand. As a result, certain concepts—sublimation, for instance—are explained more than once. This has been done deliberately, not only because of readers' habits of selective reading, but because overlapping explanations can actually be helpful to the writer as well as to readers in strengthening one's understanding of difficult ideas. Of course I would much prefer for people to read the book all the way through, because it presents a continuous argument. Its essentials can be found summarized in the Conclusion, 300–303.

Lacan is an abstruse—indeed, sometimes an impossible—writer. In presenting my own understanding of those parts of his teaching which I think are illuminating for medieval literature, I have, for the most part, done just that. It would (I thought) be tedious to preface each explanation with reminders of how difficult, ambiguous, etc., the material is, and therefore how tentative, provisional, etc., my interpretation is. By saying once, emphatically, that I think he is infuriatingly difficult and slippery, I hope that can now be taken as read throughout the book.

An important dimension of the argument presented here is that it is historical or, at least, literary–historical. For this reason, the first mention of any author or text is accompanied by a suggested dating. However, dates are relatively unmemorable; so rather than keep repeating them, I have included an Appendix which gives approximate dates for all the texts or authors discussed at any length. It is, in any case, the chronology of texts relative to one another, rather than their date in absolute terms, which is important to my argument.

The literary texts from which I cite have been edited by scholars from all over the world and over the span of at least a century. Although I have always respected the orthography of the editions cited, I have standardized their punctuation in two ways: direct speech is represented using modern American punctuation; and I do not use capital letters at the beginning of lines of verse unless the syntax requires it.

I wish to thank the following. Boydell and Brewer for permission to reuse material previously published as "The Sublime Body of the Martyr: Violence in Early Romance Saints' Lives," in *Violence in Medieval Society*, edited by Richard W. Kaeuper (Woodbridge: Boydell and Brewer, 2000), 3–20. For financial support and periods of research leave: the University of Cambridge, Girton College Cambridge, and the Arts and Humanities Research Board. For help with the content: Colin Davis, Matthew Bardell, Mathilda Bruckner, Tom Caldin, Penny Eley, Simon Gaunt, Miranda Griffin, Peter Haidu, Ruth Harvey, James Helgeson, Sylvia Huot, Peggy McCracken, Dominic Selwood, Ian Short, Jocelyn Wogan-Browne, and a great number of long-suffering students and conference audiences at home and abroad.

Contents

Introduction 1

1. The plait of contradictoriness in twelfth-century texts 40

2. "High" and "low": a conduit of contradictoriness 72

3. At the edges of reason 109

4. From the riddle of the subject to the riddle of the object: the Occitan *devinalh* and the *romans antiques* 143

5. The Virgin and the Lady: the abject and the object in Adgar's *Gracial* and the *Lais* attributed to Marie de France 179

6. The sublime body: the "zone between the two deaths," belief, and enjoyment in hagiography, the *romans antiques*, and *Cligés* 216

7. Sublime and perverse objects: love and its contradictions in *Yvain* and *Partonopeu de Blois* 259

Conclusion 300

Appendix. Approximate chronology of works or authors discussed 315

Notes 319

Works cited 351

Index 375

COURTLY CONTRADICTIONS

Introduction

The success of courtly literature in the twelfth century is an astounding phenomenon. The interlinked themes of courtly love, courtly living, and chivalry, which seem to burst out of nowhere in the early 1100s, come to dominate the genres of lyric and romance around the middle of the century and enjoy extraordinary cultural prestige by the end of it. The apparently irresistible advance of courtly literature is the more remarkable given that its favored tone, far from being one of brash arrogance or insolent appropriation, is decorous, restrained, even reticent. This is an elite movement, firmly invested in the social and moral gulf dividing the refined (*courtois*) from their antithesis (the *vilain*); but the lure of exclusivity seems to have ensured that the class of the self-styled *courtois* would ineluctably expand, so that courtliness spilled out further and further from the small, local courts that first fostered it and eventually merged with the broad stream of Western culture. Boosted by nineteenth-century fascination with the medieval inheritance, courtliness has diffused its way into our own modern rhetorical, literary, and sexual practices. So it is that our continuing interest in medieval courtliness and courtly love is also a concern with the history of our own social and sexual identities and the tensions that inevitably flare between them.

Courtly literature inaugurates enduring themes, but its significance as a cultural innovation is equally far-reaching. At the beginning of the twelfth century, such vernacular texts as exist devote themselves to didactic purposes of one kind or another, mainly edification and religious instruction, or the cementing of a common history. By the end of the century, however, a literature of public entertainment has been created for the first time in medieval Europe. Although its links with didacticism are not altogether severed, the literary "object" is henceforth established as a source of pleasure and diversion. The production and consumption of literary artifacts in the vernacular is a new and prestigious social institution whose importance—because it survives to this day—can be too easily overlooked.

The origins and rise of courtly literature have been the object of sustained investigation for a hundred years or more. What I believe is different about the approach adopted in this book is that it studies what has previously been seen primarily as an historical problem from a theoretical viewpoint: that of contradiction. I argue that contradiction is central to the makeup of courtly literature, to the intellectual environment which gave rise to it, and to its critical reception today. I thereby recast investigation into the origins and development of courtly literature in these terms: Why are medieval authors and audiences, and modern readers and thinkers, so absorbed with contradiction? What is it about the courtly text that makes it foster contradiction, and why are we so excited by it? And what circumstances, in the twelfth century, produced just that kind of contradictory text which would continue to influence the subjectivities of readers in the twentieth?

Why attribute such a key role to contradiction? This project started from an observation whose implications grew the more I thought about it, namely that what crucially differentiates various ways of understanding courtly texts is the way different critics react to the presence and role of contradiction within them. Courtly texts exhibit a particular pleasure in contradiction. The rhetoric of the lyric favors figures of speech involving paired contraries, according to which the lover is both joyful and downcast, exalted and abject. In courtly romances there are likewise many passages which elaborately explore oppositions. Both genres also exhibit the widespread use of contradiction as a figure of thought. The love lyric, for example, has long been seen as balancing desire to possess the lady against willing renunciation, a contradiction which Spitzer famously termed "le paradoxe amoureux" (*L'Amour lointain*, 1–2). Love in courtly romances may be represented as simultaneously sensual and spiritual, normative and transgressive, secret and known. The ecstatic and, indeed, frequently religious imagery of both lyric and romance invites comparison with religious texts such as miracles and saints' lives. These too are frequently patterned around major paradoxes, such as that loss is gain, death is the key to life, the lowly are exalted, and the apparently powerful are humiliated. Some texts are ambiguous between religious and erotic interpretations, apparently deliberately exposing themselves to conflicting interpretations. This is particularly true of early troubadour poetry, but some romances have also been read both as secular works and as religious allegories. Critics cannot fail to respond to this overwhelming fascination with the contradictory. And yet there is surprisingly little discussion of why one view of contradiction is espoused over another, or why contradiction is so central to the composition and reception of these courtly texts.[1] It is as though critics seek out their contradictoriness only to look straight *through* it, rather than *at* it. The centrality of contradiction as a critical issue is too obvious to be visible and lies too much at the heart of interpretation to be itself interpreted.

This Introduction will examine the intellectual background of courtly poetry in medieval thinking about contradiction and then the role played by contradiction in contemporary theory. This will provide the opportunity to refine the understanding of the various kinds of structures and operation which the term "contradiction" is used to cover. First, however, I will present two brief case studies which show how different readings of major texts reflect critics' differing reactions to the contradictory patterns they contain. The first—a survey of some critical reactions to the poetry of Bernart de Ventadorn—illustrates how contradiction is often used as a springboard to interpretation without itself being the focus of investigation. A range of different kinds of phenomena—rhetorical, historical, psychological—fall pell-mell under the heading of contradiction. The second—a selection of responses to the *Chevalier de la Charrete* by Chrétien de Troyes—shows to what an extent our current critical vocabulary can be used precisely in order to close down contradiction or avoid confronting it.

Reading contradiction in courtly texts I: Bernart de Ventadorn

It is impossible to overlook the centrality of contradictoriness to the poetry of Bernart de Ventadorn, a major troubadour.[2] As Pierre Bec ("L'Antithèse poétique") observes, Bernart's rhetoric continually draws on elaborate antitheses such as the following:

Introduction 4

> Tostems sec joi ir' e dolors
> e tostems ira jois e bes,
> et eu non cre, si jois no fos,
> c'om ja saubes d'ira que.s es.
> (XXXVI, 41–44)[3]

> Distress and suffering always follow joy, and joy and well-being always follow distress, and I don't believe, if it weren't for joy, that one would know what distress is.

For Bec, these notions of "joy" and "suffering" are in perpetual tension in Bernart's poetry; they are the poles of an opposition that is simultaneously formal (expressed through figures of speech) and thematic. Because this "contradictory vision" (107) is also found in other poets, Bec ascribes it to what he calls "a rhetorical tradition which transcends any possible subjectivity in the poem" (108): antithesis is part of the impersonal, formal "register" (to use Zumthor's term) in which lyric poetry is cast and to which alone it refers. Bec describes this register as "dialectical" in the sense that the antitheses give rise to an inferred middle ground where the opposing terms interact and exchange their values: "ill-defined shadow zones where joy becomes painful and pain becomes joy" (108). This interaction results in paradoxes such as that death is sweet and suffering is to be embraced. Drawing on a formulation of Dragonetti's (*La Technique poétique*, 55), Bec summarizes: "the negative becomes positive and vice versa" (108). The fundamental opposition *joi–dolor* incorporates hosts of others (success–downfall, life–death, loved–unloved) whose terms, thus sucked into convergence, acquire what Bec delightfully calls "semantic elasticity" (119). Bec stresses that this passage of terms into their contrary is not a narrative structure ("first happy, then sad"), but a formal and intellectual one endowed with what he sees as a vital and incantational dynamic (137). Clearly Bec's reading of Bernart is shaped by the formalist tradition.[4] This aesthetic leads him to base his account of contradiction in Bernart's surface rhetoric, stressing its impersonality and attributing to it a structuring role as generator of a whole series of homologous paradoxes.

David Carlson's study ("Losing Control") of Bernart's most famous song "Can vei la lauzeta mover" (XXXI) is, like Bec's, broadly structuralist in inspiration, but draws attention to "deep" rather than surface phenomena. It is based on the semiotic square of Greimas, which plots four positions interrelated by contradiction and contrariety (I will be defining these terms shortly). Carlson argues that the song is built on implied contradiction between (on the one hand) loss of control and loss of self and (on the other hand) self-control and self-possession. These latter are present only by inference; they constitute "an unmentioned norm of behavior, of self-control and self-possession, in view of which the behavior and situation of the lark and speaker are intelligible" (272). In contrast to this ideological norm, the poet's eccentric condition is expressed through what Carlson (questionably) identifies as the contraries of ecstasy and death, which themselves contrast with their implied opposites, normality and life. Discerning the same "contrariety" of ecstasy and death in medieval mystical writing, Carlson maintains that its erotic treatment in the lyric enters into the same dialectic as occurs in the religious context. By "dialectic" he means that the opposition of ecstasy and death is mediated and resolved through the emergence of a third term, the theme of the poem, namely loss of control/loss of self. Carlson states that his interpretation resembles Bec's, but actually their conceptions of dialectic are quite different because for Carlson contradiction is mediated by recourse to a superordinate term or "hyponym," whereas for Bec, antithetical terms coincide in paradox.[5]

The term "dialectic" is also invoked by Erich Köhler in his interpretation of "Can vei."[6] The poem serves to illustrate his basic contentions about the Occitan lyric: spoken in the interests of *joven* (youth), it is addressed to a heterogeneous courtly class comprising nobles and lesser knights. It unites them by transposing to the level of the "paradoxe amoureux" (the erotic "have and have not" described by Spitzer), a celebration of nobility as *both* a claim to social advancement justified by merit *and* a willingness to renounce reward as an expression of gentility. Contradiction in the lyric, then, derives first and foremost from the conflicted reality of political life, in which the lesser knights feel that they both are, and are not, integrated to the nobility; and that they both should, and needn't, be materially rewarded. These contradictions in the knights' historical situation are seemingly harmonized (Köhler's term is "mediated") by the ideology of love and by the contrivances of poetry, but they nonetheless remain perceptible in the verbal substance of song.

Köhler's preparedness to envision contradiction as an attribute of material reality rather than of thought is what marks his criticism as Marxist (see Wilde, *Marx and Contradiction*). His method of reading involves shifting contradictions upwards through successive layers of mediation (*Vermittlungsschichten*) in a way that presents analogies with Carlson's notion of dialectic. The point for Köhler, however, is that these layers, far from being higher levels of meaning, are so many mystifications of an underlying reality; for Köhler, furthermore, unlike for Carlson, no resolution is ever achieved. Thus although Carlson reads "up" the contradictions he discerns in order to arrive at the poem's "true" theme, Köhler reads "downward" to uncover the poem's material origins.

Köhler is a major theorist of literature; he cannot be faulted for failing to expound his method.[7] In discussing "Can vei" he acknowledges his debt to the formalist tradition of Bec ("'Can vei,'" 452) with whom he shares attentiveness to a text's formal surface patterning. Unlike Bec, however, Köhler sees contradiction as operating most significantly not in rhetorical ornament but in underlying political circumstance. Thus although for Bec contradiction is one of a series of formal conventions which efface subjectivity from the text, for Köhler it is a clue to the historicity of subjects in a class torn by conflicting conditions.

The psychoanalytical approach to Bernart's poetry adopted by Jean-Charles Huchet (*L'Amour discourtois*, 182 ff.) starts, like Carlson's semiotic and Köhler's Marxist readings, from a contrast between what is manifest and what latent in the text; like these critics, Huchet is less concerned with the contradictions of surface rhetoric that attract Bec than with underlying contradictions that generate Bernart's peculiar fusion of the poetic and the erotic. Like Köhler, Huchet in no way neglects the surface rhetoric of the lyric; but it is read by him as symptomatic of the major aporias of psychoanalytical thought, which turn, for Huchet, a disciple here of Lacan, on the irresolvable impasse between body and language and the impossibility of figuring the sexual relation.[8] In Bernart, for Huchet, this impasse results in repeated scenarios of disavowal.[9] Huchet suggests the importance of the gaze in Bernart as a means of looking *elsewhere* than at the genitals (thus avoiding the contradiction whereby woman is/is not castrated). This poetry, he argues, needs to make the body less corporeal by placing it off-limits; the lover thereby comes to resemble the mystic. Huchet represents "Can vei" in particular as an instance of quasimystical self-effacement (195–97). The approach to contradiction adopted by Huchet is formally similar to Köhler's in that both rely on simultaneous affirmation and negation (is/is not) rather than on the terms in opposition (joy–pain, ecstasy–death) explored by Bec and Carlson.[10] For Huchet, however, this contradiction characterizes psychic processes that are "metahistorical" (*L'Amour discourtois*, 40), whereas for Köhler it captures the particularity of material existence at a specific historical turning point.

My final examples of reading contradiction in Bernart de Ventadorn's poetry are taken from the writings of R. Howard Bloch. Bloch's argument in *Etymologies and Genealogies* is that textuality is a privileged site of anthropological investigation. Of the other critics surveyed here, he most closely resembles Bec in his concentration on surface rhetoric. But whereas Bec sees antithesis as a dynamic that generates intermediate meanings— extending a paradoxical "both–and" between the two poles of an opposition—Bloch discovers "a static map of conflicting images, emotions, and states held in constant tension with each other, but without the prospect of resolution" (119). Such "self-canceling opposites" (120) have the effect of closing the poem in upon itself (123), and as each term generates its counterterm, so the text's meaning is endlessly self-referring: "Poetic closure and psychic closure work hand in hand to create a pervasive atmosphere of entrapment" (123–24). In Bloch's ingenious reading, the formalist tradition of Bec has taken a deconstructive turn. The textual aporias thrown up by this network of verbal oppositions encapsulate, for him, the problematic of "courtliness." For both Köhler and Huchet, by contrast, the nub of contradictoriness lies outside language rather than primarily within it.

In his later book *Medieval Misogyny*, Bloch offers another reading of "Can vei" (146–48). Here again the logic of contradiction is perceived as lying on the surface of the text. Now, however, rather than confining the text in the self-canceling rigidity discerned in *Etymologies*, this logic assumes a specific propositional content. Bloch represents the singer as caught in paradoxes of knowledge and ignorance, utterance and silence, which reflect the impossibility to which "courtly love" is condemned as a result of love and language being radically incommensurable: "There is no way of loving that does not imply the incongruity of persistent singing about dissatisfaction that 'Can vei la lauzeta mover' makes explicit" (147). The discreet pressure of psychoanalytical thought is discernible in this invocation of sexuality as impossible, but neither here nor elsewhere (to my knowledge) in his writings on courtly love does Bloch make this explicit. The studies of Bernart de Ventadorn contained in these two books treat the troubadour's contradictory rhetoric in similar yet significantly divergent ways.

The point of this brief survey, which gives some indication of the range and quality of troubadour criticism, is simply to point out that what these critics have in common is, at the same time, precisely what separates them. All take as their starting point the importance of contradiction in Bernart's poetry, and yet once it has been sighted, it ceases to be at the forefront of their attention, becoming instead the springboard for the kind of criticism each critic is drawn to write. By the same token, the critical approach of each writer clearly influences which kinds of contradiction are seen as most significant, and even what forms those contradictions are said to take. It is, I submit, a contradiction deserving further study that the stimulus to interpretation should also constitute a blind spot within it.

Reading contradiction in courtly texts II: Le Chevalier de la Charrete

Many readers of Chrétien's *Lancelot* or *Chevalier de la Charrete* have similarly set off from the recognition of contradiction and thus effectively turned their backs on it. This romance has, not surprisingly, been the object of critical approaches similar to those which I have just documented with respect to Bernart de Ventadorn. For example, Frappier's famous review article ("Sur un procès," 77) invokes an "oscillation" between the poles of fleshly and spiritual love which recalls the way Bec analyzes Bernart's "dialectic." (Frappier does not specifically address his remarks to the *Charrete* but this seems to be among the texts he has in mind.) Köhler's enormously rich and difficult study of Arthurian romance in *L'Aventure chevaleresque* contains detailed and explicit theorization of contradiction in the genre as a whole, and in the *Charrete* in particular, from a perspective similar to that which he adopts in reading the lyric.[11] The major psychoanalytical reading of the romance by Charles Méla underlines how "ambivalence lies at the heart of all the high points of the narrative" (*La Reine et le Graal,* 282). Influenced by Kristevan semiotics, Mathilda Tomaryn Bruckner offers a complex and sophisticated view of the *Charrete* as problematizing both truth and meaning, because the fiction proposes not opposition but the intertwining of contradiction in a way that resists separation: "the rumors about Lancelot as cart-rider are both true *and* false, Bademagu's love for his son is both good *and* bad, Lancelot is the worst *and* the best at the tournament, love makes Lancelot appear as an adulterer who betrays his lord and king *and* as the best of Arthur's knights because he is the most faithful lover of his Queen" (*Shaping Romance*, 107).[12] But the case of the *Charrete* differs from that of Bernart in that critics have evinced so much disquiet at the potential for contradiction between the text's erotic and religious discourses that they have actively sought to minimize or suppress it. Such critical terms as "parodic," "ironic," or "symbolic" have often been deployed (at least partly) in a way which seeks to contain or disguise this disquiet.[13]

This seems to be the pattern of C. S. Lewis's classic study of the romance in *The Allegory of Love*. Lewis first identifies the scene where Lancelot reverently withdraws from Guenevere's chamber as an extreme instance of "the irreligion of the religion of love," a contradiction Lewis finds "revolting" (29). Yet by the end of this chapter, he has found a means of neutralizing his disgust by interpreting the relations between love and religion as parodic and as a seat of analogy or figuration: "That very element of parodied or, at least, of imitated religion which we find so blasphemous, is rather an expression of the divorce between the two. They are so completely two that analogies naturally arise between them: hence comes a strange kind of reduplication of experience. [. . .] Love is, *in saeculo*, as God is, in eternity" (42). Naming the space between two conflicting discourses in the *Charrete* "parody" rather than "contradiction" is a recourse adopted by several subsequent critics. In "Profanity and its Purpose," for example, Roy Owen argues that the liberation of the prisoners from Gorre in the *Charrete* parodies the Harrowing of Hell as narrated by the Gospel of Nicodemus. After hesitating as to the interpretation to be placed on such a parody, he pleads for "a burlesque intention" on Chrétien's part, with Lancelot as "a mock-heroic figure" (47).

D. W. Robertson Jr. offers a particularly clear case of arguing from apparent contradiction to ultimate unity of literary intent. For him, "The incoherence of the surface materials is almost essential to the formation of the abstract pattern, for if the surface materials—the concrete elements in the figures—were consistent or spontaneously satisfying in an emotional way, there would be no stimulus to seek something beyond them" (*Preface* to *Chaucer*, 56). For Robertson, the unifying concept invoked to "satisfy" his reading of the *Charrete* is that of irony. The point of the religious imagery in the *Charrete* is, he thinks, "to make the significance of Lancelot's misdeeds apparent and to emphasize the extent of the inversion to which a submission of the reason to sensuality may lead" (452). It is, in other words, to be interpreted ironically as marking the depths of Lancelot's misconception of erotic love while also indicating the truth to which that love blinds him. (The Augustinian thinking which underpins Robertson's interpretation is discussed below.) Although subsequent critics have sought to distance themselves from "Robertsonianism,"[14] Robertson's empowerment of the reader to discern such radical irony has proved widely attractive. An illustration is Green's monumental *Irony in Medieval Romance*, which also embraces the concept of irony in the *Charrete* as a clerical author's attack on misconceived secular values (in Keu's trial, 87–88).

A final example of a critical term whose deployment may serve to disarm the problematic of contradiction is that of "symbolism." Whereas for Robertson the religious motifs in the *Charrete* denounce love as idolatrous and are to be read ironically, Ribard takes those same religious motifs at face value and reads the secular plot as "symbolic" of the Christian doctrine to which they point: "It is the history of human salvation which the author invites us to rediscover beneath the transparent veil of a chivalric and courtly 'adventure'" (*Chrétien de Troyes*, 22). In this light, Lancelot's love for Guenevere is radically reread as a messianic redemption of the human soul, whereas her love for him signifies the mystical love of the human soul for Christ (33, 37, 47–48): "The spiritual experience that Guenevere will undergo—this encounter with divine love by means of the Christ-Lancelot—is a means of access to a higher truth" (48). This reading strategy, like Robertson's, is remarkably empowering, and although few critics would follow Ribard in the claims which he makes for the *Charrete*, the attraction of symbolic or allegorical reading still persists.[15] Even recent studies of the *Charrete* which owe nothing to Ribard's religious commitment may be prepared to unite the romance's conflicting discourses into an expression of a single ideological concern, such as women's desire or gender identity (Krueger, *Women Readers*, 51–52; Gaunt, *Gender and Genre*, 96–97). As David Hult has shown in his important essay "Author/Narrator/Speaker," duality and duplicity are uncomfortable aspects of the experience of reading the *Charrete*. His own solution to their presence—the hypothesis that Godefroi de Leigni is a pseudonym for Chrétien—allows him both to maintain and dissolve such duality by subdividing one "author" into two distinct "narrators."

The purpose of this brief survey is to show how some of the terminology used by scholars earlier this century can be traced, in some instances at least, to disquiet with the coexistence of religious and erotic motifs in the *Charrete*. Although the critics who responded in this way are all motivated by Christian conviction, similar terminology and reading strategies are used by later writers whose reading stance appears secular or agnostic, or whose commitments lie in quite different directions. I do not mean to suggest that terms such as "parody" are in any way less valuable because they respond to, while also in some degree evading, the potential contradictoriness of courtly texts. These terms have become part of our general critical baggage for approaching courtly literature, and we could not manage without them. My point is simply that the critical vocabulary evolved for writing on courtly romance is bound up with contradictoriness, and that one of the consequences of using it can be that we defuse or neutralize the problems which that contradictoriness presents. Once again, contradiction can serve as a light to interpretation while itself remaining in darkness.

The context of composition: medieval views of contradiction

An obvious way to seek to illumine the contradictoriness of courtly texts is to examine the intellectual context of the twelfth century, and doing so will in turn refine our understanding of the term "contradiction," which so far I have been using loosely to cover a range of types of clash of signification.

Contradiction results from the various structures of opposition which are inherent in language. Defining the exact nature, scope, and implication of these different kinds of contradiction was at the forefront of academic life in the twelfth century. This was a period of intense interest in the science of logic, or "dialectic," as it is usually called by medieval logicians. We have dozens of surviving treatises on dialectic from the twelfth century, as opposed to only one on rhetoric (by Matthew of Vendôme).[16] In the 1120s and 1130s, it was as a result of a determination to recover a wider corpus of logical works that Boethius's translations into Latin of Aristotle's *Prior Analytics*,

Topics, and *Sophistici elenchi* (Sophistical Refutations), were searched for and recovered in the West.[17] The *Posterior Analytics* followed shortly after in a translation by James of Venice, but it was not widely studied in medieval Europe. Until then, the logical canon had been dominated by Aristotle's *Categories* and *De interpretatione* and Porphyry's *Isagoge* ("Introduction"), also in Latin translations by Boethius, plus Boethius's own works on syllogistic and topical logic. The discovery of the wider Aristotelian corpus gave rise to the so-called New Logic, attesting to intellectual effervescence in scholastic milieux, fueling interest in the refinements of argumentation for its own sake but also provoking a conservative reaction in favor of the Old Logic. In 1159 John of Salisbury, Anglo-Norman humanist and friend of Thomas Becket, wrote the *Metalogicon*, which recalls his experiences as a student at the many schools of logic that were thriving in Paris. A partisan of the Old Logic, he regrets that dialectic is becoming a discipline in its own right rather than a tool with which to approach other disciplines. The *Metalogicon* vividly portrays the central role of dialectic in twelfth-century education, the lively competition for students among Parisian teachers, and the attraction which the New Logic exercised for aspiring intellectuals. In the twelfth century, indeed, dialectic "achieved in Western Europe a pre-eminence within the field of secular learning that it had never achieved before in the West and that it would never achieve again."[18]

For these intellectuals, the most influential and prestigious tradition of thinking about contradiction was that of Aristotle, who identifies its fundamental structure as "opposition." Aristotle defines opposition in this way: "I speak of statements as opposite when they affirm and deny the same thing of the same thing" (*De interpretatione*, 17a, 34–35/§6/27).[19] Scrutinizing the impact of different instances of opposition, Aristotle points out that some do not contradict the affirmation they relate to; they actually assert its contrary. You can disagree with someone, contradict him in the sense of not thinking as he does, without having to maintain the opposite, or the contrary, of what he thinks. The proposition "every man is white" is contradicted by the proposition "not every man is white," but "every man is white"–"no man is white" are contrary propositions (*De interpretatione*, 17b, 2–7/§7/27). Here and elsewhere Aristotle devotes meticulous care to distinguishing the scope of an opposition.

Fundamental to the argumentative system which Aristotle constructs on the basis of these observations is the principle of noncontradiction, whereby neither contradictory nor contrary statements can be true of the same thing at the same time. Aristotle enunciates this most clearly in the *Metaphysics*: "The firmest principle of all is one about which it is impossible to be mistaken, for necessarily that sort of principle is most knowable [. . .]: It is impossible for the same thing both to belong and not to belong at the same time to the same thing and in the same respect."[20] The *Metaphysics* became available to medieval readers in the course of the twelfth century,[21] but the standard reference for Aristotle's teaching on the principle of noncontradiction remained the *De interpretatione*, §§6–end. In the course of a long dissection of the oppositions involved in contraries and contradictories, Aristotle considers between what pairs of propositions it can be contended that, if one is true, the other is false. Contrariety is more negating than contradiction. For example, if a man is unjust, this implies he is not just; but if he is not just, this does not mean he is positively unjust. The Aristotelian principle of noncontradiction applies *a fortiori*, then, to contrariety: "For contraries are those which enclose their opposites; and while these latter may possibly be said truly by the same person, it is not possible for contraries to hold of the same thing at the same time" (*De intepretatione*, 24b, 7–9/§14/38).

In §10 of the *De intepretatione*, relations of contradiction are mapped onto what was to become known as the "square of opposition," an elementary logical cell linking four interrelated propositions in such a way as to authorize a series of inferences. (It will be familiar to some readers today through the "semiotic square" of Greimas.[22]) Aristotle's examples here rely on systematic negation of the elements of a proposition so as to produce four variant forms of it. But the canonical form in which the "square of opposition" was used in medieval Europe used the combination of contraries and contradictories which Aristotle had outlined in §7; the example given below is from Apuleius, the first logician actually to present the square diagrammatically (Gersh, *Concord in Discourse*, 167). Following Greimas's usage, I have labeled its four terms s_1, s_2, $-s_1$ and $-s_2$. s_1 and s_2 are contraries, and $-s_1$ and $-s_2$ are the contradictories which correspond to them; $-s_1$ and $-s_2$ are also contrary with respect to one another and are known as "subcontraries." The stronger form of contradiction is thus placed on the horizontal axes and its weaker form is expressed via the diagonals (Figure 1).

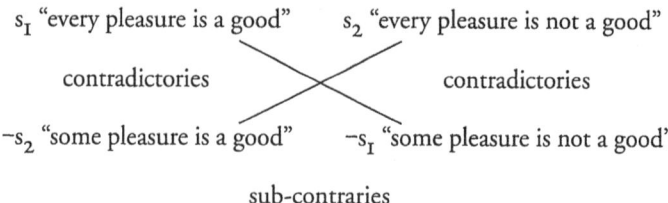

Figure 1. The square of opposition (Gersh, *Concord in Discourse*, 169)

The principle of noncontradiction enables arguments to be framed by referring to each of the sides of the square and its diagonals. The two vertical sides authorize inference of the kind s_1 implies $-s_2$ (e.g., "every pleasure is a good" implies "some particular pleasure is a good"); s_2 correspondingly implies $-s_1$. Note that these inferences are valid in the downward direction only. The top horizontal axis presents propositions both of which cannot simultaneously be true: if either one is true, then the other is false. However, depending on circumstance, it is possible for both to be false. As for the bottom axis, that of the subcontraries, both cannot be false but both may, depending on circumstance, be true. The diagonals of the square, which present relations between contradictory terms, convey a further set of inferences. If s_1 is true, then $-s_1$ is false, and vice versa. Variations on the makeup of this square and the arguments which could be construed by using it were a basic part of training in medieval logic; Boethius, for instance, includes discussion of it in his *Commentary on Aristotle's Categories*, I, 169B ff., and a series of twelfth-century examples which, like Apuleius's, focus on the relations between universal and particular statements can be found in the *Abbreviatio Montana* (§8c), an elementary textbook of the Old Logic from the school founded by Abelard on the Mont Sainte Geneviève.[23]

In the *Categories*, 11b, 18 ff./§10/18, Aristotle specifies the four forms which opposition can take:

> Things are said to be opposed to one another in four ways: as relatives or as contraries or as privation and possession or as affirmation and negation. Examples of things thus opposed (to give a rough idea) are: as relatives, the double and the half; as contraries, the good and the bad; as privation and possession, blindness and sight; as affirmation and negation, he is sitting–he is not sitting.

These distinctions make possible reflections not only on truth and falsehood, but also on the nature and direction of change. Under certain circumstances, contraries can change one into the other (something hot into something cold, for example[24]); possession may be transformed into privation but not usually vice versa (the bald man will not recover his hair). Furthermore, some kinds of opposition contain a middle ground, such as gray between black and white, or the intermediate distance between near and far. These considerations all have implications for assessing how far one proposition contradicts another to which it is opposed. Aristotle returns to these distinctions in the *Prior Analytics* in the course of arguments about the "middle term" (beginning 25b, 26 ff./I, 4/41 ff.). The "middle term" is the point of intersection of the various propositions in a syllogism; for example, if all men are animals and all creatures capable of learning grammar are men, then all creatures capable of learning grammar are animals: "men" here is the middle term which is found in both "animal" and "creatures capable of learning grammar."[25] Aristotle's presentation, already sufficiently intimidating with his introductory examples, becomes truly virtuoso when the changes are rung on all the various patterns of opposition and their concomitant conditions of noncontradiction (e.g., in 50b, 5 ff./I, 45–46/81–84).

The term "dialectic" was sometimes used to designate not the whole of logic but its application to practical contexts in the form of prescribed argumentative strategies (or "topics"). A topic, says Boethius, is the "seat" (*sedes*) of an argument, the "place" (*locus*) from which it is drawn (*De topicis differentiis*, 1184D, 16–17/II/46).[26] The New Logic added to Boethius's *De topicis differentiis* the *Topics* of Aristotle, enthused over by John of Salisbury in Book III of the *Metalogicon*. In his opening chapter to the *Topics*, Aristotle draws the distinction between "demonstrative" and "probabilistic" logic. When the premises from which arguments are constructed are true, then further truths can be demonstrated if the arguments are properly conducted (e.g., if they are constructed in accordance with the square of opposition). Such logic is "demonstrative" because it is capable of proving its conclusions. Not all subjects of argument are susceptible of demonstration, however; some fall under the logic of probability ("dialectic" in the narrower sense) which deals in opinion rather than uncontested truth. Dialectic in this sense involves honing our views with rational argument, testing their bases and seeking to persuade others to hold them through appeal to rationality and acknowledged principles of argumentation.[27] Because promoting a reputable opinion may involve denying what is contrary to such opinion, a thorough understanding of the mechanisms of opposition—and of the rules governing the relations of contrary and contradictory utterances—is as important to probabilistic logic as to the demonstrative kind (*Topics*, 104a/I, 10/173; cf. 112a, 27 ff./II, 7-8/188-90 and 123a, 20 ff./IV, 3/206-8). There is, for example, a whole category of topics in Boethius called "from opposites" which includes a subdivision involving argument from contraries: "Suppose there is a question whether *being praised* is a property of virtue. I might say: not at all, for neither is *being reviled* a property of vice." The reasoning is sustained, Boethius says, by the general rule whereby "contraries are suited to contraries" (*De topicis differentiis*, 1191B, 8-12/II/56). Learning to manipulate topics was a standard part of medieval logical training. In the *Abbreviatio Montana*, topics form a prescribed framework for argumentation, including demonstrative arguments.

For many writers, topical argument is not merely an intellectual exercise; to practice it without regard to truth is tantamount to sophistry. In seeking to influence opinion, the dialectician must not lose his sense of values. The sort of questions, according to Boethius, that dialecticians most frequently address are ethical ones: "for example, 'Is pleasure the greatest good?' [or] 'Should one marry?'" (Boethius, *De topicis differentiis*, 177C, 1-13/I/35).[28] And their purpose is to urge on everyone the principles of reason; in this respect, dialectic is antiparadoxical:

> Now a dialectical proposition consists in asking something that is reputable to all men or to most men or to the wise, i.e. either to all, or to most, or the most notable of these, *provided it is not paradoxical*; for a man would probably assent to the view of the wise, if it be not contrary to the opinion of most men. (Aristotle, *Topics* 104a, 9-12/I, 10/173, my emphasis)

The ambition of topical argument is to expose the potential contradictions within other peoples' opinions, thereby causing such opinions to be rejected, and so eliminate contradiction (including the sense here also of "disagreement") in favor of universally held, rational views.

Very different from this desire is the excitement of logicians pursuing the subject for its own sake down the multiple paths of argument which logic opened up to them. John of Salisbury records of his teachers Alberic and Robert of Melun that for Alberic "not even a plain surface that was polished smooth could be entirely free from objectionable roughness," whereas Robert "would never complete his discussion of a proposed point without [first] choosing to take up the contradictory side, or showing with deliberate variety of speech that there was more than one answer" (*Metalogicon*, II, 10/96).[29] Elsewhere John mocks the convolutions to which the New Logic gives rise. More and more negations are piled up in propositions, he says, making it very difficult to keep track of whether they are positive or negative:

> ... one had to bring along a counter whenever he went to a disputation, if he was to keep apprised of the force of affirmation and negation. For generally a double negative is equivalent to affirmation, whereas the force of a negation is increased if it is repeated an uneven number of times. At the same time, a negation repeated over and over usually loses its effect, and becomes equivalent to contradiction, as we find stated in the rules. In order, therefore, to discriminate between instances of even and uneven numbers, it was then the custom of those who had prudent foresight to bring a bag of beans and peas to disputations as a reasonable expedient. (*Metalogicon*, I, 3/15)

John is referring here to the "chaining" of propositions which was unavoidable for those who wished to pursue research into the structures of argument: lacking the formalized logic in use today, logicians had no recourse but to proliferate propositions in their examples. Venturesomeness with respect to contradiction was so great that some researchers went so far as to disagree with Aristotle's teaching on the rules of noncontradiction (*Metalogicon*, II, 10/98–99). Even the theologians of the later twelfth century seem to have been drawn to reasoning for its own sake, and to controversy rather than synthesis (Marenbon, *Later Medieval Philosophy*, 12). Polemicizing against such developments, John recommends a basic training in logical method from Aristotle's *Categories* and clings old-fashionedly to the belief that its main deployment should be in disputation and persuasion, especially of ethical questions.

The image John uses to condemn logical self-indulgence suggests that he saw its pleasures as analogous to those of self-abuse: "For if it is to fecundate the soul to bear the fruits of philosophy, logic must conceive from an external source" (III, 10/100). Tony Hunt and Eugene Vance have both, in different ways, suggested that courtly texts reflect the preoccupation with dialectic, and especially topical argument, in intellectual circles at the time of their composition. Courtly literature may, then, be the product of dialectic doing as John recommends and copulating with another: the courtly world and its concerns. Certainly the questions cited by Boethius, "Is pleasure the greatest good?" and "Should one marry?", questions echoed by John himself (*Metalogicon*, II, 11/100-1), are ones which are addressed (not necessarily reverently) by courtly authors, who would not need to have pursued very advanced studies to come into contact with (at the very least) the *Isagoge*, the *Categories*, and *De intepretatione*.[30]

Tony Hunt outlines three main aspects of courtly texts which show the impact of dialectic and which reflect the preoccupation with dialectical argument in intellectual milieux at the time of their composition—with audiences, that is, as well as with writers:

> First, the very concept of "courtly love" and the experience which it embodies appear to be of a dialectical nature and susceptible of dialectical treatment. [. . .] Second, there is the construction of poetic works themselves on the dialectical model of oppositions and correspondences. [. . .] Finally, there is the part played by ratiocination itself in the frequent debates found in the romances. (Hunt, "Aristotle, Dialectic," 108)

Vance suggests that the nature of universals may also have been addressed by courtly authors. He reads the interpretative cruces of *Yvain* (what does the herdsman represent? what is the relation between the hero and the lion?) in terms of the example omnipresent in logic textbooks from Aristotle onward: "if it is a man, it is an animal" (*From Topic to Tale*, 54).[31] The point of the example, for the logician, is to define the scope of universals by studying the relation between genus (here "animal") and species ("man"). Vance suggests that the hideous herdsman is a deliberate *mise en oeuvre* of this example, and that through him, Chrétien confirms man's animal and passional nature as the generic basis on which his species-specific humanity is founded (63).

But if courtly literature is a child of logic, it is scarcely one which would be accepted as legitimate by John of Salisbury.[32] For courtly texts reproduce precisely that intellectual playfulness which he disapproves of in logicians. Moreover, they combine it with a commitment to ethical values whose own value is dubious while leaving it notoriously hard to calibrate to what extent the commitment is undermined by the play. Courtly literature, in short, may entwine itself along all three branches of logic as traditionally defined: not only demonstrative (proving a point) and probabilistic (promoting an opinion), but also sophistical (having "no care at all for facts," aiming "only [. . .] to lose its adversary in a fog of delusions" [*Metalogicon*, II, 3/79]). As a result, although courtly contradictoriness may reflect the views current among twelfth-century dialecticians, it may also contradict—in the sense of flout—the principles of rightful argument which many of them extolled.

The Aristotelian position on contradiction was not the only one available in the twelfth century. Some logicians, as we have seen, sought to redefine the principle of noncontradiction. And religious writers, at least when they are speaking of God and Scripture, follow a Neoplatonist tradition in which contradictions are ultimately resolvable. God, for Augustine, is one who is present everywhere and unites everything (except for evil which, because it cannot be ascribed to God, must be nonexistent). God's mysterious excess with respect to the principle of noncontradiction is celebrated in the opening book of the *Confessions*:

> Do heaven and earth contain you because you have filled them? Or do you fill them and overflow them because they do not contain you? Where do you put the overflow of yourself after heaven and earth are filled? Or have you, who contain all things, no need to be contained by anything because what you fill, you fill by containing it? . . . etc. (*Confessions*, I.iii/4)

With comparable rhetorical pleasure, Augustine elsewhere rehearses traditional paradoxes of the one and the many, the temporal and the eternal, also found in St. Paul[33] and in Boethius.[34] Indeed, the use of paradox to point to higher truth is found throughout the Gospels—most famously in the Sermon on the Mount (Matthew 5–7)—and, in a less exalted spirit, in the tradition of riddles and enigmatic sayings.

Catherine Brown has examined the practice of exegesis with respect to the possibility that there may be contradictions in the Scriptures (*Contrary Things*, chapter 1). For its devout readers, what Scripture contains is true and "truth cannot be contrary to truth" (23). The apparent contradictions scattered across the two Testaments must therefore be capable of reconciliation, for one part of the Bible could not be true at the expense of another. Yet these seeming contradictions, because they are on the *Sacra Pagina*, also have indisputable importance. They can be read in contrary ways, *in bono* and *in malo*, just as individual images and episodes are read (29). From man's point of view, apparent contradiction, like opacity or ambiguity, is a reflection of the confused operations of the human mind. If we find these features in the text of Scripture, it is because they mirror our own confusions and limitations, and our response must be to accept our own unworthiness and trust in the contradictions to lead us to enlightenment.[35] In this respect, submitting to contradiction is a sign of humility. From the point of view of the divine Author, however, what appears contrary is mysteriously combined in a higher unity:

> However noisy the apparent clash of meanings, we may rest assured that, since truth may not be contrary to truth, statements appearing adverse are only in fact diverse, and what seems to be logical incoherence, a harmonious and congruent showing of divine generosity. Says Hugh of St. Victor: "The divine deeper meaning can never be absurd, never false. Although in the sense, as has been said, many contrary things are found, the deeper meaning admits no conflict, is always harmonious, always true." (*Contrary Things*, 29)

The ways Scripture teaches us are multiple, but its truth is ever One, as Hugh says elsewhere (cited in *Contrary Things*, 30). The medieval practice of collecting together passages from the Bible or patristic writings which appear contradictory in order to meditate upon and seek to reconcile them was a common one. Abelard's *Sic et Non* is the most famous casebook of this kind. One hundred fifty-eight instances of contradiction are prefaced by an introduction which outlines the various means by which reconciliation may be effected: they include attention to historical context, stylistic detail, writerly intent, and even (on occasion) the possibility of scribal error.[36]

The admission of contradiction within a higher unity is also to be found in manifestations of Neoplatonism that are more strictly philosophical than theological. Some scholars address their exegetical expertise to teasing out the contradictory meanings in pagan myths and writers of antiquity, a notable example being the *Aeneid* commentary attributed to Bernardus Sylvestris (Gersh, "(Pseudo-?) Bernard Silvestris"). Neoplatonist thinkers were also themselves engaged in producing richly ambiguous and potentially contradictory texts. Steven F. Kruger's remarkable study of the dream-vision tradition, to which many striking instances of this literature belong, shows how they exploit the middle ground of a Neoplatonic scale between two contraries in such a way as to invoke the opposite poles of the spectrum concerned and the double significance they convey. In Alan of Lille's *De planctu Naturae*, for example, the figure of Hymen reconciles (though without eliminating them) the contradictions which threatened harmony in the earlier part of the work.

Just as the Aristotelian tradition has shaped critical readings of medieval texts, so has that of Christian Neoplatonism. The dream-vision tradition described by Kruger includes courtly, vernacular poems to which his interpretative scheme can be extended. I have already cited D. W. Robertson Jr.'s interpretation of the *Charrete* as exemplifying an Augustinian approach to medieval literature. Invoking the authority of Augustine's famous assertion (*De doctrina christiana*, III, 10/76)[37] that "Scripture enjoins nothing but love and censures nothing but lust," Robertson argues that what the modern reader sees as contradictions in medieval texts are apparent only, a stimulus to moral reflection and ultimately resolvable as recommendations to embrace divine love. Robertson exhorts us to see seemingly opposing elements as in fact ranged hierarchically; proper understanding will reveal that one term is inferior to the higher and uncontested value, to which it should be subordinated; put crudely, charity rules OK. Thus Robertson contends, in total disagreement with Hunt and Vance, that "The medieval world was innocent of our profound concern for tension" (*Preface to Chaucer*, 51).

More widely accepted is the practice of viewing courtly love texts as analogous to Christian devotional (or mystical) literature. Spitzer, for example, explains his understanding of "le paradoxe amoureux," referred to earlier in this Introduction, as transposing into a secular context the Christian aspiration to unity with, along with acceptance of separation from, the beloved.[38] Just as Hunt's meticulous scholarship makes it obvious that courtly authors were influenced by the discipline of logic, so too it is incontrovertible that they were affected by the language of the Bible, by the tradition of meditation upon and exegesis of it, and by devotional writings more generally. But as in the case of courtly literature's response to medieval logic, here too its troublesome combination of ethical seriousness with intellectual play may make its debt to the Christian and Neoplatonic tradition as much subversive of that tradition as conforming to it. There is a case for seeing much courtly literature as paradoxical in the sense that the "higher truths" which it proposes run counter to the opinions of "all men or [. . .] most men or [. . .] the wise" in the twelfth century (Aristotle, *Topics*, 104a, 10/I, 10/173): adulating women and courtship, for example, might be seen as fanciful and even dangerous, whereas elevating the absurdities of *fin'amor* to the status of a prestige cult may parody as well as echo Christian representation of its paradoxes as the ultimate orthodoxy.[39]

※

Studies of the history of contradiction have tended to take these two positions, which in shorthand one could call Aristotelian and Augustinian, as their starting point, because they are so manifestly in contradiction with each other. Vance's *From Topic to Tale*, to which I have so far referred only in connection with logicians' interest in universals, analyzes the balance in Chrétien de Troyes between the dialectical tradition and a charitable, mystical, Augustinian hermeneutic; the coronation of Erec in *Erec et Enide*, for example, is described by Vance (40) as "a moment of precocious harmony between fundamentally distinct trends in Western culture, Aristotelian rationalism and Neoplatonic mysticism." Brown, for her part, maintains that the focus on contradiction in the works she studies—in the exegetical tradition which entertains contradiction ("both–and"), in the logical one ("either/or") which contests it, and in the interaction between the two—shows how central to medieval culture is concern with the operations and limitations of thought, and especially of the communication of thought (*doctrina*, the activity of teaching). Brown's argument recalls Rosalie L. Colie's magnificent study of contradiction in the Renaissance, *Paradoxica Epidemica*. Colie likewise argues that paradox (the figure of thought whereby received opinion is contested by what looks like an untenable alternative) comprises two strands: the biblical–mystical and the philosophical–skeptical. The first challenges commonsense views from a position outside human temporality, and the second sets about questioning belief and knowledge on rationalist grounds. Literary paradox, her argument runs, draws on both of these strands but also undermines the difference between them because the effect of paradoxical thinking is to both insist upon and to undermine the limits of the rational.

These antecedents are impressive. But we should nonetheless be wary of their binarism; the very neatness of the opposition between "both–and" and "either/or" is characteristic of the traps which the topic of contradiction lays for the reader. The temptation to identify two contrary positions which between them define a total field of possibility is a strong one and risks fettering interpretation by the very gesture which appears to free it up. Indeed, as these authors show, it is the way contradiction puts in question the frontiers of rationality that makes it so fascinating to study. Moreover this binary approach entails a risk of passing over examples of contradiction or contrariety which do not readily fit on this particular map. Julia Kristeva ("Le texte clos") has shown how this dyad can be extended if one places it on the top axis of a Greimasian square. That is, the terms "conjunction" (both–and) and "disjunction" (either/or) are each susceptible of negation, as shown in Figure 2.

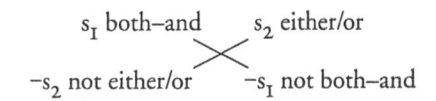

s_1 both–and s_2 either/or

$-s_2$ not either/or $-s_1$ not both–and

Figure 2. Kristeva's semiotic square of conjunction and disjunction.

Kristeva's argument is that the novel, from its beginnings in the late fifteenth century until the epistemic break of the late nineteenth or early twentieth, privileges the option of "nondisjunction" (not either/or); that is, it *both* suggests closure through invoking the closed relation of either/or, a gesture toward a totalizing Aristotelian rationality, *and* suspends it, permitting categories to float into metaphorical interference. (It is this suspension of the enforcement of the either/or rule that Bruckner appeals to in her analysis of the *Charrete*, referred to above.)

Of course Kristeva's square of opposition, by virtue of its rigorous mapping of a rational system of relations, remains firmly within the Aristotelian frame of reference. An example of a tradition of thinking about contradiction which departs more radically from the binaries she invokes would be the logic of negative theology, precisely because that of which it wishes to speak is, by definition, off the map. Negative theology patrols the limits of human reason to assert that, whatever such reason may comprehend, God lies beyond it. His nature is affirmed not through the play of antitheses and the reunion of contraries but through the systematic negation of our necessarily limited thoughts. Thus with self-conscious paradoxicality, Augustine writes, in *De doctrina*, I, 6/10, of the ineffability of God:

> Have I spoken something worthy of God [. . .]? No, I feel that all I have done is to wish to speak; if I did say something, it is not what I wanted to say. How do I know this? Simply because God is unspeakable. But what I have spoken would not have been spoken if it were unspeakable. For this reason God should not even be called unspeakable, because even when this word is spoken, something is spoken. There is a kind of conflict between words here: if what cannot be spoken is unspeakable, then it is not unspeakable, because it can actually be said to be unspeakable.

Although in the Middle Ages the most systematic exponents of negative theology were Jewish philosophers (such as Maimonides), its arguments were essayed by otherwise Neoplatonist Christian writers such as Eriugena and Anselm.[40] Graham Priest cites Anselm's *Proslogion*, §15/104, as an example:

> Therefore, O Lord, not only are You that than which a greater cannot be thought, but you are also something greater than can be thought. For since something of this kind can be thought [viz., something which is greater than can be thought], if You were not this being then something greater than You could be thought—a consequence which is impossible.[41]

Such passages resonate with troubadour claims about the "unspeakable" nature of courtly love and its "impossible" status between adoration and sacrilege.

Clearly the various strands of thinking about contradiction which I have just briefly outlined were not sealed off from one another. Anselm can also write in what I have been calling an Augustinian rhetoric (in his *Meditations*[42]), and in the Aristotelian one (when refuting a nominalist critique of the Incarnation), showing that even a philosopher could approach contradiction in divergent ways.[43] Augustine himself wrote in a variety of modes in which different attitudes to contradiction are implied, and a treatise on dialectic was ascribed to him. Such variation characterizes the protean world of clerical learning whose activities range from treating antique logic as a playground for exercising intellectual agility to standing awestruck before the mysteries of eternity.

This book will argue that it was precisely this elasticity of clerical culture that was formative of courtly literature. The fundamental importance of dialectical training meant that every schoolboy was taught to think about the nature, scope, and implications of different forms of contradiction, whatever intellectual course he subsequently followed. Individual courtly writers may have been drawn, some to one and some to another, of these different traditions of thought, but what was more important was the fact that these traditions coexisted, interacted with one another, and together pressed home awareness that contradiction lay at the heart of intellectual life. The fact that the emergent literature of entertainment often treated themes far removed from those of serious clerical disputation only contributed further tension, and enjoyment, to the contradictions involved.

The context of reception: contemporary views of contradiction

Such is the intellectual context in which courtly literature was composed. But we as readers are also formed by our own intellectual environment. The later twentieth century has been seething with arguments about the resolution (or not) of contradiction. In a book first published in 1988, Poundstone wrote that "the past few decades have been a very fruitful time for paradoxes of knowledge" because "by their very nature, paradoxes expose the cracks in our structure of belief" (*Labyrinths of Reason*, 15). The hallmark of French "theory" from the late 1960s onward has been the rooting out and relishing of paradox, questioning humanist belief in the self-sufficiency, self-legitimizing, self-grounding nature of reason.[44] Many current critical approaches, whether explicitly appealing to such theory or not, rely on discerning contradiction in the literary text as an initial step in its analysis; witness the examples I cited earlier of the critical discourses addressed to Bernart de Ventadorn and Chrétien de Troyes. In his flamboyant essay "Is There a Text in This Class?" Stanley Fish famously contends that interpretation is a matter not of construal but of construction; we create a literary object—"a poem"—by applying to a text a set of reading procedures, primary among which is the search for contradictions: "You will," asserts Fish, "be on the lookout for latent ambiguities [. . .], you will search for meanings that subvert, or exist in tension with the meanings that first present themselves."[45] Fish is referring here to deconstruction, but his remarks apply as well to other critical protocols, such as Marxism or psychoanalysis. Medievalists influenced by one or another modern theory will tend to locate and interpret contradiction in the light of that theory and, if Fish is right, may even be responsible for generating the very features they then set out to analyze.

Just as understanding of the scope and status of contradiction varies from one body of medieval thought to another, likewise the notions of contradiction deployed by modern "theory" are not all equivalent to one another. When I began work on this project, I looked at a wide range of theoretical approaches, from Bourdieu (who holds that, in practice, individuals steer their way through their various activities with scant concern for whatever contradictions they might imply) to Derrida (who introduces the notion of *différance* to disrupt the logical square of opposition, and who relentlessly tracks the least implication of contradiction down to its ultimate aporia). As I did so, I found myself increasingly drawn to the writings of Lacan and his commentators as a means whereby to understand the contradictoriness of courtly texts. Because Lacanian psychoanalysis is still not a widely accepted way of approaching medieval literature, this choice requires some explanation.

One reason for the use of psychoanalytic theory is that Lacan has shown a sustained interest in the phenomenon of courtly love, as have also to a lesser extent Kristeva and Žižek.[46] Lacan sees modern subjectivity as deriving from the erotic configurations of medieval courtly love poetry: "I do believe the influence of this poetry has been decisive for us" (*Ethics*, 153). Although Lacan is frequently accused of disregarding historical difference, he is in fact very emphatic that the various ways in which we unconsciously situate ourselves, and our conscious representations of our concerns, are all historically conditioned. The emergence of courtly love is identified by Lacan as a significant factor historically because its entire framework is secular. Instead of being subject to religious law, the lover subjects himself to a rule which is ascribed to a woman. In this way, the whole problematic of sexual difference and the sexual relation, on which (in Lacan's view) subjectivity is founded, is made explicit as the central concern of a prestige literature. Lacan is thus led to reflect on our link with the medieval past and our debt to it, echoing the concerns which I voiced myself in the opening paragraph of this Introduction. He points out, for instance, how tangible is the continuing influence of courtly love poetry on the writings of Freud (even though Freud himself doesn't mention it).[47] Similarly Lacan's own theories, to which the exploration of desire is central, may themselves form a part of the tradition with whose emergence this book is concerned. Of course Lacan, who despised specialists, knew relatively little about the Middle Ages. I would like to use my rather greater knowledge to contribute to the psychoanalytical understanding of courtly literature.

In addition to perceiving a historical link between medieval poetry and the modern self, Lacan specifically sets out to address the contradictoriness of courtly love literature (as of everything else he analyzes) in the light of his overwhelming conviction that our psychic life is caught up in a series of contradictions. So much is this the case that to give a brief outline of Lacan's attitude to contradiction will also serve as an introduction to the main lines of his thought (or at least to those of his works upon which I have drawn). Although this outline may seem a digression from enumerating the reasons for choosing a Lacanian approach to courtly literature, it will in fact make those reasons clearer.

In the early years of his Seminar, Lacan's teaching is based on the mutual incompatibility of what he identifies as two fundamental registers within the mind: the imaginary and the symbolic. This incompatibility is represented in a schema ("schema L") that recurs throughout his early writings and which strikingly recalls the "square of opposition": four terms are arranged in a square in such a way as to display the relations of contradiction and implication which exist between them (Figure 3).

This schema represents how the various parts of the psyche are interrelated. The two intersecting diagonals, which recall those in the square of opposition, mark the conflict between what Lacan calls the "imaginary" relation and the "symbolic" relation. The "imaginary relation" is constituted by the two terms a–a' and the axis between them. This is a relation of mirroring or imitation which leads to one element being patterned on the other; here, the perceptual self as a fragmented body (a') becomes modeled on an-

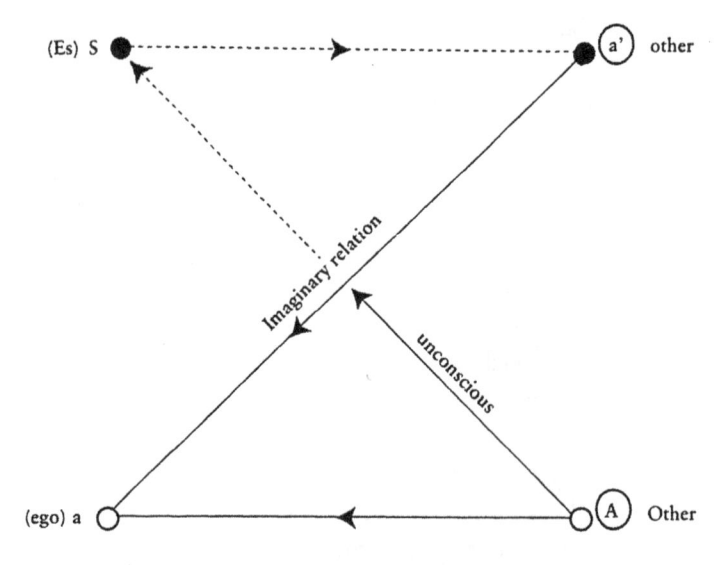

Figure 3. Schema L (reproduced from Evans, *Introductory Dictionary*, 169)

other image, such as one seen in a mirror, or on the perception one has of another person, which is then adopted as a "self" (the ego, *a*). This relation, although largely unconscious, can include conscious imitation. It results in the delusion that the self is a whole and autonomous entity, like the body-image reflected by a mirror. What Lacan calls the "symbolic relation" is defined by the terms *A*–*S* and the axis linking them. Here the subject of the unconscious—*S* or *Es* (*Es*, "it," is Freud's term for the *id*)—is constituted by the imprint of the big Other subject, *A*, the repressive authority of language and law. The two axes are represented as intersecting because Lacan sees the imaginary axis as interrupting and impeding the symbolic one. Deludedly identifying with the imaginary self (*a*), we become cut off from the truth of our unconscious subjectivity. So, for example, we trust in our conscious perceptions rather than recognizing that they may be distorted by our unacknowledged desires. Another way of saying this is to describe the imaginary order as a "lure," or decoy, away from the symbolic.

Thus the horizontal axes, also as in the square of opposition, oppose the contraries of the imaginary and the symbolic: on the upper axis the symbolic subject (*S*) and its perceptual counterpart, the fragmented body (*a'*); on the lower axis an imaginary alternative self, reassembled as an integrated body (*a*) and the symbolic Other subject (*A*). The positions on the lower axis could be said to originate outside the individual (i.e., initially they are not the self, and so they correspond to the contradictories in the Aristotelian square). The whole self is constituted by its integration of these alien positions, which is why it is said to be "decentered."

In this example of the schema, the use of broken or solid lines represents how the four positions are intricately interrelated. Relations which are more dominant are represented by solid lines; these tend to override those represented by broken lines. The direction in which the arrows are pointing indicates how these relations are formed. The big Other subject (*A*) ultimately determines all of the other positions: that of the imaginary other self, the ego (*a*), most immediately; that of the subject of the unconscious (*S*) in a way that is interrupted by the lure of the imaginary; and finally, via the subject, the self as fragmented body (*a'*). Whether we recognize it or not, all our categories stem from the symbolic order.

The two intersecting diagonals, which both connect what is initially self to what is initially other, describe the two contrasting forms of alienation to which we are subjected, a contrast indicated by the fact that the arrows on these two diagonals point in opposite directions. The alienation which leads to the identification of the self as another (the ego, *a*) is the opposite way around to the alienation which leads to the constitution of the subject of the unconscious (*S*) through the repressions of the symbolic order (*A*): in the imaginary relation we identify ourselves as another; in the symbolic relation the Other is what determines the subject. The relation of what is "self" to what began as "not self" is the opposite way around in the two cases. The use of solid lines is intended to show how utterly overwhelming this double alienation is.

Aware of what he himself calls the "dialectic" of these interactions, Lacan often seeks to make explicit the different kinds of contradiction they involve. The symbolic relation, dominated by the structuring force of language, is a domain dependent on differentiation. All of the linguistic patterns capable of constructing contradiction—the various kinds of opposition and negation—are contained within it. The symbolic also stands in a relationship of conflict with the reality beyond it, which is "nihilated" (*néanti*) by symbolization (*Psychoses*, 148)—that is, the presence of a term in speech takes the place of the thing in reality and banishes it. Increasingly, Lacan becomes preoccupied with the incapacity of the symbolic to take account of what is there in reality; this lack in the symbolic both reflects and generates a sense that reality has a profoundly traumatic dimension which exceeds language. Thus, although the symbolic orchestrates all the resources of language, it also itself stands in a relation of negation, and contradiction, to the real.

Communication along the symbolic axis involves temporality and process. The chief characteristic of this process is inversion: Lacan keeps insisting that the subject (S) receives the message of the Other, or rather receives its own message back from the Other (A), in an inverted form. In the Seminar on the Psychoses, he gives two examples of what he means by this (*Psychoses*, 36–37). The first is an example of commitment. If I say "You are my woman" or "you are my master," what this implies if communication is effected is that you to whom I speak already unconsciously recognize yourself as the one whom I recognize as my woman or my master, and you recognize me as such because unconsciously you return the message in an inverted form, for instance: "I am the one who is recognizable to you as your woman because you are recognizable to me as my man" (cf. 51); you are committed to me, and me to you, by your inversion of my message. Lacan's second example involves deceit: it is Freud's well-known Jewish joke about the man who says, "I am going to Cracow" only to meet with the rejoinder, "Why are you telling me you are going to Cracow? You are telling me that to make me believe you are going somewhere else" (*Psychoses*, 37). What is happening is that each speaker postulates the other as meaning the reverse of what is said. Both assurances and lies, therefore, have the same structure whereby "he sends me, and I receive, the message in an inverted form." Speech is only possible because we recognize the Other as being able to speak back to us in the same terms, but the other way around.

Such inversions are a response to the lack in the symbolic order which makes any message unstable; each inversion is a response to the potential lack in the other's message and hence to the unspoken question, "Why are you telling me this except to mask the lack in what you say and which, in my response, you expect me to fill?" They are further enabled by the fact that in the depths of the unconscious, contradiction does not exist. Terms can be inverted into their contraries and negatives substituted for affirmatives without a change of meaning; in dreams, for instance, the surface narrative may often appear to contradict the dreamer's underlying preoccupations, but this does not mean it is any the less a pointer to them. In the imaginary relation too, the bases of which are preverbal, the relation of contrariety is suspended in favor of unity: "high is equivalent to low, the back is equivalent to the front, etc." (*Psychoses*, 165). Polar opposites, rather than obeying the differential structure of the symbolic, are pulled into complementarity, an imaginary unity.[48]

Schema L dominates Lacan's early teaching; the seminar volumes from this period on which I draw are III (*The Psychoses*) and IV (*La Relation d'objet*). The ultimate purpose of psychoanalysis at this stage is to enable the patient to disengage the symbolic from the imaginary registers. In later seminars (primarily for my purposes volumes VII, *The Ethics of Psychoanalysis*, and XI, *The Four Fundamental Concepts*), although he is still interested in the interaction of the symbolic and imaginary orders, Lacan concentrates more attention on the third order, that of the real. The purpose of analysis is now to establish our dependence upon it, how we are "subject to the real." The real in Lacan's thought is a combination of what, in everyday parlance, we think of as external reality and the inner reality of our bodily drives. What these have in common is that they cannot be subsumed into language but on the contrary resist it; our bodily particularity, indeed, is something that we have to sacrifice in order to gain access to language in the first place. For we can only become subjects as part of a social fabric; but our doing so involves a loss because language is inherently Other to ourselves—it is an alienating, public institution far removed from private experience. Indeed, entering language creates the sense of loss by cutting the infant off from union with the mother and by always leaving out of account (literally not being able to account for / give an account of) all its intimate bodily experiences. The real is thus a traumatic residue which infuses speaking subjects with the anxiety that language is "not everything" but rather breached by a gaping hole (*Four Fundamental Concepts*, 25–26). Unlike the other orders, the order of the real has no structure either of differentiation (the symbolic) or unification (the imaginary). Nothing is lacking to it; it is an unstructured, unrepresentable threat which haunts us everywhere. Lacan keeps saying of it that "it always returns to its place," suggesting that we can neither escape nor confront it (e.g., *Four Fundamental Concepts*, 49). In language which seems to parody the language of negative theology, he concedes that such a concept is strictly "impossible" (*Four Fundamental Concepts*, 167). Lacan's account of the real thus adds a further, distinctive element of contradictoriness to his theory.

Against this background of trauma (in the real) and lack (in the symbolic), Lacan explains that we inevitably become dependent on objects. Referring to the *fort-da* game (Freud's account of how a child alternately throws and hauls back a cotton reel as a way of coming to terms with his mother's departures and returns), he says: "This is the place to say, in imitation of Aristotle, that man thinks with his object" (*Four Fundamental Concepts*, 62). The teaching of these later seminars is to a large extent devoted to explicating this crucial role of the object. The object itself, for Lacan, belongs in the imaginary order, because it acts as a lure, that is, a decoy, for the subject. But like the ego as represented in schema L, it can only be positioned relative to the subject via the mediation of the symbolic order. And the reason why we desire objects at all is because we want to fill the aching hole in the symbolic; or, to put it another way, we want to mask the threat of the real behind that hole. All our objects are imaginary surrogates for the originary lost object, the loss of which gave rise to that gap. Because the object is organized with respect to the symbolic, the imaginary and the real, it manifests all of the kinds of contradictoriness associated with those three orders.

The distillation of these properties of the object is termed by Lacan *objet a*. *Objet a* is a slippery construct, difficult to understand precisely because of its contradictory makeup. Essentially it is an abstraction of all that underlies our obsessive fabrication of objects. It is thus, in its *imaginary* dimension, an endless lure for the subject; at the same time, it is a position set up for us by the deceits of the *symbolic*, a presence summoned to plug the absence behind it; third, it is an alarming marker of the *real* beyond. In its complexity, *objet a* is what prompts all our desire, the point about which our drives turn but which they never attain, and the support of all our fantasy.[49] In *The Four Fundamental Concepts* (273–74), it is through confronting his own relation to *objet a* that the analysand can "go through the fantasy" and discover his subjection to the real.[50]

As a final example of the way Lacan's teaching not only depends on contradiction but also explicitly confronts the forms which that contradiction takes, I would like briefly to discuss his presentation of the formula of fantasy $ \$ \lozenge a $ in *The Four Fundamental Concepts* (209–15). Note that "fantasy" here does not have the popular sense of a kind of idealized escape route from some more disagreeable reality. As Žižek puts it, "the relationship between fantasy and the horror of the Real it conceals is much more ambiguous than it may seem: fantasy conceals this horror, yet at the same time it creates what it purports to conceal, its 'repressed' point of reference" (*Plague of Fantasies*, 7). The formula represents the structure of fantasy as a relation between *objet a* and the "barred subject," $. $ is the subject of the unconscious, which Lacan represents as split because it can never pass into consciousness or assume knowledge of itself. On the contrary, it always remains internally divided by its subjection to language in such a way that the "I" that speaks is split from the "I" that is spoken. For example, in the paradoxical utterance "I am lying," the subject which is spoken—the person referred to by the utterance—can truthfully say that the Other that constitutes the subject who speaks is deceiving him, and that he is returning the Other's message in inverted form (*Four Fundamental Concepts*, 139–41).[51] The formula $ ◊ *a* means, roughly, that in fantasy the subject uses the object in order to conceal or fill out this split. But the part of the formula where Lacan's interest in contradiction is brought to the fore is in his analysis of the symbol ◊.

This symbol is said to comprise two elements which designate how the relation of the barred subject to *objet a* is at once alienating and isolating. The alienation is figured by the lower half of ◊, which Lacan fancifully proposes is a *v*, standing for *vel*, "or." This "or" is not an exclusive either/or, nor yet an indifferent one or the other, no matter which; it is an "or" that designates a hierarchy between the alternatives such that, in practice, only one choice is possible. The example Lacan gives is "your money or your life"; if you chose money you lose your life, but if you lose life you effectively lose the money too, and so the only possible choice is life, even if it is a life of deprivation (without money). The example is more telling in French, "la bourse ou la vie," because *bourse* in French is also understood as referring to the testicles. Lacan's point is that to enter the symbolic order one must pay the price of what he calls "castration"; although this may look like a willing sacrifice, in reality we have no choice because there is no life except in the symbolic, and so we have to live as deprived ("castrated") subjects. This *vel* is thus an either/or which can result in a neither–nor. Lacan represents the subject as following this logic and being constrained to "choose" *objet a*: it has no option but to give itself up in favor of an object constituted by the double alienation of the imaginary and symbolic orders.[52] Invoking set theory, Lacan depicts the subject's relation with the Other as one of overlapping circles in which one circle, representing the subject, half vanishes behind the circle of the Other which overlies it. Lacan does not actually say that *objet a* is positioned in the overlap between the two circles, but this must be what he means because, as we know, the object (like the ego) can only be positioned relative to the subject via the mediation of the symbolic order, that is, in the intersection of the two. *Objet a*, then, is that point at which the subject succumbs to, or slides under, the domination of the Other. Insofar as the subject is "being" and the Other provides it with "meaning," the subject has no choice but to opt for meaning, because being doesn't mean anything without the imaginary and symbolic orders, whose potential for providing meaning for the subject is crystallized in *objet a*.

In the upper section of $\lozenge$, however, $\wedge$ figures a relation which is the opposite of this. Whereas the v represents $\$$ as altogether given over to (and thus alienated in) the object, $\wedge$ holds subject and object apart. The point of intersection between the two circles of the subject and the Other is now not an overlap but a hole which reduces each circle to a crescent. Or rather, each circle now overlaps the other in an empty space, in a space of lack. This space, which is still the locus of *objet a*, restores $\$$ to being, albeit in a defective state; and it also exposes the lack in the Other:

> A lack is encountered by the subject in the Other, in the very intimation that the Other makes to him by his discourse. In the intervals of the discourse of the Other, there emerges in the experience of the child something that is radically mappable, namely, *He is saying this to me, but what does he want?* (*Four Fundamental Concepts*, 214, original emphasis)

Thus separated from the Other, $\$$ can then offer his own lack as a recognition of and response to the lack in the Other: the empty space of *objet a* defined by the intersecting circles is where these two lacks are acknowledged.[53] Whereas in the mode of alienation the subject $\$$ has no meaning except what comes to it from *objet a*, now it can realize that such meaning is an illusion and that the Other is no more in a position of strength than the subject himself.

These two relations of alternation and separation are depicted by Lacan as rotating so that the v and $\wedge$ join together to form $\lozenge$, and $\mathcal{S}$ is alternately gulled and granted independence by *objet a*. The symbol thus marks a complex play of relations between the subject, the Other, and their meeting point in *objet a*. The rich combining of different strands of contradictoriness in this account, reinforced by appeals to logic and set theory, are a good example of Lacan's constant focus on the nature and operation of contradiction.

I embarked on this exposition of Lacan's teaching in order to show its relevance to medieval texts. Not only does Lacan periodically interest himself in the content of courtly love, but his attention is constantly addressed to the contradictions of the theoretical framework by which this interest is defined. In the course of describing Lacan's treatment of contradiction, a number of other justifications have emerged for applying Lacan's writings to the study of courtly poetry. The sheer range of different kinds of contradiction which are combined together in the different areas of Lacan's analysis parallels the variety of approaches to contradiction which we found in twelfth-century thought and which, I have suggested, impacted collectively on courtly compositions. Indeed, formally, the writings of Lacan and those of late twelfth-century courtly poets are surprisingly similar in that both are characterized by an interplay between what (from an Aristotelian perspective) would be considered the "rational" and the "paradoxical." Both can "make the most heterogeneous, or even the most discordant, systems exist simultaneously in our minds, in a simultaneity in which [acknowledgment of the principle of noncontradiction from formal logic] seems completely forgotten" (*Psychoses*, 67).

Reading Lacan alongside medieval logic makes one appreciate what a scholastic thinker he is. I have found him a most radical and lucid theorist of contradiction, as well as being one of its most infuriating practitioners. The indignation he provokes in his critics is, indeed, exactly like that expressed by John of Salisbury toward the New Logic; both Lacan and the New Logicians are accused of being obscurantist, jargon-ridden, and fraudulent.[54] Moreover Lacan's analysis of our subjective dependence on fantasy objects might help explain not only the fictions of quest or passion within courtly texts, but also why audiences then, and readers today, find these texts rewarding and absorbing. As Lacan himself asserts, the truth as he describes it has the structure of fiction (*Relation d'objet*, 253). His theory, in other words, engages with questions of fantasy and desire, loss and trauma, which both make up much of the substance of medieval texts and also help to define our relationship to them.

The content and organization of this book

So far I have referred to "courtly literature" or the "literature of courtly love and chivalry" as though it were self-evident what they were. In this final section of the Introduction, I will briefly explain what materials are discussed in this study, why, and in what way.

There have been very many accounts offered of the origins and rise of courtly literature.[55] Most persuasive among these, in my view, is Reto R. Bezzola's, for whom the impetus to this rise is provided by the interaction between aristocracy and clergy in medieval aristocratic courts. Of course Bezzola is here elaborating on an established view of courtliness as resulting from the alliance between clerk and knight[56]; but the unprecedented scale of his research commands respect.[57] In the five volumes and more than 1500 pages of *Origines et formation*, Bezzola charts the decline of literary production in the imperial courts of the former Carolingian realm (present-day France and Germany) and its gradual reemergence, between ca. 1100 and 1170, along the quite different geographical axis of Poitou–Anjou –Norman England. In the courts of this oddly peripheral territory—which winds, far from traditional royal or imperial centers of power, through the princely and aristocratic courts of what are now western France and southern England—literature in both Latin and the vernacular is reborn.[58]

In this study, Bezzola writes about any and every text which can be associated with court patronage, but the "courtly literature" whose origins really interest him is lyric—primarily the troubadour love lyric, which signals the birth of "courtly love"—and, above all, courtly romance from the *romans antiques* through the Tristan romances to the great Arthurian and Byzantine romances of the later twelfth century. A third genre extensively represented in his study is historiography, much of it in Latin. Although I have followed him (uncontroversially, I am sure) in according a central role to lyric and romance as manifestations of "courtly literature," I have confined this study to vernacular texts (except where comparison with Latin sources seems called for) and I have chosen to devote space to hagiography instead of to the writing of history—a choice which could be supported in Bezzola's own terms, given the importance he ascribes to the interaction between aristocracy and clergy, and also given the interplay of religious and secular elements in lyric and romance texts.[59] In particular, it seems to me that one can't explain the history of contradictoriness in twelfth-century romance without reference to hagiography. We know that saints' lives were performed in courts; for example, Orderic Vitalis recounts that the deeds of warrior saints were recited at the court of Hugh of Chester.[60] I am not claiming that saints' lives are "courtly literature" in the same sense as lyrics and romances, but they were clearly sometimes created by the same authors for the same audiences as were courtly texts more narrowly defined, and they form a vital part of the literary context of courtly composition.

This book, then, incorporates a reading of pre-1200 vernacular saints' lives in Occitan, Anglo-Norman, and French; of twelfth-century troubadour poetry; and of the romance tradition likewise in the twelfth century. I have not dealt with the poetry of the *trouvères*, partly because in the twelfth century (unlike in the thirteenth) it is heavily derivative of the troubadours, and partly because the formative influence of troubadour poetry on Anglo-Norman and French romance is still an underresearched field. I have taken 1200 as a cutoff point—one which needs to be interpreted flexibly, given that medieval texts are so difficult to date—because by then "courtly literature," however exactly one draws the line around it, has unquestionably achieved canonical status.

How did this extraordinary phenomenon come about? This book seeks to illumine the development of courtly literature by charting how the various patterns of contradiction available to medieval writers interact and combine in twelfth-century vernacular literary texts so as to produce, by the end of the century, a distinctive social artifact which had never existed in medieval Europe before: works of literary entertainment. And it suggest that the success of courtly literature may lie in the way the contradictions which it embodies appeal to the contradictoriness of our own impulses and desires: at some point, and in some respect, audiences and readers of courtly literature have been able to see in it their *objet a*.

The first three chapters work primarily from the perspective of the medieval context. Chapter 1 describes the interaction between the three different genres of hagiography, lyric, and romance over the course of the twelfth century and observes how their approach to contradiction evolves; at key moments in the latter half of the century, patterns of thought appear to migrate from one genre to another. In Chapter 2, I focus on a case study in order to illustrate in detail the more general observations of Chapter 1. A series of interrelated texts from all three genres are adduced to show how the opposition between "high" and "low" mediates different ways of treating contradiction. In Chapter 3, a further group of texts from each genre is studied as embodying responses to specific issues in medieval thought. Collectively, these analyses suggest that the concentrated address to contradiction in the second half of the century results in experimentation with, or exposure of, the limits of rational thought.

Chapter 4 then serves as a turning point between analysis of the medieval context and the introduction of Lacanian theory. This chapter continues the theme of the limits of reason from the preceding one, focusing on the use of riddle and enigma in the troubadour lyric and the *romans antiques*. The riddling language of the medieval texts is set beside Lacan's similarly enigmatic reflections on issues similar to those dealt with by the medieval poets: problematic issues of violence, sexuality, or incest. The purpose of this chapter is to argue that, as the twelfth century advances, contradiction is increasingly shifted from the subject to the object—both within the text and to the text itself as an object.

Each of the last three chapters then leads up to the analysis of a courtly text from the later part of the century: Marie de France's *Lais* (in Chapter 5), Chrétien's *Cligés* (in Chapter 6), Chrétien's *Yvain*, and the anonymous *Partonopeu de Blois* (in Chapter 7). Each of these works is examined from the perspective of different concepts of the object as elaborated by Lacan: phobic and fetish objects (Chapter 5), sublime objects (Chapter 6), and sublime and perverse objects (Chapter 7). In this way, I examine Lacan's contention, echoed by Žižek, that the modern subjectivity whose roots can be traced back to medieval courtliness is perverse. In Chapters 5 and 6, additionally, courtly texts are compared with religious ones. The relations between them (already explored in Chapters 1 and 2), situated in this different theoretical perspective, can be seen to exemplify, precisely, a shift toward perversity. An Appendix indicates the approximate datings of all the texts discussed, so that the shape of my literary-historical argument is pinned to a rough chronology.

I began this Introduction by asking why contradiction was absorbing and appealing to medieval courtly authors and their audiences, and to readers today. By working between the contradictions of twelfth-century thought and those of Lacanian analysis, I hope to provide some answers to these questions. I am not, of course, claiming that Lacan's approach to contradiction is the same as that of medieval thinkers; the influence of Hegel on all of modern thought licenses tolerance of self-contradiction in rational and even logical inquiry in a way which radically departs from the Aristotelian tradition (Priest, *Beyond the Limits*, 1). My point is that Lacan's interests sufficiently overlap those of medieval thinkers to provide a productive space for critical reading. The nature and results of this interaction are addressed in my Conclusion. My aim overall is to locate twelfth-century courtly literature between the concerns and desires of its producers and those of its readers, including ourselves, in the hope of further promoting our understanding and enjoyment of our literary objects.

CHAPTER I

The plait of contradictoriness in twelfth-century texts

At the beginning of the twelfth century, vernacular hagiography is well established, the Occitan lyric is apparently just emerging, whereas romance narratives are barely hinted at in the divagations of saints' journeys (such as the *Life of Saint Brendan*) or tucked away in the folds of history-writing (such as the Haveloc narrative in Gaimar's *Estoire des Engleis*, 193–816). By the end of the century, the lyric tradition has run a vast course through experimentation to canonicity, romance has absorbed many lyric and hagiographic features in its rise to become a prestige genre, and hagiography, influenced perhaps by romance, turns increasingly to the narration of biography rather than martyrdom. These three genres are plaited together, their mutual interaction sparked in part by the expectations of overlapping audiences—notably those in the Angevin sphere of influence, whether in England or in France and Occitania—and also by their responsiveness to the currents of twelfth-century intellectual preoccupation. This chapter picks out the strands in this plait which are constituted by the structures of contradictoriness. In some respects, all three genres develop along a parallel course; in others, however, they exhibit complementary shifts. As they move in different directions to one another, the strands cross and the plait takes shape. All start from an awareness of being drastically at odds with commonsense expectation—that is, of being paradoxical; all three cultivate a rhetoric of opposition (especially that of contraries),[1] which seems to reach its apogee around the 1160s–1170s; and all three subsequently develop a greater emphasis on negation. This parallel course affects the different genres differently, however. Whereas in hagiography and lyric, opposition consists primarily in simultaneously affirming contraries or privatives (*both* life *and* death, *both* joy *and* sorrow), in romance it is initially associated with the need to map a terrain of possible alternatives between which the audience is exhorted to choose (*either* sense *or* folly, *either* good *or* bad). Conversely, as the role of negation increases, in hagiography it is marshaled in favor of a rationalist impetus toward noncontradiction, whereas in lyric and romance, it often contributes to a pattern of disavowal whereby beliefs are playfully undercut and rationalizing claims flouted.

The literary history presented in this chapter cannot be more than summary, but many authors or texts omitted here, or accorded only brief treatment, are given detailed discussion in other chapters. To avoid ambiguity, I use the term "contrariety" to refer to the relation between propositions opposed by the use of contraries ("He is good"–"He is bad"), "contradiction" to refer to the relation between propositions which dialecticians would see as "contradictories" ("He is good"–"No he isn't"), and "contradictoriness" to cover both types of structure.

The beginnings

Hagiographic works predominate among the oldest surviving vernacular Romance "monuments." Several of the earliest have links with Occitania: a martyrdom of *St. Stephen,* a *Life of St. Faith* (ca. 1070), a couple of Marian hymns preserved in the late eleventh-century Limousin manuscript containing the *Sponsus*,[2] and a tenth-century *Life of St. Leger* which, although (like the *Sponsus*) a text of Northern French origin, survives only in an eleventh-century manuscript from Clermont-Ferrand.[3]

Saints' lives are a home to contradictoriness because they record, in an exceptional individual, a point of contact between God and humanity. Thus they are the meeting ground of dichotomies: Christian and pagan, divine and human, eternal and temporal, spiritual and physical, nature and grace (Heffernan, *Sacred Biography*, 10, 94). The saint is the site where most of these dichotomies are confronted, and who, through his or her experience, demonstrates that beyond what we call death lies another Life where the values of our world are countered and reversed. Saints who are martyred bear witness also to the paradoxes of the mighty humbled and the victim triumphant (Heffernan, 213). In most hagiographic texts, whether they recount a life that ends peacefully (the genre of the *vita*) or one ended in martyrdom (that of the *passio*),[4] the revelation within the saint of the divine order alongside the human one is confirmed by miracles. In a further staging of opposition, grace reverses the order of nature by causing the sick to be well, the blind to see, the lame to walk, the dead to live, and so forth.

The 240-line *St. Leger* illustrates how hagiography is conceived paradoxically because at its climax the saint speaks miraculously, impossibly, in defiance of all human expectation. The young child Leger is presented by his parents to King Clothaire, who has him educated. A young man of outstanding qualities (31–36), he becomes a royal courtier and bishop of Autun (44, 48). When Clothaire dies Leger becomes the counselor of his successor, Chilperic. This sparks enmity between Leger and Ebroïn, who had supported Chilperic's brother for the succession. Thwarted, Ebroïn enters a monastery. Leger, meanwhile, falls victim to court intrigue (73–76) and takes refuge in the same monastery as Ebroïn. Although Leger and Ebroïn apparently make peace, Ebroïn's anger against him smolders. When Chilperic dies, Ebroïn and Leger are exhorted to return to their *honors* (120, "offices, estates"). Leger resumes his bishopric, but Ebroïn's evil nature is confirmed by his forsaking his orders and letting his tonsure grow out. He ravages the kingdom with fire and the sword, leading his evil followers against Autun, where he takes Leger prisoner and has him tortured. Leger's eyes are put out, his lips are cut off, and his tongue is amputated. By these means, Ebroïn silences him so that he can no longer praise God (vv. 161–62). However, Leger's saintly nature takes no account of this mutilation:

> Sed il non a lingu' a parlier,
> Deus exaudis lis sos pansaez;
> et si el non ad ols carnels,
> en cor los ad espiritiels;
> et si en corps a grand torment,
> l'anima·n awra consolament.
> (169–74)

If he does not have a tongue with which to speak, yet God hears his thoughts; and if he does not have eyes of flesh, he has spiritual ones in his heart; and if he suffers great torment of body, his soul will have consolation.

Although physically dumb and blind, spiritually he can speak and see, the contrast reinforced by the rhymes *carnels–espiritiels*. God then miraculously restores to Leger in the flesh what he has never lost in spirit. Able to speak again, Leger speaks, prays, and arouses people's faith (181–86). The impossible is manifested in him. Furious, Ebroïn has Leger martyred by having his head cut off. His story is brought to an end.

Dramas of the eloquent saint are a recognized subtradition of Latin hagiography.[5] In the vernacular, too, the courtier saint is a recurrent figure (see below). Such saints are positioned from the outset as opposing worldly expectation. A paradoxical challenge to other people's values is also mounted by the martyrs. Most of them are beheaded, so that their final wound—like Leger's—is to the throat, the organ of speech (see Chapter 6); this draws attention to the way they have been speaking out of line, at least in the eyes of those secular powers which repress them. Thus in vernacular texts, where the saint's eloquence contributes to the prestige of the vernacular tongue, he or she is also a prototype of the vernacular author, and composition in the vernacular is posited as standing in a paradoxical relation to some (not necessarily stated) norm.[6] The clear lines of influence connecting early saints' lives to subsequent courtly literature confirm that the hagiographer is a forerunner of the courtly author and his protagonists. And the early examples of lyric and romance likewise have a strongly paradoxical cast to them.

The earliest surviving secular poetry in the vernacular—the lyric production of the troubadours—follows hard on the heels of the Southern hagiographic texts. At the very start of this tradition (or at least, of what survives of it), the songs of Guilhem de Peitieu (1071–126) seem pugnaciously to assert the contrary of what some unspecified interlocutor might expect. Their subtext runs, "Contrary to what all of *you* may think, I maintain. . . ." This oppositional structure is alluded to when "una domna s'es clamada de sos gardadors a mei" (II, 3, "a lady has complained to me about her guards"); in the aggressively anticlerical assertion "Donna non fai pechat mortau / que ama chevaler leau" (V, 7–8, "a lady does not commit a mortal sin if she loves an upright knight"); in the irritated contesting of commonplaces such as "D'amor no dei dire mas be" (VII, 7, "I should speak only well of love"); or in the aggressive sidelining of other peoples' opinions: "Eu, so sabetz, no·m dei gabar [. . .] mas. . . ." (IX, 7–9, "I should not boast, I know, [. . .] but. . . .") or "eu non ai soing d'estraing lati" (X,

25, "I have no care for the talk of strangers"). The sense of debate among the other early troubadours—Jaufré Rudel (...1125–1148...),[7] Bernart Marti (mid-twelfth century), Marcabru (...1130–1149...), Peire d'Alvernha (...1149–1168...)—is urgent as they lay siege to courtly opinion. Throughout the subsequent tradition, and however great the increasing weight of convention upon it, troubadours will retain a sense that they are crazy to sing of love as they do and that therefore they are inevitably at odds with the commonsense attitudes of others.

Although the first medieval romances are latecomers to vernacular literature compared with hagiography and lyric, they almost entirely lack the surface rhetoric of contradictoriness which makes those other genres so dazzling and intriguing. They do nonetheless share with early examples of lyric and hagiography the sense of confronting their audiences with material that will conflict with their expectations. The oldest Alexander romance, surviving only in a Franco-Provençal fragment, is thought to have been written by Alberic de Pisançon in the first third of the twelfth century. Alberic's prologue suggests that his narrative will sit uncomfortably with the Christian tradition:

> Dit Salomon, al primier pas,
> quant de son libre mot lo clas:
> "Est vanitatum vanitas
> et universa vanitas."
> Poyst lou me fay m'enfirmitas,
> toylle s'en otiositas!
> solaz nos faz' antiquitas
> que tot non sie vanitas!
> (1–8)

Solomon said, in his opening passage, when he sounded the knell in his book: "Vanity of vanities, all is vanity." Since infirmity gives me space, away with idleness! Let antiquity be our consolation that all may not be vanity.

The citation from Ecclesiastes, with the Speaker's crushing assertion that all is vanity, is oddly juxtaposed with the poet's confidence that antiquity will at the very least keep us agreeably occupied and may even produce something that is not "vain" at all. He does not go so far as to assert that Solomon was wrong; but a space is hollowed out for pagan culture in the midst of Christian religious authority. Alberic is typical of other authors of *romans antiques* in encouraging his audience to see antiquity as a strange, other world from which we can learn.[8] The *translatio studii* (the "transfer of learning" whereby antique texts are transmitted to twelfth-century audiences) involves not just an adaptation of the pagan past to the Christian present but also the imaginative transporting of the audience out of their own culture into the very different world of classical civilization, where their received opinions may be challenged and rethought.

In the oldest of the *romans antiques* to survive in its entirety, the *Roman de Thebes*, the effect of this probing at the border between experience and experiment is to immerse the audience in a world which is shockingly contrary to moral expectation. Its protagonists, Eteocles and Polinices, are the sons of the incestuous union of Oedipus with his mother, whose story prefaces the *Thebes* and is examined in Chapter 4. The two brothers agree to share the rule of Thebes by taking the throne in alternate years, but Eteocles, once ensconced, refuses to yield up power to his brother. Their mutual hostility becomes so implacable that when finally they kill each other and their bodies are burned on a pyre, the two halves of the fire separate and appear to fight; their ashes, placed in an urn, fight on and burst the urn apart (10497–524). In conclusion we hear that their great city is laid waste because "contre Nature furent né" (10555, "they were born contrary to Nature").

The narrative bristles with reminders that it is paradoxical, in the sense that its events run counter to expected beliefs and practices. One of the main functions of the poet's preferred character, Thideus, is to register shock on behalf of the audience. When, for example, at the end of the first year he goes as a messenger from Polinices to Eteocles, he forthrightly condemns Eteocles's breach of faith in refusing to give up the throne:

> Cest couvenant, tu li juras;
> se tu nel tiens, parjur seras.
> (1317–18)

You swore this agreement with him; if you don't keep it, you will be a perjurer.

The worse the war fares, the more others find themselves in a no-win situation. This is especially explicit in the episode of Darius the Red, where the accumulation of injustices leaves no right way forward. Darius cannot avoid breaking faith with one of the brothers once they have broken faith with each other, as his wife says:

> parjurer nous estuet vers l'un,
> quant juré l'avons a chascun.
> (7413–14)

We are bound to perjure ourselves to one of them when we have sworn [the same thing] to each of them.

The text depicts disaster on a vast scale, with the deaths of all of the heroes of Thebes and Greece: "Tuit i sont mort et fol et sage" (9989, "Everyone died there, wise and foolish"). Early on we hear Isiphile's horrified tale of how all the women of Lemnos killed their menfolk (2318 ff.); at the end, it is the men who have all killed one another, so that only women are left to run councils (9925 ff.), bury the dead (10177 ff.), and fight for revenge (10435 ff.). That the unnatural behavior of men should lead ultimately to such unnatural behavior in women illustrates how the tide of paradox ultimately engulfs everything in this text: all this horror ensues from Oedipus's initial crime.

The texts considered here can all be seen as speaking in defiance of expectation. This speech is staged as miraculous in hagiography, as a polemic over love's value in lyric, and as an imaginative exchange with the pagan past in the *romans antiques*, but a self-consciously paradoxical cast is common to the oldest exemplars of all three genres.

Contrariety in the 1150s and 1160s: romans antiques *and lyric poetry*

The *Thebes* is the work of a Poitevin poet, the *Eneas* is thought to be the work of a Norman, and the *Troie* is signed by Henry II's court poet, Benoît de Sainte-Maure. All three texts were composed between ca. 1150 and ca. 1165, probably in that order and under Plantagenet patronage; Eleanor may be the patron referred to both in the *Thebes* (see lines 6273–74 and notes) and the *Troie* (13457–70).[9] These texts are thus contemporary with many of the troubadours, who also had connections with the Plantagenets (Lejeune, "Rôle," Bec, "Troubadours"). The two genres of lyric and romance are, however, stylistically very different. Whereas the figures most favored by the *romans antiques* are those of repetition (especially anaphora) and set-piece descriptions, by the same period one of the most obvious stylistic features of the lyric is the exploitation of antithetical structures involving contrariety.

Awareness of negotiating contraries characterizes the structure both of individual poems and of troubadours' relations with one another; for example, in the debate between Marcabru and Ugo Catola (Marcabru Song VI), one contends that love is good, the other that it is bad. Oppositions such as *cortes–vilan, fin'amor–fals'amor, viu–mort, joi–dolor* are familiar to every reader of Jaufré Rudel, Marcabru, or Bernart de Ventadorn (...1147–1170...). We have seen that Bec identifies the polarity *joi–dolor* as the founding opposition whose dialectical interaction governs the poetic of Bernart's entire corpus ("L'Antithèse"; see Introduction). His study also reveals the preeminence, in Bernart, of contrariety because his examples include only one of antithesis structured by negation:

> Per midons m'esjau no-jauzitz,
> don m'es l'afans greus a portar.
> (XLII, 9–10)

I rejoice not-rejoicing in my lady and the pain of it is hard to bear.

As Bec shows, Bernart exploits the seeming collision of opposing terms; the lover can seem both joyful and downcast, wise and foolish:

> Amors, aissi·m faitz trassalhir:
> del joi qu'eu ai, no vei ni au,
> ni no sai que·m dic ni que·m fau.
> Cen vetz trobi, can m'o cossir,
> qu'eu degr'aver sen e mezura
> —si m'ai adoncs, mas pauc me dura—
> c'al reduire·m torna·l jois en error.
> Pero be sai c'uzatges es d'amor
> c'om c'ama be non a gaire de sen.
> (XIII, 19–27)

Love, you make me tremble so violently with the joy that I feel that I can neither see nor hear nor do I know what I say or do. A hundred times, when I reflect, I find that I should have sense and moderation—and I do have it, but it doesn't last long for me—for when I contemplate it my joy turns to pain. But I know that it is the custom in love that the man who loves well has little sense.

This stanza describes how the lover's *joi* is so intense that to become aware of it is to realize how painful it is. It cuts him off from reason and moderation, yet he has to accept this as a consequence of love's law. The point is even more pungent in Song XV: "car, qui en amor quer sen, cel non a sen ni mezura" (31–32, "whoever looks for sense in love has neither sense nor moderation"). The superimposing of contraries in a troubling and unstable union remains a feature of later poetry, though toward the end of the twelfth century the device can come to seem ritualized and parodic.[10]

The *romans antiques* also occasionally feature a rhetoric of paired contraries, especially those of wisdom and folly, but in an altogether different spirit. The prologue of the *Troie* is typical in emphasizing not the collision of polar terms but the need to separate them. It would be wrong of the learned to keep their knowledge quiet, says Benoît:

> Se fussent teü, veirement
> vesquist li siegles folement:
> come bestes eüssons vie;
> que fust saveirs ne que folie
> ne seüssons sol esguarder,
> ne l'un de l'autre desevrer.
>   (11–16)

If they had kept silent, truly the world would live foolishly: our lives would be like those of the beasts; we would not even know how to see what was wisdom and what folly, or how to separate one from the other.

Benoît's concern here to put mental discrimination at the service of moral understanding reads like an illustration of John of Salisbury's contention (*Metalogicon*, II, 6/84) that logic "provides a mastery of invention and judgment, as well as supplies ability to divide, define, and prove with conviction."[11] Dido is used by the *Eneas* poet as an exemplum of the failure to distinguish sense from folly. His account of her feelings shuns antitheses of the kind cultivated by the troubadours, the rare exceptions inciting not sympathy with rapture but wry condemnation: "Amor l'a fait de sage fole" (1408, "Love has turned her from a wise person to a fool") and "tel tient l'en sage qui est fole" (1592, "You may think someone wise when they are a fool"). Even the instruction in love given by Lavinia's mother to her daughter later in the same poem, though rehearsing love's traditional dichotomies, situates them in alternation: love's pleasures come from its pains (7957 ff.) and it wounds and later heals (7976 ff.). Her only concession to the kind of simultaneous contrariety found in the contemporary love lyric is in line 7937: "Cist maus est buens, ne l'eschiver" ("This ill is good, don't avoid it"). (Contrast the scene imitated from this between Fenice and Thessala in *Cligés* 3017–38, discussed in Chapter 6.) The *romans antiques* are thus strikingly reluctant to be drawn into the passionate relation with contrariety attested in the mid-twelfth-century lyric. The only troubadour whose practice resembles the *romans antiques* is Marcabru, who likewise devotes an ethical attention to discriminating (for example) "pure" from "false" love (XXXI) or "broken" from "whole" thought (XIX; and see my "Contradictions," appendix I).

Contrariety in saints' lives

By the same token, the experimentation of *romans antiques* with alternative worlds does not result in the diametrical reversal of the conditions of our own, such as we find in saints' lives, but rather in cautious discrimination between one world and another. Saints' lives, however, offer a terrain where contrariety flourishes. In the earliest texts, it is present primarily as a structure of thought whereby the perspective of the saint is systematically opposed to that of the world. But already in the *Leger* it can sporadically flower into figures of speech (*contentio*). This tendency increases in the second half of the twelfth century in such texts as Guernes de Pont-Sainte-Maxence's *Becket*. Guernes wrote his text in England in 1174 after extensive research and an earlier draft.[12] Becket's life and death follow the same pattern of the disgraced courtier as Leger, but Guernes's work is more ambitious, and his use of wordplay, especially of figures involving contraries, is elaborate, not to say obsessive.

Guernes's Becket, like Leger, shows early signs of being "wise and courtly" (245). He is exceptionally canny, and God advances him in "wisdom and counsel" (251–52). He speaks excellent Latin and expounds his points (or articulates his sentences?) with skill (2362, 2369), to the pleasure of clerks and laymen (2379). He is always attentive to the linguistic accuracy of his arguments (e.g., 3343). Thanks to these qualities, Becket becomes the most trusted courtier of Henry II, his chancellor, and tutor to the Young King. Becket enjoys the king's confidence to such an extent that Henry always follows his counsel and prefers him to all other men (379–80). Inevitably, however, Becket and the king fall out. The substance of their disagreement is Becket's championing the right of the clergy not to be subject to secular jurisdiction, but enmity is fueled by envy. Becket's riveting attraction and the glamour of his court excite the king's jealousy (419–20). Plunged into open conflict with Henry, Becket is exiled to France, but then returns to be reconciled with him. All goes wrong and Becket is instead killed inside his own cathedral. Miracles confirm that he is indeed a saint.

Far more than in the *Leger*, the theme of eloquence in *Becket* is paralleled by Guernes's own practice as a writer. The narrator's views are expounded at length in commentaries of his own devising whose didactic tone recalls that of Thomas in the *Tristan*[13]; for example, we find reflections on the theme "low is high" in lines 81–120. In another passage, the description of miracles accumulates what dialecticians call oppositions by privation (such as "sighted"–"blind"). Aristotle's principle ("from privation to possession [. . .] is impossible" [*Categories*, 13a, 34/§10/21]) is here repeatedly overridden so as to foreground the countering of the natural order by the divine:

> Li muët i parolent, li surt i unt l'oïe,
> e de lepre i guarissent maint, e d'ydropisie,
> li contreit i redrecent, li mort i unt la vie,
> li avogle i alument; seint Thomas tost aïe
> celui ki par bon quer le requiert e deprie.
> (71–75)

The dumb speak there, the deaf hear, many are healed of leprosy and dropsy, the crippled stand again, the dead have life, the blind are illumined; St. Thomas comes at once to help whoever sincerely calls on and beseeches him.

The coincidence of the contraries of worldly and spiritual status is represented throughout the text by wordplay on *corune*, which can mean both "crown" and "tonsure." A king should never, the prologue affirms, oppose the will of the clergy or take what is theirs, for his crown and laws derive from the church (57–59).[14] The king's crown is material, on his head (1241), but the tonsure is worn on the soul (1246–47); the clerk is "tunduz cumme fous" (1248, "shaved like a fool")—an outcast from the perspective of the world, but crowned ready for the next. One of Becket's dreams, when he is living a life of extreme privation in exile, is of his *curune* being shaved with swords: a prophecy of martyrdom to follow (3648–49). In the second version of this dream, his head is flayed (3877). At the end of the text, Becket stands accused of trying to deprive his lord (the Young King, whose coronation is being contested) of his *curune* (5762), while he himself is killed by a blow to the *curune* (5586). Thus

> . . . li bons corunez pur sa gent corunee
> sa corune en dona as armez desarmee.
> (5701–2)

The good tonsured one, tonsured/crowned for his people, yielded up his tonsure/crown unarmed to the armed men.

The wordplay illustrates the convergence of contraries in a single signifier and confirms the text's conviction that the tonsure, mark of humility and exclusion from worldly affairs, is at the same time the authority to which secular crowned heads should submit.

By the 1160s and early 1170s, then, we can see in both hagiography and lyric a willingness to override the principle of noncontradiction and affirm contraries simultaneously, which contrasts with the more cautious, discriminating approach of the *romans antiques*. In the terms advanced in my Introduction, the romances are more Aristotelian, whereas both lyric and hagiography are more Augustinian. The next decade, however, will witness a transformation of this pattern.

Romancing the matter of Britain in the 1170s

This is roughly the period of composition of romances exploiting a Celtic *merveilleux*: Thomas's *Tristan* (early ?1170s) and the romances of Chrétien (early ?1170s onward). Whereas it is hard to detect any impact of lyric or hagiographic material on the *romans antiques*, both these authors seem to respond to both genres while also making the influence of dialectic—

which is only discreetly felt in the *romans antiques*—much more palpable. For instance, the influence of hagiography has been seen in the *Tristan* in the episode of the hero's living under the stair at his lover's house, just as St. Alexis lived under the stair in the house of his former bride (see Chapter 2), and is unmistakable in *Cligés* when Fenice is "martyred" (see Chapter 6). The impact of troubadour poetry on Chrétien at least is also a matter of record.[15] The debt of Marie de France's *Lais* to both lyric and hagiographic traditions has also been noted (and see Chapter 5).[16] It is here, then, that strands first cross to initiate the plait: the practices of what I have been calling "Augustinian" contradictoriness associated with hagiography and lyric cross over into romance, whose debt to "Aristotelian" contradictoriness is simultaneously emphasized.

An example from the *Tristan* illustrates how Thomas both endeavors to discriminate contraries (in the manner of the *romans antiques*) and allows his characters to get caught up in their convergence—or rather, in the collapse of the opposition as the positive pole is contaminated by its opposite.[17] Tristan is regretting that his failure to consummate his marriage with the second Isolt will cause her love to turn to hatred:

> Ço ere a dreit qu'en haür m'ait
> quant m'astienc del naturel fait
> ki nos deit lier en amur.
> Del astenir vient la haür:
> issi cum l'amur vient del faire,
> si vient la haür del retraire;
> si cum l'amur del ovre vient,
> e la haür ki s'en astient.
> (Sneyd¹, 517–24)

It will be right for her to hate me, given that I abstain from the sexual act which ought to bind us together in love. Hatred comes from abstaining: just as love comes from doing the act, so hatred comes from its withdrawal; just as love comes from the deed, so hatred comes to whoever abstains.

This passage applies the argumentative strategy of the Topic from contraries (see Boethius, *De topicis*, 1191B, 8/II/56): if love comes from the act of love, then hatred, love's contrary, follows from the contrary of that act, its withholding. Hatred brings countless other undesirable consequences in its wake (suffering, unhappiness, the decline of nobility and prowess into failure, the collapse of everything he values [526–34]). This argument (redolent of the Topic from causes, *De topicis* 1199A, 7–14/III/69) should lead to Tristan embracing the more reasonable option, but desire dictates otherwise. In following his desire (to abstain), Tristan thwarts his new wife's desire (for consummation), and so it follows that he desires hatred more than he desires love (543–44). Lucidity enables him to chart the consequences of his behavior with excruciating precision, but not to change it. The more Tristan seeks to divide one alternative from the other, the more inevitable is the corruption of Isolt's love by hatred, just as in the passage quoted the word *amur* is repeatedly replaced in the second line of each couplet by *haur*.[18]

In Chrétien, similarly, antithetical terms struggle together in a mixture of convergence and separation. But whereas the use of dialectical structure in Thomas's *Tristan* is relatively static (see also Chapter 3), Chrétien's engagement with contrariety is dynamic. It is the *process* of narrative unfolding, as "Chrestien develop[s] and structure[s] his tale through oppositions," which provokes what Hunt describes as the "Abelardian *interrogatio*," the inquiring response, of his audience (Hunt, "Dialectic," 288).[19] An example is the famous passage in *Yvain* deliberating whether Yvain and his lady are *ami* or *anemi*. The changing contexts in which the lady might view Yvain position him now as her *anemi* (slayer of her husband) and then as her *ami* (the man who loves her and will defend her fountain), whereas her alleged inconstancy as a woman is invoked to justify her reversal from hostility to passion. As these shifts gradually take effect there is an oscillation whereby one can be both *ami* and *anemi*, and yet also distinguish one position from the other (*Yvain*, 1453–64, and see Chapter 7). Similarly, the passage in which it is debated whether Yvain and Gauwain love or hate one another (5996 ff.) does not merely play on the contrary contexts in which they find themselves at that moment (good friends who unknowingly find themselves defending opposite sides in a court case and are therefore obliged to fight to the finish, each unaware who their opponent is), but also calls to mind their interaction throughout the romance. When Gauwain encouraged Yvain to leave his wife and accompany him to tournaments, for example, did he act out of love or out of hatred? The more we think about it, and the more considerations we include from different points in the narrative, the harder in practice it becomes to distinguish love and hatred.

Relating contradictoriness to the conduct of an argument over time remains a constant of romance from Chrétien until the end of the century (Nolting-Hauff, *Liebeskasuistik*, especially 44–64). Both Hunt and Vance see this as a direct influence of logic. But I wonder whether this development in romance was (also) affected by lyric poetry and represents another twist in the plait. The wordplay highlighting opposition, especially at the rhyme, which we have just seen in Thomas and Chrétien, is anticipated by the troubadours, for example in the use, from Marcabru onward, of derived rhyme balancing masculine against feminine, or constative against injunctive. Such rhyme schemes point to the need to examine opposition in the structure of entire songs. Bec's analysis of contraries in Bernart de Ventadorn is restricted to local, verbal ornament. He describes Bernart's balancing act between joy and suffering as not temporal but psychological. Attention to the organization of whole songs reveals, however, that the role of time deserves more emphasis. Finding how folly is the lover's moderation, sensuality his spiritual vocation, or pain his joy is not a matter of sudden revelation to Bernart but the provisional outcome to an emotional, often lengthy hesitation. The relatively high proportion of Bernart's songs to have a stanza order that is to some degree fixed enables us to see this process in operation over an entire song, as for example in "Tant ai" (IV), which works through the oppositions *joi–dolor* and *cor–cors* ("heart"–"body") to arrive at a love of willing renunciation (*amor de lonh*) that is both exquisitely painful and emotionally satisfying (on the progressive treatment of antitheses in this song, see also Gaunt, *Gender*, 151–57). In the final stanza, Bernart describes a fragile synthesis of these oppositions whereby love inspires tears, which in turn season and enhance love:

> Tan l'am de bon' amor
> que manhtas vetz en plor
> per o que melhor sabor
> m'en an li sospire.
> (69–72)

I love her with such good love that I often weep because of it, for weeping adds savor to my sighs.

Several other troubadours whose work bears the imprint of dialectic also compose a significant proportion of songs with relatively stable stanza orders: Marcabru, Peire d'Alvernha, Raimbaut d'Aurenga (...1147–1173), Giraut de Bornelh (...1162–1199...). All of these are early enough to have influenced Chrétien.[20]

By whatever route this interest in the dynamic dimension of dialectic found its way into romance, we here see a treatment of contradictoriness common to both lyric and romance but not yet shared by hagiography.[21] For in saints' lives, the immensity of eternity dwarfs temporal processes; from the beginning of time, we know that humanity's perspective is always already reversed by that of God. It is not until the very end of the twelfth century that contradictoriness in saints' lives begins to be mapped in relation to narrative progression (see below). Thus in the matter of Britain in the 1170s we see the strands in the plait cross over as features of lyric and hagiographic writing are taken up in romance. Whereas previously the treatment of contradiction in the lyric more closely resembled hagiography, now it has more in common with romance. The two secular genres now stand together, differentiated from the religious one. This is a significant moment in the establishment of courtly literature.

Contesting contrariety in hagiography

Shortly after the 1170s, we reach another significant point in the plait where the strands appear to cross again. Just as romance writers are beginning, albeit uneasily, to accord space to the simultaneous affirmation of contraries and thus admit to courtly narrative what had been essentially a trope of lyric and hagiographic writing, we find suspicion toward contrariety emerging in hagiographic texts. It seems as though the rationalism of the *romans antiques*, contested in Celtic-derived romances, finds a new outlet in saints' lives.

This development can be illustrated by comparing Guernes's *Life of Becket* with the *Life* written by Beneit, a monk of St. Alban's, about a decade later (between 1183 and 1189, according to Walberg, "Date et source"). Whereas Guernes exploits Becket's consummate eloquence to highlight the contradictoriness of the saint's relations to the world, Beneit is more concerned to eliminate contradiction for the sake of advancing an argument.

The contrast between the two texts emerges most sharply in their accounts of negotiations between Becket and Henry. In Guernes's text, contrariety predominates as the exiled Becket writes to Henry at length commending to him the value of submission to God (i.e., to the Church and to himself as its mouthpiece):

> Tes privileges as e leis e poesté;
> ne toil al devin ordre rien encontre sun gré.
> Se par mal conseil as contre Deu meserré,
> que Deus ne traie a tei, chié en humilité:
> se tost ne te repenz, envers tei ad tesé.
>
> Que que dient li tuen e li Deu traïtur,
> ne te turne a vilté mais a mult grant honur
> se del tut t'umilies vers le puissant seignur
> qui l'orguilus abat, met l'umble el sié hauçur.
> E rei e prince deivent de li aveir poür.
>
> (2921–30)

You have your privileges, laws and power. Do not take anything from the divine order against its will. If, ill-advisedly, you have acted wrongly toward God then, lest God shoot you low, fall down in humility: he has his bow aimed to strike you if you do not at once repent.

Whatever your supporters and traitors to God may say, it brings not debasement but high honor to humble yourself completely to the powerful lord who casts down the proud and puts the humble in the highest seat. Both kings and princes should fear him.

Furious, Henry has a reply written by his bishops demanding that Becket show submission to *him*. By humility he will regain the king's favor; humility wins more than high office (3231–40). Each disputant, then, urges the other to be humble on the grounds that the lower you are, the higher, and vice versa.

The disagreement between Henry and Becket is quite differently handled by Beneit. His Becket's arguments invoke not the simultaneous affirming of contraries but the principle of noncontradiction. When the king demands from Becket accounts of his various benefices, Becket claims to be quit of all dues to the king and denies that the court has any jurisdiction over him. The count of Leicester counters that this court is composed of lay and clerical members and that they are his peers. Becket then launches into an argument alleging that it is impossible for the laity to judge members of the clergy. The lesser should not have jurisdiction over the greater (625–26). If they did, it would be like the sheep beating the shepherd, the disciple the master, the son his father, or the vassal his lord (631–36). The two jurisdictions are like gold and lead. Both are metals, but far from being equal in value, they have antithetical qualities, one fair, the other foul (637–42). The enlightenment of Holy Church is like gold and the willful selfishness of the king's rule like lead (643–48, cf. 655–60). One is bright and the other black, one inner and the other outer, one spiritual and the other physical (649–54).[22] It follows that Becket is in no way subject to their jurisdiction; rather, they should be subject to his:

> Coment dunc voleiz pruver
> ke la curt me deive jugier,
>   kant sui legat?
> E si vus ai tuz a governer,
> e fei me devez partut portier
>   cum a primat.
>
> (661–66)

How then do you intend to demonstrate that the court is entitled to pass judgment on me, given that I am a legate? Rather, I have all of you under my rule and you should keep faith with me in everything, as to your primate.

This argument, far from allowing contraries to co-refer, is grounded in their rigorous separation. It proceeds by invoking what will be believed as truisms in order to establish general principles from which the particular case can then be argued. It is conceived in the spirit of topical argument (cf. the Topic from a similar, *De topicis*, 1197B, 20–28/III/66), its call to discrimination echoing the either/or assumptions of the *romans antiques*.

Contesting contrariety in the lyric

There are examples of a similar change in the lyric. Again, I will use two texts on the same theme in order to point a shift from the affirmation of contraries to their separation. These two *tensos* between a Bernart and a Peire/Peirol about whether or not to continue as a singer of love songs were composed at least two decades apart. "Amics Bernartz de Ventadorn" can confidently be assigned to Bernart de Ventadorn's corpus (XXVIII); its Peire may be Bernart's contemporary Peire d'Alvernha. In "Peirol, cum avetz tant estat?", however, the references to works by Peirol (...1188–1222...) rule out the participation of the historical Bernart (last known of in 1170). This second poem, then, probably involves the historical Peirol and a fictional Bernart (Marshall, "Dialogues").[23]

In the earlier *tenso*, Peire reproaches Bernart for abandoning love poetry. Bernart's defense (stanza ii) that love is mere folly is brushed aside by Peire in a triumphant résumé of Bernart's most memorable declarations of love's value (cf. especially his Song II):

> Bernartz, greu er pros ni cortes
> que ab amor no·s sap tener;
> ni ja tan no·us fara doler
> que mais no valha c'autre bes,
> car, si fai mal, pois abena.
> Greu a om gran be ses dolor,
> mas ades vens lo jois lo plor.
> (XXVIII, 15–21)

Bernart, a person can hardly be worthy or courtly who does not know how to conduct himself in love, nor can love cause any suffering which is not worth more than well-being in another domain—for if it hurts, it then gets better. You can hardly have great good without pain, but joy always overcomes weeping.

This stanza scintillates with antitheses about good and ill, joy and pain, which position love as a quasiecstatic experience. The dismissal of it as folly is thus met, implicitly, by its contrary: love, which the world calls folly, is better seen as a higher wisdom. Unrelenting, Bernart insists that henceforth men should no longer court women; it will be up to women to court them. These contraries are countered by Peire with a further pair: it is not seemly for ladies to woo; rather, men should implore their favor. Returning to an earlier point in the argument, Peire advances a contrary definition of folly to that offered by Bernart. For Bernart, folly lies in loving women; for Peire, in hostility to them. The meticulous oppositions of the *tornadas* encapsulate the principle of argument by contraries which has been followed throughout this *tenso*:

> Bernartz, foudatz vos amena,
> car aissi vos partetz d'amor,
> per cui a om pretz e valor.
>
> Peire, qui ama, desena,
> car las trichairitz entre lor
> an tout joi e pretz e valor.
>   (43–48)

Bernart, you are being carried away by foolishness in leaving love which is the source of merit and worth.

   Peire, whoever loves loses his wits, for the deceiving creatures between them have taken away merit and worth.

For Peire to abandon love (*amor*) is folly (*foudatz*), because love is the source of merit and worth ("pretz e valor"), whereas for Bernart, whoever loves (*ama*) acts foolishly (*desena*), and women are what have deprived us of merit and worth ("pretz e valor"). The *tenso* both celebrates love and deflates it, wittily combining appeal to a wisdom higher than mere logic with rejection of the folly of unrequited passion.

Although the subject of debate in the later "Peirol, cum avetz tant estat" is the same, a Bernart here entreating a Peirol to return to singing, the strategies of argument are altogether different. The Bernart of the earlier *tenso* was not offered a choice between *mal* and *ben*, *ira* and *joi*, but told that they were mysteriously inseparable contraries whose interaction consecrates the supreme value of passion. Here, however, though these antitheses ornament the opening stanza, they are presented as alternatives:

> Peirol, cum avetz tant estat
> que non fesetz vers ni chansso?
> Respondetz mi, per cal razo
> reman que non avetz chantat,
> s'o laissatz per mal o per ben,
> per ira o per joi o per que,
> que saber en vuoill la vertat.
>   (1–7)

Peirol, how have you abstained so long from composing a *vers* or *canso*? Answer me why you have refrained from singing, whether you are abandoning it for ill or for good, for grief or for joy or some other reason, for I wish to know the truth of the matter.

Peirol's reply alleges the need for song to be sincere and to express the joy of love which is lacking to him. This blatant reference to the songs of the historical Bernart is objected to by the fictional one (drawing on the Topic from similars again, as in Beneit's *Becket*) on the grounds that if love is one good, song is another; to lose one is bad, so why lose both? Peirol concurs (perhaps sarcastically[24]): Bernart has made him see the light: he will sing from now on, and, with a new addressee, he will not do so in vain. As for Bernart, Peirol hopes he will waste his song and his affection alike on his unresponsive lady. But Bernart is ready with his reply: he too has moved on and found a new lady to be the object of song and provider of *joi*.

The shift in attitude toward contrariety between the two *tensos* is identical to that between the two *Lives of Becket*. In both cases the later text inclines toward topical argument and respect for the principle of noncontradiction. But the implications of the change in the lyrics are very different. The effort to refine argument in hagiography offers an additional means of persuasion but does not impair the genre's fundamental conviction that the perceptions of this world are countered and reversed by those of eternity. Several saints' lives from the end of the twelfth century—those of Lawrence, George, and most notably Catherine—show the influence of dialectic on Christian apologetic but still retain the traditional hagiographic framework whereby the lower the higher, the worse the better, and so on (Clemence's *Life of St. Catherine* is analyzed in Chapter 3). Reason may support faith, but it ironizes desire. Although in the first *tenso* the rhetoric of contrariety is poised between commitment to irrational passion and humorous dismissal of it, in the second, rational argument leads to both "lovers" pursuing their interest with cynical calculation. There is no room left for "love."

From contraries to contradictories in lyric and romance

The ending of the second of the two *tensos* has a further feature characteristic of late twelfth-century lyrics: a preference for arguments structured by contradictories rather than contraries. Peirol compares Bernart with a fox who complained that cherries were worthless because he couldn't reach them. Marshall interprets this as a variant of the fable of the fox and the grapes in which the fox reviles the inaccessible grapes as sour:

vi   Bernat, ben es acostumat
     qui mais no·n pot, c'aissi perdo,
     que la volps al sirieis dis o
39   qan l'ac de totas partz cercatz:
     las sirieias vic loing de se
     e dis que non valion re.
42   Atressi m'avetz vos gabat.

vii Peirol, sireias sont o be,
     mas mal aia eu si ja cre
45   que la volps no·n aia tastat!

viii Bernat, no·m n'entramet de re,
     mas pesa.m de ma bona fe
48   car non hi ai ren gazaignat.

Bernart, it is usual for someone who has done his utmost to no avail to give up at that point, for that is precisely what the fox said at the cherry-tree when he had examined it from all sides: he saw the cherries were out of his reach and said they were of no value. In just the same way you have made a fool out of me.

Peirol, cherries they may be, but damn me if I ever believe the fox never tasted them!

Bernart, I say no more about that; but I am annoyed that I have gained nothing through acting in good faith. (Marshall's translation)

The point of the fable is to cast doubt on the fox's claims: he was in no position to know if the fruit was sour or not. Peirol's reason for citing it is, by analogy, to undermine the vituperation of the disappointed lover: how does he know if a lady he was unable to win is worthless? Bernart's response meets skepticism with skepticism. Are we really to believe, he asks, that the fox *didn't* taste the fruit?

This *tenso* thus ends quite differently from the earlier one. Whereas "Amics Bernartz" exhibits carefully balanced structures of contrariety, this works through a series of contradictions as each discussant, rather than affirming the contrary of the other's position, evinces disbelief in it. The predominance of negative particles from stanza v onward in "Peirol, cum avetz tant estat" is an index of this; there are none in the equivalent stanzas of "Amics Bernartz." Although the earlier text admits that contraries *may* coexist to produce a troubling, higher-order truth, the later one doubts whether it has any reliable relation to any truth whatever.

This move from contrariety to contradiction is attested in a number of later Occitan debate poems. In "Peire Vidal, pos m'ave," for example, Peire concludes by asserting that Blacatz's conceptions of a lover, a lady, and love are all unacceptable:

> Non es fis drutz cel que·s camja soven,
> ni bona domna sela qui·l consen;
> non es amors, ans es engans proatz,
> s'oi enqueretz e deman o laisatz.
> (XLV, 29–32)

A man who is often changing is not a true lover, and a woman who puts up with it is not a worthy lady; this is not love but manifest trickery if what you woo today you leave tomorrow.

Similar examples of contradiction can be found in other late twelfth-century *tensos*.[25] The *partimen*, a late twelfth-century debate genre, consistently operates by balancing contrariety with contradiction,[26] as for instance in the series of debates on whether a man should go to bed with his lady by agreeing to restrictions imposed by her, only to flout them once they are in bed. In these discussions, one of the participants must defend the option of not keeping one's word, thereby foregrounding the corrosive impact of negation on the text.[27] Later love lyrics may also pursue the path of negation. This exchange between internal voices sounds almost flippant in "Entr' ir' e joy" (Song VII of Peire Rogier, from the last third of the thirteenth century):

> Dompn' ay.—Non ay.—Ia·n suy ieu fis!
> —No suy, quar no m'en puesc jauzir.
> —Tot m'en jauzirai, quan que tir.
> —Oc, ben leu, mas sempre n'a tort.
> (7–10)

I have a lady.—No I don't.—I'm sure of it.—No I'm not, since I can't enjoy her.—I certainly shall do so fully, even if she makes me wait.—Yes, maybe you will, but she's still in the wrong.

Song VII of Raimbaut de Vaqueiras (...1180–1205...), similarly, balances arguments for and against commitment to love (Lecoy, "Notes," 29); and

Song V of Guilhem Ademar (...1195–1217...) picks up the theme of "amor de lonh" only to contradict the expectations he himself sets up in the song by abandoning his distant lady.

Debates in romances exhibit a similar shift later in the century, as witness the changes in the self-questioning love monologue in *Eneas* (ca. 1155), *Cligés* (ca. ?1173) and *Ipomedon* (between 1180 and 1188). Lavinia in the *Eneas* examines her motives, weighs her options, and plans her moves (8083–334, 8426–44, and 8676–774); Eneas wittily discourses on the arrow with its message that she sent to him and its implications for him (8940–9099); but neither of them shows a marked preference for arguing through either contraries or contradictories. In *Cligés*, however, we find a self-consciously balanced use of both, as Soredamors ponders her reactions to Alixandre:

> Or me grieve ce que je voi.
> Grieve? Non fait, einçois me siet.
> (478–79)

Now what I see grieves me. Does it grieve me? No, rather it agrees with me.

Are her eyes to blame? Rather, her heart, a poetic "contrary" of the eyes:

> Doi les en ge blamer? Nenil!
> Cui donc? Moi, qui les ai en garde.
> Mes eulz a nule rien n'esgarde
> s'au cuer ne plest et atalente.
> (504–7)

Should I blame them? No! What then? Myself, who have then under my control. My eye looks at nothing if it doesn't please and attract the heart.

The influence of dialectic in *Cligés* has been studied at some length by Hunt ("Aristotle," 108–19; see also Nolting-Hauff), who demonstrates its working through of oppositions and the weaving in amongst them of affirmation and denial. When we get to *Ipomedon*, however, we find both La Fiere and Ipomedon resorting to what seems to be its author's favorite argumentative structure, namely a "yes it is" met with a "no it isn't" and vice versa (cf. Peire Rogier VII, cited above). Thus La Fiere says of her heart,

>   —Il ne puet mes.—Certes, si poet!
>   —Nanil, quant si fere l'estoet.
>   (965–66)

It can't do more. Yes it can. No it can't, not even if it had to.

Did Ipomedon take leave last night just to go to his lodgings, she wonders:

>   Noun fu! Si fu! Y pensa de hel!
>   (1052)

No he didn't! Yes he did! He had some other plan!

Did she act rightly in rejecting him?

>   —Si avez.—Non ay, si Deu plest!
>   (1067)

Yes you did. No by God I didn't.

What about her words to him?

>   Ceste parole rien n'amonte;
>   si fet! Jeo eüse fet qe sage
>   si eüse dit mon corage.
>   —N'estes pas sages. . . .
>   (1084–87)

That doesn't carry any weight. Yes it does! I'd have been wise to say what I felt. You're not wise. . . .

Similarly, Ipomedon is unsure whether to leave or not:

>   Jeo ne sai pru qe jeo quer si,
>   si sai! pur estre maubailli.
>   (1141–42)

I don't know what advantage I can look for here; yes I do, to be ill used.

This insistent "yes it is—no it isn't" dominates the entire text, and seems to be making fun of conventions of argument already no doubt made ironic in *Cligés*. The fact that the later scenes are modeled on the earlier ones makes these changes in argumentative technique all the clearer.

Both the secular genres of lyric and romance—the major genres of courtly literature—thus keep pace with one another through the 1180s–1190s in their common disengagement from the heady "both–and" register they had formerly entertained. As they do so, they also play with the possibility that the whole courtly edifice may be unpersuasive, unimportant, or indeed—who knows?—a lie.

Disavowing, reneging, and downright lying in lyric and romance

Already the narrators fielded by Thomas and Chrétien mark an aesthetic distance from their tales. But this distance expands alarmingly with the appearance of romancers who admit to manipulating the plot in order to gain favor with their beloved. The date of the oldest such text, *Partonopeu*, is a matter of controversy; composed perhaps as early as 1170, it may have been written considerably later.[28] It is uncertain, then, how much time separates it from the next known instance of the same device, Renaut de Beaujeu's *Li Biaus Desconneüs* (1185–1190, and anyway before 1210–1214). Both narrators interject and comment on their stories, comparing them with the purported "reality" of their own love affairs and thereby underlining their romances' fictive character; in particular, they declare the endings of both to be negotiable subject to the responses of their ladies (see Krueger, "The Author's Voice," 122–29, and Walters).

The possibility that the text of a romance might be quite different from what it is finds equally radical expression in *Ipomedon*. Previous narrators may be masters of irony, but they leave actual misrepresentation—deceit, forgery, and lies—to their protagonists. Hue de la Rotelande's narrator, however, admits that he is a liar:

> Ore entendez, seignurs, mut ben;
> Hue dit ke il n'i ment de ren,
> ffors aukune feiz, neent mut,
> nuls ne se pot garder par tut.
> (7175–79)

Now listen very well, lords; Hue says he is not lying about anything except sometimes, and then not very much; no one can avoid it all of the time.

Admitting that the poet may mislead is also characteristic of the late twelfth-century lyric. Hints at unspoken words that might undermine and even contradict those which are pronounced are common throughout the corpus of Arnaut Daniel (...1180–1195...,; e.g., Songs II, VIII, IX, and XV). This crystallizes in a disquieting *arrière-plan* of contradiction in Arnaut de Maruelh (...1195...), occasionally surfacing in explicit admissions of dissimulation and downright lying (see, e.g., X, 35; XVI, 42; and Chapter 3). The same is true of Peire Vidal (...1183–1204...). In "Una chanso ai faita" (XXVI) Peire Vidal represents himself as both deceived and self-deceiving. Struggling to interpret his lady's behavior, he wryly puts her in a no-win situation where the more pleasing she is, the less she is trusted.

> Mas ges no·m par qu'ill n'aja bon talen,
> e non per tan, quan me parla, e·m ri
> e promet me; mais anc mais no menti
> nulha dona tan azaut ni tan gen.
> Pero·l bels ditz me torn' en alegransa,
> e si·m disses vertat, ab tota Fransa
> non estera ta suau ni tan be;
> mas non a cor ni voluntat en re.
>
> (17–24)

But it doesn't seem to me at all that she is well disposed, and yet she speaks to me and smiles, and makes promises, but never did a lady lie so cleverly or convincingly; nevertheless her fair word cheers me, and if she *were* speaking the truth, then I wouldn't be so comfortable or so well-off if I had all of France; but her heart and will are not in it.

Peire's thought here is convoluted. His lady is ill disposed to him, *and yet* his lady behaves kindly to him, *and yet* his lady is lying to him, *and yet* he is cheered by her behavior; *if* she were sincere, he would be really pleased, *but* no, she isn't sincere. The theme of deception licenses this parody of an argument in which, paranoiacally, the conclusion is assumed to be the same as the premise (his lady does not care for him). Against logic such as this, the evidence of the senses—the fact, for example, that Peire's lady is actually very nice to him—has no value. (See also Peire's Songs XXIII, XXXVII, and XLII; the latter two feature in Chapter 2; and on the topos of the "true lie," see Chapter 3.)

By the late twelfth century, then, negation in both lyric and romance operates not only in the way arguments are explicitly conducted, but also as a persistent undercurrent insinuating the contingency, unreliability, or downright mendacity of the text. The previous generation's reliance on topical argument to frame ethical or political debate has given way to a more whimsical interest in fictionality and in the ways arguments can generate both sense and nonsense. Allusions to the "liar paradox" (that is, the difficulty of ascribing either truth or falsehood to the statement "I am lying") may reflect dialecticians' interest in such logical puzzles (known as *insolubilia*) precisely at the end of the twelfth century (see Chapter 3). Courtly texts have evolved as complex artifacts, recognizable as the antecedents of imaginative literature today.

Romancing hagiography

There remains one final twist in this plait to be described: the attraction exercised by this now highly elegant and elaborate courtly literature on hagiography. *The Life of Saint Evroul* was composed in the latter part of the twelfth century and is representative of a shift from *passio* to *vita* also found in the late twelfth-century lives of *Giles* and *Genevieve*.[29] The biographer's concentration on experience and the passage of secular time means that contrariety—the countering of the human perspective by the divine—is less prominent in the thought of *vitae* than in earlier martyrology. Through its emphasis on lived human reality, the *Evroul* is open to contradiction and even to irony.

Like Leger, Evroul starts out as a successful courtier at the court of Clothaire but then decides to enter a monastery. The story seems indebted to the Alexis legend in that Evroul recognizes his monastic vocation when on the point of marriage and persuades his intended bride to leave the world at the same time as he does.[30] However, the text distances itself from the isolationist cast of the Alexis by vigorously upholding community, whether of court or monastery. Evroul keeps leaving monasteries because he is the object of too much veneration, but his attempt to live an eremitical life results in disaster for his monks. In the last years of his life, Evroul brings to monasticism the qualities of the ideal courtier: he is charitable, forgiving, eloquent in resolving disputes (2221–26), generous, and *cortois* (2239). After a saintly life, he dies at the ripe age of eighty. The lengthy account of the social anarchy following his death underlines the importance of good leadership and communal responsibility.

Evroul eschews the rhetoric of contrariety, mainly by introducing the image of a ladder (*l'eschiele*, 443) to mediate the contraries of temporal and spiritual values.[31] The ladder's steps consist of the virtues by means of which one ascends from earth to heaven. It is made

> de charité,
> sobrieté et castité,
> de l'amour dieu et de son prisme.
> (453–55)

of charity, sobriety and chastity, of the love of God and one's neighbor.

When Evroul describes this ladder to his prospective wife, she agrees to work with him on "preparing" and "making" it (507–12), so that they can ascend it together to glory. The image recurs as Evroul seeks

> a proier dieu secreement,
> et monter viguerousement
> de vertu en vertu drechant
> et a dieu toujours aprechant.
> (1491–94)

to pray secretly to God and to climb strenuously, rising from virtue to virtue, and always getting closer to God.

Just before he dies, its rungs of *charité*, *sobrieté*, and *castité* are recited once more (2420, 2427, and 2428), along with other virtues Evroul has acquired in the course of his ascent. The ladder image inserts a space between the contraries of "earthly" and "heavenly," which earlier texts, as we saw, tend to superimpose. It recasts contraries as a hierarchical progression with mediating elements and thus holds them apart while also asserting their interconnection. This kind of gradualism as a means of mediating contrariety has a long history in medieval thought (see Kruger, *Dreaming*), but this is the only example I have found of it in hagiography. A means of resolving contraries through time, such as I discerned earlier in the twelfth century in lyric and romance, has found a place in hagiography. But the passage of time, as well as enhancing control over contraries, can also insinuate contradiction of the text's claims.

When he leaves the monastery of Deux-Jumeaux to start a new community in the wilderness, Evroul and his monks are challenged by bandits who oppose the usurpation of what they see as their territory:

> Vostre preu point ci ne ferez,
> ci n'a pas bonne demouree
> a gens de vostre renommee,
> n'est pas demeure a hermitez,
> mes a larrons. . . .
>
> (968–72)

It won't be to your advantage to be here, this isn't a good place for people of your reputation to stay, it is not a dwelling place for hermits but for bandits. . . .

Evroul rebuts them point for point:

> Quant le larron out ice dit,
> saint Evroul a tout contredit;
> son propos a tout retourné
> et dit, que pas ne sunt tourné
> en ce bois par forcenerie,
> mes pour miez amender leur vie,
> non pas pour usurper leur terre,
> mes pour dieu devotement querre. . . .
>
> (989–96)

When the bandit had said this, Saint Evroul gainsaid[32] him; he turned every word upside down and said that they had not come to this wood from lack of sense but in order to live better, not to usurp their land but devoutly to seek God. . . .

The *Evroul*, like Beneit's *Becket*, constructs its arguments with care. But whereas the logic of Beneit's *Becket* polices the separation of clergy from laity, in *Evroul* attempts to separate monks from bandits are undermined by experience. The bandits convert and become monks, so that over time the dichotomy between them breaks down; subsequently more robbers are attracted to Evroul's monastery by its *renommee* (1395) and, more concretely, its pigsty; later again, Evroul goes into a spiritual retreat and the monks, deprived of his strong leadership, are led into evil ways. After Evroul's death the ground claimed by the monks returns to the control of bandits. So although Evroul himself denies any similarity between monks and bandits, the story, for its part, rather suggests that they are situated on a continuum on which there is room for movement and exchange: bandits may rise to become monks, and monks sink to become bandits. In permitting this implication, the narrator of *Evroul* allows a chink of irony into his text.

The passage of time—a great deal of it in some cases, as these saints can be long-lived—provides the subject matter of saintly *vitae*. *Evroul* is far from admitting to deception, but the very device it has used to eliminate contrariety—the image of the ladder—has had the ironic effect of linking the terms "monk" and "bandit," whose connection it denies. In its investment of the temporal process with contradictoriness, as well as in its biographical impetus, hagiography has grown closer to romance.

Thus concludes the plait which I see woven in the course of the twelfth century by the genres under study. As patterns of contradictoriness shift, all three genres undergo changes that draw them into changing relationships with one another. Because of the uncertain dating of medieval texts, the chronology of these changes cannot be grasped with precision. But even if we knew the date of every text, precision would still be lacking given that we cannot expect all twelfth-century texts to conform to a single neat pattern: we are faced with gradual shifts rather than abrupt switches, and even if a development were datable, it is unlikely that all poets would be affected by it simultaneously. My image of the plait is intended rather to suggest an evolving interaction.

These caveats aside, there seems to be a general progression from paradox toward a peak of contrariety in the 1160s and 1170s and then away from it toward explicit negation and its implicit counterpart, an ironic undermining of the text. As these developments unfold, relations between genres alter. Initially the genre which has the most straightforward relationship with contradictoriness is romance; early examples of hagiography and lyric are more elaborate. In about the 1170s, however, romance responds to these other genres. Perhaps because of the relatively early influence of dialectic on both lyric and romance, and maybe as a result of its own impact on romance, the lyric, which previously had more in common with hagiography, plaits across to join romance. The two secular genres join forces, following similar patterns of contradictoriness to one another and establishing the growing cultural ascendancy of "courtly literature." Subsequently, the influence of dialectic permeates to hagiography. By the 1180s the prestige of logic is apparent in all genres, even though it has to compete with other models of contradictoriness. Under what looks like the influence of romance, hagiographic texts gradually disengage themselves from the strongly contrary framework, eternal versus temporal, of the early poems, and focus instead on the saints' experiences in the world. As this last strand in the plait crosses over, all vernacular texts have become less static, less caught in structured oppositions, and more able to engage progression, argument, and irony. Instead of embracing the topical schemes beloved of the midcentury texts, they seem increasingly seduced by the New Logic as they play with complex chains of reasoning and the fun of argument for its own sake. Detailed studies of particular aspects of this history follow in the next two chapters, and critical and theoretical implications in those that come after.

CHAPTER 2

"High" and "low":
a conduit of contradictoriness

The last chapter identified certain points in the twelfth century at which conceptions of contradictoriness cross over from one genre to another. The significant periods for these exchanges seem to be the early 1170s, when romance takes on features of lyric and hagiography, and the 1180s onward, when hagiography increasingly admits the rationalism and interest in human temporality associated with romance. Before the 1160s, lyric has more in common with hagiography than with romance but subsequently, lyric and romance move closer to one another. This move gives new solidity to the phenomenon of "courtly literature," which in turn appears to exercise an attraction over hagiography. Central to these changes is generic treatment of the form of opposition known to dialectic as "contrariety." By examining the use of contrariety in a motif that links texts across the century, we will obtain a close-up of how responses to it pass from genre to genre and thus of how part of the plait of contradictoriness is formed.

One of the most common oppositions in twelfth-century texts is that of the contraries "high" and "low," which can be articulated in a number of different ways (cf. Gravdal, *"Vilain"*). "High" and "low" can be terms with spiritual significance (celestial distinction may await those who seem in earthly terms to be insignificant); spiritual values can readily be aligned with moral meaning (humility and self-abnegation may indicate moral superiority); moral meaning, in turn, can easily take on social coloration (the lowly but deserving person may turn out to be of noble birth); and this can slide into material implications (not just noble, but also rich . . .). Manifold situations can be conjured up in which lowliness may be the sign or harbinger of its contrary, so that what seems low is in fact already high, or is destined to become so; and the reverse process may also be precipitated whereby the high can fall back into the low (pretensions punctured, pride punished, secular position toppled, wealth forfeited, and so on). In consequence, the opposition is adaptable to many literary contexts. Saints who are despised or degraded in human terms will reap a heavenly reward and may, indeed, already enjoy special divine favor; their debasement typically results from the sacrifice of the worldly status and wealth into which they were born, the surrender of which is the index of their moral and spiritual superiority. Lyric lovers who humble themselves deserve to be raised up by the Lady's love. Knights who undergo humiliation or rejection can rebuild their reputation; their internalization of debasement can be the springboard of their subsequent return to favor. The high–low opposition, in short, serves to knot together concerns of different kinds—religious, erotic, social, moral—all of which lend themselves to the defining, or contesting, of the hierarchical frameworks so dear to twelfth-century thought. As a result, it is an ideal vehicle for transferring preoccupations from one genre to another.

There are a number of motifs relying on this opposition whose movement we can trace over the course of the twelfth century. One is martyrdom. Originating in hagiography, moving into lyric poetry from about Bernart de Ventadorn onward, and then being taken up by romance (e.g., in *Cligés*), martyrdom is a sacrificial wager whereby utter subjection is embraced in hopes of lasting glory. Another motif exploiting the polarity of high and low is that of a protagonist exiled and stripped of all humanity only to be subsequently raised up: like Mary the Egyptian, a noble girl who leads a life of sexual degeneracy but then atones for it by a lifetime of destitution in the wilderness. The protagonist cast out of society but enabled thereby to gain enhanced stature is a familiar figure in genres other than hagiography, such as the troubadour exiled literally or metaphorically from his homeland and his love, or the heroes of *Yvain* and *Partonopeu* who forfeit their Ladies' love, go mad in the forest, and wander incognito, but eventually win her back. A third high and low motif which likewise transmits patterns of contradictoriness across genres is that of the unacknowledged "great one" concealed in lowly surroundings. This motif can be traced back to the earliest vernacular *Life of St. Alexis*, a saint who ends up dying literally "under the stair" of his parents' house where he has lived unbeknownst to them for seventeen years. It occurs in a wide range of texts in which a protagonist is abjected and despised among people who should properly recognize him as their own; after his debasement, or because of it, the hero may emerge as superior to them all.

I devote this chapter to the motif of the great one "under the stair," reserving martyrdom for Chapter 6 and *Yvain* and *Partonopeu* for Chapter 7. One reason for this choice is the suitability of the Old French Alexis material: the oldest *Alexis* texts (*L* and perhaps *A*) predate the rise of lyric and romance but are then followed toward the end of the century by another redaction (*S*). We are thus able to observe the motif as it travels both *out* of hagiography and *back* into it again. Another reason is that in between these versions of the *Alexis*, the motif of the great one "under the stair" finds expression in several major texts: Thomas's *Tristan*, Chrétien's *Charrete*, Hue de la Rotelande's *Ipomedon*, as well as a number of troubadour songs. My interest is not in the history of the motif as such, but in analyzing how its underlying framework, its configuration of high and low, becomes modified as it passes between genres, thus providing a case study in how generic strands cross over one another to form the plait of contradictoriness outlined in Chapter 1.

St. Alexis (*L text*)

The version of the *Life of St. Alexis* preserved in the Hildesheim manuscript (*L*) may be as old as late eleventh century[1]; the status of *A*, which contains a text similar to that of *L* but shorter and more irregular, is more controversial and I use it for comparative purposes only.[2] The narrative of *L* is as austere as its implacable protagonist; we are given minimal explanation of his motives, and there is little direct speech until the three set-piece laments by his father, mother, and abandoned bride. Alexis leaves his wealthy Roman background in order to escape marriage and devote himself to God. He sails to Alsis (Edessa), where he leads a holy life as a beggar until he is miraculously hailed by a statue of the Virgin Mary as "l'ume Deu" (the man of God); thereupon he leaves because "d'icest' honur nem revoil ancumbrer" (188, "I do not wish to be burdened once more with this honor"). Alexis takes a ship bound for Tarsus but storms drive it instead to Rome. He is fearful of encountering his family lest they once again burden him with honor ("de l'honur del secle ne l'encumbrent," 200). Although he recognizes their longing for his return and seeks to satisfy it by living under their protection, he does not risk his salvation by revealing himself to them (206–10); indeed, he asks his father to look after him for the sake of the lost son for whom he grieves (216–20). With tears in his eyes, the father agrees and Alexis is installed "under the stair" of the parental home (218, 231, 246, 261, etc.[3]). Although he observes his relatives' incessant mourning, his devotion to God is so single-minded that he remains unmoved by it (241–45).

I have paraphrased this episode in detail to bring out its paradoxical cast. So as to escape worldly honor, Alexis goes from being a stranger in Alsis to being a stranger in his own home, secure at last from recognition in the very place where he might most have expected to find it. He asks his parents to show him charity as though for their son, thus indicating that there is a sense, contrary to ordinary understanding, in which he no longer is. He is trying to accommodate his relatives' human desire (though he himself has left such ties far behind), but contrary to the way they themselves would have chosen and without their knowing that their desired object is at hand. The saint he is becoming has replaced the son and husband he once was, so that his family cannot recognize him and yet neither, with their worldly eyes, can they see the emergent saint.

The spatial opposition of low and high is the chief vehicle of this paradox: Alexis "under the stair" is too low to be perceived as a man of rank, whereas the proximity to saintly glory of his lowliness is too contrary to human expectation to be apprehended. Only at one point does the paradox crystallize in a figure of speech: "a grant poverte deduit sun grant parage" (248, "in great poverty he leads his life of high rank"). Elsewhere it is presented in narrative terms. "Low" beneath the stair, Alexis is thrown table scraps, mocked and insulted, drenched in household water by his father's slaves, his sufferings ignored by all. He endures these indignities with Christlike fortitude, praying for his tormentors to be forgiven "since they know not what they do" (270). Seventeen years of this befit him for the glory which God intends for him (295). Hailed after his death as the "man of God" (297), he is publicly acclaimed as savior of the city. Physical debasement was the sign, all along, of the spiritual splendor that awaited him. His abject humility in this world, and his rigorous refusal of every human gratification, are the pledges of his spiritual distinction and the joys of paradise to come. As Johnson and Cazelles put it, Alexis imitates "Christ's achievement of victory through humiliation" (*Le Vain Siecle*, 38).

THOMAS OF BRITAIN, ALEGRET, MARCABRU

An episode "under the stair" occurs in the Douce fragment of Thomas's *Tristan*. Following Isolt as Blanches Mains's revelation to her brother Kaherdin that her marriage to Tristan is still unconsummated, Tristan explains to Kaherdin his love for the first Isolt and shows him the statues he has made of her and Brengain. This rouses Kaherdin's interest in Brengain, and the two of them travel to England to see their Ladies. Brengain, however, is led mistakenly to believe that Kaherdin is a coward, and she angrily resists the proposal that she should marry him. The Douce fragment opens with her raking up old scores with Isolt; Isolt's attempts to pacify her only inflame her further. Furious, Brengain denounces Isolt to King Mark—not for Isolt's love for Tristan, which Brengain dismisses as never having amounted to anything, but for being at risk of seduction by Cariadoc. As a result, Brengain is given complete charge over Isolt, who becomes virtually a prisoner (Douce, 477–80). Tristan and Kaherdin depart, but Tristan, desperate to see Isolt, steals back disguised as a leper. Isolt recognizes him and wants to give him her ring; Brengain, however, recognizes him too and quickly intervenes to prevent it. Desolate, Tristan slinks away and huddles under a stair wanting nothing but to die (603–6).

A protagonist has escaped from an unconsummated marriage and travels to die as an outcast under a stair near the people to whom he is closest: it is hard not to see this as an allusion to the Alexis legend, if not to the actual text(s) just discussed.[4] The phrase "under the stair" recurs repeatedly, as it does in *L*, as though to urge the connection (598, 604, 626, 647). But how are we to read this allusion? Critics agree that Tristan's "lowliness" lacks any corresponding spiritual elevation.[5] At best he may hope for some reward in love (Cazelles, "*Alexis* et *Tristan*," 93); at worst, his sensuality stands condemned in contrast to the ascetic purity of the saint (Delcourt, *Éthique*, 63–65). Delcourt rightly points out that Thomas's scene reverses the *données* of the *Alexis* in a number of ways. Tristan has come to be with his sexual partner, not to avoid her, and she is someone else's wife, not his own. Instead of being unrecognized, his presence is known to Isolt but she dares not meet him. Rather than sacrificing himself by lying under the stair, Tristan retreats there consumed only by despair. Far from being despised, as Alexis was, by household servants, it is servants who rescue him; he is taken for a devil (633), not a saint. And instead of dying and being united with God, Tristan does in fact subdue Brengain's anger and enjoy a night of love with Isolt before riding away. Rather than turning his back on the *Alexis* narrative, Thomas actively resists and recasts it.[6]

Does Tristan's suffering, when he is "low" under the stair, justify the "high" of the two lovers' union afterward? Is Tristan in some way love's "saint," his sufferings rewarded by love? The Douce fragment narrative loosely evokes many early troubadour songs where the lover is unable to approach his Lady and yet where the more he abases himself for love, the greater his anticipated joy in her favors becomes. A song by Alegret (...1145...), a *joglar*-composer who was either a predecessor or an early contemporary of Thomas, will serve as example. The lover in this song is not literally "under the stair," but he is an abject figure, "vencutz e sobratz" (1, "vanquished and overwhelmed"), prepared to be slain for love (5?,[7] 9–10). He would be satisfied just to be allowed to kneel before his Lady like her serf, weeping and with joined hands, but he dare not risk her rebuff (stanza iv). Any favor she shows him seems to him fabulous wealth:

> Pauc n'ay de be e meyns cre que n'auria,
> qu'era·m fai tan de gaug un vostre ris
> que si·m davon Tors, Angieus e Paris,
> ni re ses vos tan de gaug no·m faria.
> (I, 37–40)

I have little good (favor/well being/property) and fear I might have less, for a smile from you gives me more joy than if they gave me Tours, Anjou, and Paris, nor would anything apart from you give me such joy.

The song concludes that the height of elevation for him would be "to have conquered the entire world," and then "wish [his Lady] to have lordship in everything" (43–44).

Alegret's song thus swings between utter debasement and extravagant self-promotion. One is transformed into the other through metaphors of strength and wealth which represent him simultaneously as having servile status and as enjoying universal domination, as a man defeated and as world conqueror. The poorer he is, the richer his Lady can make him; the more he suffers, the more he can enjoy; the lower his assumed position, the higher his deserts and his eventual reward. Although the terms in which Alegret couches these contraries are secular, their operation resembles that of the *Alexis*: both embrace the logic whereby the lower you are, the higher your merit.

The conclusion to the leper episode in Thomas, by contrast, fails to deliver a "high" anywhere near equivalent to the protagonist's "low." Reconciled with Brengain, Tristan goes with her to join the queen:

> suz en une chambre marbrine.
> Acordent sei par grant amur,
> e puis confortent lur dolur.
> Tristan a Ysolt se deduit.
> Apres grant pose de la nuit
> prent le congé a le enjurnee
> e si s'en vet vers sa cuntree.
>
> (720–26)

high in a marble chamber. With great love they are reconciled and then they console their suffering (pain/grief). Tristan takes pleasure with Isolt. After a long part of the night, when day is breaking, he takes his leave and departs in the direction of his land.

I assume that my translation of line 720 is correct because the expression "sus en une chambre" is a common one. There is, then, a purely spatial elevation when Tristan goes "up" to the chamber which, as the most private part of the interior of a residence, is the contrary of the outdoor stairway at its entrance which previously he was "under." The scribe, however, has written not *sus* ("up") but *suz* ("under") exactly as in the phrase "suz le degré" ("under the stair"). So even the spatial "high" is canceled by the text; while emotionally all the lovers are said to achieve is some pleasure and redress of their sufferings. The relation of high and low is thus quite different than in Alegret. Able to cultivate thoughts of bliss after merely fantasizing servility, the troubadour would not need almost to die of exposure before earning his reward; preferring his Lady's smile to Tours, Anjou, and Paris, a night in her arms would surely have filled him with rapture. The heights achieved by Thomas's Tristan seem very moderate by comparison, while the lowliness he endured was disturbingly, genuinely painful.

When, therefore, Thomas resists the *Alexis* episode as much as echoing it, his resistance does not take the form of substituting for its high–low opposition an equivalent, erotic one from the lyric. "Low" is not presented as the presage and justification of "high"; rather the negative low is sustained and intensified, while the positive high is placed in suspension. The only one of the early troubadours of whose practice this is reminiscent is Marcabru, who, like Alegret, is probably an early contemporary of Thomas. Marcabru keeps emphasizing the need to draw moral distinctions (in this, as we saw in Chapter 1, he resembles the authors of the *romans antiques*). Yet his pessimism about our ability to do so successfully, or to follow the right option afterward, blinded as we are by our carnal natures, means that he constantly privileges low over high. As a result, the distinctions he tries to establish tend to collapse into their negative pole.[8]

There are no literal stairways under which abject figures cower in Marcabru's songs, although there are kitchens (XXXI) and corridors (XXIV) where outsiders and social undesirables lurk. Song VII, however, chimes with the Douce fragment episode, including the motif of Tristan's disguise as a leper, because Marcabru represents all those who suffer from Love as plunged into disease and destitution[9]:

> A nuill home que dompnei
> no quier peior malavei:
> be mor de fam e de frei
> qui d'Amor es en destrei!
> (5–8)

For any man set on courtship I could not ask for a worse sickness; whoever is in Love's grip certainly dies of cold and hunger.

Tristan under the stair is likewise colder than ice (Douce, 645), while his feigned leprosy has become actual infirmity, leaving him

> pale de vis, de cors endeble,
> megre de char, de colur teint.
> (704–5)

pale-faced, his heart sickly, his flesh skinny, his complexion discolored.

Marcabru goes on to speak of Love's folly as a weight which drags the lover "low":

> Ben es cargatz de fol fais,
> qui d'Amor es en pantais.
> Senher Deus, quan mala nais
> qui d'aital foudat se pais!
> (21–24)

The man tormented by Love is well laden with a foolish burden. Lord God, how the man who feeds himself on such folly should regret the hour of his birth!

Subsequently his imbecility turns him from the cabbage of life to its stalk (*sic*, 48). Instances of lowliness accumulate as these physical images of intellectual and moral decline also invoke social degradation to the condition of peasants or even of beasts.

Is there a high to match this low? Only one which has been canceled:

> C'Amors es plena d'enguan,
> per aver, s'o vai camjan,
> e·ls plus pros torn' en soan
> que·l malvatz l'aura enan.
> (25–28)

Love is full of deceit on account of money, and ever fickle, and it despises the most worthy/the bravest so that the base/bad/cowardly man will have it [Love] sooner.

In Love's toils, the good end up worse than the bad. Although Marcabru's own sense of social exclusion may sometimes be harnessed to justify the moral authority of his voice, Marcabru does not speak from the position of one whose lowliness supports a claim to elevation. The vocabulary of falling, declining, and degeneracy runs through his poetry, and typically he is compromised by the downward tug himself. In Song VII, for example, he speaks as an angry and disappointed lover, one who has only just escaped the thrall of what he now denounces (11–20). Even for the poet himself, the dichotomy of high and low tends to collapse downward, the negative term prevailing.

Thomas's third-person narrator may have more detachment from his material than Marcabru's first-person moralizing voice, but his treatment of opposition is very like the troubadour's. In his revision of Alexis under the stairs, "down" means really "down." Tristan is brought low by the animosity and deceit of Brengain, he has wrecked his life to the point where he has reason to despair, and even his assumed illness becomes real. The suspension of the opposite term, the high, does not mean that Thomas's narrative is merely literal and lacking a moral dimension. No one would say that Marcabru, for all the savage coarseness of his humor, lacked a moral outlook. To overlay an episode from the life of an ascetic with Marcabrunian pessimism on the theme of love is, on the contrary, a particularly powerful means of underlining the guilt and moral limitation of lovers. The saint's transcendence, after all, is exceptional, whereas most human beings aspire to be lovers at some point. Unable to reconcile the aspirations of love with the ubiquity of obstacles and deceit, lovers should hesitate to appropriate the saint's wager that low is really high and just accept their lowliness, the sickliness and debasement of sensual desire.

In the texts considered up to this point in the century, then, the love lyric and hagiography are allied in treating high and low as ultimately equivalent—what appears debased already encodes a supreme elevation—even though their subject matter is utterly opposed, insofar as the lover seeks precisely what the saint shuns. Thomas, however, like Marcabru, seeks a separation of high and low that is compromised by the precariousness of the positive term. This situation will change markedly in the slightly later texts I consider next.

Chrétien de Troyes, Giraut de Bornelh

It may seem odd to include the Lancelot of Chrétien's *Charrete* in this series. He does not lodge "under the stair"; nor does he die in destitution. But when he attends the tournament at Noauz, he seeks out shockingly humble accommodation ("petiz et bas," 5509) where his bed, described at surprising length as poor and rough (5530–35), recalls Alexis's wretched bed, emblem and witness of his sufferings. The narrator professes astonishment at so fine a man as Lancelot lowering himself in this way (5507–11). Like Tristan in the episode just examined, Lancelot does so in order to avoid recognition; and like Tristan, he is unsuccessful, being recognized at the outset by the feckless herald and gradually, in response to her testing, by the queen. Although Alexis differs from both romance heroes in remaining unrecognized by everyone, the enigma attaching to the saint's identity is echoed in the *Charrete* more than it is in the *Tristan*. Alexis is both the son of wealthy parents and *l'ume Deu* with no worldly attachments; Lancelot at the tournament famously veers between covering himself with glory and accepting ignominy at the queen's behest. Unrecognized by most people there, he arouses a fever of curiosity as he provokes by turns the admiration and jeers of the onlookers.

Chrétien's debt to hagiography is clearest in the way he assigns to his hero the sacrificial spirit of a saint. In Thomas's *Tristan*, the lovers suffer because their desires are incompatible with their human situation. The plot of the *Charrete* could have lent itself to similar treatment, depicting Lancelot as Love's tragic victim. But instead Lancelot seems inured to suffering, displaying rather a saint's sublime endurance. Already before the Noauz tournament, Lancelot has acquired stigmata by crossing the sword-bridge and liberated the prisoners of Gorre in scenes recalling the Harrowing of Hell (Owen, "Profanity"; Kay, "Who Was Chrétien?"). Guenevere's recognition of his identity earlier in the text, when he first fights Meleagant in Gorre, has been likened to the Virgin's declaration that Alexis is *l'ume Deu* in the Alsis section of the *Alexis* (Nichols, "Amorous Imitation," 57). Like Alexis, Lancelot willingly casts aside secular honor and degrades himself in the eyes of the world. He does so at the start of the romance in the cart episode and he does it again at the tournament. Love, or Guenevere's whim, takes the place of the divine. Lancelot declares his will entirely subject to hers (5655–56, 5891–93).

By the same token, the polarity of low and high, flattened by Thomas, is reinstated by Chrétien. The ladies of Noauz have engineered the tournament as a device for testing possible husbands:

> De cels qui le feront noauz
> ne tandront parole de rien,
> mes de ces qui le feront bien
> dient que les voldront amer.
> (5370–73)

Of those who perform badly there will be no more talk; but of those who perform well, they say they will have a mind to love them.

Presented here in the antithetical terms *noauz–bien*, the tournament is also framed antithetically given that the ladies' hopes of marriage at its outset are countered by their despair of achieving it at its end. The action itself is carefully built around antitheses. On the first day Lancelot, incognito, fights so well that everyone asks, "Qui est cil qui si bien le fet?" (5635, "who is that who is performing so well?"); and Guenevere answers the question to her own satisfaction when Lancelot obeys her instruction to fight "au noauz" (5645, "as badly as possible"). On the second day, both terms of the antithesis are imposed by her: he is to fight first "au noauz" (5853) and then "au mialz (5879, "as well as possible"); he willingly complies "del bien come del mal" (5914, "with good and ill alike"). And so he alternates between cowardice and prowess, while observers' reactions swing wildly in response. This insistently antithetical patterning underlines the extent to which the whole scene is conceived according to the contraries of high and low. Just as the elevation of the saint results from God's releasing him from his sufferings and crowning him with splendor, so the blaze of glory in which Lancelot exits the tournament results from Guenevere deciding to end his cowardly performance and inspire him to the height of worth. The episode concludes with the admission that he has no equal (6025).

Hagiographic influence does not, of course, account for all of the features of this scene. Something of Thomas's analytical aloofness persists in Chrétien's account of an imperturbable Lancelot being bounced by Guenevere between disgrace and acclaim. Chrétien's narrative also has a comic side to it, which presents an even greater deviation from hagiography. Detachment and comedy may serve to palliate what might otherwise be seen as the flagrant impiety of the *Charrete*. For whereas Thomas's overlaying of romance and hagiography reinforces orthodox misgivings about sexual passion, the same generic combination in Chrétien's hands could strike readers as anything from hilarious to blasphemous. The moral tenor of the episode, like that of the entire romance, is notoriously hard to judge. Indeed, the tournament crystallizes interpretative problems from throughout the text (Bruckner, *Shaping Romance*, chapter 3). In the initial cart scene, for instance, Lancelot's apparently unchivalrous behavior likewise sets up antithetical reactions, some condemning him as disgraced, others hailing him for his redemptive role.

What relationship does the *Charrete* posit between these extremes of high and low in which the protagonist is placed? In the *Alexis*, as we saw, high and low are in an important sense the same; low is not really low but a sign of spiritual elevation and a pledge of heights to come. Similarly, a courtly poet such as Alegret represents submissiveness as a mark of excellence in a lover. The Lady ought to raise up one who has thus shown himself already to have deserved it. The poles of antithesis coalesce in these texts, whereas in the *Tristan*, as in Marcabru, low is low, its distinctiveness being compromised only in so far as little is, or can remain, high. Transferring this problematic to the *Charrete*, is Lancelot's ignominious behavior an expression of the selfsame qualities which make him a superlative knight or does it detract from his excellence?

The Noauz scene implies mixed answers to this question. Its readers within the text, the various onlookers at the tournament, arrive at different verdicts. The ladies of Noauz devise the tournament as a framework for discriminating between good and bad knights, and thus between eligible and ineligible husbands. Although they declare at the start that anyone who fights *noauz* will be ruled out (5370), they continue to find Lancelot absorbingly attractive even after his abysmal performance (5714–15); at the end, they all set their hearts comically and self-defeatingly on him. The mechanism has malfunctioned and the tournament shown itself as *noauz* as its name in establishing difference in these ladies' eyes. Any lowliness on Lancelot's part is ignored, swept up into his utter exaltation "high" above their reach:

> Car tant ne s'osoient fier
> en lor biautez n'an lor richeces,
> n'an lor pooirs, n'an lor hauteces,
> que por biauté ne por avoir
> deignast nule d'eles avoir
> cil chevaliers, que trop est prouz.
> (5996–6001)

For they dared not so far trust to their beauty or wealth or power or high rank, as to imagine that this knight would stoop to have any of them, whatever their beauty or possessions, for he is too worthy.

If the collapse in the ladies' analytical skills is mocked, so are the attempts by other participants to rationalize their wildly veering judgments of the unknown knight. On the first day, they suggest that his initial display of knighthood may have been beginner's luck, but that his lack of true courage is revealed once he has experienced the reality of fighting (5689–99). In a little flight of allegory, they explain to themselves that Lancelot is *malvés* because *Malvestiez* (Evil/Cowardice) lodges within him and *Proesce* (Worth/Courage) does not:

> Mes en lui s'est tote reposte
> Malvestiez, s'a trové tel oste
> qui tant l'ainme et qui tant la sert
> que por s'enor la soë pert.
> (5753–56)

But all Evil/Cowardice has taken shelter in there and found in him a landlord who loves and serves her so well that for the sake of her honor he forfeits his own.

If we compare this passage with one from *Yvain*, we can see how it is as much an instance of underachievement in dialectic as Lancelot's presumed cowardice is in chivalry. For in *Yvain* Chrétien uses the same image—familiar from biblical exegesis[10]—to explore the same question of whether a single person may accommodate contraries. How is it, he asks, that both love and hatred for each another can coexist in Gawain and Yvain?

> Dex! Meïsmes en un ostel
> comment puet estre li repaires
> a choses qui si sont contraires?
> (*Yvain*, 6020–22)

God! How can the home of two things which are such contraries be in the selfsame lodging?

Chrétien is not slow to arrive at the answer which the image itself provides

> Mais en un [chas][11] a plusors menbres,
> quë il i a loges et chambres.
> (*Yvain*, 6029–30)

But a dwelling place has many members, for there are lodgings and apartments there.

Perhaps, the analysis continues in similarly light-hearted vein, Love is in one room while Hatred is in another?

> Ha! Amors, ou iés tu reposte?
> Car t'en is! si verras quel hoste
> ont sor toi amené et mis
> li ennemi a tes amis.
> (*Yvain*, 6041–44)

> Oh Love, where are you concealed? Come out! and then you will see what fellow guest your friends' enemies have brought up against you!

The knowing juxtaposition of friends and enemies in the last line of this quotation reminds us how amity and enmity are complex states which can be construed from different points of view. Beside this virtuoso performance in *Yvain*, the analytical efforts of the onlookers at Noauz, undermined by the very image in which they are couched, are exposed as amateur and unconvincing. They have not gotten very far in sorting out the relation of high and low; indeed, on the second day of the tournament, they abandon the attempt and simply wring their hands over their mistakes (5984–85).

Just as the love–hate passage in *Yvain* resonates with other parts of the romance (see Chapter 1), so the onlookers' judgments at the Noauz tournament are a catalyst to further reflection. The image of *Proesce* refusing to lower herself by taking poor lodgings ("Onques voir tant ne s'avilla / Proesce qu'an lui se meïst," 5750–51) recalls Lancelot's choice of humble accommodation at the start of the scene, where he was presented precisely as "Prowess . . . lowering herself": "Einz si prodom n'ot mes itel, / car molt estoit petiz et bas" (5508–9, "Never did a man of such prowess have such lodging, for it was very small and low"). Earlier again, Lancelot explicitly repudiated *Malvestiez* by daring to take on the four rapist-assailants of the Hospitable Damsel, thereby showing that he preferred death with honor to shameful flight (1102–15; contrast the accusation of dishonor in 5756). Meleagant, by contrast, is represented throughout the romance as *Malvestiez* incarnate.[12] His most recent behavior—treacherously imprisoning Lancelot to prevent his attending the duel agreed between them—is the antithesis of good or courageous.

And yet Lancelot's willingness to fight badly at a tournament also recalls his preparedness to withdraw from the two previous duels with Meleagant, both fought, like the tournament, under the eye of the queen and their outcome controlled by her interventions. Effectively she has already twice instructed him to act "au noauz" and to spare Meleagant's life at the risk of

Lancelot's own (3788 ff., 5016 ff.). From the point of view of justice and order, then, Lancelot's subservience to the queen may not be without *Malvestiez*. Fortunately, her discretion causes her to be absent from the final battle where Lancelot finishes Meleagant off; we are told she has learned, at last, to submit to Reson, and put aside her follies (6846–47). This passage takes the reader back to the celebrated confrontation between Amor and Reson just before Lancelot mounts the cart. His sacrifice of honor to Love in defiance of Reason contrives to give the impression that Love and Reason are contraries; the conclusion to the romance reminds us that the usual antonym of reason is folly. In opting for Love over Reason, was Lancelot actually embracing foolishness? His passionate love for Arthur's wife is open to censure, different scenes encouraging its reading, variously, as silly (his mooning around at the ford), sacrilegious (his night of love in Gorre), and illegal (the trial of Keu).

In the light of these considerations, Guenevere's own reading of the tournament scene may seem the least adequate of all. She asserts that Lancelot is all hers and she all his, thus defining the identity of each of them in purely reciprocal terms:

> . . . c'or set ele sanz dote
> que ce est cil cui ele est tote
> et il toz suens sanz nule faille.
> (5873–75)

For now she knows beyond doubt that he it is to whom she entirely belongs and that he is entirely hers without fail.

Such self-absorption ignores the legitimate interests of others: Arthur, the former prisoners in Gorre, the people of Logre who await Lancelot as their champion against Meleagant, even the unfortunate ladies of Noauz. Whereas these last ignore the very differences they set out to look for, Guenevere deliberately effaces the distinctions of *bien*, *noauz*, and *mialz* in the totalizing rapture of love. She is blind to the moral or political significance of difference.

The various readers of the Noauz tournament thus all present us with partial and limited readings of the relationship between high and low, and we can be sure that, if we are to improve on their performance, we must look beyond to what they do not say, but what the whole fiction itself performs. Drawing on threads from all over the romance, we weave them into intricate and constantly changing configurations. Sometimes these are conducive to the view that Lancelot's humility really is the sign of its opposite, his superlative excellence, and at others that his "low" really is "low," his exposure to ignominy in some respects justified. This approach to dichotomy as open to fluctuating readings, and as shaped by process rather than stasis is, as I suggested in the last chapter, a characteristic of the lyric of the period immediately preceding and contemporary with Chrétien. The treatment of high and low in the *Charrete*, although closer to that of hagiography than was the case in Thomas, can also be shown to share common ground with lyrics of the troubadours of the generation immediately after Alegret and Marcabru.

Although the opposition of *vilain* and *cortois* is found from the beginnings of the lyric tradition, for the troubadours of the late 1160s and 1170s the opposition of high and low focuses on more specifically social and material meanings, perhaps as poets are drawn from an increasingly wide range of social backgrounds. Although none situates himself, Alexis-like, under the stair, there is no lack of examples of songs where the issue of what is high and what is low takes concrete social and material form, and where representations of wealth and eminence are countered by those of abjection and contempt. The question whether one should love a *ric ome* ("wealthy/powerful man") is raised in the circle of Raimbaut d'Aurenga by such poets as Giraut de Bornelh, Azalais de Porcairagues (...1173...), Guilhem de Sant Leidier (...1165-1195...), and Peire Rogier.[13] And the idea of poetry/love as an alternative form of *ricor* ("wealth") emerges in the same circle, initially in relation to the *trobar clus–trobar leu* debate in which imagery of wealth (or cheapness) is used to figure poetic exclusivity (or accessibility). Although the expression *trobar ric* ("rich composition") is not used before Peire Vidal's "Ajostar e lassar" (III, 1–5), the idea that poetry may be *ric* is first explored in this period, as is also the conception of it as *car* ("dear/rare/precious").[14] "Wealth" in poetry expresses itself in an abundance of meanings which need to be carefully teased out of the text and reflected upon by the careful listener. Raimbaut d'Aurenga and Giraut de Bornelh were both relatively learned poets, so it is not surprising to see a more argumentative approach to contradiction taking shape in their songs and Raimbaut at least seems to have been in contact with Chrétien.[15]

I have chosen to concentrate on Giraut de Bornelh's "Si·m sentis fizels amics" (XXX) as an example of the kind of song which may have influenced romance, because it was composed in this circle in the very late 1160s, appears to have been successful with medieval audiences, and condenses many themes which are prominent throughout Giraut's corpus (cf. III, IX, XI, XII, XXIII, and XXXVI).[16] In particular, the song's complex manipulation of the high–low opposition anticipates what we find in the *Charrete*.

The song stages a lover unsure whether his fidelity entitles him to reproach Love for the humiliations he endures or debars him from doing so. His debasement has a painful materiality, and he experiences a keen sense of social rejection, adopting what Žižek was to call "the excremental position of a saint" (*Metastases*, 93)—not literally "under the stair" but anguishedly abject. The song reflects on his predicament. What makes a lover faithful? How much should he be expected to suffer? To what extent should his abasement—his humiliation even—be treated with derision or taken as an index of his high deserts? Eventually he decides that those responsible for his amorous setback are the inevitable false lovers and *lauzengiers* and so reproaches them instead; at this point, we get the sense that his own moral worth passes unrecognized—that he is, if not "a great one," at least a figure of authority. As the song unfolds, it develops a poetics of high and low in which the concept of *ricor* shifts from worldly status to poetic achievement where meanings are "rich" and equivocal, requiring a dynamic engagement on the part of the listener to tease out the various strands. Indeed, "Si·m sentis" is far from easy and provokes hesitation over alternative possible meanings as we struggle with its contradictions.[17]

The opening stanza poses itself as a puzzle, the first four lines suggesting that the lover is less faithful than he might be and reluctant to suffer, whereas the remaining ones assert that he never had an unfaithful thought and has suffered inordinately.

>   Si·m sentis fizels amics,
>   per ver encuzer' Amor,
>   mas er m'en lais per paor
>   4 que·m dobles l'ant' e·l destrics.
>   Mas aytan puesc dire
>   senz dan
>   c'anc d'enian

> 8   ni de no-fe
> no·m menbret pueis amiei be,
> per c'ay soffert de grans mals;
> c'aisi s'aven als lials!

> If I felt I were a faithful lover I would indeed bring charges against
> Love, but I refrain from so doing because I am afraid she might
> double my shame and distress. But this I can safely say: that no
> infidelity or deceit has crossed my mind since I loved well; that is why
> I have suffered such great ills, for that is the lot of those who are loyal.

If the contradictions in this stanza are to be resolved, it must be through a retrospective assessment of the meaning of fidelity and its relation to suffering.[18] What is a faithful lover? Is it one who is completely undeterred by the humiliations heaped on him by Love? Or does the faithful lover have a right of protest? In short, as in the *Charrete*, is the one who is debased raised up, or is he really, in some ways, just debased?

Uncertainty concerning the relationship of fidelity and suffering is explored throughout the song. Stanzas ii and iii continue to elaborate the dilemma of stanza i. Stanza ii suggests that a lover who has invested in love, like a lord with his land, has a right to expect to harvest a reward. The beginning of stanza iii recalls times when the lover was "wealthier," more able to be indignant about the mortification which he now abjectly endures; but then, in a move antithetical to that of stanza ii, he enjoins humility and long-suffering:

> Eu vi l'ora qu'era rics
> segon lo temps qu'era cor,
> que·m teni' a desonor
> 26   mainz plaitz don ar son abrics.
> Qar vencutz suffrire
>   qui blan,
>   suffertan,
> 30   —quar no·s recre—
> so que plus li descove
> a segon que s'es egals
> l'amors, e l'amics cabals.

> I see a time when I was wealthy in relation to how it stands at
> present, when I used to regard as humiliating many conditions

which, now, I admit[19]; for the long-sufferer who has been defeated but who solicits with long-suffering—provided he doesn't give up—that which damages him [i.e., the ongoing unsatisfactory response from the Lady], receives love, in such measure as is equal [to his love for his Lady?],[20] and [as he is] a perfect lover.

These two stanzas between them, then, hesitate between a "down is down" position (indignation at a lack of reward, rejection of love's outrages) and one where "down is up" (you reap a return, in the form of [the rewards of] love, exactly what you put in of [the suffering of] love).

In stanza iv the dilemma takes a further turn. If you are a perfect lover, but despite the optimism of stanza iii you remain dissatisfied, what are your options?

> iv   E si uns si feynh enics
>   per espaventar l'os lor?[21]
>   Quan plans volers no·y acor
> 37   pauc li val precs ni chastics.
>   Per so fay bon rire
>   d'aman
>   qui l'afan
> 41   d'amor soste,
>   e no·l sap loynar de se,
>   pois ve que·s vira venals;
>   es lo doncs Amors aytals?

Yet who would feign hostility [i.e., not submission, as in the preceding stanza] in order to instill fear in his Lady (?)[22] then? If not supported by straightforward desire, his prayers and rebukes would be valueless. And so one can only laugh at the lover who endures the misery of love and cannot escape it, even when he sees that it is turning exploitative.[23] Is, that, then, what Love is like?

The lover is in an impasse. He faces two choices: insincerity, which will convince nobody, and being an object of general derision because he can't call a halt to the extortionate treatment he receives. Is that what love has to offer? This stanza conveys an acute sense of inescapable social stigmatism. Like Lancelot, the lover is branded as the embodiment of *Malvestiez*. The image of love as exploiting him (*venals*, 43) connects with other financial images in the song to suggest that the lover is truly reduced to destitution by his passion. Love brought him *ricor* in the past; but, as the next stanza will go on to argue, there is no advancing your capital (*captals*) through love (55). Stanza v reflects bitterly on this plight. It is impossible for the lover to know how to choose the lesser of two evils (45–48)—that is, to make a choice between insincerity and being a laughingstock. Thus suffering is inevitable; and though the more one suffers the more right one has to entreat one's Lady (51), the less chance one apparently has of success (55).

Antithesis is subsumed in the thought of this song. It describes a series of impasses in which the themes of fidelity and suffering are looked at from contrary points of view and found to be fraught with contradictoriness: long-suffering provokes rightful indignation and deprives the lover of status, yet it is the only means of reward; sincere devotion is the only option for a lover and yet risks making him look ridiculous; true love is both the key to success and an impediment to it. Its concluding stanzas propose two ways out of these contradictions, neither of them straightforward, as we shall see. The first is the value of the song itself; the second, the relative superiority of the lover to others.

Stanza vi proposes that the only wealth that can be gained through courtship is the wealth of meanings which accrue, through these conflicting experiences, to poetry:

>   Oymais semblara prezics
>   mos chans, e, s'ieu Dieu azor,
>   anc mais non vitz trobador
> 59 cui meins noz'anta ni trics!
>   Mas, per miels assire
>   mon chan
>   vau cerchan
> 63   bos motz en fre
>   qui son tuit cargat e ple
>   d'uns estrayns sens naturals,
>   e non sabon tuit de cals.

Henceforth my song will look like a sermon, and, as truly as I worship God, never did you see a troubadour less vulnerable to humiliation and deceit! But the better to position my song, I go in search of good words that can be led by the bridle and that are all laden with a set of meanings which are foreign but at the same time native, and not everyone knows what they are.

In the first line, Giraut humorously asserts his song is like a sermon. Perhaps he means no more than that it is becoming a homily exhorting others to moral effort. At least he can be satisfied that his own conduct is unimpeachable (58–59). But he may also have in mind that the paradoxes he is working with are reminiscent of those in religious texts, that the problematic relation of effort to reward he has outlined is like that of the sinner to grace.[24] Sharman certainly interprets the thematic of wealth in this song as shifting from material to spiritual or moral value: "the poem teaches the courtly paradox that it is the faithful lover who is ill-used (10–11) and who has no material gain (*captals*) from Love (54–55), but that worth and happiness lie precisely in the humble acceptance of unmerited suffering" ("Introduction," 39).[25] There is some truth in this account. At the same time, however, the "redemption" from lowness to a moral height is not uncontested. The sting of disgrace still hurts; there may be worth in this song, as Sharman says, but where is the happiness? In the next stanza (stanza vii), those who lack the lover's lifelong dedication are branded as *mendics* (67, "beggarly"): this is a "down" which remains "down." And the image which concludes this stanza (60–66)—that of a man on foot, merchant or squire perhaps, leading words like docile packhorses, laden with meanings from home and abroad—also admits a comic abasement in the poet alongside the "wealth" which his poetry can bring. Such riches are clearly better than the "foolish burden" borne by Marcabru's pack animal (VII, 21), but the image nevertheless jars with that of the sermon and underlines the social exclusion of the lover: he may be worthy, but he is still risible.

At the end of the song, the truly low ones are exposed as false lovers or *lauzengiers* (stanza vii onward), the moral gulf between the first person and these others captured in the antithesis whereby the true lover worships God (57) while false ones are accursed (82). The vocabulary earlier applied to courtship is ironically recycled in order to vilify these deceivers (*suffrire* 71, cf. 27; *egal* 74, cf. 32; *chastics* 78, cf. 37; *no-fezat* 87, cf. *no-fe* 8). Lacking the capacity for long-suffering, they deserve nothing but contempt. This stanza reinforces what has been largely implicit earlier in the song, that the lover's qualities are fundamentally misrecognized by those detractors among whom he lives. He has some claim, in his own view, to be admitted as "a great one under the stair." The lover's abjection and loss of prestige may bring public disgrace on him, but those who deride him are lower than his "low."

This song, in conclusion, exemplifies important trends in the troubadour poetry of the late 1160s and early 1170s. Giraut is an educated troubadour, and his manipulation of the dichotomy of high and low is complex. He maps concepts of success and failure in conflicting ways onto images of wealth and status. He acknowledges kinship between amorous and religious discourse, and here his treatment may hark back to narratives such as the *Alexis* in which high and low are both contraries and interchangeable. At the same time, it preserves a keen sense of the social and material reality of humiliation, which it concludes is inescapable, and which it refuses to deny. From these two movements, the song constructs a rich dialectical debate. Its development proceeds within carefully balanced antithetical arguments and is spiced with humor. The contraries are preserved in muted form in their resolution, where even the heights of poetry are risible, and the depths plumbed by other courtiers show the extent to which society is flawed. Songs such as this would have been known to Chrétien. In their knowing combination of dialectical and religious discourses, these learned troubadours form a bridge between the reversible high–low opposition of earlier lyric and hagiography to Chrétien's more complex deployment of it in the *Charrete*.

Hue de la Rotelande, Peire Vidal

Similarities between Hue de la Rotelande's *Ipomedon* and Peire Vidal's lyrics confirm the crossing over of lyric to the same side of the plait as romance, so that what has come into being as "courtly literature" henceforth steers a common course through contradictoriness. These later poets continue to allude to the metaphysical harmonization of opposites found in early hagiography and lyric, but they do so with increasing irreverence and delight in the humorous potential of contrariety.

The three-day tournament in *Ipomedon* owes much to Chrétien, notably the Oxford tournament in *Cligés* and the Noauz episode in the *Charrete*.[26] The Noauz tournament is staged by women hoping to marry the winners, and likewise Hue's heroine La Fiere calls the three-day tournament with herself as prize in order to entice Ipomedon (or rather, the unknown page boy with whom she earlier fell in love) to enter it and thereby win her. And Hue's tricky hero Ipomedon plays a game similar to Lancelot's in that drawn there by love of his Lady he does indeed fight superlatively, but simultaneously covers himself with ignominy by pretending to be an utter coward. These contrary performances are differently structured in *Ipomedon*, however, because whereas everyone can see that the unknown scarlet knight in the *Charrete* is both worst and best, Ipomedon's identity is fragmented by his multiple disguises. He has persuaded Meleager, king of Sicily, La Fiere's uncle, to accept him into his service under the title "le dru la reine" ("the queen's darling"); his duty is the unmanly one of escorting the queen from and to her apartment morning and evening, and his reward is to kiss her when he does so. In this role, he pretends to be such a coward that he dares not even go near the tournament. He claims to go hunting, but in fact he commissions others to pile up mounds of dead game as evidence of his sport. Meanwhile, like Cligés, he fights incognito in three different suits of armor on each of the three days of the tournament and so is taken to be three different unknown knights, each better than the last.

The account of the three days self-consciously recycles the same narrative material, underlining its dichotomies of high and low. Each day we are told of Ipomedon's pretended departure for the hunt, his arrival in disguise at the tournament, his feats on the field, and La Fiere's attraction to the unknown knight. These prompt her to misgivings about her fidelity toward her earlier, unknown, beloved; and her confusion is increased by the teasing messages sent her by Ipomedon, which offer clues to his identity too late for her to act upon them (indeed, she does not always understand them[27]). He meanwhile returns to the queen's court, where he listens to tales of the admirable feats he himself performed at the tournament. Feigning disinterest, Ipomedon counters with offers of venison to the king and burlesque accounts of his dogs' hunting exploits, which are derided by all the other courtiers.

This elaborately camp narrative, although it more obviously recalls the *Charrete*, also contains distant reminiscences of the *Alexis*. For unknown to anyone, Ipomedon is the half-brother of one of the finest members of this household which so reviles him: the king's nephew and seneschal Capaneus.[28] And although he ought by rights to marry La Fiere, he refuses to identify himself as any of the successful knights until after he has left the Sicilian court, but instead runs away, leaving his intended bride sorrowing behind him—a trick he will play again subsequently when he returns disguised as a fool to liberate her from an aggressor and win her for himself, only to walk out on her once more. Like Alexis, though for different reasons, Ipomedon subordinates marriage to his quest for perfection, a perfection paradoxically sought in the depths of ignominy.

In *Ipomedon*, however, the opposition of high and low is social and amorous rather than moral or spiritual. The protagonist is the object of both the highest plaudits and the deepest contempt. To the "high" and "low" estimations of his worth correspond the parallel roles of La Fiere and the queen, the first falling for his prowess even though she has given her heart, as she thinks, to a different man whom she misguidedly scorned, the second finding him adorable even though she sees him in the worst possible light. High or low, then, the hero is irresistible to women. And each woman's responses involve her in her own drama of humiliation. On the first day of the tournament, the queen's courtiers mock her favorite to her face:

> Dame, veez la vostre dru!
> Cist cunquerra mut ben la Fiere
> par suvent aler en rivere.
> (3284–86)

Madam, look at your darling! He'll certainly win La Fiere by going hawking all the time!

On the third evening, the queen "ki mut volenters de amur fine / l'amast senz fere trop lunc plet" (6574–75, "who would not have put up too much resistance to loving him with true love") calls Ipomedon back to her apartment after he has kissed her goodnight, asking him to be with her early in the morning. However, he abruptly refuses, preferring the company of his dogs, and leaving her despondent (*murne*, 6588). In La Fiere's case, shame and self-reproach at the failure of her plan are repeatedly expressed in the motif of pride brought low. On the second day, she even compares herself with Lucifer, who was also cast down by excessive pride (4595–604). She cites proverbial wisdom:

> Redient: ki munte trop haut
> tost pot descendre a mauveis saut;
> jo meisme sui trop haut muntee,
> a grant hunte sui devalee,
> abatu est tant mun orgoil,
> or me faut quanques jo plus voil.
> (4609–14)

And people also say: whoever climbs too high can quickly descend to a dreadful plight; I myself climbed too high and am brought low in disgrace, my pride is so dashed down, now everything I most want is lacking to me.

La Fiere's shame is compounded by her having undertaken to marry the winner or else give up her estates (2485–510): an unfavorable outcome may bring a "low" of total destitution.

La Fiere's decision to call the tournament results from an earlier dilemma in which the opposition of high and low also plays a defining role. At the start of the romance, she publicly vows never to marry anyone

> si il ne fust chivaler si pruz
> ke il as armes venquit tuz,
> ke en totes terres ou entrast
> le los e le pris en portast.
> (129–32)

unless he were such a valiant knight that he could defeat everyone at arms so that in every land he entered he would carry away the glory and the prize.

This solemn undertaking earns her the name "La Fiere" ("proud, unapproachable, fierce") and causes her to scorn the young Ipomedon when, as yet not knighted, he visits her court incognito. Already he attracts unfavorable notice for his apparent indifference to fighting and, in a scene anticipating the "dru la reine" episode, La Fiere rebuffs him for his apparent interest in her while in fact falling in love with him herself. So impassioned does she become that even though he leaves her court in humiliation, she confides to her sister her resolve to marry no one except him (1556–57). Publicly claiming to aim "high," then, La Fiere has also committed herself to loving someone about whom she knows nothing and who may prove wholly undeserving ("low"); he is simply known to her to as "the foreign page boy" ("l'estrange valet"). Her hope is that the tournament will tempt him back and prove his valor; but the succession of attractive and seemingly unknown knights who keep winning plunge her into agonies of self-doubt.

Feminist scholarship on *Ipomedon* has shown how the plot attributes a range of typically misogynist faults to the women characters, especially La Fiere—pride, cunning, fickleness, sensuality—and then punishes them for these faults.[29] And yet as Penny Eley ("Anti-Romance of *Ipomedon*") points out, although La Fiere fears she is fickle, in fact her heart does not mislead her and the succession of unknown knights to whom she is drawn are the same as the so-called foreign page boy she first loved. Furthermore, although she suffers during the tournament, its outcome is a success for her. Her two vows, to marry the best knight and to marry the *valet*, which had been incompatible, are reconciled at the end of it when Ipomedon's identity under his various disguises is revealed (though his name remains unknown) and all the members of the court ratify La Fiere's determination to marry him (6890, 6894). The figure of contempt is accepted as the same as the best knight; those who mocked his "low" performance discover they themselves were the objects of his mockery, and the "high" opinion prevails: La Fiere is vindicated. Indeed, the narrator himself endorses La Fiere's initial vow, pointing out that it can be wise to hold out for the best (160–64). Although tricked and tormented, she eventually gets what she wants.

She does not succeed through her own agency, however, nor through that of Ipomedon: the romance's denouement is brought about when Capaneus recognizes his half-brother by accident. By contrast, the lovers' actions seem, with perverse logic, to drive them ever further apart. The tournament episode is typical: even though by the end of it the couple know that each loves the other and their love is publicly approved, Ipomedon refuses to accept his prize. This impossibility of resolution arises from the impasse in which the opposition of high and low places the two principal characters. The romance is given over in large part to the playful manipulation of these terms.

The problem with La Fiere's initial vow is that its fulfillment depends on identifying who is the best knight. The same problem affects her subsequent calling of the tournament. Much of the fighting there consists in Ipomedon worsting various of La Fiere's declared suitors. Their intention is to show that they are the best knight; and such an intention, the narrator suggests, is doomed to backfire. For the narrator, Ipomedon's show of ignominy is a mark of his real worth. His refusal to boast of his prowess indicates "duble chevalerie" (4270), and his skill in concealment shows his wisdom and cunning (5335–37). The only way to be best is not to want to appear so, because otherwise one falls victim to complacency and vainglory. Thus the less Ipomedon appears to be the best, the more deserving he will be. Only, of course, he must not think of himself as deserving; to do so would be instantly to become undeserving. He can only be best by being convinced he isn't. Thus at the end of the tournament he tells his astonished landlord that he is too young to claim La Fiere and still needs to seek his reputation ("quere mun pris," 6648).

His words here recall his self-reproach when rebuffed by La Fiere at the very beginning of the romance:

> Eschar est grant de nous bricons
> ky *querrom* d'amer achaisons,
> ke unqes n'eümes *los ne pris.*
> (1149–51)

We oafs are ridiculous who seek opportunities for love without ever yet having any distinction or reputation.

This monologue, in turn, picks up La Fiere's taunts against

> uns fous qi n'ad quei despendre,
> ainz q'il con*querge los e pris,*
> veit suspirant e trespensifs.
> (882–84)

A fool with nothing to spend [and who] before he wins distinction or reputation goes round sighing and lovesick.

Ipomedon's behavior throughout the romance is a perverse rehearsal and reversal of the terms of this taunt. Does she think him too much of an unworthy fool to aspire to her love? He will show her what it means to be an unworthy fool while simultaneously exciting her love for him regardless. Does she think that one should acquire a reputation before seeking love? Then he will punish her by utterly failing to acquire one, ensuring by constant recourse to disguise and incognito that his prowess cannot be acclaimed, while at the same time teasing her with hints that he has the means to win renown did he so choose and proving himself irresistible even when unknown.[30] Ipomedon's double move both to justify La Fiere's disdain and to repudiate it by actually meriting her admiration lends itself to psychoanalytical reading: by acting out her scorn of him, he returns her own message in an inverted form and thereby presents himself to her as the object of her desire.[31] But his antics can also be looked at from the perspective of medieval dialectic. Sophistically, his behavior proposes that if to *be* the best knight, one must appear *not* to be the best knight, then to set out to appear to be the *worst* knight will lead to his really being the *best*. This parody of deductive logic relies on the elementary error of confusing a contradictory (best–not best) with a contrary (best–worst). What makes this fallacy the more piquant is that it guys precisely the identification of low and high which, as we have seen, characterizes religious and ecstatic thinking in literary texts earlier in the century. Such an identification may work as long as it enjoys metaphysical support, but from the perspective of secular logic, low and high can only be equated through sophistry. Being fallaciously persuaded that to be the best knight he has to go on appearing to be the worst, the hero—even though he really *is* the best—can't possibly marry La Fiere because there is always more reputation or ignominy for him to achieve

The mystery of the unknown knight's identity is thus constructed by recourse to sophistical argumentation; and it is also resolved sophistically, by arguments which rely on the misuse of a supposed identifying feature as a middle term.[32] How are Ipomedon's various masquerades to be reconciled and referred back to him? On the second day of the tournament, the white knight who had seemed supreme the day before is not thought half so good as the red knight who is now winning (5429–34); by the third day, only the black knight is deemed praiseworthy (6291–94). In *Cligés*, where the Oxford tournament follows similar lines, Arthur's knights realize that the three mystery knights in different colored armor are all the same man because he fights so well: he is identified by the positive quality of his superlative prowess (4821–22, 4827–28, 4834–36). The problem with the identifying characteristics proposed in *Ipomedon*, however, is that they are negative or nonexistent. On this final day, Ipomedon hints to La Fiere that what links all three knights is the fact that none of them was present together at the same time as the others:

> Si jo i fusse des avant er,
> n'eüst pas le blanc chevaler
> ne l'autre vermeil er choisi,
> mes or pert ben ke jo sui ci
> [...]
> et quant jo m'en serrai parti
> o mei en menrai sun ami.
> (5775–78, 5787–88)

Had I been here as early as the day before yesterday, the white knight would not have been seen nor, yesterday, the other one, in red; but now it is obvious that I am here [. . .] and when I leave I shall take her lover with me.

This riddle offers as a clue to the identity of the three knights the fact of the absence of two of them. And it is argument by reference to a nonexistent middle term which eventually leads, similarly fallaciously, to the denouement. Because nobody knows who the best knight is, they eventually realize that the one nobody knows, and who seems to be the worst knight, must in fact be the best knight. Capaneus follows this sophistical logic when he eventually cracks Ipomedon's disguise as a madman: someone who can disguise his worth so well, Capaneus intuits, can only be the same person as the other person who disguised his worth so well earlier:

> Ne se poüst covrir si nuls
> se ne fust li druz la reïne.
> (10070–1)

No one could have disguised himself so well, unless it were "the queen's darling."

When La Fiere learns that Capaneus and Ipomedon have accidentally discovered that they are brothers, she proceeds with the same reasoning. Will the one who is other than she thought he was turn out to be the same as the other one who wasn't what he seemed?

> Ha, Deus, car fust ço mis amis!
> mes ne sai se il est mort u vifs;
> issi se soleit il covrir
> e sul aler e sul venir.
> (10355–58)

Oh God, if only that were my love! But I don't know if he is alive or dead; he used to disguise himself in just such a way and come and go on his own.

Discovery that the unknown is the known and the worst the best allows her uncle officially to declare that the terms of her vow can be fulfilled: she can marry Ipomedon, "ke el mund n'ad meuldre chevaler" (10473, "for there is no better knight in the world"): a happy outcome for the lovers because

> or se entreaiment tant par amur
> ke il se entrefoutent tute jur.
> (10515-16)

now they love each other with so much love that they fuck each other all day.

How are we to read the treatment of high and low in *Ipomedon*? Critical responses to the romance vary, but my own view is that it adopts two ways of dealing with contrariety, both of which withhold belief in any higher-level synthesis or equivalence of opposites. The first, as I hope my commentary has shown, is to revel in intellectual froth and nonsense, parading delightful sophistries whereby the best knight can only be the worst one, and someone no one can recognize can only be the same as others no one can recognize either. The second is to counter all this intellectual posturing and the chivalrous etiquettes in whose service it is invoked this with a no-nonsense emphasis on the "realities" of sexual attraction, frankly celebrated in the denouement and epilogue of the romance. Coward or champion, the hunky hero—as Hue leeringly reminds us—has what it takes where women are concerned.

Lifting contrariety to the forefront of the text, making fun of the mechanisms of argument, and casting doubt on the possibility of transcendent resolution are characteristics Hue de la Roteland shares with his contemporary Peire Vidal. Peire promotes his poetry as *trobar ric* ("splendid/rich/powerful composition"), which I understand as meaning that his songs both exhibit and solicit *ricor* ("splendor/wealth/power") of different kinds. The opposition of high and low recurs throughout as Peire humorously assumes by turns the role of emperor and poverty-stricken supplicant. Peire's most obvious reminiscence of the Alexis legend is the poor man huddled in a rich man's house in the opening stanza of "Plus qu'el paubres" (XXXVII):

> Plus que·l paubres, quan jai el ric ostal,
> que noca·s planh, sitot s'a gran dolor,
> tan tem que torn az enuech al senhor,
> 4 no m'aus plaigner de ma dolor mortal.
> Be·m dei doler, pos ella·m fai erguelh,
> que nulha re tan no dezir ni vuelh;
> sivals d'aitan no·lh aus clamar merce,
> 8 tal paor ai que no s'enueg de me.

No more than the pauper lying in a splendid house who does not complain at all, even if his suffering is great, he is so afraid it may annoy his lord, do I dare to complain of my mortal sorrow. I ought by rights to be sorrowful, given that she treats me arrogantly, and I do not desire or want anything as much as I do her: and yet I am afraid even to ask her pity, I am so afraid she will be irritated with me.

The abject tone continues in stanza ii, but in stanza iii, Peire unexpectedly criticizes his Lady for her sinful behavior in failing to succor him, and reveals that his only complaint against her is for withholding "so don plus mi duelh" (22, "what I am really grieved about"). His situation is now dramatically reversed from what it was in stanza i: suddenly he represents his love as a rich estate from which he risks being banished (29, *faidit*, a term usually denoting someone who has been evicted from their lands). Moreover, he expects still more "wealth" to follow—better than all the possessions of the Plantagenet princes (stanza iv). We see then that low and high in this song are not terms which chart spiritual meaning and together conduct mysterious exchanges, but rather motifs strategically deployed in fantasy narratives of a lover who sees himself as destitute or enriched, depending on how he reckons his chances of sexual success. As in *Ipomedon*, the opposition is expressed in the humorous pursuit of exaggeratedly contradictory plot lines, the resolution of which lies not in transcendence but bodily satisfaction. A later poem "Quant hom honratz" (XLII) likewise displays bravura play with the low–high opposition.

As in "Plus que·l paubres," the lover in "Quant hom honratz" initially presents himself as a rich man made destitute and, deeply embarrassed by this reversal of circumstance, groping for ways to regain favor:

> Quant hom honratz torna en gran paubreira,
> qu'a estat rics e de gran benanansa,
> de vergonha no sap re com si queira,
> ans ama mai cobrir sa malanansa. . . .   (1–4)

When a man of position/respect, who has been rich and happy, falls into great poverty, in his shame he does not know how he might ask for anything; instead, he prefers to conceal his unhappiness. . . .

In stanza ii, it appears that his lost wealth was metaphorical, consisting in his Lady's good will, now withdrawn. Indeed, she has become an implacable enemy (stanza iii). We later learn that she has good reason to be annoyed. He called her a liar, a mistake he now regrets:

> Tort ai quar anc l'apellei messongeira,
> Mas drutz cochatz non a sen ni menbransa.
>
> (36–37)

I was wrong ever to call her a liar, but an anguished lover has no judgment or presence of mind.

The song, it becomes clear, has to solve the problem of how someone who has behaved as badly as he has can possibly request a return to favor (3). Peire's solution is metaphorically to reverse the relations of high to low between himself and his Lady and thus "conceal his unhappiness" (4) beneath a cloak of fabulation. Whether or not *she* was a liar, *he* can create fantasy scenarios whose fictions are the opposite of the literal truth. She has cast him low from high but, by means of the image of warfare (stanza iii onward), he turns the tables on her:

> Ren no·m val forsa ni genhs qu'eu·il enqueira,
> plus qu'a l'enclaus, quant a de mort duptansa,
> que bast dedinz e trauc' e fa arqueira
> e contra l'ost pren del traire esmansa.
> Mas l'autr' arquers de fors es plus ginhos,
> que·l fier premiers per aquell luec rescos:
> e ma dona·m ten en aital balansa.   (21–28)

No force nor wit I might have recourse to helps me against her, any more than it would to a man besieged (shut in) who is afraid of death, who builds, drills, and creates arrow slits on the inside facing the army and takes his aim to shoot; but the other bowman on the outside is more cunning, and strikes him first through the concealed opening: and this is how my Lady holds me in the balance.

His supposed destitution is reversed into the metaphorical wealth of a man in charge of a castle who fortifies and defends it against assault. This in turn contrasts with the social demotion of his Lady to the position of a bowman ("l'autr' arquers de fors," 26). This strategy continues in the following stanza (v), where she is metaphorically presented as a fowler, another low-class occupation. Peire Vidal thus represents himself as the victim of an ignoble opponent.

His admission, then, that when he said she was a liar, he was not speaking the truth, does not lead to his being more truthful. He praises his Lady for her truthfulness in having rejected him!

> Qu'a pauc no muer, quar tan m'es vertadeira,
> que loignat m'a de la paubr' esperansa,
> don ieu era a las oras joios;   (38–40)

for I am almost dying, she is so truthful, since she has cast from me the poor hope which I at times rejoiced in;

he asks her to make peace with him (42) and then, in a further flood of self-aggrandizing fantasy, starts delivering corrective advice to his genuinely rich and powerful addressee, King Alfonso II of Aragon. Just as Ipomedon, reproached with not having a reputation, sets out to disgrace himself ever more completely in the public eye, so Peire atones for misrepresentation with ever more outrageous imaginings, in which he plays on extremes of wealth and poverty.

The fantastical exploitation of contraries, and the ring of humor in Peire's songs, mark their kinship with the developments we have seen in *Ipomedon*, confirming the crossing over of lyric to the same side of the plait as romance. Both these authors puncture the spiritual, ecstatic or moral pretensions of earlier treatments of the dichotomy of high and low, disengaging themselves from the possibility that low could mean high while at the same time burlesquing the logical procedures which serious dialecticians deployed to avoid such contradiction. Where intellectual issues are concerned, Hue and Peire will run with both hare and hounds, provided they have a good run for their money. As they do so, they turn courtly themes—the "chivalry topos" and devotion to one's Lady—into dialectical pranks. "Courtly literature" is constituted not only as the alliance of lyric and romance but also as the object of its own humorous reflection.

(v) Alexis (S text)

In the last section of this chapter, we see how a redaction of the Alexis legend from later in the twelfth century differs from the version with which we began. Unfortunately, it is impossible to assign a date to the *S* text; Elliott implies a range ca. 1160–1187 but also stresses its oral-improvisational and hence open-ended textuality.[33] Preserved in a thirteenth-century manuscript, *S* is an expanded version of *L,* apparently influenced both by the *chansons de geste* (because it is in *laisses*) and by romance. These expansions mitigate the bleakness of the earlier narrative and make it less confrontationally paradoxical (Elliott, 28–43). Attempts are made to soften and justify the saint's behavior and to lessen the chasm between him and his family.

This *rapprochement* between the saint and ordinary humanity is effected partly on Alexis's side. The saint's icy indifference in *L* toward his family's plight is replaced in *S* with compunction at the grief he has caused. As he leaves Alsis, Alexis regrets his cruel treatment of his bride (*S,* 494–96). He feels guilty at how he is treating his parents when installed in their house (*S,* 736–42). Just before his death, he has a final exchange with his mother in which he begs her pardon and receives forgiveness from her and his bride (*S,* 859–71). And partly this *rapprochement* arises from an answering flicker of recognition on his family's part. When his father asks Alexis, "Biaus crestïens, ne savons vostre non" (795, "Fair Christian, we do not know your name"), Alexis accepts the name given him by his father:

> "Sire," dist il, "Crestïens ai a non,
> et trestout cil qui levé sont des fons."
> (797–98)

"Sir," he said, "my name is Christian, as it is for all those who have been baptized."

This assumption of a generic identity helps to heal the painful separation of son from saint. His mother comes closer to recognizing him:

> Quant jel regart, membre moi de mon fil;
> pour un petit nel resamble del vis.
> (842–43)

When I look at him, I am reminded of my son; their faces are almost alike.

The way the text treats the polarity of high and low also marks a retreat from the stark confrontations of *L,* because in *S* the motif of the saint "under the stair" is much less prominent. Line 231 of *L,* which contained the phrase, is not preserved in *S.* Other lines are altered:

> L 218   Suz tun degrét me fai un grabatum
> S 720   Un grabeton me fai sour ton degré
>
> L 246   Soz le degrét ou il gist sur sa nate
> S 765   Sour le degré u gist sour une nate
>
> L 261   Suz le degrét ou il gist e converset
> S 778   Sous le degré ou il gist et converse

Note how in two out of three cases, *S* has substituted *sour* ("over") for *suz* ("under"). In passages added by *S*, when the father goes to ask Alexis's name, he goes *up* the stair to find him:

> Monta li pére les degrés contremont
> et voit gesir son fil el grabaton.
> (792–93)

The father climbs up the stairs and sees his son on the mattress.

Conversely, when Alexis is avoiding all contact with his mother and former bride, he sees them climbing up and down the stair *above* him (825, cf. 817). The spatial relation has become blurred. In passages added by *S*, Alexis's quarters are referred to not as being "up" or "down" but by the verb *herbergier* ("lodge") or its cognates (666, 682, 686, 703, 706, 718, 726). The idea is repeated that his family's lodging him will be rewarded by God lodging them (678, 692) or their lost child (729). The paradox whereby low is high is replaced by a language of nonhierarchical inclusion and exchange.

The text seeks by these means to mediate the terms of what, in *L*, was the paradoxical relation between the perspective of the world and that of eternity. *S* is not only more realistic, as Elliott has pointed out, but also more rationalistic, keener to reconcile and smooth out contrariety. The Alexis story has become more willing to compromise with the secular world.

This chapter has traced the history through the twelfth century of a story line organized around the contrary terms "high" and "low." At first, texts crucially depend on upholding both terms simultaneously. In *L*, Alexis's abjection is a mark of spiritual distinction. In Alegret, and more problematically in the *Charrete* and Giraut de Bornelh, lowness is also a pledge of future elevation. To uphold contrariety is to point to something transcendent: God, love, moral or courtly worth. Already for Thomas in the *Tristan* and the moralist Marcabru, however, contrariety is suspect. These poets enjoin practicing discernment in order to contain our human follies; sadly, we often prove unequal to choosing what is higher and end up confined in our own debasement. Perhaps both authors are shocked at the way secular love poets appropriate the Christian trope of lowliness rewarded. When Jesus spoke of the meek inheriting the earth, he probably did not have in mind self-styled lovesick troubadours extracting sexual favors from their Ladies. But the trope is inherently ambiguous between spiritual, moral, social, amorous, and physical highs and lows. These ambiguities are exploited down to the last equivocation by poets such as Giraut or Chrétien. Chrétien's Lancelot is the best knight because he loves Guenevere so much that he is willing to pretend to be the worst knight, but he is also the worst knight because he loves Guenevere when he ought not to. Earlier practices in the treatment of high and low leave their trace in *Ipomedon*, whose hero finds exaltation in ignominy and who chivalrously performs a series of sophistries with his contrary identities. Although the riddles posed in *Ipomedon* may likewise spur some readers to a quest for moral meaning, I think they reflect the crossover in the plait whereby late twelfth-century poets—such as Peire Vidal—disavow the fervors of earlier generations, undercut them with a current of negation, and turn strategies of reasoning into a game. The success of the combined mass of courtly texts may be legible in the kinds of revisions made to the Alexis story by the redactor of the *S* text. The domains of God and the world may still be contrary to one another, but room is found for accommodation and compromise. Thus a chapter which began with the stark separation and conflation of high and low ends with attempts to rationalize the middle ground between them. Contrariety is a medium which, whether embraced, resisted or mocked, serves to plait religious and secular texts tightly together.

CHAPTER 3

At the edges of reason

The opening chapters have outlined an evolution in the forms of contradictoriness used in twelfth-century texts. Such forms probe at the very processes of thought, for how can one think without recourse to the fundamental mechanisms of opposition (such as negation and contrariety) on which language depends? To draw on these mechanisms is to rehearse the operations of understanding, affirming its capacities or exposing its limitations.[1] The notion of what is and what is not contradictory maps the contours of the rational and thereby implies, or defines, areas of the non- or superrational; dividing "sense" from "nonsense" is among its effects.[2] The forms which contradictoriness can take in the twelfth century include what the Introduction identified as the Aristotelian principle of non-contradiction (whereby "it is impossible for the same thing both to belong and not to belong at the same time to the same thing and in the same respect") and a Neoplatonist or Christian tradition in which writers such as Augustine admit the coexistence of contraries or contradictories in a higher harmony. These two traditions imply contrasting positions on the relationship between rationality and ontology: as one of Aristotle's most-used propositions affirms, for him "man is a rational animal,"[3] whereas for Augustine this rational self is in fact darkened and deluded so long as it fails to see according to God's light. Experimenting with different forms of contradictoriness can lead, then, to questioning the status of the rational function and how far the subject can be identified with it. Such questioning is taken further in negative theology, which relies on negating what we think we can understand. Exploring how truth may exceed the intellectual framework which we bring to it illustrates how the contradictory, in addition to defining subjectivity, can structure the objects of our thoughts. Contradictoriness also mediates our relation to temporality: is the passage of time integral to argument as process, or does understanding depend on recognizing structures which hold independently of time? In short, forms of contradictoriness draw attention to the edges of reason and point beyond them, interrogating the reliability of the analytical categories in which we try to frame our understanding.

These effects are emphasized in literary texts where rational control can be subordinated to ecstatic abandon or analysis combined with fantasy and nonsense, "reason" with "folly," to cite one of the most-used contraries contained in twelfth-century texts. Awareness that contradictoriness is integral to their own textual substance is discernible in many of the works of this period. The influence of dialectic, or the debt to biblical, mystical, or theological registers of argument, will indeed have been more obvious to medieval writers and audiences than it is to us. We do not need to suppose that all twelfth-century authors and their publics had completed advanced courses in logic to surmise that they would have had some knowledge, even if elementary or second-hand, of the major intellectual preoccupations of their day. I have suggested that the gradual shifts discernible in vernacular texts over the twelfth century attest to the increasing prestige of the logical tradition over other ways of negotiating contradictoriness; to playful experimentation with different traditions of thinking about contradictoriness; and eventually to the rise of the New Logic in favor of the Old. Such changes suggest that authors were aware not only of there being an edge to reason to which they were drawn, but also of a desire to keep the edge, to make sure that they did not fall behind prevailing opinion, and that whatever the gratifications of working with contradiction might be—transcendence, control, passion, sophistication, danger, humor—they should be ready to exploit them.

The first chapter traced the interlacing of more or less rationalist impulses through the various genres. In this chapter, I will examine specific instances where texts draw attention to the edges of reason and thus, as in Chapter 2, offer a close-up of issues raised in Chapter 1. Starting with the most "rationalist" end of the spectrum, that represented by the *romans antiques*, I suggest how the sense of a limit to reason is depicted by Benoît and Thomas through reference to the square of opposition. Then I examine how, in the late twelfth-century *Life of St. Catherine* by Clemence of

Barking, the traditionally paradoxical cast of hagiography is combined with dialectical defense of the Incarnation. The chapter concludes by reconsidering the notion of a "dialectic of composition" elaborated by Jörn Gruber. Starting from the relatively "irrationalist" cast of the early troubadours, I argue that later ones preserved the enigmatic quality of "true" love and its deceptions by emulating the New Logic's interest in *insolubilia*. These three sets of examples will enable us to perceive the impact of intellectual changes on particular texts. They reveal the interaction between the philosophical complexity of the twelfth century and its great literary themes of history, knighthood, love, and faith: all areas whose claims on the individual go beyond the limits of the rational.

Boundaries and the square of opposition in Benoît and Thomas

All of the *romans antiques* contain lengthy descriptions of fabulous edifices (on which see also Chapter 6). These descriptions "monumentalize" the antique past, functioning as an architectural *translatio* which preserves its splendors for posterity. Not only are they metaphors of the enduring value of the ancient tradition which the *roman* in question commemorates; they also draw attention to the intricacy, the marvels, and the unprecedented achievements of which art is capable.

Of the many such descriptions contained in the *Roman de Troie*, the longest is that of the Alabaster Chamber ("la Chambre de Labastre/Labastrie," 14631–958).[4] It falls at the midpoint of Benoît's great romance and is, as Penny Sullivan has pointed out, a *summa* of the cultural achievements of Troy, ironically positioned at the fulcrum of events leading to their destruction ("Medieval Automata," 12). We are told that it was given by Priam to Helen when Paris stole her from Menelaus (14952–54), thus provoking the major siege of Troy narrated in the romance. It is described when Hector's wounds are being tended there after the eighth battle, and shortly before his death at the hands of Achilles in the tenth, the heroic disaster which will eventually lead to the fall of Troy.[5] The Chamber is significantly placed, then, in relation to defining moments of Benoît's history; and its role as a metaphor for his poetic undertaking is supported by the loving account he gives of its astonishing artistry.

The Chamber's design is square. Four pillars mark its four corners, each wonderfully beautiful and precious, and each adorned with an automaton which seems angelic (14680). Two are of boys and two of girls. The smaller of the girls holds a mirror in which those who enter the Chamber can see themselves and check whether there are any faults in their appearance or demeanor (14681–710). The other embodies courtly merriment. She dances and tumbles, and conjures up spectacles on a table before her:

> fait merveilles de tel semblant
> que ne porreit rien porpenser,
> [. . . wild animals, battles, monsters . . .]
> que n'i face le jor joër,
> e lor natures demostrer.
> (14722–23, 14737–38)

She conjures up marvels such that there is nothing one could imagine [. . .] that she doesn't make a spectacle of at once and display its nature.

Her marvelous distractions make all who see them forget their cares and watch, riveted.[6] The first of the two boys, regally seated and crowned, performs music on a wide repertoire of musical instruments to accompany whatever is going on in the Chamber. His music is so spiritual that it soothes away unpleasant emotions and pleases lovers (14780–804). He also strews flowers. Above him an eagle dodges the small club hurled at it by a little satire and, when it flies, the wind from its wings withers and sweeps away the flowers so that they can be renewed; in this way the Chamber is always freshly scented with sumptuous blooms. The final automaton, the second boy, shows those in the Chamber what they most need to do and how best to act so as to avoid faults and cultivate virtue. He carries a censer, the smoke from which guards those who smell it from deceit, suffering, and evil (14896–913). These artistic creations enable those in the Chamber to forget the horrors of the war outside and take pleasure instead in the courtly qualities which the automata provide: elegance, entertainment, ethical and even spiritual improvement.

The description of the Chamber is rich in implications for the conception of the *Troie* as a literary artifact. Its alabaster walls function in such a way that from inside one can see out but not the other way around (14926–31): art provides a means of viewing the world outside, whereas those without are not privileged to view the world through the lens of art. It is no coincidence that its automata are said to be the work of poets (14668–69). They transfer the reader away from the violence of historical experience into the timeless aesthetic of art.[7] But art is not just beautiful; it also provides an intellectual and ethical framework. Between them, the four figures define a number of significant relations. The order in which they are described represents a hierarchy of different levels of perception. Those embodied in the girls are physical, starting from external appearance (the mirror) and progressing to an external representation of the nature of the created world. Although all the automata are said to be angelic, the impact of the two boys is described as "spiritual" (14787, 14911) and their effect is felt inwardly, whereas that of the girls is not. The first boy inspires pleasant emotions and offers the opportunity for discretion; the second boy guarantees proper behavior.

This hierarchical progression from the two female automata to the two male ones is combined with a series of correspondences and dichotomies in the interrelations between the four. The spectacle-mounting girl and the boy with the musical instruments both provide courtly distractions. The girl makes people forget their troubles, whereas the boy favors beneficial emotions and his music helps to safeguard secrets: so the girl's appeal is to vision, the boy's to feeling and expression. The mirror girl and the boy with the censer both recommend courtly behavior, and indeed the mirror is a standard medieval metaphor of right conduct, but again the boy offers enlightenment in relation to action and the girl to physical appearance. Thus the whole Chamber offers an image of the work of art as didactic: as proposing, through its oppositions, a framework for judicious discernment in all areas of experience.

Now a square whose four corners between them create a framework for rational reflection is precisely what is offered by the square of opposition. As we saw in the Introduction, this is a basic logical tool for configuring the relations between four interrelated ideas; the example given there was the influential Aristotelian one involving universal and particular propositions (see Introduction, 13–14). Throughout the Middle Ages, the square of opposition was also used as a device classifying things in general, and in such cases, its four corners present not propositions but interrelated terms, as in this example from Macrobius (Figure 4):

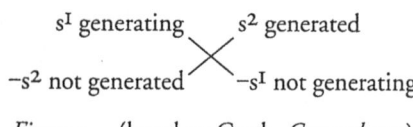

```
    s¹ generating      s²  generated
                   ╲ ╱
                   ╱ ╲
   –s² not generated   –s¹ not generating
```

Figure 4. (based on Gersh, *Concord*, 140)

As in the propositional example, each of the two upper terms is negated (i.e., contradicted) by the diagonally opposite term, but the terms on the top horizontal axis, although opposed, are not contraries in the sense of being mutually canceling; rather, they represent a preliminary stage in the classification of Beings. From this square, one can proceed to posit a more complex structure by combining its terms as follows (Figure 5):

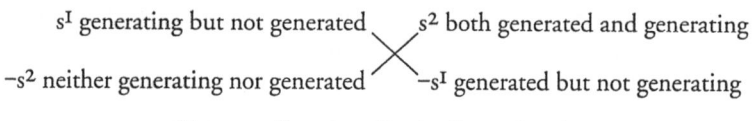

```
  s¹ generating but not generated    s² both generated and generating
                                 ╲ ╱
                                 ╱ ╲
 –s² neither generating nor generated   –s¹ generated but not generating
```

Figure 5. (based on Gersh, *Concord*, 140)

Studying the common ground between contrary terms was a route to identifying universals. Neoplatonist thought was especially interested in their interaction; Augustine, for example, stressed the interrelation of contrary terms rather than their incompatibility. As a result, "discussion of contrariety can be blended with that of parts and whole." The combination of contraries resulted in the "coincidence of opposites" as a means to higher unity (see Gersh, *Concord in Discourse*, 122–28).

Benoît's Chamber can be understood as a square of opposition similar to that of Figures 4 and 5 in that it is designed primarily for classification rather than argumentation (see Figure 6):

masculinity (spiritual)

ethical boy	musical boy
heightened perception of self	*distraction and diversion*
mirror girl	conjuring girl

femininity (physical)

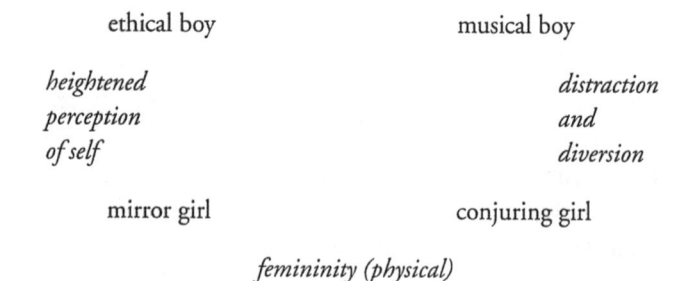

Figure 6. Benoît's Alabaster Chamber as a square of opposition

Like logicians' squares, this arrangement maps a set of differential relationships which between them structure a totality, insofar as each of the four corners is the product of the oppositions indicated in italics on its four axes; and like them, it is hierarchical in that the terms on the top axis take precedence over those beneath.[8] But what kind of oppositions are these exactly? As in the logical models, those on the top axis clearly involve contrariety: that is, the ethical boy is the contrary of the musical boy because heightened self-perception is the contrary of diversion. In the same way, on the bottom axis, the mirror girl is the contrary of the conjuring girl. If one were to take femininity in Benoît as the negative of masculinity and physicality as the negative of spirituality, this square would be just like that in Figures 4 and 5 because each of the two lower points could be seen as contradicting the diagonally opposing one above: that is, the mirror girl would contradict the musical boy by virtue of being not-a-boy and not-distracting, and the conjuring girl likewise would contradict the ethical boy by being not-a-boy and by not-promoting-self-awareness.

I have not adopted this course because, unlike the logicians' squares, Benoît's description seems to me to favor contraries on all four axes. That is, I see the ethical boy as the contrary of the mirror girl because the perception he affords is spiritual and masculine whereas hers is physical and feminine; and *mutatatis mutandis* for the musical boy and the spectacle-mounting girl. It is the four walls of the Chamber—so attentively described (14919–36)—which define the significant relations between its corners, rather than the inferred diagonals.[9] Whichever wall one paces from one automaton to another, one encounters a relation between contraries. The whole structure of the Chamber enables one to progress through its ordered terms, thereby acquiring greater value and an enhanced sense of discrimination. Benoît has rewritten the "square of opposition" as a "square of contrariety" that is also a "square of art": by discerning and progressively assimilating its systematically organized oppositions, one may perfect one's pleasure and understanding.

Identifying the square of contraries as a four-sided building provides a clear outline to the concepts which it organizes.[10] The Chamber walls demarcate the outer limit of the intellectual structure, as well as displaying its splendid contents. Inside is the prospect of accumulating all the improvement art can offer. What about the outside? To what extent can Benoît's entire romance can be seen, in the light of the Chamber, as a vast architectural edifice that offers structured opportunities for educating the reader's intellectual, moral, and aesthetic judgment?

Outside the peaceful Chamber is the Trojan war, narrated in tones of desolation at its endless battles and terrible carnage. It thus appears to be the contrary of the Chamber which is a haven of calm and a place of healing for the wounded Hector. Interlaced with the horrors of the war is Benoît's account of four successive amorous relations between Greeks and Trojans. Critical analyses of the relations between these four couples have varied, although it is generally recognized that Benoît seeks to ring the changes.[11] Certainly they describe between them a kaleidoscope of possibilities. Women may be seized as booty or given by treaty; they may be wives or concubines; they can be kidnapped in retaliation or volunteered as peace offerings; their consent may be crucial, withheld, or ignored. But rotate as the narrative may through these various permutations of the exchange of women, it remains locked on a seemingly inevitable course of destruction.

Here is a summary of these four relationships[12]:

> 1. The Trojan princess Esiona is seized in a Greek raid on Troy and given as a war prize to the Greek Telamon who keeps her as a concubine, inflaming Trojan fury and inspiring the raid on Greece, which results in (2).
>
> 2. The Greek queen Helen, wife of Meneleus, is seized by the Trojan Paris, who marries her. This provokes the Greeks to lay siege to Troy in order to win her back.
>
> 3. During the siege, the Trojan lady Briseida has as her *ami* the Trojan prince Troilus; but she then transfers to the Greek camp, which her father had already treacherously joined, and the Greek knight Diomedes becomes her *ami*. This inflames personal animus between the two camps.
>
> 4. The Greek warrior Achilles falls in love with the Trojan princess Polyxena and successfully asks for her to be given him in marriage in exchange for ending the war. This places Achilles in conflict with his own greatest qualities—those of a heroic warrior—and with his own men. Eventually he resumes fighting, whereupon the Trojans conspire to murder him.

Now it is easy to plot this foursome of relationships on another square (Figure 7). Like the Alabaster Chamber, what we have here is a square of contraries, except here the multiplication of oppositions make it a more advanced structure (cf. Figure 5).

gift

Briseida (gives herself, has two lovers)	Polyxena (given by parents, relation never realized)
already united to a partner on one side of the war when transferred to a partner on the other	*both single, unmarried daughters before being seized/courted by the opposing side*
Helen (married, has two husbands)	Esiona (unmarried, becomes a concubine)

raptus/booty

Figure 7. Benoît's square of women

I have indicated by the glosses in italics and the material in parentheses how I see these contraries as constituted. Their proliferation here means that whichever corners of the square are compared, they exhibit multiple interrelations. Thus, for example, Helen and Briseida are contraries in that Helen has two husbands in succession and Briseida two lovers, one Greek and one Trojan in each case. Both women are presented as acting in accordance with their own desires (in Helen's case this takes some doing but Benoît manages to depict her as consenting to her kidnapping by Paris [4371–72]). Polyxena and Esiona are contraries in that Polyxena is loved and requested in marriage, but never united with her lover, whereas Esiona's fate is the opposite: she is taken into concubinage and denied the honors of marriage. The treatment of Esiona sparks retaliation, whereas attempts are made through Achilles's love for Polyxena to secure peace. Initially, neither of them is consulted as to their desire, but Polyxena is later shown to be favorably disposed to the match and mourns Achilles's death (see Chapter 6). Helen and Esiona are both taken as booty, whereas Briseida and Polyxena are gifts; however, Briseida's claim to be able to give herself shocks the poet whereas the gift of Polyxena ends in a trap to murder the would-be recipient, Achilles. Whatever form of relationship is attempted, the war goes inexorably on. To invoke a more recent pair of contraries, Eros is overwhelmed by Thanatos: woman, however you approach her, leads to death.

Benoît's romance thus describes, alongside the "square of art," a "square of historical reality" which could also be described as a "square of catastrophe." Like the Alabaster Chamber, this square maps relations between contraries. How is the reader supposed to react to the two squares? Their juxtaposition recalls Neoplatonist philosophical systems in which relations of ratio and proportion serve to link different levels of reality (mathematical, musical, cosmographical, etc.) to one another, so that harmony on one level resonates with harmonies on higher levels (as in the *De planctu*; see note 9 above). However, in Benoît's text, the square of historical reality seems to have an effect contrary to the square of art. Whereas the Alabaster Chamber represents an orderly progression of qualities, history enumerates instances of failure. In both, the systematic oppositions convey an impression of exhaustiveness, so that history, like art, appears as a totality; but instead of perfecting experience, history blocks all paths to success because whichever form of the exchange of women the protagonists embark upon, the relentless tide of war remains unstilled.[13] The only solution to the problems posed by the historical couples are the boy and girl automata within the Chamber: lifeless figures which abstract moral and aesthetic values from their historical setting, leaving desire, blood, and death outside.

Benoît's poem thus offers us two systems of classification: one of art, the other of the reality on which art reflects. We may want to see the Chamber as the haven it is presented as being, but its boundaries are not secure because its structure of contrariety is exactly echoed outside it. If this replication were faithful to Neoplatonist models, it might bring us enhanced understanding of harmony; but instead, the world outside reverses all the values which prevail within the Chamber. Benoît's text thus leaves us with a sense of disquiet concerning the "edge of reason" defined by the alabaster walls. Although they mark a limit to the forces of destruction, ironically they do so only by the elimination of life: the substitution of automata for people. The Chamber's entrancing spectacles are all effects of clockwork; even ethics and religion are furnished by machines. Although the automata may be an escape from the deathly impulses that reign outside, they are also an unconscious reminder of death itself. In Lacan's phrase, for those in the Chamber they are "the memory of those things [they] forget," replicating the horrors outside in a disguised, but no less troubling, form (*Ethics*, 231).

The rationality of Benoît's poem is thus achieved at a price. He adapts the elementary structures of the square of opposition to the analysis of art and of history in such a way as to enable us to discern the framework of contrary values which make up the first, and the relentless pattern of contrary experiences which impel the second. We may of course learn to eschew the destructiveness and passions that make up the historical process. The risk is, however, that this act of rational discrimination leaves us with nothing but a world of lifeless simulacra.[14]

It is interesting to find a variant of this problematic in the roughly contemporary *Tristan* by Thomas. Not enough survives of the account of Tristan's Hall of Statues for us to know its shape.[15] The first Turin fragment to survive of Thomas's romance, however, shows Tristan's only consolation, after his misguided marriage to the second Isolt, being with the statues he has made of the first Isolt and Brengain:

> Car ne sot vers cui descovrir
> ne son voler, ne son desir.
> (Turin[1], 49–50)

For he didn't know to whom to reveal his longing and desire.

Immediately afterward, Thomas analyzes the unhappy situations of his four protagonists (Turin[1], 71–151):

1. Mark is aware that Isolt is not true to him and loves someone else; he loves her and possesses her body, but another has her heart.

2. Isolt has King Mark, whom she does not want; she does not have what she does want; therefore, her sufferings are twice those of Mark.

3. Tristan also has twice the load of suffering. He is married to someone he does not love and cannot leave; and he does not have what he does want.

4. The second Isolt has neither the heart nor the body of her spouse, but she does love him.

Thomas's four protagonists can be positioned, like Benoît's women, on what we realized above was also a square of catastrophe (Figure 8):

frustrated matrimony
(single torment)

Mark
(has body but
doesn't have heart)

Isolt as Blanches Mains
(has neither heart
nor body)

consummated　　　　　　　　　　　　*not consummated*

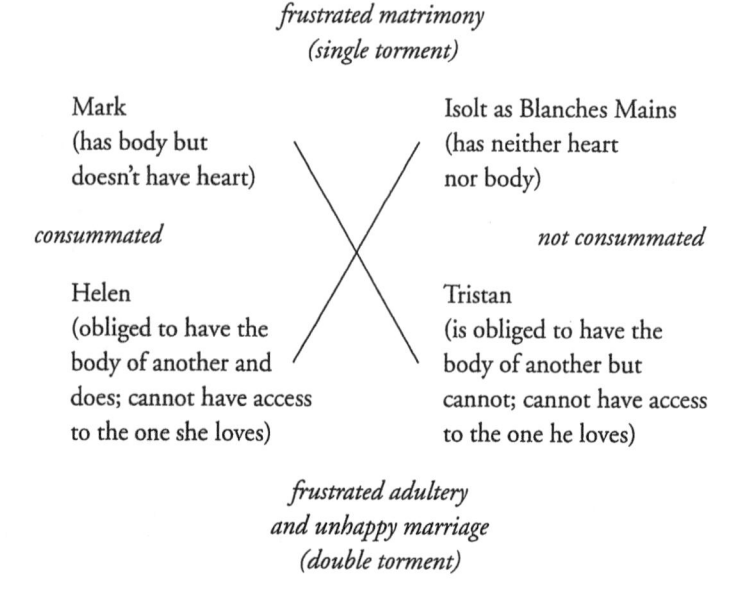

Helen
(obliged to have the
body of another and
does; cannot have access
to the one she loves)

Tristan
(is obliged to have the
body of another but
cannot; cannot have access
to the one he loves)

frustrated adultery
and unhappy marriage
(double torment)

Figure 8.　Thomas's square of lovers

Like Benoît's, Thomas's square is designed to exercise discrimination and promote reflection. At the conclusion of this passage, we are specifically asked: who is best off in love or worst off without it (148–51)? But unlike Benoît's square, where the women's positions are all definable in terms of contraries and relatives, here the characters are most clearly differentiated by the way the situation of each negates the situation of the others. Thus Thomas's square tilts toward contradiction; contradictory relations are indicated in the parentheses, and in the opposition (in italics) consummated–not consummated (see also the number of negative constructions in lines 71–151 of the text). Contrariety may be attested by the opposition (also in italics) between marriage and adultery (unless one is thought of as the negative, rather than the converse, of the other). However, the opposing corners of Thomas's square—as in the traditional logical square—return us to the contradictory: Isolt La Blonde's situation is the negative of Isolt Blanches Mains's because the former has the body of the man she does not love whereas the second does not have the body of the man she does love. Tristan's situation is the negative of Mark's because Mark can have intercourse with his wife and loves her whereas Tristan cannot bring himself to have intercourse with his wife and does not love her. In addition, because of the accretion of different factors, all four corners find grounds for contradiction with one another. Whereas Benoît adapted the logical square to map failure, here it maps suffering. The idea that, to escape misery and frustration, you can only talk to a statue, offers a gloss no less dismal than Benoît's on the limitations of what artistic endeavor can achieve.

These texts are comparable in date, and both respond to the prevalence of dialectic in clerical milieux by their approximations to the elementary logical construct, the square of opposition. Both, however, deform it to some extent, Benoît in the direction of contrariety and Thomas in that of contradiction. When they use the square to depict real-life circumstances, both authors suggest the inexorable failure of warfare and love (the *roman de Troie*) or simply of love in a world where knighthood seems no longer to have any function (*Tristan*). Both authors also set off from this disaster we call reality a privileged space of art where phenomena are the product of rational control. In both texts, this space is strongly demarcated from external reality, by wondrous walls or the otherworldly space of the cavern. In the *Troie*, the Alabaster Chamber offers a particularly rich account of the benefits which such control can offer.

Also in the *Troie*, though, echoes between the way the Chamber and the world outside are structured make more striking the contrast between beauty and order within, and violence and destruction without. In the *Tristan*, given its fragmentary state, the only link we have between inner and outer worlds is Isolt la Blonde in her contrasting roles of serene statue and wretched lover. What is clear is that in both texts the control of art is achieved only through the elimination not just of passion, but also of life. The limits of reason are etched tragically into these poems by the realization of its failure to cope with all that lies beyond it. The very depiction of "reasonableness" by the square of opposition is deformed in order to accommodate the material it is designed to classify. In the Alabaster Chamber and the Hall of Statues, clerically educated authors both celebrate the achievements of rational organization and mourn its deathly limitation, its sterile impotence. Through them, we see romance beginning to open itself to impulses at odds with the dialectical tradition on which it draws.

Shifting the frontiers of reason in the Life of St. Catherine

Saints' lives do not usually see it as their duty to reconcile contradictoriness. In Guillaume de Berneville's *Life of St. Giles*, when the saint celebrates Mass for Charlemagne before hearing his confession,[16] he emphasizes the mysteries of Christian belief: Christ is eternal but died for us; God is both in heaven and his body down here and yet he is not divided; anyone who does not receive God in the Mass eats and drinks his own death (2980–3002).

A few late twelfth-century texts, however, although in their overall structure preserving the paradoxical cast of the genre, nonetheless feel a responsibility to defend Christian doctrine against the charge that it is contradictory. The *St. George* by Simund de Freine has the Roman emperor Dacien challenge George with such questions as these: When Christ was crucified, where were the other two members of the Trinity (i.e., why weren't they all together)? How can a God die? And isn't a Virgin birth just a contradiction in terms? As Dacien sees it,

> Ceste lei est tote fause
> e ma reison bien la fause.
> (311–12)

This religion is all false and my reasoning show up its falsehood.

George replies that the Father and Son are as inseparable as fire and light (351–52); God had to become man because of Adam; the Virgin birth is like sunshine passing through glass (385–90)—all compatible, in short, with reason. Clemence of Barking's *Catherine* contains comparable, more extended, and intellectually more sophisticated scenes, and similar arguments also occur in the anonymous *St. Lawrence*, although Lawrence is not explicitly asked to resolve contradictions. All three saints defend the doctrines of the Virgin Birth, the Incarnation, and the Resurrection. All three texts may be related, and the *Lawrence* and the *Catherine* are so certainly because they contain some identical material.[17] All three are, like *St. Giles*, assigned a date after 1170; the *George* may be as late as the early thirteenth century, and the *Catherine* is sometimes thought to postdate the *Lawrence*. I will concentrate on Clemence's text because its literary qualities are now well acknowledged[18] and its arguments are the most fully developed.

The St. Catherine legend relies on generic paradoxes: here is a young girl threatened with death by imperial might and yet predictably wresting victory from defeat, life from death, triumph from humiliation. The story cannot be told without triggering these hagiographic tropes, and Clemence knowingly deploys the rhetoric of antithesis to set them off.[19] Thus, for instance, Catherine warns pagan sympathizers:

> Ceste mort m'est espeir de vie,
> mes vostre mort a mort vos guie.
> La vostre mort a mort vus meine,
> mais la meie iert vie certeine.
> (1997–2000)

This death is, for me, a hope of life, whereas your death takes you toward death; that death of yours leads to death but mine will be certain life.

(The contradictions associated with martyrdom in *Catherine*, *Lawrence*, and *George* are further explored in Chapter 6). Yet at the same time Clemence's text gives an exceptionally prominent role to dialectic. Catherine is unusual in having been given a most advanced education by her father:

> D'escripture la fait aprendre,
> opposer altre e sei defendre.
> El munt n'out dialeticien
> ki veintre la poust de rien.
> (141–44)

He has her taught writing skills, countering the arguments of others and defending her own. There was no dialectician in the world who could defeat her in anything.

Catherine seeks out the emperor Maxence, eager to demonstrate to him that his religion is erroneous. Exasperated, he summons fifty trained philosophers to debate with her. They are mortified by the commission (476–98), but Catherine rebuts all their objections to Christian teaching, convincing them that they are reconcilable with reason. The success of her arguments leads them all to convert. She also converts the emperor's wife and his friend Porphyry, the latter admitting he was especially impressed by her performance against the philosophers:

> Jo la vi as clers desputer
> e lur argument issi falser,
> qu'ele sule fist tuz recreanz
> cinquante clers bien desputanz
> (1567–70)

I saw her disputing with the scholars and rebutting their reasoning in such a way that she, on her own, confounded all fifty scholars, who were proficient at arguing.

Clemence's text thus admits two different approaches to contradictoriness, one involving the maintenance of paradox, the other its dialectical resolution. The simultaneous presence of these two conceptual frames produces frontiers between them which shift in the course of the text. The pagans perceive there to be a frontier between reason (their beliefs) and nonsense (Christianity), until they are induced to accept Christian beliefs as reasonable. The other frontier at stake is that between faith and reason, a frontier Catherine seems both to affirm and deny. Analyzing how Clemence negotiates these frontiers, we find her text differs systematically from its Latin source.[20] Clemence withdraws dialectical competence from the pagans and confers it on Catherine; the Latin text is more vehement in its denunciation of pagan philosophy, whereas Clemence's Catherine both relies on it and stresses the need for it to be subordinated to Christian faith. The value of dialectic thus fluctuates, and the limits of reason are alternately affirmed and played down.

Clemence starts the debate with Catherine alleging to Maxence that he and his religion are damnable. His response is to ogle her (222): throughout the text, his carnality will be equated with stupidity as well as idolatry, making him the butt of clever Catherine. Despite his intellectual limitations, Maxence finds two counterarguments: (1) his religion is traditional, and (2) hers must be false because it posits belief in a god who died and then was resurrected, whereas his gods—the sun and moon—are *nun mortel* (immortal). Maxence, with a rather basic understanding of dialectic, is confident that the distinction between "mortal" and "immortal" is integral to the definitions of "man" and "god."[21] Catherine's position, he thinks, relies on a category error because it ascribes divinity to the mortal and denies it to the eternal. He stigmatizes this as an *errur* (247; the Latin text has him say how alien it is to human reason, "ab humana ratione tam alienum," 152, line 157). Catherine claims reason back for herself by riposting that Maxence is the one making the category error, because he fails to recognize the subordination of the created to the creator. All phenomena, she says, including Maxence's own power, are effects of God's will; recognition of the Son requires prior recognition of the Father, but Maxence prefers to worship the creature rather than the creator, an *errur* (299, 301) for which he may fear punishment. Stupefied by this onslaught,[22] the emperor fantasizes about marrying her before calling for intellectual reinforcement from the fifty "best clerks in the world" (488).

Confronted by their vainglorious contempt for her, Catherine, who was supreme in the exercise of *clergie*, scorns it now that she has embraced faith in Jesus (690–94). This rejection is, however, much more insistent in the Latin text, which expatiates on the fatuousness of pagan philosophy.[23] Furthermore, the Latin text condemns the pursuit of secular wisdom by conflating it with the Fall,[24] whereas Clemence's Catherine states that God created men and women as rational creatures (701) and attributes the expulsion from Eden to man's folly (i.e., failure to exercise reason), which she equates with disobedience (705–7). Reason may be practiced in vain arts, but it is also God given. Catherine's retelling of the Fall leads to her account of its redress: God, whose nature is immortal, saved us by suffering death in the flesh of his Son by means of the Virgin birth (715–23). (The corresponding passage of the Latin makes rather briefer reference to these doctrines.[25]) She concludes this speech with the words:

> E ço est de mun sen la sume,
> que cestui crei Deu e hume.
> Iço est ma filosophie.
>
> (729–31)

So here is the sum of my understanding: that I believe him to be both God and man. This is my philosophy.

That is, belief in the Incarnation has taken over the place in her understanding formerly occupied by pagan philosophy.

When the pagan philosophers are challenged by Catherine to find "pruvance raisnable" (776) why they should disagree with her, one of them immediately homes in on the problem of contradiction:

> "Par fei," fait il, "par ço te pruis
> qu'en tes diz verté nen truis.
> Se il est tel cum tu nus diz,
> e Deu e hume e a Deu fiz,
> cument pot le fil Deu murir
> ne nun mortel la mort suffrir?
> Murir ne puet pas par dreiture
> quant nun mortele est sa nature.
> Se hume fud, dunc est mortel
> e nient a nun mortel uel (etc.)."
> (783–92)

"In faith," he said, "I can demonstrate to you that I find no truth in your words in this way: if he is, as you assert to us, both God and man and son of God, how could God's son die or an immortal suffer death? He cannot rightly be capable of death if his nature is immortal. If he was a man, then he is mortal, and not at all the equal of an immortal (etc.)."

In the Latin text, one of the clerks (a *rhetor*) underlines the technical character of this objection.[26] In Clemence's text, however, it is Catherine who makes the link with dialectic explicit[27]:

> Unes cuntraires nus mustrez.
> Se il est huem, dunc n'est pas Deus.
> Se il est Deus, n'est pas mortels.
> Granter ne vels que ço seit dreit,
> que Jhesu Deu et hume seit.
> (810–14)

You point out to us a set of contraries: if he is a man, then he isn't God. If he is God, he isn't mortal. You do not wish to concede that it could be right that Jesus could be both God and man.

Catherine is here citing the precept familiar from Aristotle's *De interpretatione* according to which "It is not possible for contraries to hold of the same thing at the same time" (Aristotle, *De interpretatione*, 24b, 7–9/§14/ 38). She sets out to show how, in this case, the precept is not infringed. What is wrong with her opponents' objection is their treating the nature of God as if it were on a par with the nature of man. God made the whole universe from nothing; his nature is to be omnipotent; thus if he wishes he can become man (829-34). The problem of contrariety does not arise; God's power is such that he can pass from the role of creator to that of creature,[28] from invisibility to the visible, die as a man and live as God (837-42). Catherine goes on to give supporting illustrations about how what we assume to be the properties of things may be reversed into their contraries under the effect of God's power: miracles of healing, resuscitation, release from hell. She points out that even pagan philosophers such as Plato prophesied the birth of Christ. Her opponent is still not satisfied, and Catherine explains once more that the Son is equal to the Father and thus immortal; but that in his power, he joined his nature to ours (953-62). She ends with a highly rhetorical meditation on the interrelation between the Fall and the resurrection, hymning the transformations of fruit and tree from one story to the other.

Catherine defeats the pagan philosophers in argument in both the Latin *Passio* and the Anglo-Norman text; but Clemence represents her as better informed about dialectic than her Latin model. When Clemence's Catherine converts the philosophers, then, they are defeated with their own tools; they are persuaded that what their own reasoning had defined as beyond reason in fact falls within it: the frontier of reason is redrawn in order to include Christianity and exclude unbelief. In the Latin text, by contrast, both pagan unbelief and pagan philosophical practices (i.e., dialectic) are subject to attack. Having invested dialectical skills in its protagonist, the vernacular Life is, not suprisingly, less scathing about philosophical activity than its Latin source. Reservations regarding dialectical skills are expressed solely by Catherine; she repeatedly stresses that reason must be subordinate to faith. While persuading the philosophers to convert through reason, thus pushing forward the frontier of reason, she also draws it back again, to assert the primacy of faith.

Partly this concentration of faith and reason in her protagonist is a feminist move on Clemence's part: the learned nun author celebrates their union in a female saint. It may also reflect logical inquiry into questions of faith, prestigiously practiced by such intellectual stars as Anselm, Abelard, or Gilbert of Poitiers.[29] Little has been done to unearth the sources of Catherine's dispute, whether in the *Passio* or the Anglo-Norman text.[30] Although aware that I am not best equipped to remedy this deficiency, I would like briefly to examine a text which provides philosophical bases for

Catherine's argument even if Clemence did not know it: St. Anselm's letter *De incarnatione Verbi* ("The Incarnation of the Word"), the final recension of which was published in 1094.

Anselm, like Clemence, is explicit in this letter about the desire to reconcile apparent contradictions in faith by means of reason: "even though the faith [of many people] surmounts the reasoning which to them seems inconsistent with faith, I do not think it superfluous to resolve this inconsistency" (11). He writes in order to attack Roscelin for thinking that, if the Trinity is one God in three persons, then all three persons must have been incarnate and not just the son.[31] Anselm condemns Roscelin as a "heretic of dialectic" because his grasp of the nature of universals is more at fault than his religious beliefs.[32] Anselm here shows his "realism" as opposed to Roscelin's "nominalism."[33] For Anselm, proper understanding of the universals would lead to our seeing that by "incarnation" is meant the assumption by the Son of a generic humanity, not of the personhood of an individual man:

> Finally, someone who cannot understand a human being [*homo*] to be anything except an individual shall not at all understand a human being to be anything except a human person, for every individual man is a person. How, then, shall he be able to understand that a humanity [*homo*], though not a person, was assumed by the Word? That is another nature, but not another person was assumed. ("Incarnation," 13–14.)

Arguments about contraries, such as those Catherine undertakes, also involve the status of universals; the point for both Catherine and Anselm ultimately is that "divinity" (and "immortality") is not the contrary of "humanity" (and "mortality") because the concept of "God" does not have common ground with that of "man."

Much of Anselm's argument resembles Catherine's. Anselm stresses, just as Catherine does, that what is defining about God's nature is his power. God's power is an aspect of his substance, and not an accident:

> Assuredly, it is a characteristic of the Divine Nature so to exist always and everywhere that never and nowhere does anything exist without its presence. Otherwise, it would not at all be powerful everywhere and always; and that which is not powerful everywhere and always is not at all God. ("Incarnation," 24.)

Compare here *Catherine*:

> En tutes [sc. criatures] mustre sa poissance;
> il sul est a tuz sustenance.
> Des qu'il tute rien fist de nient
> e tute rien par sei maintient
> e sur tute rien est poissant
> e tut ad fait a sun talant
> Ne pot cil dunc hume devenir?   (827–33)

He manifests his power in all his creatures; he alone sustains all. Because he created everything from nothing and maintains all things by himself and is powerful over all things, and has made everything according to his will, could he not become a man?

Also similar to Clemence is Anselm's assertion that the two natures, human and divine, of Christ remain distinct: "For whoever rightly understands His incarnation believes that He assumed a human nature [*homo*] into a unity with His person, rather than into a unity with His nature" (26). Anselm expands on this, explaining that Jesus was one person with two natures: "Indeed, God assumed a human nature not in such way that the divine nature and the human nature were one and the same but in such way that the person of God and the person of the man were one and the same. But this [assumption of a human nature] can only occur in the case of one person of God. For it is incomprehensible that different persons be one and the same person with one and the same man" (27). Thus God is three persons, and one of those persons has two natures. Clemence likewise says that God assumed the role of creature as a sign of his power, not of his nature (837–38, "Par poesté, nient par nature / devint li faitres criature"). It was the Son as an all-powerful person who assumed humanity, not the nature of God which became united with human nature:

> Jo di que Deu nostre salvere
> est par nature uel al pere,
> e des qu'il est al pere uel,
> dunc n'est il pas en sei mortel.
> [. . .]
> Sa nature pas ne muad,
> mais nostre par soe honurad.
>   (951–54, 961–62)

All this section of Clemence's text (942–1010) is much expanded relative to the *Passio*, which "provides only the skeleton of the argument for this climactic speech."[34] Clemence's text as a whole thus embodies a spirit of "fides quaerens intellectum" (faith seeking understanding), as Anselm had subtitled his *Proslogion*.

With the weight of figures such as Anselm behind her, it is surprising that Clemence follows her Latin model as far as she does in allowing Catherine to denounce the "false arts" of dialectic:

> Tutes voz falses arz guerpi
> des queles ere ainz si sage
> que el munde n'oi per de mun eage.
> Ben soi que de fei furent veines
> e [de] dreite veie lointaines.
>
> (690–94)

I relinquished all your false arts in which formerly I was so wise that I had no equal of my age in the world; I knew they were empty of faith and far from the true path.

The frontier of reason may be pushed forward, but it is also drawn back; it advances to encompass the nonsense of the pagans but withdraws to respect the mysteries of faith. The text's approach to contraries thus fluctuates: when they are objected to by pagans, they are resolved, but when they form part of the traditional expressions of faith adopted by hagiography, they are endorsed. It is hard not to see this as representing a contradictory attitude toward contradictoriness, and not to be struck by the similarity between faith and nonsense, given that both are instances of contrariety which define the frontiers of reason. In this extended and intellectually sophisticated weaving together of the traditions of paradox and dialectic, those frontiers are always in play. Clemence of Barking's *St. Catherine* enables us to see in detail how the rise in prestige of dialectic overtakes late twelfth-century hagiography, which both embraces and resists it.

The "dialectic" of the troubadours: "True" love and its lies

We owe to Jörn Gruber's *Die Dialektik des Trobar* the idea that troubadour songs constitute a dialogue whereby successive compositions seek both to absorb, and to surpass, their predecessors in a Hegelian sublation (*Aufhebung*). Gruber conceives this *Aufhebung* primarily in rhetorical and hermeneutic terms: one text struggles to exceed another by elaborating, ornamenting, and more deeply encoding it.[35] He also occasionally envisages this process, however, in terms of dialectical reasoning. For example, he contends that the opening stanza of Jaufré Rudel's "Non sap chantar" (I) creatively rewrites the final stanza of Guilhem de Peitieu's "Pos vezem" (VII) by reversing Guilhem's claims and the order of his key terms; and that Rudel contradicts his own assertions but then resolves the contradiction by positing the song as the "sublation" of his source (89–91, cf. also 200–9). It is this engagement with argument on the part of troubadour poetry that I want to focus on here, with reference not to Hegelian dialectic but to that of the Middle Ages. An overriding preoccupation of medieval logicians was to determine the truth or falsity of propositions, just as for love poets, protesting the truth of their own declarations, and the falsehood of other people's, is an abiding theme. But falsehood is so pervasive that from the early troubadours forward disentangling the truth is conceded to be a problem—a risk, too, because it may expose what would be better concealed. All kinds of argument are deployed in love poetry in order to persuade the intended audience of its truth: deductive ones drawn from universalizing claims about the nature and effects of love and inductive ones inferring the likely consequences of particular behavior. The songs I consider here address the precariousness of the lover's truth despite such efforts at demonstration. In chronological order of composition they are Cercamon's "Quant l'aura doussa" (I), Bernart Marti's "Companho per companhia" (IV), and Arnaut de Maruelh's "Anc vas Amor" (XV); they can be associated with the early, the early to mid, and the late twelfth century, respectively.

Cercamon's song opens with an image which was to prove influential[36]: as summer gives way to winter and his love remains unfulfilled, the lover is overwhelmed by feelings of disempowerment (1–6). The irony of his situation is not lost on him: it is precisely because what he wants lies out of reach that he desires it so much (9–12). His one pure joy is a love so intense that when he is with his Lady he is unable to reveal his desire to her yet, when he departs from her, he feels as if he loses all sense and understanding (13–18). She is his only light, and he yearns to be close to her or watch her going to bed (19–24). The next group of stanzas, whose order varies between manuscripts, recite pell-mell the conflicting emotions which follow from this impossible situation—for example:

> No muer ni viu ni no guaris,
> ni mal no·m sent e si l'ai gran.
> (31–32)

I neither die nor live nor recover nor feel suffering and yet I undergo it greatly.

The lover actually prefers this irrational world, where his Lady turns everything back to front, because it encourages the hope that eventually ill will reverse into good:

> Bel m'es quant ilh m'enfohletis
> e·m fai muzar e·n vauc badan;
> de leis m'es bel si m'escarnis
> o·m torn dereire o enan,
> c'aprob lo mal m'en venra bes,
> ben leu, s'a lieys ven a plazer.
> (37–42)

I like it when she drives me crazy and makes me gape and muse like an idiot; I like it if she derides me or turns things back to front for me, for after the ill, good will come to me perhaps, if that is her wish.

Putting all his faith in her, he declares in what is the final stanza in all seven manuscript versions:

> xi 49 Totz cossiros, m'en esjauzis
> 50 car s'ieu la dopti e la blan,
> 51 per lieys serai o fals o fis,
> 52 o drechuriers o ples d'enjan,
> 53 o toz vilas o totz cortes,
> 54 o trebalhos o de lezer.

Even though yearning [for her], I am joyful, for if I submit to her and serve her, through her I shall be false or true, upright or full of deceit, wholly rustic or wholly courtly, in laborious misery or in leisured enjoyment.

One of the *tornadas* concludes with the aphorism that without persistence in love, you cannot be courtly:

> Cercamons ditz, "Greu er cortes
> hom que d'amor se desesper."
> (57–58)
>
> Cercamon says, "Anyone who despairs in love can scarcely be courtly."

The word *cortes* in line 57 picks up *totz cortes* from line 53, making it appear the most important term among all the oppositions in the preceding stanza. This impression is reinforced by the contraries *trebalhos–de lezer* (54), for leisure is the privilege of the aristocratic world while labor is the peasants' lot. Yet for what "Cercamon says" (57) to be true, his Lady must somehow make it so because, as lines 51–52 state, it depends on her whether his words are reliable or not.

These lines present oppositions between *fals* and *fis*, *drechuriers* and *ples d'enjan*. *Fals* and *fis* imply falsehood or truth of intent; they could be rendered by "insincere" and "sincere," respectively. What does it mean that Cercamon's Lady has the power to make him sincere or insincere (51)? If she ultimately fails to reward him, will he turn away from her and thus revert from having been a "true" lover to being a "false" one? Does the fact of his aspirations remaining unfulfilled make them, in a sense, "false," even though he remains faithful? The second two terms, *drechuriers* and *ples d'enjan*, might likewise refer to the truth or falsehood of intent (distinguishing, e.g., sincere from deceitful promises) but more than the first pair, they also imply propositional content (distinguishing, that is, true from misleading statements), an implication confirmed by the variant *vertadiers* ("truthful") for *drechuriers* in five manuscripts (52). Cercamon's Lady, he claims, can make his statements truthful or deceitful.[37] How? Maybe he means simply that, if disappointed in love, his character will degenerate so that he ceases to uphold the integrity she now inspires in him: up to her, then, if he remains upright or not. But his words also mean that whether what he is saying now is truthful rather than deceitful depends on her: for his love to be "true" she must respond to it. If she does not—and according to stanza ii she does not—how truthful is anything he says? Cercamon invokes what we now call "the liar paradox" (as in "ego dico falsum," "what I say is false"), an utterance to which we are at a loss to know how to respond.[38] This kind of logical conundrum was known as "insoluble" by medieval dialecticians ("paradox" having a different sense; see Introduction, 16), and so I refer to it by that term.

The first known twelfth-century reference to the insoluble of the liar is by Adam of Balsham (also known as Adam of Petit Pont) in 1132: "Such also is that question 'whether he speaks truly who says that he lies [qui se mentiri dicit];' but also that question 'whether he says the truth who says nothing but that he lies'" (Spade, "Origin," 294–95). There is no sustained discussion of insolubles until late in the century, although there are references in the second half of the twelfth century to the existence of such discussions.[39] Adam's rephrasing of the problematic utterance, to "who says *nothing but* that he lies," suggests that for him the crux of the problem was the scope of the statement. Cercamon's song is ambiguous on precisely this score. The future tense of "per lieys serai o fals o fis" (51, "through her I shall be false or true," etc.) may suggest that he is being truthful now but could, at some future time, be untrue. He doesn't say *nothing but* that he lies; he might even be taken to imply that he is now speaking the truth about lies he might pronounce in the future. Cercamon skirts, but does not confront, the insoluble as formulated in his day (it is unlikely, indeed, that he came across Adam's teaching); and so anxiety about this interface between true love and lies persists. It is possible that Marcabru responds to this unease if, as Gruber suggests, his Song XLII is a parodic response to Cercamon's "Quant l'aura doussa." For here Marcabru recommends the season before the bitter breeze invoked by Cercamon as "the time to choose a true love, one without lies, and which does not quarrel with its lover" (5–7, "ladoncs deuria hom chausir / verai' amor, ses mentir, / c'ab son amic non barailla"). Cercamon's equivocation is resolved and truth affirmed.

Another song which may be related to Cercamon's is less optimistic. In "Companho, per companhia," Bernart Marti, like Cercamon, delivers himself of an aphorism on the nature of love, but his is surprisingly damning:

> Bernart Martin lo pintor
> que ditz e trai guirentia:
> "Greu er amor ses putia
> comjairitz,
> tro que.l mons sia fenitz."
> (38–42)[40]

Bernart Marti the painter who says and guarantees, "Love will scarcely ever be without fickle whoring until the world ends."

Bernart's song records the confusion of a lover at the deceptions which love brings. His experience is so topsy-turvy that the spring *topos*, instead of occupying the first stanza, comes last: Bernart looks forward to Easter as a time when he may master some happiness in love. Like Cercamon, then, he is singing in the bitter season, and it shows. Like Cercamon, he is caught up in the folly of love: "ma part ai en la folia, / chantador" (8–9, "I have my share of folly, fellow singers"); effectively, he is moralizing at his own expense. For Bernart, too, "folly" designates a state of confusion where contrary states obtain (e.g., the lover laughs and weeps, 43–44). For Bernart, however, the greatest contradictions result from the omnipresence of falsehood. Its effects are set out in three stanzas (iii–v) dealing, respectively, with lies, cheating, and deceiving. These stanzas are not easy to understand, and their obscurities are aggravated by the fact that the single manuscript is defective, but their general drift is that because deceit is rampant, there is no point withholding from it—on the contrary, one can only gain by joining in. The lines which particularly interest me are those about lying:

iii 15 Mas ab bel mentir prendia
16   ses clamor
17 no tem mais escarnidor,
18 qu'ela ditz ver quan mentia
19 et ieu ment can ver dizia.
20   A envitz
21 rema lo drutz esbaitz.

Since she [Love] was able to capture [one, i.e., me] with fair lying, and without uproar (on her part)/protest (on mine), I no longer fear anyone who might deride me, for she speaks the truth when she was lying and I lie when I used to speak the truth. Against his will, the lover is left dumbfounded.

This recalls stanza ix of the Cercamon song, but Bernart's deliberate clashing together of the contraries of truth and lying intensifies the problematic posed by his predecessor, obliging his listeners to address the conundrum. A similar formulation occurs in his "Quan l'erb'es reverzida" (VII),[41] where his deceitful Lady:

s'es de bel mentir garnida
que mon ver fai mensongier.
(VII, 45–46)

is so armed with fair lying that she makes my truth mendacious.

What is Bernart saying? First, the lover becomes completely entangled in the captivating delusion of love, so that he no longer cares if love makes him a laughingstock (IV, 15–17). Values of truth and lying become reversed for him. Previously (he knew that?) love lied but now (under her malign spell he believes?) she speaks the truth (18). Previously he told the truth but now (again in the grip of the distortions effected by love?) he finds himself lying (19). Alternatively, those things which formerly seemed to him to be true now (under the distorted perception of love?) seem to him to be lies (19 again, cf. VII, 45–46). He is left bewildered, disoriented by this transformation (20–21).

The tenses used in Song IV (unlike in Song VII) distinguish "then" from "now": what *used to be* love's lies are *now* accepted as truth and what *used to be* his truth is *now* a lie. The effect of this may be to demarcate the general nature of the truth—namely the moralist's condemnation of love—from the particular experience of succumbing to love's falsehood. This distinction is of interest because when insolubles began to be discussed in the twelfth century, it was with respect to a passage in the *Sophistical Refutations*—a work which formed part of the New Logic of Aristotelian writings recovered in the 1120s and 1130s—where Aristotle discusses the logical difficulties posed by exceptions to a stated rule. There is a difference, he says, between something being true absolutely (*simpliciter*) and in some particular respect (*secundum quid*). Aristotle cites as example a perjurer who habitually breaks his word; on one occasion, however, he swears that he will break his word, and then does so; on this occasion, therefore, there is a sense in which he did not break his word, and indeed his utterance confirms the more general truth of his being an oath-breaker. The fact of his keeping this oath therefore does not prevent his being a perjurer "absolutely," "for he who swears that he will break his oath, and then breaks it, keeps this particular oath only; he is not a keeper of his oath" (*Sophistical Refutations*, 180a, 39–41/§25/307). Aristotle continues: "The argument is similar for the problem whether the same man can at the same time say what is false and what is true; but it appears to be a troublesome question because it is not easy to see whether it is saying what is true or saying what is false which should be stated without qualification" (180b, 2–5/§25/307), but he does not explain the difficulty or flesh out the example of the liar. (This was done later in the twelfth century, but probably too late and in too isolated a case to be known to Bernart Marti; see Spade, "Origin," 303.)

To philosophers, the differences between the cases of the perjurer and the liar raise a number of problems,[42] but for vernacular authors, there is at least one difference fewer given that the vocabulary of failing to keep one's word and of saying what is not the case overlap in Romance languages. Bernart seems to be talking about misrepresentations rather than false promises, but the crucial verb *mentir* can mean either, and we noted a similar ambiguity in the language of truth and falsehood in the Cercamon passage. A particular problem with Aristotle's two examples is that the perjurer example relies on the passage of time—he says he will break his oath, and subsequently does so, thereby keeping it—whereas the example of the liar involves "the same man [. . .] at the same time say[ing] what is false and what is true." (Thirteenth-century logicians eliminated this discrepancy by revising the perjurer's words to "By God, I am committing perjury"![43]) By emphasizing the temporal difference between a time of undistorted perception ("then") and the world of deceit ("now"), Bernart may perhaps be adapting to his own case the temporal dislocation of the perjurer example.[44] Indeed, his "ieu ment can ver dizia" (19) is curiously poised. On the one hand, it directly invokes the liar insoluble (*ieu ment* = "ego dico falsum"); on the other, it draws attention to the resolution by recourse to the *secundum quid–simpliciter* distinction: "I lie" now, in this particular respect, but by nature "I used to tell the truth," so much so that it is true (*simpliciter*) that I am lying (*eu ment*).

The *secundum quid–simpliciter* resolution was not found generally compelling in medieval discussions of insolubles,[45] and the listener to Bernart's song would be justified in asking how, even if Bernart is only lying now, and only with respect to love, we should not have problems with his utterance since now is when we hear it, and love is what it is about. (The replacement of truth-telling by lies is especially corrosive if we understand *ver* "true" as resonating with *vers*, "song."[46]) So if Bernart is lying, surely we must disbelieve him; but then, that would be assuming that he is telling the truth about lying. . . . We are right back with the conundrum looking as insoluble as its name. And like an old wound, it flares up again in the work of subsequent troubadours. Arnaut de Maruelh, whose tone of submissive passion has much in common with Cercamon's, and whose poetry knowingly redeploys many of the same motifs, is a good example.[47]

The opening stanza of Arnaut de Maruelh's "Anc vas Amor" depicts a lover unable to resist love. The vocabulary of conflict (*guerra, conquis*) and dominion (*poder, domengiers*) initially suggests that *contradire* (line 1) is being used, not with its most familiar meaning of "gainsay, contradict," but as a synonym of *contrestar*, "withstand"[48]:

> Anc vas Amor no·m poc res contradire,
> pois ben i volc son poder demostrar;
> per qu'ieu non puosc sa guerra sols atendre,
> a sa merce mi rend totz domengiers;
> e ja vas lieis mos cors non er leugiers,
> c'anc nuills amans, pois lo primier conquis,
> ni aquel eis, non fo de cor plus fis.   (1–7)

Never was I able to resist (?) Love in anything, once she decided to show me her power; because I cannot face her onslaught alone I give myself up, as one submissive to a lord, to her mercy; and my heart will never be fickle toward her, for no lover, ever since the first vanquished man, and not even that one, was more true-hearted [than I am].

This truest-ever lover goes on to protest his sincerity; and as he does so, we gradually come to appreciate that this talk of struggle is, at least in part, a metaphor of persuasion. As equivocation between combat and argument continues we increasingly feel the dialectical meaning of *contradire* reassert itself. Consider the beginning of stanza ii:

> D'amor no·m feing, ni sui de plus jauzire,
> mas sol d'aitan c'ab ferm cor et ab clar
> a lei d'aman mi fai en tal entendre,
> don es sos pretz sobr' autras tant entiers.
> (8–11)

I am not feigning in love, neither do I have enjoyment of anything other than the fact that she [Love] makes me aspire with a clear and constant heart to one whose merit is so entire.

Feing (8) is ambiguous. *Fenher* can mean "to give up (on a project)," a sense which accords with the previous stanza's active metaphors: despite the pressure, Arnaut is not about to throw in the towel. Or it can mean "to be hypocritical, deceitful," which would reaffirm the truthfulness of Arnaut's love earlier stated in line 7. But it might also refer to the inability to declare one's suit, as in the Occitan recasting of the lover's *gradus amoris* ("steps in courtship"), which begin with the position of *fenhador*:

> Cel qu'a ben cor de domna amar
> e la vai soven cortejar
> e si no l'auza razonar
> fenheres es espavantatz.
> (cited in Akehurst, "Étapes," 136)

He who is actually inclined to love a lady and often goes to court her and yet dare not speak to her is a fearful *fenhador*.

The next "step" is to declare one's love (*pregador*) and thereafter to become an acknowledged admirer (*entendador*), the last stage being that of *drutz* or lover in the physical sense. Arnaut's lines 8–11 may invoke this progression: he has passed the stage of not daring to pronounce his love ("no·m feing") but not reached that of physical enjoyment ("ni sui . . . jauzire"), still being on the footing of a suitor ("mi fai . . . entendre"). So when Arnaut declares "d'amor no·m feing," he could mean that he is still ready to withstand love's onslaught, that he is truthful, and that he is capable of pressing his suit.[49] After praising his Lady's beauty in stanza iii, Arnaut continues his double reference to language and power through stanzas iv and v. He congratulates himself on his Lady's *avinen respos* (23, "pleasing response") and his own discretion toward busybodies, however ingratiating (33–35); he also uses terms denoting strength or courage (*conquis* 24, *sobranciers* 26, *m'afortis* 27).

In the final stanza, the two registers resound together still. However, language is increasingly spoken of in literal terms while the military/political terms *defendre* and *se trahir* have become figurative:

> Aitan si pert qui·m cuja plazer dire
> ni lausengas per mon cor devinar;
> c'atressi ben o mieills m'en sai defendre
> qu'ieu sai mentir e remaing vertadiers;
> tal ver hi a qu'es fals e messongiers,
> e qui ditz so per c'Amors avilis
> vas sidonz ment e si mezeis trahis.
> (36–42)

> Thus anyone who imagines they can flatter or deceive me into revealing my heart is wasting their time. For I know how to defend myself as well or better [than they], for I know how to lie and remain truthful; there is some truth that is false and mendacious; and whoever says something that debases Love lies/breaks faith toward his Lady and is a traitor to himself.

It is here that the kinship emerges between this song and those of Cercamon and Bernart Marti as Arnaut twice, apparently, equates lying with telling the truth.[50] He too has played the insoluble card. What does he mean by it?

The thinking in this final stanza appears to be this. In frustrating the *lausengiers*, Arnaut can deny his love while in fact remaining truthful to it; anyone, though, who seeks to debase love, corrupts truth to the point where their so-called truth is false and mendacious; love is so supreme that it makes what supports it true.[51] The earliest surviving tract actually to try to resolve *insolubilia* (late twelfth century) proposes the solution *nil dicis*, "you are saying nothing,"[52] known as *cassatio*. It is interesting that Arnaut's position is the opposite of this: far from meaning nothing, the statement "I lie," when said with respect to love, derives meaning (and truth) from love's power.

Arnaut's vision of love consecrating the truth directly reverses Bernart Marti's of love corrupting truth into lies. (Of course if one reads Arnaut from the position of Bernart Marti, then Arnaut's delusion is complete and *he* is the one taken over by lies.) Arnaut does, however, share with Bernart an attempt to restrict the reference of the terms of truth-telling and lying. Whereas in Bernart the medium of demarcation is tense usage, in Arnaut the restriction is conveyed in the formulation *tal ver* (40): it is truth (verse?) of a particular kind (namely spoken against love) which is untrue. Thus when I lie (by denying my love) I remain truthful (to love) because my denial is relative only to a particular purpose, which includes serving love's cause. Could it be that here Arnaut is making explicit awareness of one interpretation of the *secundum quid–simpliciter* distinction, that associated with the so-called *restringentes* because they sought to restrict the reference of the troublesome term and prevent it undermining the entire proposition?[53] (Note also in line 42 how perjuring and lying, Aristotle's two examples, converge in the terms *mentir* and *trahir*.)

Whether or not Arnaut is aware of the dialecticians' debates, it follows from his final stanza that the claim lodged in the opening one relies on the dialectical sense of *contradire*: namely, the claim that it is impossible to speak truly against love. The insoluble is thus the culminating argument in favor of love's irresistible truth. When Arnaut says he is lying, we are love's detractors (cf. 41) if we don't believe he is actually telling us the truth about a certain *kind* of lie. . . . Has he, better than his predecessors, succeeded in taming the insoluble? If so, he has succeeded in patrolling the limit of reason only by pointing beyond it to the limitless mystery of love.

The three songs which I have discussed represent different stages in an argument about love's truth. Cercamon's Lady holds the power to make the lover truthful or untrue. Bernart Marti intensifies and generalizes the conundrum by claiming that love turns truth into lies and vice versa. Arnaut de Maruelh then reverses Bernart's position by making love, on the contrary, the touchstone of truth. In miniature, we see in these three songs the rebuttal of early love song (Cercamon) by a moralist (Bernart, and cf. Marcabru) and the incorporation of the moralist's objections back into love song (Arnaut). This "dialectic of composition," in Gruber's phrase, also resonates with medieval discussion of what we now call the "liar paradox." Of course, poets anxious to persuade of the truth of their own feelings in a world of deceit did not need prompting by philosophers in order to light upon the intricate conundrums of truth and falsehood. Nevertheless, all three of the troubadours considered here invoke the idea that the poet's truth may be a lie in ways which parallel logicians' interest in *insolubilia*. It is not easy to tell how far the poets seek to resolve the insolubles' problematic. The likelihood of Cercamon's knowing Adam of Balsham is slight, and there is no evidence that he was aware of philosophical issues which were in any case not well known at the time. That Bernart Marti could have come across the *Sophistical Refutations* is less unlikely. If his treatment of the liar is at all indebted to Aristotle's discussion, this would have the interesting implication that Bernart recognizes love as an exceptional (indeed, aberrant) state of affairs. In Arnaut de Maruelh, the interplay between the vocabulary of argument and that of force makes engagement with dialectic more likely; he too seems the one most drawn to a dialectical resolution which will rationalize and resolve the insoluble when, restricting the reference of terms in human language, he gestures toward the higher domain of love. Yet this appeal to love's mystery is as much a displacement of the problem as a solution, and equivocation as to the lover's truth is preserved. Whether or not these troubadours knew the philosophical debates, all three draw on the insoluble *ego dico falsum*, exploiting its contradictoriness to challenge the limits of reason and reliability within their texts, and to summon up powerful, dangerous, or ineffable forces beyond them. The term "dialectic" is appropriate to them in ways Gruber did not foresee.

⁓

The case studies presented in this chapter attempt to capture genres in the process of change. Romance strains at the rational systems of categorization and deforms them toward new ways of dealing with contrariety and contradiction. Hagiography and lyric respond, in different ways, to the prestige of logic: as a way of wrestling with the expression of faith for Clemence of Barking, as a means of ratcheting up the playful problematic of "true love" for the troubadours. In their various interactions with scholastic thinking on contradiction, these texts succeed both in being analytical and in exposing reason's shortcomings; in their different ways, they manage to have the cake of contradiction and eat it too. This double move is encapsulated in the insoluble of the liar, in which utterance undermines its own foundations and lodges impossible claims. The study of riddles in the next chapter again takes us to the limit of rational coherence to ask what lies beyond: the answers—creativity, sex, incest, death—take us further still from the edge of reason. These topics belong in the heartland of psychoanalysis and will be pursued in harness with Lacan's riddling thought.

CHAPTER 4

From the riddle of the subject to the riddle of the object: the Occitan *devinalh* and the *romans antiques*

The last chapter showed how, as patterns of contradictoriness interact in particular texts, they play along the limits of rationality and coherent thought, exposing the raw edge beyond which language sheers off into the irrational or collapses in a tumble of nonsense. One form in which this edge of reason is especially exposed is the riddle, because the solution to a riddle is traditionally found by resolving what at first sight seems a contradiction.[1] Much of the lyric tradition in Occitan can be thought of as cultivating enigma insofar as its apparently confessional manner in fact draws us into a world of mystery, or of mystification. A subtradition is designated by the generic name *devinalh*, or "guessing poem," the earliest instance being among the oldest surviving songs (Guilhem de Peitieu's "Farai un vers de dreit nien," IV). The romance tradition also starts with riddles—those posed by Antiochus in *Apollonius* (ca. 1150–1160)[2] and by the sphinx in the *roman de Thebes*—and the opening episodes of the *Eneas* and the *Troie* likewise confront their protagonist with a dilemma or mystery. These opening scenes of the *romans antiques* prepare the way for the enigmatic marvels of adventure in later romance. The presence of riddles in these early texts is unsurprising given that riddles are among the oldest literary forms in existence. In this chapter, I examine the riddles posed by lyric and romance as a key to the way the various texts which contain them position themselves with respect to contradictoriness. In the lyric tradition, indeed, the riddle is often coextensive with the text and thus posits the text as simultaneously riddle and solution, as in this Swedish example cited by Taylor: "When one does not know what it is, then it is something; but when one knows what it is, then it is nothing" (*Literary Riddle*, 4).

As the twelfth century advances, there is a shift in the nature of lyric and romance riddles. Initially, the enigma centers on the first-person subject of the protagonist, but in later texts, attention shifts away toward an object presented as perplexing or mysterious. In different ways, both genres illumine through this progression an evolving conception of the literary text as artifact. In analyzing this development, I will draw on Lacan's writings on the "riddle" of art and on the contradictions of subjectivity. Lacan's own practices of, and reflections on, contradiction will contribute to making this chapter a hinge between the three preceding ones (which dealt with formal manifestations of contradiction) and the three following (which analyze our relation to the contradictory object).

Medievalists often resist using Lacan to inform their readings on the grounds that it is anachronistic to apply his views to the Middle Ages. Lacan himself, however, insists on the historicism of his theory. With respect to art, for example, he says: "Note that no correct evaluation of sublimation in art is possible if we overlook the fact that all artistic production [. . .] is historically situated" (*Ethics*, 107). Indeed, there is no doubt that Lacan's conception of the imaginary and the symbolic orders is historical. The imaginary is historical in that who we think we are, what we think we want to be, what we persuade ourselves we love or hate, and the totalities within which we imagine we function, vary from one time and place to another.[3] The symbolic is likewise historically contingent; it resides mainly in the frameworks of language and social institutions that make up the structures fleshed out into our sense of "everyday reality" by the imaginary order.[4] Only the order of the real, the traumatic world of inadmissible impulse, of all that is unrepresentable and resistant to language, the black hole on the edge of signification which we have to plug with fantasy objects so that we don't disappear down it like water down the bathtub drain, is represented by Lacan as ahistorical.[5] These three orders are intricately interrelated in Lacan's extensive writings, but what is relevant to this chapter is the way they interact to define Lacan's concepts of the "Thing" and of subjectivity. Bringing these concepts to bear on two different genres, the Occitan riddle and the *romans antiques*, will highlight rather than obscure the historical changes which they undergo.

The riddle of composition in troubadour lyric

The outlines of the riddling tradition in Occitan have been much debated.[6] In this discussion, I restrict myself to the twelfth-century examples by Guilhem de Peitieu, Raimbaut d'Aurenga, Giraut de Bornelh, Guillem de Berguedà, Guilhem Ademar, and Raimbaut de Vaqueiras.[7] My primary interest is in the development which takes place between Guilhem de Peitieu's "vers de dreit nien" and Raimbaut de Vaqueiras's "Las frevols venson lo plus fort" (XXVI). Although the chronology of the other *devinalhs* discussed here cannot be known exactly, the careers of both Guilhem IX and Raimbaut de Vaqueiras are firmly dateable to the beginning and end of the twelfth century, respectively. The end points of the historical changes charted here are therefore secure. As both Guilhem IX and Raimbaut de Vaqueiras center their riddle on a concept of "nothing" which is nestled in the crisscross of contradiction, they enable us to observe historical changes in the way the "riddle of art," as Heidegger put it, is conceived:

> The foregoing reflections are concerned with the riddle of art, the riddle that art itself is. They are far from claiming to solve the riddle. The task is to see the riddle. ("Origin of the Work of Art," 79)

Specifically, I will contrast Guilhem's formulation, whereby the poet recasts "nothing" as song, with its reversal by Raimbaut de Vaqueiras for whom "nothing" is the agency by which things are made and unmade, and which leads not to creation but to death:

> Us niens es qu'adutz a mort
> so qu'el fai e qu'el pot desfar.
> (XXVI, 15-16)

> There is a nothing which leads to death whatever it makes and has the power to unmake.

In the course of this comparison, I will explore further the notion of an "edge" of reason beyond which the lines of contradiction converge on the unthinkable by drawing on Lacan's discussion of creation *ex nihilo* in Book VII of his Seminar (*The Ethics of Psychoanalysis*), itself a meditation on (among other things) Heidegger's essay on "The Origin of the Work of Art" (see Lacan, *Ethics*, 139–42.) In this way, the relation of singer, text, and love to a "nothing" which may also be a troubling "something" can be more fully analyzed; at the same time we can explore, if not the "origin" of the work of art, at least the evolution of the literary artifact in the twelfth century.

The theme of nothingness epitomizes the ambiguities of contradiction in the courtly lyric. If contrary or contradictory predicates cannot truthfully be applied to the same subject, as Aristotle maintained, then when we encounter them we need either to pressure them to discover that there is a "something" which they have in common (in which case they cease to be contradictory in Aristotle's terms), or else we need to recognize them as mutually canceling (in which case their presence is conducive to an absence of meaning: there can be no real-world subject of contradictory predicates; the rhetoric collapses on nothing, on emptiness). If, however, the word "nothing" designates not just an absence, but a mystery that lies behind the contradictory affirmations of the human mind, and a way of gesturing toward alterity, then it possesses a fullness in excess of what we can imagine. "Nothing" may be the best way to conceptualize the supreme "something" that embraces all of our contradictions in powerful harmony; or it may be that, in its very negativity, it offers the best understanding of a spiritual Being which is all that we are not. Most of the analyses of Guilhem de Peitieu's *devinalh* have opted for one or another of these alternatives or have declined to decide between them.[8] The poem famously opens "I shall compose a *vers* about strictly nothing" before unleashing a welter of paradoxical and contradictory assertions about the singer's love, or lack of it. Later songs in the same tradition also have as their subject love, the song about love, or both. Love and song are thus whirled in a spin somewhere between ultimate vacuity and supreme significance. But the patterns of contradiction differ between the earlier and later texts.

Patterns of contradiction in the devinalh

Guilhem's *vers* is typical of early twelfth-century poetry as it sets out to counter an unspoken orthodoxy, whether it be philosophical, moral, or amorous (Holmes, "Unriddling," 25). The opening stanza implies expectations about the content of song which the singer will frustrate. Negation is rife, but for the most part it does not take the form of self-contradiction. Instead, it negates what might be taken as norms of knowledge and conduct: "No sai en qual hora·m fui natz" (7, "I don't know what hour I was born"), "No sai cora·m fui endormitz / ni cora·m veill" (13–14, "I don't know when I'm asleep or awake"), "Malautz soi e cre mi morir; / e re no sai mas quan n'aug dir. / Metge querrai al mieu albir, / e no·m sai tau" (19–22, "I'm sick and afraid of dying but I don't know about it except what I'm told and I'll look for a doctor to suit my taste but I don't know what kind"), "Amigu' ai ieu, non sai qui s'es: / c'anc no la vi, si m'aiut fes; / ni·m fes que·m plassa ni que·m pes, / ni no m'en cau" (25–28, "I have a girl, I don't know who: for I've never seen her by my faith; she has never done me good nor harm, and I don't care"), etc. The singer is constantly puncturing the pretensions of a set of values whose nonsensical makeup the opening line qualifies as *nien* (Pasero's edition of Guilhem de Peitieu, 86).

The midcentury riddle songs by Raimbaut d'Aurenga and Giraut de Bornelh both shift toward reliance on contraries. Throughout "Un sonet fatz," Giraut uses antithesis obsessively. The terms of each opposition are savagely added together, their contradictoriness defining the impossibility of the lover's situation. However dedicated and faithful he may be, he cannot escape wrongdoing:

> per malvestat cui *e*·m levar[9]
> e mais valer per sordeiar!
> (41–42; cf. 26)

I imagine that through wickedness/baseness/cowardice I can advance myself and that, through getting worse, I shall be worth more.

Thus he is *both* good *and* bad, *both* right *and* wrong. Such contrary states are due, the final stanza explains, to the lover's going mad with disappointed love:

> No sai de que m'ai faich chansso
> ni cum, s'autre no m'o despo;
> car tant fols asabers m'ave,
> re no conosc que m'aperte.
> Cella m'a faich outracuiar
> que no·m vol amic apellar!
> (43–48)

I know neither what my song is about nor how I have composed it unless someone else explains it to me; such foolish wisdom falls to my lot that I don't know the first thing about my own affairs. She has driven me senseless who refuses to call me her lover.

The song leaves no clue as to whether, as in "Si·m sentis" (see Chapter 2), we can unscramble these contraries by invoking the different perspectives of the lover and other people (what seems right to him is unacceptable to others and vice versa) or whether the lover truly combines all excesses of behavior in his own crazy derangement. After a paradoxical opening, Raimbaut's riddle similarly exhibits an assemblage of contraries: he is both sad and joyful, courtly but a foolish *joglar* (stanza v).

In the next group of songs, chronologically speaking, the riddles by Guillem de Berguedà and Guilhem Ademar both retreat from the use of antithesis to place more stress on negation and contradictoriness. The enigmatic "weight" into whose nature Guillem de Berguedà inquires is one he carries but cannot touch (2), one which is called "wolf" but is not one (5). The opening stanza of Guilhem Ademar's *sirventes* also relies on a play of negation:

> Ieu ai ja vista mahnta rey
> don anc no fis semblan que vis,
> ez ai ab tal joguat e ris
> don anc guaire no·m n'azautey,
> ez ai servit a manht hom pro
> on anc no cobrey guazardo;
> ez a manh nesc' ab fol parlar
> ai vist trop ben far son afar.
>
> (1–8)

I have seen many a thing I have pretended not to see and enjoyed myself and had fun with plenty of people I couldn't stand and served many a man of worth without ever being rewarded and seen many an idiot, by speaking stupidly, get his way.

The negations are used satirically, to underline how the courtier's life travesties or negates true values.

Compared with these last two, Raimbaut de Vaqueiras's "Las frevols venson lo plus fort" may at first seem more reminiscent of midcentury riddles in its reliance—its insistence, even—on antithesis as a challenge to reason. (The song is, indeed, so systematic in its use of contraries that I believe we should take the order in which they appear in the *tornada* as an indication that somewhere in the tradition before the two surviving manuscript copies, *CE*, were made, stanzas ii and iii were interverted. The stanza order presented here is thus different from that printed by Linskill and Tobler.[10]) The form which this confrontation of contraries takes differs, however, from that found in midcentury texts in that Raimbaut pressures each term to make it yield ground to its opposite. The poem thus relies on the view that contraries are mutually excluding and represents what Linskill rightly terms "an exercise in dialectical reasoning."[11] In stanzas i and ii, as I have ordered them, the strength of the strong is sapped by the weak, and bitterness driven away by sweetness[12]:

i		Las frevols venson lo plus fort
		que fortz frevol non pot durar;
		quar frevol vey fort frevolar,
	4	aissi bat frevols contrafort,
		e·n frevol trop tan de vigor
		quez a fort tol sa gran valor.
	7	Fortz a frevol non a poder.
ii		Vist ai e trobat en ma sort
		que d'agre potz doussor gitar
		ab breu aten ses ajustar;
	11	doncs agr' e dous eysson d'un port.
		E fai tant agres ab doussor
		que l'ivern mescla ab calor;
	14	mas l'agres fuy al dous parer.

The weak creatures overcome the strongest man, for the strong cannot withstand the weak; for I see the weak weaken the strong, and so the weak defeats its mighty adversary, and I find an excess of vigor in the weak because it can deprive the strong of his great worth. Against the weak, the strong man has no power.

I have seen and found, in my lot, that you can bring forth sweetness from sourness, promptly, and without adding anything to it. Thus sweet and sour issue from the same passage. And the sour is so successful against the sweet that it mixes winter with warmth; but at the appearance of sweetness, sourness takes flight.

Raimbaut thus approaches the "nothing" of stanza iii in a way that invokes the great "something" of the *coincidentia oppositorum*, but he does so from the perspective of dialectic according to which the coincidence of contraries cannot occur, there is strictly "nothing" to which it can relate.[13] Instead of being summative (as in Giraut), it is negative:

> iii   Us niens es qu'adutz a mort
> so qu'el fai e qu'el pot desfar,
> que es so que lo mons ten car;
> 18   doncx al mon fai niens gran tort.
> E·l mons, cum suefre tal folhor?
> Quar niens a tan gran sabor
> 21   que·l mons l'acuel el cartener.

> There is a nothing which leads to death whatever it creates and can destroy, for it is what the world holds dear. Therefore nothing greatly harms the world. And the world? How does it endure such folly? Nothing is so attractive that the world receives it into its affection.

This nothing/something may mean many things, but among them is surely love, which has been "something and nothing" in riddle poems throughout the century. The "nothing" to which the world is deludedly enslaved recalls the negative portrayal of love in the satirical tradition. Indeed, the images of strength–weakness and bitterness–sweetness in the preceding stanza are found repeatedly in Marcabru.[14] Such "nothing" also mimics the creator because it can make and unmake (15–16): Raimbaut's language here harks back to Guilhem de Peitieu's parodic posing as one who can create, like God, *ex nihilo* (cf. Spence, *Rhetorics*, 115–16). But lines 17–21 puncture this inflation of nothing into something and collapse it back into sheer absence: nothing is something that the world loves/there is nothing the world really cherishes, the world may suffer this nothing, but it is also the case that there is nothing wrong with what the world does. Raimbaut's joke is like that of the schoolboy claiming that Saint Nobody is really powerful because "Nobody can overcome God."[15] His wordplay causes the powers of love/nothing alternately to inflate and deflate between divine force and empty delusion.

An advantage of restoring the stanza order implied by the *tornada* is that the two stanzas in which death figures (ii and iv in Linskill, here iii and iv) now form a sequence. Stanza iii, as we saw, introduces the theme of "nothing" and its role in all human affairs; its powers of annihilation lead in stanza iv to the opposition between the dead and the living. Given that the nothing that kills a man *is* in a sense nothing at all, he springs back to life:

> iv Soven mi do gaug e conort
> que vey lo mort ressuscitar.
> Mais pot mortz que vius acabar,
> 25 per qu'ieu ab lo mort be m'acort.
> Et el mort a trop gran ricor,
> per que mortz non deu far paor,
> 28 per que·l mortz no notz e pot valer.

I am often pleased and consoled when I see the dead resuscitate. A dead man can accomplish more than a live one, and so I get on well with the dead. And there is so much wealth/power in the dead that a dead man should not be frightening, for the dead man does not harm and can help.

The motif of the lover slain by love and restored to life is familiar, characterizing the "martyrdom" motif from Bernart de Ventadorn onward. Indeed for the conventional lyricist the man assailed by love (and thus in a sense dead) is, through love, more powerful than the living, and so he is wealthy (the topos of the lover as rich). At the same time, however, the man whose merit is corrupted and his soul lost (dead) through lust (the nothing of vain delusion) may recall the rich and powerful in Marcabru, whose marital infidelities are the source of social ills, transforming wealth into impoverishment. Indeed in "Bel m'es qan la rana chanta" (XI) Marcabru's condemnation of male adultery likewise uses the motif of the living dead:

> D'aissi nais l'avols barata,
> ric viu-mort-qe Dieus descresca!
> (57–58)[16]

This is the origin of vile trafficking, you rich and powerful living-dead—may God bring you low!

The death to which "nothing" has led may be empowering; it may be confounding; or it may be meaningless and nonexistent. One clue to understanding Raimbaut's sardonic riddle, in other words, is its address to the double tradition of love poetry as eulogy or as reprobation. By conflating these contradictory strands, it finds that love may be some thing, good or bad; but such claims cancel each other out, suggesting that rather it may be nothing at all. Whereas Guilhem de Peitieu's paradoxical "nothing" flirts with the abyssal mysteries of creation, Raimbaut's deployment of dialectic summons up Aristotelian emptiness. In this way, although his song draws much of its expression from contraries, it also plunges us into negativity.

The focus of the riddle in the devinalh

The development I have traced in these few songs from paradox to contrariety and from contrariety to contradiction, via the influence of dialectic, is one that previous chapters have shown to be typical of the twelfth century. As these changes take effect, we see the contradictions of these riddles gradually shift their focus from subject to object. It is true that Guilhem's "nothing" verse is held up as an object in the opening and closing stanzas, causing Lawner astutely to observe that "the classical riddle has an object as its answer; but the riddle in this case is the song itself" ("Notes," 147).[17] It would be more exact, however, to say that because the song is so dominated by first-person verbal and pronominal forms, it is actually the singer who is the riddle. Indeed, we could go further and say that the riddle is less the singer than the *author*; for the order in which his themes are laid out—the mysteries of his birth, his temperament, his state of health, and finally his love—anticipates that of the *vidas* and makes the song into a parodic first-person *accessus* to its own creator.[18] As Pasero ("*Devinalh*") has argued, there is an "interiorization" of the riddle in this song which contrasts with its greater exteriority in the subsequent tradition[19]: it is specifically the author's own erotic and emotional reactions, and his sense that they are at odds with those of others, which constitute the riddle.

In the later twelfth-century songs, emphasis increasingly moves away from the subject. Although the lover is still in the center of the frame for Giraut de Bornelh, Raimbaut d'Aurenga's "No-sai-que-s'es" concentrates attention on the song as object, and Raimbaut is much more impersonal in the deployment of paradox than is Guilhem de Peitieu. Both Guilhem Ademar and Guillem de Berguedà are intent on showing the nonsensical character of love, and they depict it from a more objective, increasingly satirical, standpoint than the earlier poets. They present an object of which contradictory accounts are possible, rather than exposing the conflicting feelings of the poetic subject. This is very clear in Guillem de Berguedà's invitation to reflect on the mysterious "weight" or "thought" (*lo pes*), an object whose outlines shift with the accidents of word division into a "wolf" (*lop es*; see Rieger, "'Lop es nomnat,'" 502). And Raimbaut de Vaqueiras's riddle is cast in wholly objective terms. Its contradictions, as we saw, arise in part from the way a moralistic vocabulary is combined with antitheses traditionally associated with love. The riddle in this case arises not from the singer's subjective reactions—his own contradictory attitudes or experiences—but from the "riddle" of the troubadour poetic tradition with its combination of celebration and derision with respect to love. The riddle is thus "externalized," to use Pasero's term. It has left the individual to become a system within which everyone—including the subject—are contained; the first person is no longer its focus but its witness (15, 23, 30, 34–35).

The riddle and the Thing

The contradictoriness of riddles defines an edge of rational thinking and provokes their audience to reach beyond that edge in search of a solution. The notion of an edge or limit is crucial to all of Lacan's thought, because beyond this limit lies the real, the unutterable otherness of death, destruction, lust, and madness, as well as the world outside of us.[20] The real precedes and resists the symbolic order of regulation, language, and social difference; but it also emerges as an effect of it, precisely because we are aware that the symbolic order has its limits and that to invoke or approach these limits is to conjure up the sense of a beyond. In the *Ethics* Seminar, Lacan uses Heidegger's term "das Ding" ("the Thing") to designate the point on the horizon of the symbolic where the pressure of the real is sensed. "Horizon," then, is one metaphor for the limit. Another, however, is the hole or vortex which the real opens at the heart of our systems of representation. The Thing is perceptible thus both on the distant circumference of the symbolic order and at its center. Lacan presents us with an image of the symbolic as like a vast doughnut, or, more elevatedly, as not unlike the scholastic description of God whose center is everywhere and circumference nowhere (*Ethics*, 101–2). The Thing is simultaneously a nothing, the gap within or beyond representation, and a powerful something, an irreducible kernel where the pressure of the real is condensed. It infuses the whole signifying network with its terrifying otherness: ideas conveyed in the following citations:

> "Das Ding" is that which I will call the beyond-of-the-signified. (*Ethics*, 54)
>
> [D]*as Ding* is something that presents and isolates itself as the strange features around which the whole movement of the *Vorstellung* [representation] turns. (*Ethics*, 57)
>
> In the end it is conceivable that it is as a pure signifying system, as a universal maxim, as that which is the most lacking in relationship to the individual, that the features of *das Ding* must be presented. (*Ethics*, 55)

The work of art, Lacan goes on to suggest, echoes Judeo-Christian belief in creation *ex nihilo* because it recasts in a tamed and socially acceptable form the "nothing" which is also the horrifying "something" of the Thing. He thus resituates Heiddegger's claim ("Origin of the Work of Art," 76) that art is spun from nothing within the psychoanalytical framework known as sublimation, which (from Freud onward) has been invoked to describe human creativity as redirecting the inadmissible real into cultural achievement. Lacan's account of art as the cover for "nothing" uses the historic image of the potter (also found in Heidegger) in a way which is quite helpful provided you don't worry about the fact that actual potters start not from "nothing" but from a solid lump of clay:

> [I]f you consider the vase from the point of view I first proposed, as an object made to represent the existence of the emptiness at the center of the real that is called the Thing, this emptiness as represented in the representation presents itself as a *nihil*, as nothing. And that is why the potter [. . .] creates the vase with his hand around this emptiness, creates it, just like the mythical creator, *ex nihilo*, starting with a hole. (*Ethics*, 121)

As these passages show, Lacan's riddling prose when he evokes the Thing has much in common with medieval *devinalhs*. One of his pupils, for example, interjects in truly *devinalh* fashion: "This Thing doesn't exist to start with, because sublimation is going to bring it us. The question I have is, therefore, isn't this Thing not really a thing, but on the contrary a

Non-Thing and isn't it through sublimation that one comes to see it as being the Thing?" (*Ethics*, 134). Correspondingly, in the Occitan *devinalhs* we see that what lies beyond the edge of contradiction has much in common with the Lacanian Thing.

The most obvious similarity between the troubadours' "nothing" and the Lacanian Thing is their invocation of a sexuality, or a sexual relation, which is sometimes tinged with obscenity and always branded as impossible.[21] The contradictions which Guilhem de Peitieu's *vers* sets out to deflate appear to be those of *amor de lonh*, a love of cultivated nonfulfillment. However, when the singer's grasping after a tangible love is contrasted with it,

> qu'ie·n sai gensor e belazor,
> e que mais vau,
> (35–36)

For I know a nobler and more beautiful lady, and one who is more help,

this preferred love immediately proves to be just as unlocatable and indescribable:

> No sai lo luec ves on s'esta,
> si es en pueg ho [es] en pla.
> (37–38)

I don't know the place where she lives, whether it be on a hill or a plain.

These lines seem to me to admit that the *nien* of the opening stanza extends beyond the parodic dismissal of "distant love" (*amor de lonh*) and mark the singer's own erotic aspirations as (from some points of view) trivial and vacuous.[22] As in another of Guilhem de Peitieu's songs, the possibility is faced that "tot es niens": all is vanity (VII, 18). The paradoxes of human affection are assimilated to those, irreverently invoked, of the Great Contradiction in the sky.

The songs of both Raimbaut d'Aurenga and Giraut de Bornelh are likewise concerned with the sexual interests of their authors. Raimbaut's "No-sai-que-s'es" seems to refer to the difficulty of securing promised sexual favors; their absence is thus the counterpart of a thoroughly carnal presence (Di Girolamo, "'No say que s'es,'" 266). In Giraut's case, however, ambivalence extends to sexuality. If his Lady offered to sleep with him, he would resist and withdraw his service if it risked being rewarded (stanzas vi–vii).[23] The nothingness at the heart of his song—the "re non sai de cal razo" (2, "I know nothing about what theme/reason")—thus equivocates between abstinence and sensual fulfillment. Corcoran ("Song 53," 326) unearths potentially obscene meanings in Giraut's images and examines how the song may be poised between chaste and physical love. Guilhem Ademar's poem consists of wry and misogynist observations on the absurdities of erotic relations, and similarly in Guillem de Berguedà's exchange of *coblas*, the mysterious "weight" represents oppressive sexual desire requiring release as much as emotion.[24] Guillem's declared preference for a carnal love, echoing Marcabru, invites moral condemnation. Lawner ("Riddle") has gone so far as to argue that Raimbaut de Vaqueiras's "Las frevols venson lo plus fort" is an obscene allegory of intercourse that exposes the risible and contradictory features of male and female genitalia. Although I am skeptical of some of the details of Lawner's reading and would not view hers as the sole or even chief solution to Raimbaut's riddle, she is certainly right that it is possible to discern obscene implications in Raimbaut's accounts of mingling fluids and resuscitating corpses.[25] Such implications accord with what I have identified as Raimbaut's satirical cast, his debt to the tradition of Marcabru. Here we see traces of the inadmissible, disgusting, or impossible Thing, the "beyond-of-the-signified" (Lacan, *Ethics*, 54).

The increasingly sardonic or savage view of that to which the riddle points, and the association with destruction and with death opened up by Raimbaut de Vaqueiras, chime with Lacan's location of the Thing relative to the deathly urges of the real, as in this passage where he mimics St. Paul:

> For without the Law the Thing is dead. But even without the Law, I was once alive. But when the commandment appeared, the Thing flared up, returned once again, I met my death. And for me, the commandment that was supposed to lead to life turned out to lead to death, for the Thing found a way and thanks to the commandment seduced me; through it I came to desire death. (*Ethics*, 83, cf. Paul in Romans 7:7)

At the same time, the vacuousness, the sheer nothingness, of the riddles also points to the Thing as the void by which the structure of representation is pierced, a truly empty "nothingness" which is likewise best manifested by

Raimbaut de Vaqueiras. The Occitan texts' increasingly obsessive use of contradictoriness causes them to congeal with the rigid and alien formalism of the Thing, the deranged insistence of paradox, contrariety, or negation exposing to what extent the symbolic order is infused with the nonsensical arbitrariness or perverse rigor of "a pure signifying system [. . .] that which is most lacking in a relationship to the individual" (*Ethics*, 55). Sometimes contradictoriness is explicitly related to the inescapable presence of other people: "The *Ding* is the element that is initially isolated by the subject in his experience of the *Nebenmensch* as being by its very nature alien [. . .] the absolute Other of the subject" (*Ethics*, 52). Thus Guilhem de Peitieu explores "nothingness" in his paradoxical relation to others, Giraut opens the possibility that other people's perspective creates the contradictions from which he suffers, and Raimbaut de Vaqueiras sees all beings as subject to the arbitrary and conflicting impulses of "nothing." The possibility that this Thing may be internal or external reminds us of Lacan's view of it as both on the distant horizon and also at the core of representation, "something strange to me, although it is at the heart of me" (*Ethics*, 71).

The riddle of the text

Lacan says that how we situate ourselves in relation to the Thing is a crucial factor in psychic experience, but one which varies both by individual and historical context:

> At the level of sublimation the object is inseparable from imaginary and especially cultural elaborations. [. . .] In forms that are historically and socially specific [. . .] the imaginary elements of the fantasm come to overlay the subject, to delude it, at the very point of das Ding. (*Ethics*, 99, cf. 54, 113).

So what, finally, is the historical significance of the difference between making something out of the Thing-nothing (Guilhem de Peitieu) and having the Thing-nothing make and unmake us all, even to the point of death (Raimbaut de Vaqueiras)? The opening and closing stanzas of Guilhem's "vers de dreit nien" encapsulate the psychoanalytical concept of sublimation: out of nothing/something, a work will be created which will figure in courtly discussions, and which will thereby haul what lies beyond the limits of representation into the very heart of civilized life:

> i   Farai un vers de dreit nien:
> non er de mi ni d'autra gen,
> non er d'amor ni de joven,
> 4   ni de ren au,
> qu'enans fo trobatz en durmen
> sus un chivau.
> [. . .]
> viii 43 Fait ai lo vers, no sai de cui;
> e trametrai lo a celui
> que lo·m trametra per autrui
> 46   enves Peitau,
> que·m tramezes del sieu estui
> la contraclau.

I shall compose a song about strictly nothing; it won't be about me nor about other people, it won't be about love or youth or anything else, for rather, it was composed while I was asleep on horseback.
[. . .]
I've composed the song, I don't know whom it's about; and I shall send it to the person who will send it for me via someone else to Poitou, so that he or she might give me the counterkey to his or her casket.

More accurately, rather than formulating the process of sublimation, these stanzas expose it; they do not so much enact its mechanisms as lay them bare. The riddle consists in showing the contradictions inherent in creativity in which the valueless and the nonexistent are transformed into the meaningful and esteemed. Such an account, however problematically, still posits the author as "origin," crediting him with godlike ability to create *ex nihilo*.

Raimbaut's riddle, on the other hand, proceeds to strip this activity of its agent, its "creator," and thereby exposes what Lacan would call our "subjective destitution": death and nothingness reign over us, it is not we who are in charge. Yet the pervasiveness of destruction does not rule out creativity. In the penultimate stanza of "Las frevols," the poet witnesses the interplay of "hot" and "cold," which seem to me to characterize alternative ways of speaking about love and the way they make the poet-lover at once rich and poor:

> En la canal que ditz conort
> vey caut e freyt entremesclar;
> ab l'un pot l'autre amortar,
> 32 e son abduy d'engual comport.
> Ricx ers tan cum gitaras por
> e paupres si. Te dic color?
> 35 Non ieu, ans mescle sen ab ver.

In the passageway which speaks comfort I see hot and cold mingle together; one can be stifled by the other, yet they both have the same action. You will be rich so long as you keep producing, and also poor. Am I speaking mere rhetoric? Not I; on the contrary, I mingle understanding with truth.

Raimbaut's elegant text mixes "judgment with truth" in its rhetorical "coloration." By calling attention to poetic creation in the wake of his reflections on death and nothingness and of a nothing/Thing which may be nothing at all, may be love, or may be obscene, Raimbaut points to the way the destructiveness inherent in the Thing is simultaneously creative, "a will to create from zero, a will to begin again" (Lacan, *Ethics*, 212). The idea that the work of art, coming out of nothing, is linked to death is one which is reinforced in other twelfth-century texts (see especially Chapter 6); the importance of death in the constitution of the object is further explored in the second part of this chapter and in Chapter 5.

If we read the riddle of troubadour *devinalhs* in the light of Lacan's reworking of Heidegger, we see how the play of contradiction develops over the course of the twelfth century in such a way as to shift the riddle from the singer to the Thing itself, to the social artifact of the song and the nature of the sublimation that produced it. In this way, riddle poems may be said to illumine, to paraphrase Heidegger's title, "the emergence of the work of art" in the course of the twelfth century. That this tradition was not as marginal as the numbers of surviving poems might lead us to infer will be seen in Chapters 6 and 7, where I show that both Chrétien's romance of *Cligés* and *Partonopeu* allude to the Occitan riddle. In the next part of this chapter, a study of the development of the riddle in the *romans antiques* will show that we can similarly learn from the genre of romance how the riddle of art and the riddle of the object are intimately interconnected.

The riddle in the romans antiques*:*
interpellation, the subject, and the object

Each of the three romances of *Thebes, Eneas,* and *Troie* opens with an episode which is either not in its immediate source at all, or is so in a very undeveloped form: the story of Oedipus, the apple of Discord, and the quest of the golden fleece. In each of these episodes, a call is issued to its protagonist which summons him to assume the central role in events as to whose fateful repercussions the reader is in no doubt. This interpellation, to use Althusser's term, initially draws attention to the positioning of the subject.[26] Indeed without such a summons, Althusser asserts, there would be no subject. "Interpellation" is the process by which society calls the subject to occupy its position within it; when the subject responds to this address, and recognizes itself as the "you" to which the social authority (such as a policeman) speaks, it becomes subject to that authority. For Althusser, however, this recognition is at the same time a misrecognition because the purpose of the interpellation is to integrate the subject into ideology, and thus of necessity to misrepresent the subject's real historical situation. Similarly, in each of these three episodes, the call to the protagonist involves his being to some degree misled about his situation, the element of deceit increasing from the earliest (*Thebes*) to the latest (*Troie*) of the three romances. The pagan mythological framework from which this interpellation issues should, no doubt, serve as a warning to contemporary readers of its potential to mislead; the authority which seeks to define the subject is one which, from the point of view of the medieval audience, is not literally true, although the characters may believe it to be so. These episodes are thus constructed in the experimental mode characteristic of the *romans antiques,* inviting their audiences to reflect on the continuities and discontinuities between antiquity and their own time.

Interpellation serves initially, then, to define the subject in these episodes. But a shift in emphasis from subject to object is perceptible in the very way I have referred to them: Oedipus's drama is that of his own subjective identity, the goddess Discord's golden apple involves both her as subject and the apple as object, and Jason's journey is defined by the object of his quest, the fleece. Furthermore the protagonists are each confronted with a puzzle whose focus changes from the subject to the object: the riddle of the sphinx is about what it is to be a man, whereas the marvels surrounding the golden fleece identify it as a mysterious cultural object. The lethal and threatening dimension of the enigma in these romances leads us to go beyond Althusser's concept of interpellation, to explore instead Lacan's elaboration of the symbolic mandate in Book III of his Seminar, *The Psychoses*.[27] Unlike Althusser, Lacan admits a traumatic core to the symbolic address, and indeed insists that a lethal violence underlies it (expressed in the pun "tu es"–"tuer": [*Psychoses*, 40, 275, 302 ff.]). He also asserts its necessarily triangular structure: in order to assume subjectivity, the "I" addressed by "you" needs to be convinced of the existence of "him" or "her," however delusory that existence may be.[28] The symbolic mandate, in Lacan's sense, then, creates a frame for the insertion of fantasy objects which will occupy this third-person position and explains their importance in the implantation of subjectivity. (Such "fantasy objects" include the imaginary self; see below and cf. Introduction, 27–29.) The *romans antiques*, for their part, also show how the object is adduced in an attempt to ward off the deathly aggressions of others; by exposing its fantasmatic nature, they help to explain how and why romance narratives are contrived. These romances are considerably closer in date than those of the riddle poems examined in the first part of this chapter—they range from the early 1150s to the mid- to late 1160s—but the order of their composition seems uncontroversial. Exploring the "rise of the object" that takes place in their treatment of enigma will therefore, as with studying the *devinalhs*, throw light on "the emergence of the work of art" in the twelfth century. In this discussion, I will concentrate especially on the changes which take place between the furthest apart in date, the *Thebes* and the *Troie*. As a coda, I will show that Chrétien's *Le Chevalier au lion* (*Yvain*), the opening episode of which has major debts to both the *Thebes* and the *Troie*, dispenses with interpellation altogether, leaving intersubjective aggression and the third-person object as the principal attributes of the protagonist.

The Roman de Thebes

The *Thebes* romance prefaces its main story, the war between the twin brothers Eteocles and Polinices, with the story of their parents, Oedipus and Jocasta, in order to explain the accursed nature of the brothers and the doom hanging over Thebes. The Oedipus narrative is not in Statius's *Thebaid*, the principal source of the Old French *roman de Thebes*. The *Thebes* poet took it from the second Vatican Mythographer.[29] King Laius of Thebes asks the gods what end he will have and is told by Apollo that he will beget a criminal son who will kill him (39–44). His attempted infanticide of his baby son Oedipus is, however, thwarted by the compassion of the intended assassins, and Oedipus is left exposed, hanged by his feet from a tree. Rescued and brought up in another household, then scorned by members of his adoptive family as a bastard and an outsider, he determines to discover his true identity. He too consults Apollo and is told, "When you have left here you will find a man whom you will kill; thus you will know your father" (203–6). So Oedipus sets out in the direction of Thebes; near the city, he unwittingly and accidentally kills his father at public games, but no revelations follow until much later. Continuing on his journey, he next meets a demon called Pyn (the sphinx) which confounds people by asking them a question which, so far, no one can answer. The penalty for failure is death, but when the right answer is given, then the sphinx will die. The people of Thebes have given up using the road which the demon guards, but Oedipus, all unaware, comes face to face with him and is told the riddle[30]:

> D'une beste ai oÿ parler:
> quant primes doit par terre aler
> a quatre piez vet longuement,
> et puis a trois tant seulement;
> o les trois vet grant aleüre.
> Quant ses aages li meüre,
> ce li demande sa nature
> que du tierz pié n'ait ja puis cure,
> mes quant sa grant vertu li vient,
> a deus piez vet et bien se tient;
> mes puis li ont mestier li troi,
> et puis li quatre. Amis, di moi
> se tu onques veïs tel beste.
> Se tu nel sez, perdras la teste.
>
> (317–30)

I have heard tell of a beast that, when it first walks, goes for a long time on four feet, and then only on three; with the three it goes very fast. When its age matures, its nature requires that it have no care for the third leg any longer, and when its great strength comes, it walks and stands well on two feet; but then it needs three, and then four. Friend, tell me if you ever saw such a beast. If you don't know, you'll lose your head.

Oedipus recognizes the riddle as an interpellation: "ceste question est por moi" (336, "This question is aimed at myself"). He answers in the first person, telling how in infancy he used to crawl on all fours, as a toddler he used a stick, as a grown man he can stand upright, but will later require a walking aid once more, and finally two sticks. The answer to the riddle, then, is "myself as a man," which is another way of saying that to be a man is a riddle.[31] More specifically, the riddle of man is that of being a body subject to time and thereby condemned to alarming mutations from helplessness through to maturity and back into debility once more (the "ages of man").[32] Having correctly answered the riddle of human life, Oedipus declares himself entitled to kill Pyn.

Thebes is now without a ruler, and so when Oedipus arrives with all the glory of an adventuring knight having rid the country of the sphinx, it is not surprising that he is rewarded with a wife and the throne. He does admit to Jocasta that he killed her husband, but women are quickly won over (441–42), and at her counselors' urging, they settle down to a happy marriage. Oedipus still does not know his identity, or that of his parents; indeed, he loses interest in the question precisely as reality answers it by giving to him his father's position as king of Thebes and husband of his own mother. It is not until twenty years later that Jocasta notices scars on his feet and makes inquiries that put an end to this misrecognition. In a passage spoken as an interpellation of Oedipus, she declares his identity, thus cruelly clarifying the addresses of Apollo:

> Or set Jocaste par ces trois
> qu'a estroux est ses filz li rois;
> pleure et li dist: "Mar fumes né,
> car ambedui serons dampné!
> Ton pere est cil que tu as mort,
> ta mere sui si m'as a tort."
> (523–28)

From these three men Jocasta learns that beyond doubt the king is her son: she weeps and said to him, "Alas that we were born, for we will both be damned! Your father is the man you killed, I am your mother and you possess me unlawfully."

Like Althusser's policeman saying "Hey you," she calls on Oedipus to acknowledge his transgression.[33] She forces the recognition first that the father is the man whom his son killed, and then that Oedipus's marriage to her is incestuous. She thus inserts sexual difference for the first time into the structure of interpellation and simultaneously links it to Oedipus's problematic relation to an object: "I am your mother and you have me unlawfully." Far from being the reward of adventure, his possession of a wife is its crowning horror. It has masked from Oedipus the issues raised by the interpellations of Apollo and the sphinx, and it has distracted him from discovering the identity contained in his father's death. At the same time, the very mask has also, cruelly and unbeknownst to him, been what he was in quest of all along—namely his birth and origins.

I will come back to the representation in the *Thebes* of the subject as interpellated into contradiction and yet misrecognizing his identity, but first I would like, as in the first part of this chapter, to describe the changes between this, the earliest of the texts under discussion, and the later ones in which the object is more prominent and the subject correspondingly downgraded.

The Eneas

In the Middle Ages, the *Aeneid* was commonly read as allegorizing the ages of man, and especially his progress from sensual distraction (Dido) to spiritual enlightenment (the encounter with the dead father).[34] A story about the contradictions to which humanity is subject, such as that of Oedipus from the *Thebes*, would thus have provided an appropriate introduction to the Old French *Eneas*. But the adapter chose to begin his text with a very different narrative: a version of the story of the apple of Discord, which is not in Virgil's *Aeneid*, though it may have been taken from medieval glosses on it.[35] The story is introduced ostensibly in order to explain the reasons for enmity between Venus (Aeneas's mother and protector) and Juno, despite the fact that the latter subsequently plays only a negligible role in the Old French text.

The story starts when Juno, Venus, and Pallas are conversing. Discord irrupts, throws down a golden apple, and then departs. On the apple is written that it is Discord's gift to the most beautiful of the three. Discord's challenge, like the riddle of the sphinx, is an interpellation which imposes meaning on those who hear it. Just as Pyn's addressees, sooner or later, must confront their death, Discord's are plunged into strife as each of the goddesses wishes to be the one addressed. The difference, though, is that Discord's summons involves competition for the marvelous apple; that is, it defines from the outset the subject of strife as one who is in contention for an object (Huchet, *Roman médiéval*, 50–55):

> Antr'eles en ot grant tençon,
> chascune la voloit avoir. . . .
> (110–111)

Between them there was great conflict; each of them wanted to have it. . . .

In order to reach a decision in their disagreement, the three goddesses relay the interpellation to a third party:

> . . . mais par autre voltrent savoir
> lo jugemant, cui ert la pome.
> (112–13)

. . . but they wished to know through another the verdict as to whose the apple will be.

They turn to Paris: which of the three of them does he judge to be the most beautiful? This interpellation to the man to be a judge of female beauty is certainly more gratifying than those in the *Thebes*, which offered him helplessness, old age, death, and incest. Cannily, Paris postpones his decision, counting on the three goddesses to come forward with bribes (131–35). Juno offers him wealth greater than his father's, Pallas promises him more success at arms than anyone else, and Venus offers him the most beautiful woman in existence. The object once again takes center stage as Paris ponders which offer to take up:

> car molt coveita la richece
> et molt desirra la proece
> mais molt li plot la feme plus
> que promise li ot Venus.
> (165–68)

for he greatly coveted the wealth and he greatly longed for prowess, but the woman that Venus had promised him pleased him most greatly of all.

Paris's response to the goddesses' interpellation depends on which reward he selects. In opting to accept Venus's offer, he marks the gendering of this choice: he will be a subject in relation to the object woman. That this outcome was, in fact, the cause of his decision is shown up by the insistent reduplications of the text. Paris chooses Helen as the most beautiful woman in the world by the same gesture which declares (through the award of the apple) Venus to be the most beautiful goddess; it is only because Helen is desirable that Venus receives this accolade. He chooses love from the goddess of love who is competing to be the most lovely and beloved, but he does so only because he already loves. If Venus wins her prize, it is only as a function of Paris obtaining his. The episode establishes heterosexual desire not only as compulsory (it is explicitly policed later in the poem[36]) but also as compelling. The story makes it impossible to know how beautiful Venus was in comparison with the other goddesses, for Paris's "judgment" is subject to his own desire, which in turn is governed by its object-cause, Helen.

Rather than a riddle, the reader is faced by Paris with a dilemma which is the same as that proposed to Paris by the goddesses, and the same as that proposed to the goddesses by Discord: namely, how can we exercise rational discrimination as subjects when we are in thrall to what we love? The *Eneas* thus brings us up to the limits of reason, but not via the path of contradiction. Its emphasis on the object, however, forms an important step to the relocation of riddling in the interpellations of the *Troie*.

The Roman de Troie

The story of the apple of Discord could have formed a suitable preface to the *Troie* (just as it prefaces the *Iliad*), but instead it is told in much abridged form some way into the text (3860–921). In this telling, the role of Discord is suppressed and the whole episode is relegated to the status of a dream, so that the goddesses' invitation to Paris no longer has the dignity of a divine address. Instead, the *Troie* is prefaced by the story of Jason, which is very summarily recounted in its Latin source to explain the history of enmity between Greece and Troy: Jason, traveling to Colchis, is rudely treated by the Trojan king, and the Greeks subsequently retaliate. In the *Troie*, Benoît expands greatly on his model, drawing mainly on Ovid in order to reinstate the figure of Medea,[37] and so he rings the changes in the staging of interpellation, subject, and object.

King Peleus, Jason's uncle, is fearful that Jason will depose him; how can he kill him without seeming to? In some versions of the myth, Peleus (like Laius) is forewarned by prophecy that Jason is a threat to his throne (Morse, *Medieval Medea*, 5), but in Benoît's narrative, Peleus's address to Jason is not backed by supernatural authority. Instead he sets out in basely human style to deceive him, seducing him with the ideology of knightly accomplishment and then sending him on an impossible mission. "No one," says Peleus in a classic instance of interpellation, "has more prowess or courage than you do,"

> Mais conquerre la puez mout maire.
> S'une chose poëies faire,
> s'esteies si proz ne si os
> que tu la Toison de Colcos,
> que de fin or est senz dotance
> e dont il est tel reparlance,
> poüsses par nul sen aveir
> ne par force ne par saveir,
> si avreies plus los conquis
> que hom qui onc fust nez ne vis.
>
> (835–44)

but you could win much more [prowess]. If you could do one thing, if you were valiant and bold enough to obtain the Fleece of Colchos which is of pure gold without a doubt, and so much talked about, whether by any wit, by force, or by wisdom, then you would have won more reputation than any man who ever was born or lived.

As in the *Eneas* interpellations, Peleus summons Jason as subject to a relation with an object. The object is desirable as the ultimate guarantor of reputation—in this respect, the golden fleece is the equivalent of the golden apple in the *Eneas*—but its status is that of a decoy, its whole purpose being to mask Peleus's murderous intentions from Jason and ensnare him in misrecognition.

A second instance of interpellation occurs when Jason reaches Colchos (1333 ff.). Medea, who is herself already subject to Love (1294–95), reveals she knows he has come for the fleece and that all have perished who tried before him to obtain it. She explains the dangers of the magical guardians of the fleece in order to convince him that he is on his way to his death. And she promises to help him overcome them on the condition that he agrees to be her husband. The decoy of the fleece is supplemented with another object, Medea herself, who will serve as guarantor of the subject's identity. This scene takes place with Medea in her magnificent bed, an artifact so splendid that the poet says not, as we might expect, that it is worthy of Medea, but that she is worthy of it ("Bien esteit digne d'itel lit," 1571). She thus offers herself to Jason as a sexual object and as an object in the material sense of the term: an artifact. She is also a repository of knowledge and power which alone can save him:

> Fors mei ne t'en puet rien aidier
> ne aveier ne conseillier.
> Mais jo sai tant de nigromance,
> que j'ai aprise dès m'enfance,
> que, quant que jo vueil, tot puis faire.
> (1417–21)

Nothing can help, guide or counsel you except for me. But I know so much magic, which I have studied since childhood, that I can do everything I want.

Jason accepts Medea's offer with enthusiasm. His uncle's desire to kill him has been countered: Jason really will get the coveted object and not die. Lest we believe in the permanence of this solution, however, Benoît warns that Jason will not keep faith with Medea but will instead abandon her (1636–37, 2035–42). Belief in "love" to build a lasting relation with the object is undermined, whereas in the *Eneas*, despite the notoriety of Paris's abduction of Helen, it is left seemingly intact.

The most telling comparison here, however, is between the *Thebes* and the *Troie*, both of which surround the violence latent in interpellation with an edifice of contradiction. Both Oedipus and Jason encounter a series of interpellants that cast them in the role of subject. Initially, interpellation involves intermale, intergenerational rivalry. Peleus's wish to kill Jason is similar to Laius's intended filicide; both Oedipus and Jason are, in a sense, living on borrowed time, although Jason is ignorant of his uncle's intentions, whereas Oedipus at least knows (from Apollo) that his own identity is somehow enigmatically tied to his father's death. In each romance, subsequent interpellants locate the subject in riddling and contradictory structures. In the *Thebes*, the addresses of both Jocasta and the sphinx lay the burden of this contradiction on the subject himself. True, the nature of this contradiction differs from one interpellation to the other. The apparently incompatible descriptions offered by the sphinx mean that man's identity appears impossibly protean; the passage of time between the successive ages of man means, however, that these descriptions do not apply to him simultaneously; the temporal adverbs in the sphinx's address (*primes* 318, *et puis* 320, *quant* 322, *mes quant* 325, *mes puis* 327) make this clear. The problem of incest, by contrast, is precisely that relations which are held to be incompatible ("mother" and "wife") *do* obtain at the same time. Subject to these interpellations, Oedipus is thereby summoned to identify himself as a locus of increasingly irresolvable contradiction.[38]

In the *Troie*, by contrast, an external object is surrounded by contradictions. The golden fleece is depicted as a live sheep with a fleece of real gold (1884–86), a surprising conflation of the animate and the inanimate, of livestock rearing and metal refining. To win it, Medea explains, one must tame and yoke fire-breathing bronze oxen set to guard it by Mars and plow four furrows without looking, then sow the field with teeth drawn from a fire-breathing dragon which likewise watches over the fleece, and which never sleeps. The teeth will grow up at once into armed men who will kill each other. These tasks are all figures of impossibility which hinge on the juxtaposition of cultural contraries (agriculture and war, sleeping and waking, earth and fire).[39] To obtain the fleece, the hero must do the impossible or die. Medea ensures that Jason will do the former by successfully taking on these contradictions. She gives him a figurine (*une figure*, 1665) the sacrifice of which will protect him from harm. She also gives him fireproof ointment with which to withstand the fire-breathing bronze oxen. To protect him further, she gives him a ring of invisibility which is also a ring of invulnerability, a magic text which has to be read three times facing east, and some sticky gum to seal up the oxen's noses and mouths so they can't breathe fire any longer. The nature of Medea's magic, then, is to seal up what should be open (eyes, mouth, nose); to stop fire from burning, to tame the untamable, to disable armed might but make the vulnerable invulnerable, and to look away from what one needs to see while making the visible invisible. Previously we had been told, indeed, that she can turn day into night and cause rivers to flow uphill (1223–27).[40]

This shift in focus between the *Thebes* and the *Troie* from the subject to the object is accompanied, as in the Occitan riddle poems, by a change in forms of contradictoriness. In the *Thebes*, as in the early lyric, paradox is to the fore. The riddle of the sphinx and the horrors of incest both act challenge norms of understanding or behavior. In the *Troie*, however, the contradictions surrounding the fleece—although also "marvels" contrary to normal experience—also rely on opposites (sleeping and waking, visible and invisible): differences consonant with their respective dates of composition.

In each romance, then, interpellation both problematizes and facilitates the social insertion of the protagonist, making him his father's successor (in the *Thebes*) or a successful knight (in the *Troie*), while also ensnaring him in misrecognition. In both cases, the subject belatedly accepts a relationship with a woman, which stands in a complex relation to what, in a sense, he "really wants." Jocasta is both the answer to Oedipus's quest and the reason for his failing to discover it for twenty years; Medea is both a supernatural safeguard against the death masked by the fleece and a contingent love object to be later cast aside. There is thus, for both protagonists, a degree of misrecognition of their situation in relation to the object. The woman is never the first object, and supervenes contingently, giving rise to a relationship which is never welcomed by the man. The importance of the role accorded to the woman increases, however, between the earlier and later texts, the *Eneas* functioning here—as in the status accorded to the object—as an intermediary between the *Thebes* and the *Troie*.

Lacan's riddle of interpellation

Why take this analysis further? Because, as this discussion has all along suggested, what lies behind the pattern of interpellation and (mis)recognition in these romances is the menace of death. Even the love object is positioned primarily in relation not to the subject himself but to death: Jocasta masks for a while the death of Oedipus's father, then reveals it, precipitating the return of violence against her son, and Medea interposes herself between Jason and the death intended for him by his uncle. Althusser's account of interpellation as ideological integration does not admit this lethal dimension; nor does it accord importance to a third party in the summons. Yet the woman as love object is, in both *Thebes* and *Troie*, a third party not only in the sense that she is a third character, distinct from earlier interpellants, but for the more important reason that she stands in relation not to the subject but to his death: when death summons him, she intervenes. Gender is constructed in a triangular relationship rather than a binary one: the feminine is that which wards off or masks the death of the masculine protagonist.

The reciprocal violence between addresser and addressee is one of the abiding themes of Lacan's writing. It characterizes what he calls the imaginary relation, that which obtains between what we think of as our "self" and the others in relation to whom we identify our "self." Peleus and Jason, Laius and Oedipus, are in the grip of this relation to the extent that they see one another as rivals for the same place. Both of the younger men will in fact succeed their seniors, in Oedipus's case with the most horrendous exactitude, but neither of the older men wants his junior to supplant him. As the oracle explains to Oedipus, it is through violence toward his father that Oedipus will learn his identity. Previously I quoted this passage only in translation. In the Old French, the use of the same rhyme *-ras* over two couplets, in itself unusual, links together the verbs at the rhyme and so underlines the link between identity and killing:

> Li diex respont, "Quant tu seras
> issuz de ci, si trouveras
> un houme que tu ocirras;
> ainsi ton pere connoistras."
>
> (203–6)

The god answers, "When you have left here you will find a man whom you will kill; thus you will know your father."

Lacan discusses second-person singular verbal forms such as these in two sessions of his Seminar on the *Psychoses*, "Thou art the one who wilt follow me" (271–84), and "Thou art" (295–309). The violence such mandates may convey is uncovered in the sentence "Tu es celui que je suis," meaning "thou art the one whom I follow," but also "to kill (*tuer*) the one who I am" (302).

Devotion and murder are superimposed in this imaginary competition to occupy the same place, to model one's identity on another (*je suis*–"I am what I follow"). "This is the foundation of the relationship with the other. In all imaginary identification, the *tu es, thou art*, ends up in the destruction of the other, and vice versa" (*Psychoses*, 303). If the person addressed is to survive this violence, the address must cease to be dyadic and must be mediated through the symbolic with its ternary organization of "you," "me," and "him/it." This is the basis of the symbolic mandate: for the symbolic subject to be "personalized," constituted as a person in speech, the triadic structure must obtain. In Lacan's words:

> This *he* is the guarantor of my being, without this *he* my being could not even be an *I*. (*Psychoses*, 101)

> The Other is, therefore, the locus in which is constituted the I who is speaking with him who hears. (*Psychoses*, 273)

As these quotations show, Lacan himself is enigmatic, prompting his readers to ask, as he himself does, "*What am I, if I'm what you've been saying I am?*" (279). Comparing Lacan's account with the *romans antiques*, I will draw out how both represent the subjects of interpellation and their objects as a riddle.

The ternary organization of interpellation in Lacan is difficult to understand because it is not a single structure so much as an oscillation between two competing exchanges, each of which defines its own two poles in terms of "I" and "you" while casting the other exchange in the third person. (This double structure results from the interplay of imaginary and symbolic axes as represented by Lacan's schema L; see Introduction, 28.) In the imaginary relation, as we have just seen, "I" and "you" define one another in terms of mutual devotion and rivalry. This relation speaks across, and obscures, the speech of the symbolic Other. The existence of this radical Other—the world of other people insofar as they remain utterly alien to ourselves—is, however, the reason why an "I" and a "you" can ever be held apart and recognized as distinct entities. The Other is the source of real, irreducible difference, so that however strong the lure of imaginary unity, the child nonetheless learns to say "I" when someone says "you" to him, and the child understands that "when he is told *you're going to do this* he has to say in his register *I'm going to do this*" (*Psychoses*, 273). The Other, meanwhile, is constantly addressing the unconscious which, following Freud, Lacan calls the *Es* (Latin *id*, the "it"), and which thus constitutes the third person for the "I"–"you" dialogue of the imaginary. What Lacan calls "true" speech, however, is mediated between the unconscious and the Other[41]: the "I" is spoken from the position of the Big Other subject, delivering the mandate "thou art" to the unconscious. In this interaction the unconscious *Es*, by a wordplay which works in English too, becomes *S*, the subject. From this perspective, the relation between imaginary selves serves as the third element. In a normally functioning psyche, these two relations flicker back and forth to the point where they may appear to be superimposed; the position of "I," "you," and "they/it" is thus constantly moving as the first-person subject moves between the unconscious (which Lacan often refers to as *the* subject) and the *ego*, the imaginarily constituted self.

Lacan illustrates how this psychic equilibrium may be captured in the ability to respond to the mandate: "Thou art the one who wilt follow me" ("Tu es celui qui me suivras"). The injunction involves three persons: a respondent "I" is able to pass through the screen of the third person "celui qui" and hear the second person injunction in "wilt follow," *suivras*: a second-person verb form whose ending is indistinguishable in French from the third person and so can only be supplied by the addressee's response. If the addressee receives the mandate, then he recognizes that the Other recognizes him as the one who is "you." "I" will then respond from the position of the unconscious recipient "it" (*Es*) as the subject (S) of the Other's mandate. But the ego is also involved in this response. If it is strong, it will assume the third-person role and with it the certainty of following ("thou art the one who *will* follow")[42]; otherwise it will efface itself before the second person as it enters the bond of trust ("thou art the one who *wilt* follow"). Thus the ego responds to the *thou*, but not completely (see 286–87): "The *I* is essentially fleeting in nature and never entirely sustains the *thou*" (287).

When Oedipus and Jason embroil themselves with a third party (Jocasta, Medea), they successfully escape for a while from the lethal relationship with their senior/rival. In this sense, the woman acts to stabilize their identity. Both Jocasta and Medea speak with tremendous authority, interpellating the protagonists in such a way as to define them as "you" to their "I," with other characters (the father, the uncle, Medea's father) as third parties. The success of the women's address can be gauged by the fact that they are believed, and rightly, because they tell the truth. At the same time, however, the lethal interpellations of the father/uncle are also founded: the symbolic mandate also carries the stamp of death as it crushes the unconscious subject into its mold. There is no denying the reality of death; it will infallibly overtake us at some stage. The "I" that is told that it is locked in life-and-death struggle would be wrong to ignore the truth of that warning. (This is also true of the *Eneas*, where the interpellation of Discord is a call to become subject to strife.) Apollo's words to Laius link at the rhyme *engenderra* and *ocirra*, the inevitable succession of the generations which Laius's plot is incapable of circumventing:

> et Appolo li a mandé . . .
> que a present engenderra
> un felon filz qui l'ocirra.
>
> (41–44)

And Apollo instructed him that forthwith he will beget a treacherous (violent?) son who will kill him.

Neither Oedipus nor Jason is consciously aware of this threat. Oedipus is told that his identity is linked to his father's death and then instructed to solve the riddle of the ages of man, but his own death, on the model of his father's, and in conclusion to the last age of man, is a message that is present only by implication. Jason, likewise, does not hear the murderous intent behind his uncle's mission until Medea spells it out for him. To the extent that marriage with Jocasta, or the love pledged to Medea, preserve the protagonists from death for a while, these women are a third-person distraction from the "true" speech of the ineluctable Other. There is an alternation, then, in both texts between two different lines of address. Each address is triadic, but each assigns a different position to the subject, the interpellant, and the third person.

Given these similarities, how can we then account for the shift in the focus of the riddle from the subject "I" to the object "he/she/it" that forms the third point in its address by "you"? The difference between the two texts lies in the fact that for Oedipus, the supply of imaginary objects stops short, whereas for Jason, desire is fed by a constant supply of objects which all serve as points of imaginary identification and thus keep the dialogue ongoing. Jocasta's address to Oedipus unites all the previous interpellations in its devastating revelation. Oedipus's unknown origins were, for him, the object of his quest, but Jocasta shows him that recovery of the lost object is, in fact, the very last thing to be desired. He has not found a woman to provide him with a sense of identity in the imaginary register, a woman who will serve as a fantasy substitute for the originary lost object, the abyss of the real. He has unwittingly gotten the real thing: his real father dead, his real mother as wife. This may be the answer to riddle of the subject, but it is also the cue for meltdown: Oedipus's narrative crashes to its end and his sons supplant him. The riddle of subjectivity will have to be negotiated all over again: Thideus, the most admirable character in the *Thebes*, is confronted with the same riddle as Oedipus and solves it with the generic answer "man," confirming that *all* subjects, whatever their moral circumstances, are called upon to live with the contradictions of time-bound bodies.[43] And Polinices, one of the sons of Oedipus and Jocasta, tries to conceal his father's name because he does not wish to be identified in the terms of the contradiction he has inherited:

> Cil ne dist pas le non son pere
> pour ce qu'il ert filz de son frere.
> (861–62)[44]

He did not give his father's name because he was the son of his own brother.

Thus the riddle posed throughout the *roman de Thebes* is that of our contradictory origins and nature, and the problem for its characters is that, to their own doom, they keep discovering the answer.[45]

In Jason's case, by contrast, all of the objects he is offered go to sustain the alluring image of himself as a superlative knight. In Lacan's terms, Jason's imaginary self-image is itself an object, the specular ego painted for him by his uncle's words and backed by the elite ideology of knighthood. Everything he learns about the fleece, by accentuating the dangers of obtaining it, increases the prestige which will accrue to him. His departure stirs his followers to demonstrations of devotion (1847–48) and Medea to passionate outbursts (1862–75) paralleled by their rapturous reception of his return (1977 ff., 2006 ff.). His flattering self-image, mediated by others in this way, is further supported by a whole chain of additional props: Medea's offer of herself as wife (1409) and her various magic gifts (figurine, ointment, ring, gum). Whereas Oedipus is destroyed by reality, Jason becomes a magical being (*faé*, 2002) from the possession of the magic fleece-thing (*chose fáee*, 1994). Oedipus is appalled at who he is; Jason is enchanted by what he can get. The value of imaginary objects (including "oneself as a great knight") in sustaining the forward drive of narrative could not be more strongly emphasized.

All the *romans antiques* I have been discussing interpellate the subject, placing him in a network of contradiction expressed as a riddle or enigma and underlining the inevitability of violence and death. But in displacing the riddle from subject to object, the *Troie* diverts the question from the horrific "Where do I come from? Who am I? How will I die?" posed by the *Thebes* to the mystificatory and benign "What can I achieve? What can I win? How can I make myself into a paradigm of knighthood?" Although the stay of execution may be no longer in the *Troie* than in the *Thebes* (Jason doesn't, after all, survive the first reel), narrative proliferates as imaginary objects are adduced in profusion to mask the inevitable end. In this way, the shifting role of enigma in these introductory episodes, as in the Occitan *devinalh*, illumines the development of the literary object in the twelfth century.

Coda: *Chrétien's* Le Chevalier au lion (Yvain)

These *romans antiques* were all composed before the romances of Chrétien de Troyes, which they clearly influenced, most blatantly, perhaps in the case of *Cligés* (see Chapter 6). But the opening narrative of *Yvain* is a condensation of much of the material examined here. Like Helen in the *Eneas*, the Lady of the fountain sets the seal on Yvain's successful competition with his cousin, Calogrenant, and with Kay. The meeting with the hideous herdsman in *Yvain* recalls that between Oedipus and the sphinx in the *Thebes*. The herdsman is a monstrous and paradoxical union of conflicting attributes drawn from different beasts, and yet he answers Calogrenant's inquiry with the reply that he is a man. So the subject "man" is once again encountered as a riddle of corporeality, though here in relation to animality rather than to time. Also as in the *Thebes*, the hero's winning of a wife on the heels of his killing her husband forms the main narrative thread of this part of *Yvain*, and it is treated with similar irony. Indeed, *Yvain* contains actual textual echoes of the *Thebes* when the woman's repugnance toward her husband's killer is quickly overcome, her counselors urge the marriage on grounds of expedience, and the past is soon forgotten:

> Le deul du roi est oubliez,
> cil qui mort l'a est coronnez.
> (*Thebes*, 485–86)

> Et li morz est tost obliés:
> cil qui l'ocist est mariés
> en sa fame. . . .
> (*Yvain*, 2167–69)

Mourning for the king is forgotten and the man who killed him is crowned.

And the dead man is quickly forgotten, the man who killed him is married to his wife. . . .

Other links are apparent with the *Troie*, such as the ring of invisibility given by Lunete to Yvain that recalls Medea's gift to Jason, and the series of seemingly contradictory phenomena—the tree that never loses its leaves, the fountain that boils, and the drops of water which provoke storms—that flicker mysteriously on the fantasy screen of adventure and thereby exalt the hero's prowess.

As in the *Thebes* and the *Troie*, the woman emerges only secondarily, in the wake of masculine struggle. Yvain does not even know that the Lady of the fountain exists, because Calogrenant never got that far. She is the only really new experience he has, for in every other respect he follows the model of his predecessor; and he does so thanks to having survived the battle with her husband. Esclados's bleeding corpse, over which his widow laments, is the occasion of his falling in love with her and a reminder that life with her is the alternative to having been killed by him (see also Chapter 7). Despite the echoes of the *Thebes*, union with the lady does not short-circuit the fantasy so that it collapses into the real; she remains securely separate from his maternal origin. Instead, like Jason, Yvain will abandon his wife, thus providing the impetus for a further succession of new fantasy objects on which to test his "knighthood."

All these similarities make more startling the great divergence of *Yvain* from the *romans antiques*: the absence of interpellation. The remarkable negotiation conducted with ideology by the *romans antiques*, through their dependence on pagan religion and mythology, has no place in the Christian–Celtic ambiance of Arthurian romance. Perhaps the nearest any of Chrétien's romances get to the staging of an ideological summons, or a symbolic mandate, is *Cligés*, when Alexander on his deathbed instructs young Cligés to go to Arthur's court.[46] And so the initial, lethal interpellation which sets the story in motion in both the *Thebes* and the *Troie* is omitted: Yvain's adventure is motivated by his own rivalry, pure and simple. Similarly, the revelations of Jocasta and Medea have no parallel in the words of the Lady of the fountain, whose interest revolves entirely around what Yvain can do for her. That the individual man should be a riddle and seek out objects of contradiction that screen his death, through which he discovers union with a woman, has become implicit and, as it were, "natural." The subject is no longer explicitly addressed: what remains is the framework of lethal struggle and the hope of evading death oneself through an endless pursuit of fantasy objects, including and perhaps even especially the ideologically valued "self."

The chapter has looked at two analogous transformations which take place in the course of the twelfth century in two different genres. It is possible that the authors of the *Thebes*, *Eneas*, and *Troie* were familiar with Occitan poetry, and even specifically with the riddle tradition.[47] The two earlier romancers could have known the texts of Guilhem de Peitieu, Cercamon, and Jaufré Rudel,[48] and Benoît might additionally have known Giraut de Bornelh and Raimbaut d'Aurenga. The analogy I am drawing between the two does not depend, however, on inferring influence from one to the other; their common interest in the riddling and the enigmatic may result from generic interference, as Rieger suggests, but the riddle is culturally ubiquitous.[49] By aligning the riddles of these texts with similarly teasing and enigmatic passages from Lacan, I have taken the first steps in exploring how the contradictoriness of medieval poetry may be illumined by a similar self-conscious cultivation of contradictoriness in Lacan's thought. Between them, these riddles introduce, in the configurations of subject and object, the bases of the Lacanian theory used in this book. The next chapter will take this exploration a stage further by looking at how objects are constituted in medieval texts, and why.

CHAPTER 5

The Virgin and the Lady: the abject and the object in Adgar's *Gracial* and the *Lais* attributed to Marie de France

A study of contradiction in twelfth-century literature cannot ignore the growing cult of the Virgin Mary in this period. For Mary is as contradictory a figure as one can imagine: maid and queen; virgin and mother; daughter, mother, and bride of God; human and yet unique, she embodies a clash of contraries and a challenge to reason. (Some responses to this contradictoriness in saints' lives were observed in Chapter 3.) Vast numbers of Latin texts in Mary's honor are produced in the eleventh and twelfth centuries; vernacular compositions follow in their wake. From the twelfth century we have Wace's *Conception de Nostre Dame* (a life of the Virgin) and, in Anglo-Norman, Adgar's *Le Gracial* (a collection of Mary miracles); Mary is also accorded a less central role in a number of French or Anglo-Norman hagiographic and devotional works.[1] In Occitan, there are five vernacular sermons devoted to Mary of the two dozen or so surviving, and there are Limousin rhymed prayers preserved in the *Sponsus* manuscript (see Salvat, "Sainte Vierge"). The numerous vernacular Marian lyrics—hymns, *albas*, *planctus* (see Secor, "*Planctus Mariae*"), etc.—date from the thirteenth century onward, and this period also witnesses the prolific production of vernacular miracles, most famously those of Gautier de Coinci.[2] It is Mary miracles, mainly from the twelfth century, which provide the basis for this chapter's study of the contradictions associated with her cult. These are short works based on Latin models, usually in verse and typically gathered together in cycles or collections. They treat of devotion to Mary, the ways in which she miraculously satisfies people's needs, and the reporting, reception, and celebration of her interventions. They thus associate Mary, human crisis and resolution, and the texts themselves, as distinct but interrelated phenomena.

This whole package is highly reminiscent of courtly love texts where the Lady, the lover's demand, and the text which commemorates it are similarly interlinked: a pattern which is reinforced when courtly texts, like miracles, are transmitted in collections or anthologies. A long-standing critical tradition has seen the cult of Mary as both influencing, and influenced by, that of the courtly Lady.[3] The Lady addressed (or constructed) by courtly rhetoric is, like Mary, "alone of all her sex,"[4] and she too is described in contradictory ways and is the object of ambivalent demands. If the Lady and the Virgin[5] can be assimilated to one another as well as opposed, texts can become ambiguous between devotion to a heavenly or earthly Lady, and they thereby invite contradictory interpretations. For example, many twelfth-century troubadour lyrics have been seen as ambiguous between addressing a secular Lady, or Mary.[6] Following the suggestive remarks of R. Howard Bloch (*Medieval Misogyny*, 129–42), I will look at some examples of miracle texts in relation to certain of the *Lais* ascribed to another Mary conventionally referred to nowadays as "Marie de France." Roughly contemporary with Adgar's miracles, and like them composed in Anglo-Norman England, these *Lais* also commemorate marvelous or "miraculous" events in the form of an anthology or cycle of short narratives.[7]

The purpose of this comparison is to further our understanding of the role of the "object" from the preliminary pointers established in the last chapter. We saw there that the focus of enigma gradually shifts from the subject to the object, which thereby becomes a locus of contradictoriness. Objects are often situated relative to obscenity or death, as an instance of "sublimation" or alternatively as a mask deceiving the protagonist as to his fate. And they form part of a shifting triangular structure in which a third person sometimes speaks to the protagonist from a position of truth, interpellating him into subjectivity, and sometimes figures as a fantasy propping up his idealized self-image; in such cases the object may be not only the fantasy-other but also the internalized "self" of the protagonist. In all of these areas, analogies were seen between the medieval texts and the riddling way Lacan conceives and speaks of the object.

By looking more closely at the reasons why the object is constituted in the first place, at the threats it is invoked to palliate, we will better comprehend why it should be sought out, and why it is contradictory. And by tracing its increasing textual solidity, its hold on symbolization, between religious and courtly texts, we will further understand how courtly texts come to constitute themselves as objects. This analysis will be supported by two interrelated psychoanalytical texts: Book IV of Lacan's Seminar, *La Relation d'objet*, and Kristeva's essay "Something To Be Scared Of" in her *Powers of Horror*, both (in part) commentaries on Freud's case history of Little Hans ("Analysis of a Phobia in a Five-Year-Old Boy"). Although *La Relation d'objet* (which dates from 1956–1957) was published only in 1994, Kristeva clearly had access to it because she both quotes from and paraphrases it.

The core to the thinking of both works, and of this chapter, is the following statement by Lacan:

> The object is the instrument whereby we mask and adorn/ward off [*parer*] deep-seated, residual anguish [*fond d'angoisse*]. (*Relation d'objet*, 22, also quoted by Kristeva, *Powers*, 33/43)[8]

Both Kristeva and Lacan are concerned with the development of phobic and fetish objects as responses to this anguish of the presymbolic or the nonsymbolic. For Lacan, "everything of the order of the preverbal [. . .] partakes of what we call an intraworldly Gestalt, within which the subject is the infantile doll he once was, he is an excremental object, a sewer, a leech" (*Psychoses*, 164–65); to the subject in this state, the mother appears as a devouring monster (*Relation d'objet*, 195). Kristeva terms this realm of disgust, repulsion, and aggression the "abject." It is in our efforts to escape from it, to pass from anguish to fear and thus from flux to some measure of determination, that objects are formed: we find something to be afraid of and situate ourselves as the object of its threat (*Powers*, 38–40/50–51).[9] Both phobic and fetish objects are thus defensive mechanisms. As such, they are lures of the imaginary; what form they take is contingent on the network of symbolization in which they arise. The horror against which they (half-) protect us is that of a lack in the symbolic order: "The object has a certain function of complementing what appears as an absence—or rather, an abyss—in reality" (*Relation d'objet*, 23). The crucial feature of the object, as a result, is that it is conjured up in the place of something *which is not there*. Insofar as it remains keyed to this absence, and marked by it, the phobic object is in some degree still abject for Kristeva, "this 'ab-ject' that is the phobic object": "Phobia literally stages the instability of the object relation" (*Powers*, 41/52, 43/54). In *La Relation d'objet*, Lacan identifies this absence as being that of the maternal phallus (one of his chief themes throughout this Seminar being the various forms of what he calls "castration"). Kristeva's emphasis, however, is more on how lack in the symbolic betrays the underlying pressure of the real, invoked by Kristeva as a traumatic struggle with the presymbolic mother. Our desire to elaborate objects to contain this trauma is, in her view, the reason why we painfully clamber onto the raft of language and cling to the linguistic structures that will grant us some measure of protection from the horror they enable us to repress. By the same token, entering language condemns us to leave the presymbolic state forever, subjecting us to a definitive loss, to life in a universe resonant with lack. Thus "whenever we use the faculty of speech [. . .] the language we use is that of fear. I mean a language of lack as such, the lack which positions the sign, the subject, and the object" (Kristeva, *Powers*, 38/49).

As a result, language also becomes our fetish, the object to which we cling as a substitute for that which is lost, while knowing that language is incapable of remedying that loss (Kristeva, *Powers*, 37/48–49). The phobic patient turns to the fetish of language as a way of coping with his disorder: "Language instead of the good breast. Discourse substituted for the maternal breast" (*Powers*, 45/57). This substitution is facilitated by the fact that the phobic object is so densely metaphorical as to symbolize symbolicity itself (*Powers*, 44/56). In *La Relation d'objet*, Lacan also analyzes the connection between fetish and phobic objects, both of them defenses against "the same fundamental, residual anguish [*fond d'angoisse fondamentale*]" (23). The relation of substitution, and the fixation upon "screen memories" characteristic of fetishism are, he says, fundamental to the way we constitute what we think of as "reality" (24). Lacan is interested in symbolicity of all kinds, whereas Kristeva argues that writing in particular, because of its privileged capacity for dense symbolic expression (for instance, in metaphor) is a mechanism resorted to compulsively in attempts to seal over the trauma of abjection. She thus provides a theoretical bridge between representations of "reality" in any medium and the written texts which elaborate them. This will prove useful to my discussion because in miracle stories there is, as we will see, a remarkably compulsive degree of repetition and recursion, as well as a strongly elaborated figurative relation between the elements of their narrative structure.

Although both Lacan and Kristeva argue for the proximity of phobic and fetish objects, they both identify them as different, if interconnected, structures. Correspondingly, this chapter contends that the miracles and *lais* I single out for study are both different and connected: different because the subject matter of the miracles belongs more in a Kristevan universe of abjection whereas that of the *lais* rather solicits a Lacanian, fetishistic reading, connected because stories in the two genres can be read as variants of one another and because both are transmitted as similarly literary artifacts.

Constituting the abject/object in Adgar's Le Gracial: *"powers of horror"*

Adgar's *Le Gracial*, the oldest surviving vernacular miracle collection, consists of forty-nine Anglo-Norman verse miracles framed by a prologue and epilogue, mostly translated from the Latin of William of Malmesbury. The classic outline of Adgar's narratives is as follows:

(i) The protagonist observes a cult of the Virgin.
(ii) The protagonist encounters a crisis.
(iii) The Virgin rewards the protagonist's veneration by resolving his problem.
(iv) Narration or witness of the miracle is offered for the edification of others, inside and outside the text.
(v) All who hear the miracle are exhorted to pursue a cult of the Virgin. (This permits the cycle to begin again.)

An example of this pattern is Adgar's Miracle II, which has been taken as an archetypal miracle text (Ebel, *Altromanische Mirakel*, 27–33) and which has a large number of vernacular (as well as Latin) variants: in the *Roman de Rou* (III, 337–510), in Adgar himself (see also VII, XVII), and in the second Anglo-Norman collection (Kjellmann, *Deuxième collection*, XI, XVI and XXV). In this summary, the numerals correspond to the divisions in the schema above:

(i) A salacious sacristan always salutes Mary before going to the town to indulge his appetite for "worldly pleasures."

(ii) Crossing a bridge on his way there, he is pushed into the river by the devil and drowns. Angels dispute with devils as to the ultimate destination of his soul.

(iii) Mary, claiming she was the last person he had talked to, takes his defense. He is allowed to return to life and so atone for his sinful life.

(iv) Meanwhile, the monks notice the absence of their sacristan, look for him, and pull him out of the water. He tells them how Mary has helped him. They praise God. The sacristan is a reformed man.

(v) Address to the audience: may God guard us all against the devil.

The simplicity and repetitiveness of these stories lend them to narratological analysis. Such analysis has tended to center on the notion of lack and so has drawn attention to the narrative importance of a subject–object relation.[10] In this case, for instance, the sacristan's "lack" is the unlikelihood, dying as he did, of his attaining salvation; the Virgin gives him a second chance. A similar pattern of lack compensated by miraculous provision is typical of miracles associated with all saints, such as St. Nicholas, whose life was retold by Wace. But whereas other saints tend to supply fairly humdrum needs, returning lost valuables or healing minor ailments, the Virgin's objects are tinged with horror: she specializes in lost lives and lost souls.[11] This is made explicit by Adgar:

> Li altre seint rendent santé
> as cors ki unt emfermeté,
> mais la dame ad duble vaillance,
> des cors e des almes puissance:
> les cors sainet en char e en os,
> les almes met en grant repos.
> (XXXV, 125–30)

Other saints restore health to sick bodies, but the lady has a twofold effectiveness: power over both bodies and souls. She heals physical bodies and brings souls to eternal rest.

Of the forty-nine miracles translated by Adgar, death, salvation, or both are at stake in at least half. The Virgin is often appealed to by the dying to ease their passage out of this world and into the next. Her maternal comfort accompanies death as a time of helplessness, violence, and terror:

> Uns malades mult anguissié,
> de dolur grevé et blecié,
> ne pout a autre rien entendre
> fors coment il peust l'alme rendre
> a Deu e a sa bone mere.
> [. . .]
> La dame dunc ignelement
> le cumforta mult ducement.
> Cumfort le par grant amur
> et dist lui: "N'aëz tel poür!
> Mere sui pleine de pitié,
> mere de plenire amisté;
> mere sui Deu, del ciel reïne,
> de tuz mals ferai mescine."
> (XXIV, 1–5, 21–28)

A sick man, in anguish, afflicted and cut through with pain, could think of nothing but of how he was to render his soul to God and his good mother. [. . .] Then the lady promptly comforted him most gently. She comforts him lovingly and said to him: "Do not be so afraid! I am a mother full of pity, a mother of ample affection, mother of God, queen of heaven, and will bring medicine to heal all sufferings."

If Mary's miracles effectively put her in a different class from other saints, it is because the needs she fulfills function as her attributes: that is, the story establishes an interrelation between herself as the object of the protagonist's veneration and whatever the protagonist's other concerns might be. That Mary's nature is figuratively supplied by the protagonist's actions with regard to her is plainest in the stories which don't involve some crisis on his part, but rather the provision of a further service for Mary, such as writing a book about her (Adgar I: Hildefonse) or establishing a ritual in her honor (XIX: compline). Such miracles are etiological, justifying festivals such as the Nativity of the Virgin (XVI, XXX) or her Conception (XXXI) (see Corbin, "Miracula"). Here the recursive structure of the miracle is particularly evident, the cult of Mary being reinforced and extended by means of the protagonist's activity, through which we are exhorted to redouble our cult of Mary. This linking of the Virgin with ecclesiastical ritual suggests that Mary often has a metaphorical role in these stories, designating less a person than Mother Church. Those who are saved by her intervention usually have a record of devotion expressed through liturgical texts: hymns, anthems, and psalms. The texts teach that adherence to the Church as an institution will ensure salvation for the sinner, however grievous his sin, provided he continues to practice her rites.

Conversely, however, these texts emphasize the retribution awaiting us should we fail to benefit from her intervention. This is dramatically imaged in the story of the altar boy of Clusa (Adgar XIII). The monks of Clusa insist on red wine for communion because it looks like blood, whereas white wine looks like water; during the office, the altar boy accidentally spills some of it on the altar cloth. The gory stain on the white cloth ("as though it were stained all over with blood," 47) recalls Christ's Passion and serves as a frightening reminder of the sinful nature which necessitated such sacrifice, a reminder all the more vivid for being prompted by the apparently innocent boy. He appeals to the Virgin, whom he has always served, and she miraculously whitens the reddened cloth in the course of the *pater noster*. Her miraculous housewifely proficiency ("no laundress in the world could have got the cloth so white," 75–76) combines strikingly with her power to palliate the stain of sin, the reassurance of the first underlining the terrors of the second. The stain in this miracle is similar to Lacan's horrible, guilt-inspiring real, likewise frequently imaged by a stain: "the real yawning gap always hidden behind the veil or the mirror and always standing out against the background [*fond*] like a stain" (*Relation d'objet*, 297, cf. 332). As an "object" of concern to the altar boy, the stain is all too indissociable from the abject of guilt and death. The figure of the Virgin may wash whiter than white and support the symbolic structure of the liturgy, but she also communicates "powers of horror" as effectively as she allays them, as if some vestiges of the struggle with Kristeva's presymbolic mother still clung to her.

It is striking that the horrors invoked to threaten Adgar's protagonists rarely involve adult sexuality. Most of them are male clerics like Adgar himself; sexual transgression as such is most evident in the few miracles with female protagonists, like the unchaste nun (XLI), the female sacristan who eloped with a knight (XLVIII), and the pregnant abbess (XLIX), each of whom is reproved by Mary for her offenses against the ideal of virginity.

Where male protagonists are concerned, lasciviousness is rather a part of a pattern of uncleanness. They are reproached with *ordure* ("filth"), with being *ord* ("filthy"). Even objects of sexual interest are tinged with disgust rather than titillation. Thus for example the clerk in XXXVI, a miracle discussed further below, starts by being a "good boy" who learns his lessons well:

> Mais il chaï en grant folie,
> en ordure mua sa vie.
> (11–12)

But he fell into great folly and changed his life to filth.

In VIII, a monk from Cluny who had sex with his mistress is persuaded by the devil to castrate himself and dies as a result; the Virgin restores him to life but without his genitalia, thus permanently relieving him of the temptations of adult sexuality.

Orality is as significant to Adgar's male protagonists as genitality. The *ordure* of some consists in eating or drinking too much (III, XVIII). Those who fall ill and are cured by Mary often suffer from disgusting illnesses of the mouth: ulceration and putrefaction (XV, XXII, XXX), which are cured by her miraculous breast milk.[12] In XV, a cleric with a diseased jaw is granted a vision of her in a glorious temple whose beauty and radiance exceed all human description (XV, 195–200), and Mary herself is "Plus clere ke soleil de jur; / plus fud clere, plus out clarté / ke le soleil enmi esté" (XV, 206–8, "brighter than sunshine, brighter and more brilliant than the sun at midsummer"). With milk from her breast, the disease is healed, the sick man becomes as healthy as a child, and the disgusting smell of putrefaction is transformed into an odor of sanctity:

> Delivre de enfermeté,
> sain fud e entir cum enfant.
> Del sunge esveilla a itant
> e receut clere sa lumiere
> en sa face sanz mal entiere. [. . .]
> La puur d'icele maisun
> e del malade e d'envirun
> ert ja turnee a grant duçur,
> en grant suavité de odur.
> (XV, 248–58)

Free from his sickness, he was as healthy and whole as a child. He promptly reawakened from his vision and was able to receive her bright splendor on his face which was now whole and free from disease. [. . .] The foul smell in that house from the sick man and his surroundings was now transformed into great sweetness, a most pleasant fragrance.

In Miracle XXXII, the sickness of a dying monk (known as Wettinus in the Latin tradition) revolves around his mouth, even though it is not the seat of his disease. First he drinks a potion which brings him nothing but harm (1–4); then his health deteriorates:

> Acrust sis mals e sa dulur
> si que ne pout sa bouche ovrir,
> de l'oil veer ne mot geïr.
>
> (12–14)

His suffering and pain increased so that he could not open his mouth, see, or utter a word.

This preoccupation with orality is illumined by Kristeva's stress on the pivotal role of the mouth in the development of the abject/object. The mouth is the organ of satisfaction of the most primitive of the drives and the site on which our earliest aggressions are focused in fantasies of incorporation. But the mouth is also the organ of speech by means of which these early terrors can be symbolized and mastered. As a result of this symbolization, the primitive bond with the breast becomes lost forever (Kristeva, *Powers*, 38–40/50–52).[13] In the *Gracial*, the vile or dirty mouth is threatened with awful punishment, and yet at the same time it is offered the possibility of recovering its lost object: veneration of Mary may bring about a blissful union with the maternal breast.

In Miracle XX, we find a different association of the mouth with disgust. In Toledo, a pogrom is called for by the Virgin because Jews spat at an image of her and derided it. The other end of the digestive tract features in another anti-Semitic miracle (XLV), that of the Jew who puts an image of Mary into his privy intending to defecate on it. Unluckily for him, all his bowels fall out, while the image remains free of all *ordure* and is brought out glowing with mysterious radiance. Mary's insertion in the midst of such preoccupations again chimes with Kristeva's account of the abject. The boundaries of mouth and breast, inside and outside, self and other, cleanness and dirt, are precarious and traumatic (*Powers*, 53–54/65). Their painful negotiation results in our fixing disgust on objects located on the wrong side of symbolic divides: dirt, excrement, vile smells. To counter this disgust, we have recourse to notions of the pure, the sublime, and the sacred. Thus for Kristeva abjection provides the psychic motivation for religious experience and also for racism, which (like religion) is powered by an opposition between purity and filth. The conjunction of the religious and the racial oppositions between disgust and the sublime is manifested in the miracle of the Jew who puts the image of Mary in his privy: he is all bowels and defilement and general bodily repulsiveness, whereas she is a vision of light. The prevalence of anti-Semitism in Mary miracles (this particular miracle has 106 lines of prologue denigrating the Jews; and see also Fradenburg, "Criticism") returns us to the observation that the situations in which she is invoked serve to figure her significance, which is always double: both a promise and a threat. As the resplendent mother of Christendom, she brings illumination to the faithful but she also brands as irremediably abject those who cannot or will not be included in her fold. This duality of salvation and menace is well illustrated in another anti-Semitic miracle, Adgar XIV, where a Jewish boy thrown into a furnace by his father for believing in the Virgin is saved by her, but his father is burned in his place.

In conclusion, we see how pervasive are the "powers of horror" in these stories. Despite the complex legislative scaffolding erected so as to contain human anguish—extensive moralizing, expositions of doctrine, exhortations to dedicate oneself to spiritual values, visions of bliss, etc.—the anguish remains omnipresent. Indeed, the texts' purpose is to focus it on an explicit threat, "something to be scared of" in the terms of Kristeva's title: a namable object of a fear which, if you are good, Mary will allay. But the fearful objects which the stories propose—racial outcasts, horrific diseases, death, eternal punishments—although they are part of a symbolic structure (what could be more efficiently symbolized than church doctrine?), nonetheless suggest how precarious is the detachment of such objects from the beastliness behind them. Furthermore, the accumulation and repetitiousness of the stories, structured as they are in such a way that the end of each prepares for the beginning of another, mean that we are exposed to ever more demonstrations of the Virgin's ever more glorious powers, which may enable us to escape the abject dissolution with which these stories ever more threaten us. . . . The cycle of the disgusting and the pure keeps turning, "literally staging the instability of the object relation" (*Powers*, 43/54), as it seeks both to cover over, and ward off, the anguish beyond (*Relation d'objet*, 22).

Contradictions of the Virgin: "The Virgin's betrothed" and "The incestuous mother"

So far I have adduced a framework for understanding why the Virgin should be a figure of contradiction. She stands, as it were, on either side of the object of fear, provoking it into existence (on the side of the traumatic real) and then countering it (on the side of the symbolic fabric of the Church). Now I will look closely at representatives of two groups of miracles, known respectively as the *sponsus marianus* ("the Virgin's betrothed") and the "incestuous mother" groups. These stories have been singled out because of the close correspondence between their content and stereotypical representations of the Virgin as a figure of contradiction. Although I focus on just two stories, both have very large numbers of analogues and thus a certain typicality (though of course they cannot stand for the whole miracle genre). Additionally, both will lend themselves, in the next section, to comparison with some of the *lais*.

There are occasions when the "filth" of a male protagonist is expressed in sexual desire, a theme more or less elaborated in several of Adgar's miracles, notably in XXXVI, an example of the *sponsus marianus* group of stories about a man who pledges his love to the Virgin in preference to any earthly bride.[14] The form this narrative takes in XXXVI is a sexualized variant of the Theophilus legend: a clerk forsakes his service of the Virgin and makes a pact with the devil in order to secure a desired sexual partner; but thanks to Mary's intervention, he then repents and vows love to her instead. In order to reinforce the wickedness of his infidelity to the Virgin, the tale is combined with the contrastive one of a man who renounces all temporal, sexual objects in favor of permanent religious ones.

In this miracle, the eternal security which the clerk might obtain through Mary is contrasted with the damnable effects of his dealings with the devil, and so the backdrop to the story is the struggle between Mary and the devil for a human soul threatened with eternal perdition, which was identified as typical in Miracle II. The relation between Mary and the sexual beloved is likewise presented in the first instance as one of contrast between right and wrong objects of love. However, their opposition also reveals their interconnection, pulling them into rivalry and even similarity. Mary calls attention to this when she calls on the clerk to renounce the human bride who has supplanted her in his affections and to return again to her:

> Dunc dist ele: "Jo sui Marie,
> de qui [a][15] cele hure chantastes,
> ki jadis de bon cuer me amastes.
> Jadis oi un ami vaillant,
> ki ore ne me tient covenant,
> ki ore meine femme sur mei;
> merveille est qu'il ne me tient fei.
> Laissier volt nostre drüerie.
> Mais si cum jo sui Deu amie
> e mere Deu, seinte reïne,
> preciuse e pure meschine,
> e puissante en ciel e en terre,
> jo muverai vers li tele guerre,
> ki m'at covenant depecié,
> ke ja puis lunges n'ert haitié."
> (XXXVI, 178–192)

> Then she said, "I am Mary of whom you once sang, you who used to love me with a good heart. I once had a worthy *ami* who now does not keep faith with me, who now takes a woman/wife in preference to me; it is astonishing how he does not keep faith with me. He wishes to abandon our love pact. But just as I am the *amie* of God, the mother of God, holy queen, priceless and pure maid, and powerful in heaven and earth, so I shall declare such war on him who has broken our agreement that he will never again be happy for long."

Mary's speech applies to the relationship between herself and the clerk a vocabulary redolent of the profane love between himself and his worldly bride (*ami, drüerie, covenant, tenir fei*) and underlines the competition between them by her references to rivalry (*or meine . . . sur moi*) and vengeance in which the language and tone are altogether secular.[16]

The theme of sexual love in this miracle correlates, of course, with the cult of Mary as a virgin, a cult which in turn reflects as much as it distances itself from the widespread eroticism of vernacular literature in the twelfth century. Early vernacular lives of female saints, in particular, revolve obsessively around sexual themes; saints such as Foy and Catherine will reject the husbands designated for them by their male protectors in favor of preserving their virginity for the heavenly bridegroom (see Chapter 6). The way that Mary is both compared with objects of sexual love and contrasted with them also recalls the contradictory way the lady in lyric poetry is situated with respect to sexual possession: the lover both desires to possess her and renounces such possession, aspires both "to have and have not," in Leo Spitzer's famous phrase. Indeed, the proliferation of vernacular *sponsus marianus* stories in the thirteenth century documented by Wyrembek and Morawski is fueled precisely by this parallel between Mary and the erotic object. The fact that the male protagonist's relation to both Mary and the courtly Lady is both sexualized and asexual confirms the similarity between the two. Although both the Lady and Mary are contradictory objects, however, each foregrounds a different element of the contradiction. Courtly texts claim that the subject's relationship to the object is erotic (but may then deny it by creating barriers to fulfillment). Marian texts, by contrast, promote her as pure beyond any actual sexual relations (but nonetheless persistently eroticize their relation to her); sexuality is invoked only in the form of its denial. In Miracle XXXVI, for example, when the clerk repents of his pact with the devil and his lust for an earthly bride, he declares his love for Mary in sexual terms:

> Ne ja, dame, ne vus larrai,
> kar espuse prise vus ai.
> (213–14)

And I shall never leave you, lady, for I have taken you as my bride.

But then he reforms his life for love of Mary as mother:

> Pur amur sa mere Marie
> par qui si out müé sa vie.
> (271–72)

For love of his mother Mary, through whom he had transformed his life.

My reason for examining Miracle XXXVI is that this double take in its plot exactly echoes one of the most common descriptions of Mary in Adgar's *Gracial* as being both "mother and virgin," a contradictory formulation which removes Mary from sexual activity while at the same time identifying her with its most obvious outcome. It occurs in Miracle XIV:

> ki est e mere e meschine
> (103)

who is mother and maiden

or XXVI:

> mere Deu, sainte meschine
> (1090)

mother of God, holy maiden

as well as XXXVI:

> e mere Deu, seinte reïne,
> preciuse e pure meschine.
> (187–88)

and mother of God, holy queen, precious and pure maiden.

The story of Adgar's Miracle XXXVI, and of the *sponsus marianus* group as a whole, can be read as an extrapolation of this contradiction.

A similar interrelation between the contradictory descriptions accorded to the Virgin and a plot in which she features is attested in the second group of miracles I discuss: that of the incestuous mother. This group has been much less studied than the *sponsus marianus* miracles, and yet it is at least as numerous. Poncelet ("Miraculorum Beatae") refers to eighteen Latin examples,[17] and there are also several vernacular ones (Gravdal, "Confessing Incests," 283–84). Although none of the vernacular versions that I have so far found is twelfth century, an Occitan one in a collection of thirteen Occitan prose miracles can be traced without difficulty to a twelfth-century Latin text.[18] The earliest French version I know is that by Gautier de Coinci (I.18, in Koenig, II, 130–57) whose miracle collection is dated ca. 1220. I will, however, use the Occitan prose text because vernacular prose miracles, although they may be later in date than verse ones, often go back to earlier models.[19] The importance to medieval readers of this miracle may be inferred from the fact that it figures as the concluding miracle of the Occitan miracle collection and as the initial miracle of two Latin verse compilations.[20]

The mother who figures as the subject of this story is left by her husband, who wishes to devote himself to the religious life. She resists separation from their son, prolonging breast-feeding into his adolescence and always sleeping with him. To her horror, she becomes pregnant by him, and when their child is born, she destroys it by putting it down a privy. She then is filled with self-disgust and turns to Mary, whose purity offers a contrast to her own debasement. Subsequently the woman is accused of the child's death by the devil in disguise, and she appeals to Mary for help. The Virgin takes up her defense and accompanies her to court. There Mary and the murdering woman can actually appear as one:

> ... nostra dona fo no vigiblamen amb ela e conparec denan la cadeira del jutge terrenal e defendet la fenna si que aquesta fenna amb tal companheira intres en jutgamen, laquel fo pel rei e pel pobol honorablamen receubuda. E va se seire el metz de totz e fo a totz mirailhs e clardat. E adonc tut se calero e obriro las aurelhas, e adonc lo rei va dire al clers que parles si re volia dire. E adonc el ditz que lo aguardamen d'aquela fenna era mot merevilhos e ditz que aquo no era plus la fenna prumeira, ans era autra que per la gracia del s. esperit s'era cambiada.[...] E adonc el ditz que aquo no era pas la fenna malvaja que avia coceubut de so filh e l'efan avia mort, laqual el avia accujat, an[s] era sainhta e merevilhoja entre las filhas del mon, e era aquela que s'en anera pojada sus al cel del dezert, etc. E aprop el ditz que d'aisso dire el avia gran paor, empero calar no ho podia, per so quan nostra dona lhi era decosta aquela laqual el avia accujat, que lhi ajudava e la sostenia. (188–94)

> ... our lady was invisibly present with her and appeared before the earthly judge's seat and defended the woman, so that she entered into judgment with such companionship [i.e., with Mary as invisible companion], and was honorably received by the king and the people. And she goes and sits in the midst of all and was to all a mirror and a radiance. And then all were quiet and opened their ears, and then the king tells the clerk to speak if he has anything to say. And then he said that the sight of that woman was most extraordinary and that

she was not the first woman but another who had been transformed by the grace of the holy spirit. [. . .] And then he said that this was not the wicked woman who had conceived by her own son and killed the child, the one he had accused; instead, this woman was holy and wondrous amongst the daughters of the world and was the one who had ascended to the very zenith of merit, etc. And afterward he said that he was very afraid to say this, although he could not keep it silent, because our lady was beside the woman whom he had accused, helping and supporting her.

The glorious attributes of Mary—her aura of light and her incontestable splendor—are passed on to the erring mother. As a result of her identification with the Virgin, she is acquitted. From having been contrasting figures, the mother and the Virgin are now mysteriously alike. How has this come about?

In examples of the *sponsus marianus* story, I suggested that the contradictory description of Mary as both virgin and mother represented a double move to sexualize and then desexualize her. As a result of this, Mary resembles, as well as differs from, the more obviously unchaste objects of the text that have to be renounced for her sake. Likewise, in the incestuous mother story, the anxiety over boundaries which produces the fluctuations between defilement and purity, and of which the mother-son boundary is the model, is also expressed both via relations in the plot and within the figure of Mary herself. For the most common characterization of Mary in vernacular texts is not in terms of the contradiction between virginity and motherhood, but of her contradictory relationships: she is both mother and daughter of God, and she is bride to both father and son.[21] This motif is not, it is true, expressed in the Occitan miracle, but it is found in a twelfth-century Occitan hymn:

> O Maria, Deu maire,
> Deu t'es e fils e paire.
> (*"Sponsus,"* ed. Thomas, 199)

Oh Mary, mother of God, God is your son and your father.

It occurs in Wace's *Conception* (see 539–40, 1547–48) and it is especially common in Adgar:

> Ki est clamee fille e mere,
> ki porta sun fiz e sun pere.
> Or l'aüre cum seignur,
> cum fiz e pere e creatur;
> sis peres devint sis cher fiz.
>   (XVI, 29–33)

Who is called daughter and mother, who bore her son and her father. Now she worships him as her husband, her son, father and creator, her father became her dear son.

> . . . de nostre mere
> Ki portat sun fiz e sun pere.
>   (XVII, 69–70)

of our mother who bore her son and her father.

> . . . la duce mere
> ki porta sun fiz e sun pere.
>   (XXVI, 483–84)

the sweet mother who bore her son and her father.

> ki estes mere, fille e espuse
> a celui ki tutes riens fist . . .
>   (XXVI, 1092–93)

you who are mother, daughter, bride to him who made all.

Here is a particularly extended example:

> Ki porta nostre creatur,
> nostre pere, nostre cher frere.
> Ele est nostre soer, nostre mere.
> Pur ceo que Deus de li receut
> encarnatiun cum li plot,
> nostre frere est, sue merci;
> kar de nostre mere nasqui.
> Nostre pere en divinité,
> nostre frere en humanité
> est li sires, par sa merci
>   [. . .]
> Icil sires par sa merci
> nus defende de l'enemi

> pur l'amur sa chere mere,
> dunt nasqui de fille pere.
> (XXX, 148–57, 161–64)

Who bore our creator, our father, our dear brother. She is our sister, our mother. Because God was made flesh though her, as was his will, he is our brother, thanks to her; for he was born of our mother. Our lord is, by his grace, our father in divinity, our brother in humanity. [. . .] May this lord in his mercy defend us from the devil for love of his dear mother by whom the father was born of his daughter.

These passages are almost indistinguishable from descriptions of incest. The prologue to the vernacular *Life of St. Gregory*, for example, a version of which is found not coincidentally in one of the same manuscripts (B.L., Egerton, 612) as the *Gracial*, summarizes Gregory's intriguing family tree in terms closely resembling these excerpts from Agdar. I quote from Sol's critical edition of the Egerton text:

> ke uns ses uncles l'engendra
> et la sue ante le porta.
> Uncore li fist li enemis
> a cel saint home faire pis,
> ke sorurges devint son pere
> si fud mari sa charnel mere!
> (49–54)

For a man who was his uncle begot him and his own aunt bore him. And the devil caused this holy man to do still worse: for he became his father's brother-in-law and the husband of his very own mother.

We found similar riddling language, likewise caused by the transgression of expected family structure, in *Apollonius* and the *Roman de Thebes* (Chapter 4). (Indeed, Gregory, like Oedipus, has sex with his mother while trying—all too successfully—to discover the secret of his birth.) The point of the Occitan miracle, in other words, and the reason why the mother and Mary can occupy the same space at the trial, is that the woman who conceived by her own son (in the register of abjection) is a type of Mary who did exactly the same (in the register of the sublime). In Gautier de Coinci's version of the miracle, indeed, the incestuous conception is presented in terms remarkably like these formulaic descriptions of the Virgin:

> . . . tant fist cil en sa mere
> qu'engenra son fil et son frere.
> (I, 18, 107–8)

He acted in such a way upon his mother that he begot his son and his brother.

The miracle of the incestuous mother, with its very many cognates in Latin and the vernacular, denounces the horror and shame of the abject relation with the mother at the same time as it seeks to glorify union with the mother as a sublime support and sanctuary. The various objects of the miracle are interrelated by virtue of the way Mary incarnates in a benign and disguised form the sin of incest with which the earthly mother is cursed.

Marian abjects and Marie de France's objects

What of courtly texts? How do they look in the light of this reading of the Marian material? How far are they prepared to admit the trauma which leads to the emergence of the object and to the resulting equivocation between the abject and the sublime? I will look here at just two *lais* which offer secular parallels to the two miracles I have just discussed: those of "Lanval" and "Fresne."

Similar to the "betrothed of the Virgin" miracle (and like it, a member of a group of analogous stories including the so-called anonymous *lais* "Guingamor," "Graelent," and "Désiré") is the well-known *lai* of "Lanval."[22] In this tale, the protagonist is enjoined to remain faithful to his "sublime" (here, fairy) love. The supernatural qualities of the *fée*, her beauty and dignity, all recall portraits of Mary. Her desirability, although undoubtedly erotic, is contrasted with the baser sexuality of a worldly love, the queen who, when she fails to seduce Lanval for herself, is interested only in ruining him. Lanval repudiates the advances of this worldly lover, but in so doing, he breaks the command of the *fée* never to reveal her existence, thus losing her (as he thinks) irreparably. However, as in Mary miracles, the most terrible wrongdoing can be forgiven by the sublime love; she appears to him and to the court, to universal acclaim, before taking the protagonist away with her forever from mortal ills to eternal joy with her.

I have summarized this narrative in such a way as to bring out the similarities between "Lanval" and Adgar's Miracle XXXVI. However, readers of these two tales find themselves in different worlds. By contrast with the powers of horror summoned up in relation to Mary, the *fée* in "Lanval" is barely uncanny. Her supernatural attributes consist largely of the fact that she can be summoned at will to produce limitless wealth and bliss. The only aspect of her which is remotely traumatic is her capacity to impose her arbitrary law: in order to continue to enjoy her magical favors, Lanval has to observe her rule of silence ("if you reveal it, you lose it" as Bloch puts it [*Medieval Misogyny*, 142]). The *fée*'s injunction draws attention to the interrelation of love, law, and language:

> Ne vus descuvrez a nul humme!
> De ceo vus dirai ja la summe:
> a tuz jurs m'avrïez perdue,
> se ceste amur esteit seüe;
> jamés ne me purriez veeir
> ne de mun cors seisine aveir.
> (145–50)

Do not reveal yourself to anyone! I shall tell you the essence of it: if this love were to be known, you would have lost me forever; you would never be able to see me or have possession of me again.

Her injunction echoes the originary loss effected by our entry into the symbolic: once we can speak, that which language cannot name is constructed by us as a lack, and the objects in which we subsequently invest are conjured in relation to that lack. This absence at the heart of the symbolic order can seem to infuse it with inhuman rigor, and it is this which leads Lacan to characterize the courtly Lady as Thing, "an object I can only describe as terrifying, an inhuman partner" (*Ethics*, 150). Just as the protagonists of *sponsus marianus* miracles fail to remain true to Mary, so Lanval inevitably betrays the *fée*'s rule and fears losing her forever, until she relents. To this extent, as in the miracles, the *lai* both provokes fear and allays it, both invokes the rigor of the law and averts its dire consequences.

Yet even this comparison exaggerates the similarities between the *lai* and the *sponsus marianus* miracles. Courtly and religious discourses are far removed from one another. Lanval may be wretched when he betrays his lady, but he is not invaded by the abject. Although there is transgression of symbolic boundaries (when Arthur fails to reward Lanval, the queen makes her adulterous advances and Lanval breaks the *fée*'s command), there is nothing visceral at stake in this *lai*, none of the filth which engulfs the clerk in the miracle. Whereas Lacan envisages the courtly lover subordinating himself to his lady's law with the scrupulous self-indulgence of a masochist,[23] in "Lanval" the *fée*'s law can be flouted without there being any abiding consequences. It is only pronounced in order to be overridden, as it is in every one of the story's analogues; Lanval's disobedience is not going to surprise many of the *lai*'s audience.[24] There are no "powers of horror": the lady is not ultimately unnamable, and she is only inhuman in the sense of being superhuman. I would say, then, that the *fée*'s injunction does not so much reenact the lack in the symbolic order as pastiche it. Her law is not *the* law but a *substitute* for it. This relation of substitution points to a shift from phobia to fetish between the narratives of the miracle and the *lai*. Indeed, the change from the real terrors of death and perdition to the fairyland setting of the *lai* underlines the quality of make-believe in the courtly text; the words "*fée*" and "fetish" are, we are told, historically related (Lacan, *Relation d'objet*, 170).

That "Lanval" is fetishistic in character, as compared with the phobic-abject nature of the related miracle, is confirmed by the *lai*'s final scene. When the *fée* arrives, a description of her begins in which her splendid accoutrements and clothing play the starring role. Within lines of the portrait beginning, our eyes have been directed from the *fée* to her palfrey, and from the palfrey to its splendid harness, which the richest men in the world would have to mortgage their estates to buy (555–58). From there, the portrait addresses her clothing: a close-fitting linen shift which is laced together at the sides so as to reveal the flesh behind (559–62). Next it deals with her physique, moving (in reverse order from the rhetorical norm) up the body instead of down, retreating from her bare sides and slender, flowing hips up to the safer territories of neck, eyes, and hair (563–70), then further again to her mantle, hawk, and hound. This description is fetishistic not just in its preoccupation with valuable commodities[25] and kinky accessories such as horse tackle, but also in the vivid way it confronts a limit between the seen and the unseen (the lacing) that can be lingered over but not crossed, a point at which the eye stops short, and yet beyond which its continuing movement is implied (see Lacan, *Relation d'objet*, 119, 157). A similar line between the visible and the concealed is drawn in the earlier description of the *fée* (80–106) which, after dwelling on the details and value of her clothing and her priceless tent, focuses on the way her mantle is draped across her body to divide the exposed from the hidden flesh.

The purpose of the concealment, Lacan would say, is to suggest that there is something behind it. This is illustrated by what he calls the "schema of the veil" (Figure 9).

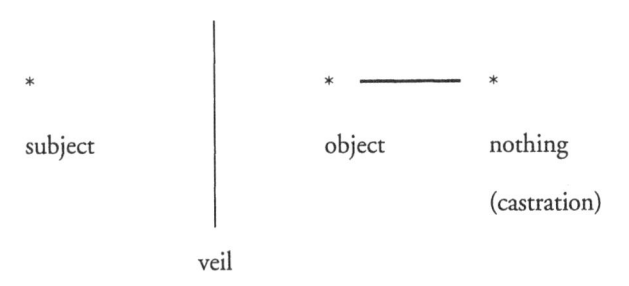

```
       *            *  ———  *

    subject       object    nothing
                            (castration)

                  veil
```

Figure 9. The schema of the veil (from *La Relation d'objet*, 156)

The veil is there less to mask an existing object beyond than to foster the subject's illusion that there *is* such an object there in the first place. Although the object may be what is loved, the fetishist's desire focuses on its veiling, which is what preserves its illusory status: for the fetishist, "that which holds fast his desire, namely the object, appears as illusory, and as valued precisely insofar as it is illusory" (Lacan, *Relation d'objet*, 156).

The change in status between the phobic abject of the miracles and the fetish object of the *lai* does not mean that the object ceases to be contradictory. On the contrary, as this discussion has shown, fetishism turns precisely on contradictory stances with regard to the opposition between absence and presence. Fixing desire on the veil involves a double take on the object behind, which is both delusory and believed in. Belief that it *is* there is the more stubbornly held for its being veiled—that is, for there being no grounds for believing in its presence. The fixation results from identification of the self (the ego) with the veiled nature of the object. For this reason, in *La Relation d'objet*, Lacan sees fetishism as an imaginary resolution of phobia, because while a phobic object is densely symbolic, so too is our relation to it; but in fetishism, we adopt an imaginary relation (that of identification) to a symbolic object.[26] Little Hans, who starts off as a phobic patient terrified of castration and who orchestrates his panic in a myriad metaphors of horses and transport systems, is seen by Lacan as becoming a fetishist when he resolves his fears by clinging disbelievingly to the belief that he is himself the missing maternal phallus.

Before taking the analysis of "Lanval" further, it is important to be clear how the structure of fetishism (as Lacan describes it) applies to it thus far. In the lingering descriptions of the *fée* with her accoutrements, it is not the fairy herself who is the fetishistic object but the "phallus" which gives her the magical powers of abundance: a phallus in which we only half-believe because we half-know that—like fairy magic—it does not exist. The fetishist, however, identifies with that phallus. Half-knowing it is not there, behind the veil, he can half-believe that he is it: by this means, he can sustain his half-belief in its existence. In fetishism, that is, the subject positions *himself* as the fetish object. (This is analogous to the imaginary identification of oneself with images promoted by the ideological interpellations discussed in Chapter 4, with the difference that identification is fixated upon this very peculiar object.)

The contradictory combination of presence and absence in the fetishistic "phallus" offers a clue to understanding the most piquant instance of contradiction in "Lanval," the fact that the only redress for Lanval's indiscretion, and thus the loss of the *fée*, turns out to be the flagrant exhibition of her to the entire court.[27] Both secrecy and display can be analyzed as turning on *what is not there*. When Arthur in the opening scene fails to reward Lanval as he deserves, Lanval loses favor at court. The *fée* immediately appears. Her suggestive clothing draws a line beyond which Lanval cannot see but which he is invited nonetheless to imagine: he is encouraged in the belief that, as a powerful, benign force, she does not lack anything. He at once becomes her darling. Empowered by her fabulous powers, embodying her magical phallus, he becomes beloved by all again; the abolition of lack is confirmed, it would seem. But he must keep their love a secret; why? The veil he has to draw over their union both affirms the identification on which it rests and calls it into question. It puts it into question in part because the fictionality of the veil is so patent: the injunction is made to be broken. It is a pretense, a lure forbidding Lanval to reveal what, ultimately, *is not there*[28]: there is no maternal phallus for him to assume and thereby live out a fantasy of plenitude and bliss: his love (with a fairy!

I ask you!) both panders to a desire "to lose oneself in the beyond of a refound unity" (the phrase is Harf-Lancner's, *Fées*, 243) and mocks it. Thus when he breaks the command and the veil is torn down, the absence is momentarily exposed: the *fée* disappears, and there is no magic thing, nothing for him (or anyone) to see.

At the end of the *lai*, however, the fetishistic solution reasserts itself. The fetishistic performance is this time staged for the benefit of everyone, displaying to the whole court the possibility that there is *nothing* there, only to enlist them all in the fantasy of its existence. When the *fée* arrives, all can see the line between the visible and the invisible and so collude in Lanval's belief in the imagined presence behind. The consecration of the fantasy comes when the *fée* declares to Arthur that Lanval is the object of her love (615–16): she is not lacking for anything, he is her imaginary completeness, and he can be exhibited to all as the substitute for the object which may—or may not be—behind the veil.

It is significant that in this, as in other "Marian" *lais*, the "fixation" of the veil is materialized through lingering attention to forms of covering—clothing, the *fée*'s tent—which also serve as figures of representation. The prominence of so much symbolic fabric corresponds to the "fixing" of the symbolic order in the texts, its capacity to conjure up an endless supply of objects of love and desire. This promotion of the role of textiles is even more striking in the *lai* of "Fresne." Here the fetishistic "logic of the veil," a cover which conjures a fullness of meaning behind it, is rampant.[29]

The narrative in "Fresne," like that of "Lanval," presents striking analogies with Mary miracles. Fresne herself, for example, recalls the nun in the well-known miracle of "la sacristine" (Adgar XLVIII) who leaves her convent in order to live with her lover but whose place there is miraculously filled by Mary in anticipation of her eventual return.[30] But the *lai* also presents common ground with the incestuous mother group examined above. Features common to both are the threat of infanticide to avoid accusation of a sexual sin; the threat of incest[31]; and most significantly, knotted with these two themes, the problematic doubling which lends uncertainty to the definition of subjects and objects, which centers anxiety around the dyad, and which brings simultaneous abasement and elevation. The contradictions worked out in this text involve—as in the incestuous mother miracle—the capacity for low and high to occupy the same space (cf. Chapter 2). Fresne is surplus twin, unwanted concubine, and self-abnegating lover; but she is also, and simultaneously, long-lost child, honored bride, and cherished love object. As in the miracle, the *lai* acknowledges the potential instability of objects and their problematic situation with respect to the mother.

However, unlike in the miracle, infanticide and incest are both dissociated and averted: although her mother wanted her killed, Fresne survives, and the incestuous marriage of her sister to her lover is aborted. The conclusion is brought about by Fresne's self-abnegation, but she is not abjected. Ultimately the significant boundaries in this *lai* are not those perilously negotiated with the mother but those imposed by the social order. The path to this resolution may be fraught, but the dénouement of the *lai*, as in "Lanval," is a triumph of figures of representation. In the passage leading to the recognition by the mother of her daughter, images of covering and uncovering accumulate, their purpose being to locate the objects conjured behind them—bodies and the bed—in the desired relationships. Fresne goes into the bridal chamber to ensure it is ready. She takes off her mantle (392). The bed is draped with cloth made from old dress material (398–99). Then Fresne, judging the fabric not fine enough, covers it over again with a silk cloth (404)—the same as the one in which she was wrapped as a baby. Meanwhile, the bride, her sister, is instructed to undress (412), but at once her mother's attention is caught by the silk cloth (413). A chamberlain, summoned to explain, reveals how the cloth came to be placed on top of the coverlet. Fresne is called to the chamber and, instead of the sister undressing, it is Fresne who removes her own mantle once more (429). Questioned by her mother, Fresne tells her how she obtained the cloth and shows her mother the ring she was given at the same time.

> "Bele, pois jeo veer l'anel?"
> "Oïl, dame, ceo m'es [mut] bele."
> L'anel li ad dunc aporté,
> e ele l'ad mut esgardé;
> el l'ad tresbien reconeü
> e le paile ke ele ad veü.
> Ne dute mes, bien seit e creit
> que ele memes sa fille esteit;
> oiant tuz, dist, ne ceil[e] mie:
> "Tu es ma fille, bele amie!"
>
> (441–50)

"Lovely one, may I see the ring?" "Yes, lady, surely." She brought the ring, and the mother looked at it closely and recognized it clearly, and the cloth she had seen. No longer doubting, she knows and believes that this selfsame girl is her daughter. So that everyone can hear, not concealing it, she announced: "You are my daughter, lovely friend!"

The miraculous ending of this *lai* is far distant from that of the incestuous mother miracles: instead of the powers of horror being invoked and countered by an all-powerful sublime figure, life's problems are resolved and smoothed over by cloths, clothes, and jewelry. Objects of adornment—the cloth and the ring—are dramatically produced in order to underwrite social identities and ensure that the right twin achieves reunion with her parents, restoration of her inheritance, and marriage to her lover: the *fond d'angoisse*, in Lacan's term, is definitively parried/adorned. The fetishistic solution has prevailed; the symbolic structure with all its problems and deficiencies is imaginatively recast in the visual field as series of covers that fix the "reality" of the objects behind them. The retreat from trauma has been comprehensively achieved.

Objects of writing

The similarities which exist between individual *lais* and miracles have helped to highlight differences between the two genres. I have contrasted the phobic–abject universe of certain miracles with the fetishistic one of some of the *lais*; the first lends itself to reading in the light of the "powers of horror," the second in function of the "logic of the veil." But both sets of texts exist *as texts*, dependent on textual antecedents and committed to manuscript. To what extent do the differences so far discerned characterize the treatment of the texts themselves, and what we can glean from how they were recorded of authors' or copyists' attitudes toward them?

The transmission of miracles and *lais* presents obvious analogies. Both genres are gathered together in anthologies; one rarely finds lone miracles or isolated *lais*.[32] There are so many miracle collections that it is possible to trace the constitution of some of the very earliest groupings. We know, for example, that although Adgar drew mainly on William of Malmesbury's *De Laudibus et miraculis sanctae Mariae*, the *Gracial* reverts to the order of one of the oldest known compilations for its opening thirteen miracles, which follow the sequence baptized by Mussafia "Hildefonsus-Murieldis" after its first and last tales.[33] Nevertheless, the precise outlines of the *Gracial* are unclear. Divergences between the two major manuscripts which transmit it prompted Legge's suggestion that it existed in two successive recensions, with two different dedicatees (Gregory and Maud), dated ca. 1165–1170 and 1175–1180, respectively.[34] In his introduction to the *Gracial* (14), Kunstmann, however, rebuts this suggestion as "a pure conjecture unsupported by any secure facts"; he thinks that there is a single text which cannot be dated more narrowly than between 1150 and 1200. A weakness of Legge's account is that she appears to think that the version in B.L. Additional 38664 (the prologue of which contains the dedication to Maud) is an abridgment of that in Egerton 612 (which contains addresses to Gregory in Miracle XX and the epilogue). This is not the case: the Additional manuscript contains the prologue plus Miracles I–X, all of which are lacking from the Egerton manuscript, plus twelve other miracles which it shares with Egerton 612, though in a different order. Moreover, the collection in Egerton 612 did not start with Miracle XI, even though this is how Neuhaus's edition presents it, because some lines from Miracles IX and X survive on the lacunary first folio. Thus the lengthy prologue of Miracle XI, although it gives the impression in Neuhaus's edition of heading Adgar's text, was only ever embedded somewhere inside a larger collection. On the other hand, Kunstmann's defense of the integrity of the *Gracial* is also vulnerable, given the different selection and ordering of miracles in the two manuscripts, and especially given the odd position of Miracle XLIX in Egerton 612. This miracle ("the pregnant abbess") is appended not only after the epilogue but also after the *Life of St. Gregory* which follows. Because the epilogue to the *Gracial* in this manuscript contains a dedication to Gregory, it became mistaken for a prologue to the *Gregory*.[35] Maybe the compiler of Egerton 612 himself was misled into taking the *Gregory* for an additional miracle; it presents significant similarities, as we have seen, with the incestuous mother group. As for the miracle of the pregnant abbess, scholars disagree whether it is by Adgar or not; Kunstmann considers that its late inclusion merely rectifies the oversight of its earlier omission (Kunstmann's introduction to Adgar, *Gracial*, 15). Whatever the *intentions* of the copyists—oversights and lost folios aside—the fact remains that Kunstmann's edition does not correspond to the contents of either of these two manuscripts.

These uncertainties concerning the number and authorship of the miracles in the *Gracial* are paralleled by debates regarding the status of the *lais* in B.L. Harley 978. Recent years have seen a spate of publications in quest of the author-narrator Marie—or in contestation of "her" existence.[36] Although the majority of scholars privilege the Harley collection over others, ascribing all the *lais* contained in it to Marie and labeling as anonymous all those which are only found elsewhere, there are reasons for doubting whether this privilege is justifiable. As with the *Gracial*, different groups of *lais* are assembled in different manuscripts and in different orderings (Baum, *Recherches*, 117–21; Masters, *Esthétique*, 102–10). Collections of *lais* being far less numerous than those of miracles, we know much less about the movements of these texts and their associations with one another; there is no evidence for there having ever been any fixed order or grouping (Baum, *Recherches*, 118; Masters, *Esthétique*, 105–7). The name "Marie" appears in only one collection (in the prologue to "Guigemar" as it appears in the Harley manuscript), the two other copies of this *lai* either omitting or altering the line in which the name occurs. It is odd that this self-attribution, if such it is, occurs in the second text of the collection, *after* the prologue. On the other hand, of course, Adgar's revelation of his name does not occur until the prologue to his Miracle XI. Arguments about consistency can be drawn for and against the integrity of the Harley collection. Reviewing these arguments leads Baum to conclude that, whereas the prologue to Denis Piramus's *Life of St. Edmund* is evidence that a "dame Marie" composed some *lais*, we cannot be at all sure which ones they are (Baum, *Recherches*, 123, cf. 58, 218). Masters is more radical still in her rejection of Marie as "author" or originator of any of the surviving texts (*Esthétique*, 141–56).

Although the size of collections of *lais* and miracles in manuscripts collections is variable, the beginning and end of each short text is clearly marked. Within the *Gracial*, each miracle is set off by its own prologue and epilogue, which mirror in miniature the prologue and epilogue that frame the entire collection in Kunstmann's edition. It is impossible to know how much of this material is of Adgar's own devising. Southern credits Adgar's immediate source, the Latin compilation made by "mestre Albri" of St. Paul's and referred to by Adgar in the epilogue, with having grouped William of Malmesbury's collection together with others and simplified its style in preparation for translation ("English Origins," 203). Maybe Aubri introduced some of the elements for which Kunstmann finds no analogue in the surviving Latin texts, or maybe Adgar contributed them all. Certainly he adopts a very different stance toward the texts he is transmitting from William of Malmesbury in the *De Laudibus*.[37] Typically Adgar's prologues expatiate on the worth of the Virgin, whereas his epilogues are a first-person plural prayer asking for her intercession; the *De Laudibus* has neither. Taken together, Adgar's framing devices reiterate the belief that service of the Virgin will assist us all in gaining salvation, that belief being, of course, what is enacted within each individual tale. Adgar also provides a substantial amount of commentary in the first-person singular. In his prologue, he speaks of the greater benefits to be earned by writing for a divine than an earthly patron. In Miracle XI he talks at some length about his two names; in Miracle XVI he contrasts his texts with more popular frivolous ones, a "prologue" which in fact takes up half of the entire text; in Miracle XX he talks about his task as a translator and names for the first time his friend Gregoire, who made him undertake it; the theme here of the "diversity" of his material is taken up again toward the end of Miracle XXXV (132 ff.), where he justifies again the intention of writing in praise of the Virgin; and Miracle XXXV opens with lengthy reflections on the importance of study, the permanence of writing, and the need to remember what one has read and so reform one's life in a way pleasing to God. In similar vein, though at less length, the Harley *lais* are each framed with introductory and concluding material, in which the need to commemorate the signal events recorded in the *lai* is a recurring theme.

In their written form at least, both the miracles and the *lais* thus present us with a contradiction whereby each story seems self-contained and sufficient to itself and yet requires to be transmitted as a part of a group. In performance, the same contradiction will have been suggested by the prologues of some at least of the miracles and *lais*, because these state that the texts they introduce belong to a wider collection. For example, "Yonec" is offered as one of many *lais*, Miracle XLIX presents itself as one of several miracles about nuns, and both Miracle XXI and "Milun" invoke the diversity and plurality of their genre:

> Mult fait Deu miracles sovent
> par tut le siecle diversement
> pur l'amur sa mere chere,

> mustré l'ad en meinte maniere;
> par ses mustiers, par ses ymages
> rent il suvent des desvez sages,
> si cum vus iert ici mustré.
> (Miracle XXI, 1–7)

God time and time again performs a great variety of miracles throughout the whole world for the love of his dear mother, and this he has displayed in many ways; through the churches and images dedicated to her he often makes madmen wise, as will be shown to you here.

> Ki divers cunte veut traitier,
> diversement deit comencier
> e parler si rainablement
> k'il seit pleisibles a la gent.
> ("Milun," 1–4)

Anyone who wishes to narrate a variety of tales should begin in a variety of different ways and speak as reason dictates so as to give people pleasure.

It is impossible to know how many *lai* or miracle texts might have been read or recited in one performance session, and thus to what extent this implied invitation to add other examples of the genre was taken up. Even in written transmission, the extent of this wider set is ill defined because its outlines are, as we have seen, uncertain in the manuscript tradition of both the *Gracial* and the *lais*; there is no point at which the number of texts a manuscript contains seems anything other than arbitrary. It is noteworthy that there is no epilogue to the Harley *lais* or to the Additional version of the *Gracial*, whereas in the Egerton manuscript, which does contain an epilogue, a miracle is appended *after* it. Thus there is an instability inhering in the individual text, a sense in which it both fulfills a lack—each miracle or *lai* is complete in itself—and creates one—each invites more of its genre to create a larger unit, the collection; and there is also an answering instability in this larger unit given that its outer limit remains indeterminate. Each miracle or *lai* is thus in a sense a substitute for another miracle or *lai*, because each one gestures toward a space which another instance of the genre can be called upon to fill. Each individual text, in short, invokes the contradiction of absence and presence which characterizes the object:

by its very presence, it invokes the potential absence which another text will make good, in turn creating an absence that calls for a further text. . . .

So far as miracles are concerned, this potential to prolong indefinitely the series of tales—whether in performance or in writing—confirms my earlier remarks about the recursive structure of their plots, whose conclusion (the need to revere Mary) reinforces their beginning (an example of a sinner who reveres Mary) and thereby sets the stage for a further miraculous intervention and another story. The compulsive, ongoing narration which these texts elicit also recalls Kristeva's observations on the fetishistic recourse to language of the phobic–abject patient. As texts (unlike in their plots), miracles are no longer caught up in the visceral, the horrific, or the compensatingly blissful: instead, they appear obsessed with the resources of textuality. Kristeva suggests that abjection is a figure of thought whose traumatic nature can be assuaged when it is transmuted into figures of speech. Writing can make bearable the anguish of our relation to our objects because it can turn the very symbolicity of the object into a defense against it; that is, language offers itself as a means both of making the object present and of distancing us from it; the sign, like the veil, can act like a fetish, both masking and invoking the object behind it:[38]

> But isn't the use of language in fact the ultimate fetish, one from which we cannot be separated? Doesn't it rely precisely on fetishistic denial ("I know very well, but all the same . . . ," "the sign is not the thing, but all the same . . . ," "the mother is unspeakable but all the same I can speak") and thereby define our essence as speaking beings? (Kristeva, *Powers*, 37/49)

In their symbolicity, then, the miracles rejoin the fetishistic universe of the *lais*; we should beware of thinking of them as in any way less "literary."[39]

Nevertheless, they certainly strike us as being literary in divergent ways. One summary characterization of this divergence would be to describe the *lais* as invoking the pleasures and pains of remembering the past, whereas the miracles see the past as alerting us to the need to look to the future. This difference is conveyed by the epilogues to the two genres. It is striking that both genres practice a compacting of meaning in their conclusions, a moment of slippage which, as the texts accumulate in the collection, causes each to end on a slightly problematic note, thus intensifying the call for another text to follow it. Both blur boundaries, but the boundaries in question are different in the two genres and situate the texts differently in relation to the father.

Agdar's epilogues foster ambiguity between the salvific roles of Mary and God. Miracle I ends "e Deu servir la nus duinst," which appears to mean "and may she grant to us to serve God there," but which could also mean "and may God grant to us to serve her." In the passage in which it occurs,[40] we are told that if we serve her, we will earn God's grace, and so it seems right that we should ask God to inspire us to serve her; on the other hand, if through her we obtain God's grace, then perhaps we need to serve her first in order to win the grace to serve him[41]? An almost identical line occurs at the end of Miracle XI. Repeatedly, the agencies of God and Mary appear as parallel and interconnected to the point where they are hard to separate—for example:

> Or nus duinst Deu, li veir sauvere,
> pur amur de sa chere mere,
> itele essanple a cesti prendre,
> ke nos almes li pussum rendre!
> (IX, 89–92)

> Dampnedeu, ki unc ne menti,
> duinst ke seium si ami
> par le pri de la gloriuse,
> ki tant est seinte e vertuuse!
> (XXXIX, 271–74)

I have not translated these passages because of the multiple ambiguities they present. In the first passage, do we pray to God that we may take example from Mary because *we* love her, or do we enjoin God to enable us to imitate her because *he* loves her? Are we to render our souls to her or to him? In the second, is Mary subject or object of prayer? Do we pray to God that she will pray to him for us, or that we may pray to her? The heavenly addressees of Adgar's efforts seem to merge with one another. By the same token, Adgar's use of the first-person plural identifies him with both the fallible human protagonists of the miracles and their prospective audiences.

The elisions operated in the epilogues of the *lais* attributed to Marie de France, by contrast, concern the origin of the text being transmitted and the question of whether or not it can be identified with an earlier *lai* whose composition it records. Instead of persons being blurred together, texts are. As is well known, these texts often center on a central core for which progressive layers of interpretation will adduce significance. The historical dimension of interpretation means that this core is sometimes equated with genealogy and, more particularly, paternity. Whereas the fatherhood of God in the miracles permeates the figure of Mary and becomes confused with it, in the *lais* fatherhood—when invoked—may be contested or in doubt. The requirement for narrative to make a father present in spite of his absence drives the plots of "Milun" and "Yonec" (cf. also the anonymous *lai* Tydorel).

It is instructive to compare these two Harley *lais* with the miracle of the pregnant abbess (Adgar XLIX), because it likewise involves a woman conceiving by a mysterious or unacknowledged father. Whereas both "Milun" and "Yonec" adduce explanations for why the father is missing and have as their conclusions revelations of his identity (realistic in the case of "Milun" but fantastic in "Yonec"), at no point does the miracle display any interest in how the abbess became pregnant. All we are told is that, although she has abandoned her chastity and fears disgrace, she refrains from flouting God's law by seeking to destroy the child. It is not the physical father but reverence for God that counts:

> maint est en pechié engendré
> qui puis demeine grant seinté.
> (47–48)

Many a man is begotten in sin who later leads a very holy life.

The Virgin spares the abbess public humiliation by delivering the baby and spiriting it away to be looked after. Eventually the bishop who looks into her case assumes responsibility for the religious education of the child: he and God become its "fathers." In this way, the miracle concludes, Mary can save us from great harm. "Milun" and "Yonec" end one with a live and the other with a dead father (or fathers), but in both cases, the question of the son's identity is crucially tied to that of his natural father. The happy family reunion in "Milun" leads directly into an epilogue recording the narrator's satisfaction in writing down this ancient tale, whereas in "Yonec," where all the fathers are dead, the *lai* is said to commemorate grief and loss.

This comparison shows how these examples of the two genres position themselves differently with respect to what psychoanalysis calls "the paternal metaphor." In the miracle, Mary and God are merged as father-mother with us poor mortals as their errant children. Our dependence on them extends to a limitless future, to the Day of Judgment and beyond. If we revere the father-mother, they will preserve us throughout eternity. In the *lais*, by contrast, the father is identified with the past; he is lacking and needs to be sought after; the text weaves narratives around him in a mixture of mourning and pleasure; our origins, in so far as they are known, are conveyed through the layering of glosses around an absent core. Both genres invoke paternity, but perhaps the miracle, in which the father's presence, though ill defined, is all-pervasive, more openly admits the father's power, whereas "Yonec" at least is more inclined to evade it, because "it becomes clear that Yonec's father is whoever Yonec's mother says he is" (Griffin, "Gender," 53). If we then recall that it is anxiety about "castration" on the side of the father which generates the need for phobic objects whereas fetishism is powered by anxiety about "castration" on the side of the mother, we may tentatively infer that—although both miracle and *lai* are "literary" objects—the quality of the object differs in the two cases. Despite the centrality of Mary to the stories themselves, the compacting of meaning at the end of miracles attests to the father's power and is imprinted with legislative zeal to invoke and ward off future menace. The endings of the *lais*, however, are entangled in overlapping efforts to invoke and repair past loss: the fetishism of textuality in the *lais* is more complete.

Whereas preceding chapters have traced chronological developments, the emphasis in this one, given the impossibility of assigning a reliable date to either Adgar's or Marie's work (or, indeed, of defining in what exactly their work consists), is on the way courtly texts are both intimately related to, yet different from, religious ones. My overall purpose has been to uncover the connections and differences between the ways each genre envisages the objects of its narratives and presents its own texts as objects too. To do so, I have drawn on Lacan's and Kristeva's writings on the abject and the object, both of which situate the emergence of our first objects as a defense against trauma.

In the miracle texts, the traumatic character of the object is to the fore. These tales are about the terror, revulsion, and attempts at sublimation that initially provoke the construction of objects. The figure of Mary is implicated in the fears which the texts seek, through veneration of her, to palliate. She remains tainted with that from which she provides an escape: the powers of horror survive in her and are invoked as much as they are eclipsed by the narrators' legislative efforts. As a result, the very formulas that describe her are themselves caught up in the contradictions between horror and reassurance which their narratives convey. She embodies in her contradictory attributes the contradictions with which the protagonists of the miracles wrestle: purity and sexuality, connection and separation, mother love, and incest.

Mary as object is also—as early scholars suggested—related to the figure of the lady in courtly texts, a relation explicitly exploited in the *sponsus marianus* miracles. However, this relation is not one of direct resemblance. Comparing selected miracles with similar stories from Marie de France's *lais* shows how the abject of religious literature is manipulated into the fetish object of the courtly. Only distant vestiges of anxiety survive. Instead, images of covering are repeatedly invoked in the *lais* in such a way as to promote complicity in the fantasy that what lies behind the covering is an object of supreme value with which we can identify, not a *fond d'angoisse* from which we need shielding.

There is no doubt that all of the texts discussed in this chapter position themselves as "literature." Miracles, like *lais*, are short stories adorned with more or less artful prologues, dedications, inscribed audiences. Adgar offers no grounds for thinking that the literature of Mariolatry, being more "primitive," was a "source" of courtly literature. The relative lateness of vernacular Mary material, and the complex interrelations between Marian and courtly texts, both argue against this and in favor of their being contemporary products of the same historical culture. All the more striking, then, is the dissimilarity in their eventual fates. Miracles such as Adgar's are now consigned to the past, an arcane topic rarely studied even by medievalists, whereas the *lais* ascribed to Marie de France are among the most widely read works of the French Middle Ages and have directly contributed (in the work of John Fowles) to modern fiction.

In the complex interconnections which this chapter has plotted between miracles and marvels, phobic objects and fetish objects, we can learn about the need for objects and the reasons for their contradictoriness, and appreciate the very slight twist of structure needed to transform an edifying story into an entertaining one. The next chapter undertakes a similar comparison between religious and related courtly texts by examining how the different treatments of the idea of the "sublime body" in hagiography, the *romans antiques*, and *Cligés* each brings a distinctive permutation to the status of the object.

CHAPTER 6

The sublime body: the "zone between the two deaths," belief, and enjoyment in hagiography, the *romans antiques*, and *Cligés*

The last chapter was concerned with the way objects (in the psychoanalytical sense of the word) are initially created for purposes of defense. It concluded that courtly and religious texts differ from one another in very slight adjustments in the structure of the object from one to the other. This chapter will, in part, address the rejoinder that such a finding entirely overlooks the different value of the beliefs conveyed in the two genres. By again examining a series of interconnected texts, some religious and some courtly, I will argue that belief is intimately interwoven with death (or rather, Lacan's idea of the "zone between two deaths") and enjoyment in all of them, but with different effects the development of which can be traced chronologically and across genres.

This argument returns to the concept of sublimation discussed in Chapter 4 in relation to the creation *ex nihilo* of riddle poems. It once more involves the situation of objects relative to what Lacan calls "das Ding," "the Thing"—a traumatic knot just beyond the limits of what we can symbolize or imagine. In sublimation, an imaginary (for example, an ideological) construct is made to occupy the position in the symbolic at which the pressure of "das Ding" is felt: it becomes the special idea (thing/person) which transfigures the whole arbitrary structure we inhabit so as to make it seem meaningful, beautiful, or morally uplifting. "Thus, the most general formula that I can give you of sublimation is the following: it raises an object [. . .] to the dignity of the Thing" (Lacan, *Ethics*, 112). Such "sublime objects" are, as we saw in Chapter 4, historically and culturally determined.

Hagiography, the *romans antiques*, and *Cligés* 217

This chapter is about a particular manifestation of sublimation, the "sublime body." The term is taken from Žižek, who uses it when he is commenting on Lacan's suggestion, in the *Ethics of Psychoanalysis*, that there exists a "second death" and thus a "zone between the two deaths," an idea Lacan in turn derives from this passage from Sade's *Juliette*:

> Nature wants atrocities and magnitude in crimes; the more our destructions are of this type, the more they will be agreeable to it. To be of even greater service to nature, one should seek to prevent the regeneration of the body that we bury. Murder only takes the *first life* of the individual whom we strike down; we should also seek to take his *second life*, if we are to be even more useful to nature. For nature wants annihilation; it is beyond our capacity to achieve the scale of destruction it desires. (Marquis de Sade, cited in Lacan, *Ethics*, 211, my emphasis)

In Sade's novel, horrendous tortures are unleashed on the woman, tortures that exceed the limits of the possible because, astonishingly, their victim does not die but remains untouched and beautiful. Lacan observes: "suffering doesn't lead the victim to the point where she is dismembered and destroyed. It seems rather that the object of all the torture is to retain the capacity of being an indestructible support" (*Ethics*, 261). Žižek extrapolates: "it is as though, above and beyond her natural body [. . .] and thus above and beyond her natural death, she possessed another body, a body composed of some other substance, one excepted from the vital cycle—a sublime body" (*Sublime Object*, 134). What Sade's fantasy of a sublime body supports, according to Lacan, is the fantasy of the torturer that he can transgress the bounds of reason, unleash all the psychotic violence of which he is capable, and yet evade its consequences.[1] Later in the *Ethics of Psychoanalysis*, Lacan explores the notion of a zone between the two deaths in relation to Sophocles's play *Antigone*. Antigone is buried alive and given up for dead for part of the play before, finally, she dies for real. As in Sade's novel, this zone between two deaths—between the treatment of Antigone as if she were dead and her actual death—is seen by Lacan as a space of the sublime, characterized in this case by unbearable beauty, moral reflection, and the whole cathartic experience of tragedy. Again as in Sade, the urge to destroy is both fed and thwarted by the fantasy of indestructibility; the cathartic experience (of terror and pity) allows us both to glimpse and deny the violence in our own hearts.

The sublime results from lethal destructiveness, and yet it also occludes the reality of death, translating its horror into the uncanny in the form of the victim's preternatural beauty or ethical significance. This uplifting quality of sublimation—the elevation of an object to a position of value in which we can believe—serves to block out the traumatic real of the death drive. However, because the object is aligned with the real, it is at the same time imbued with a sense of urgency and fringed with unease: like the moon in an eclipse of the sun, the sublimated object is surrounded with the aura of the devouring intensity of destructiveness behind it. It is thus deeply bound up with enjoyment: *jouissance*, in the Lacanian sense of the satisfaction to be derived from following the drives to their limits of sexual release or death. *Jouissance* transgresses the regulatory framework of the symbolic, which acts like a kind of thermostat to preserve us from excessive sensation; it is "enjoy-meant" in that it goes beyond the signifier of the symbolic order to the signified of the real (*jouis-sance/-sens* = "sense" as well as "the senses"; see Žižek, *Metastases*, 156). In the last resort, *jouissance* is complicitous with the drive toward destruction and death and a source of suffering and evil as well as of bliss (*Ethics*, 184–85).

The fact that this fantasy is preserved in literary texts reminds us that literature too is a work of sublimation; beauty is created out of the very process of annihilation (*Ethics*, 260–61, cf. *Sublime Object*, 134, and Chapter 4, above). The violence inhering in the sublime body of the protagonist can be read as impressing on its audience the sublime values inscribed in the text which records it, as well as affording them a glimpse of the enjoyment (*jouissance*) which underlies sublimation. The exact lineaments of the concept of the two deaths are not easy to pin down. There is some slippage between the accounts of it given by Lacan, Žižek, and Evans (*Introductory Dictionary*, 31), the main difficulty being that of materializing the second death, the ultimate annihilation, which is located as a fantasy in the Sade passage, but sometimes referred to by Lacan and Žižek as actually taking place.[2] We will see that the vernacular texts of the twelfth century deal in different ways with this possibility of a second death, but that all of them support the notion of a zone between the two deaths as the space of the sublime and as bound up—in different ways—with belief and enjoyment.

Sublime for eternity: the lives of the martyrs

It is obvious, I hope, how applicable Žižek's concept of a sublime body is to the lives of the martyrs because *passio* texts turn precisely on the conviction that there is a universe beyond the natural destruction of the "first death." The martyr who is burned, broken on wheels, or boiled in oil, yet doesn't die, possesses a sublime body analogous to that described by the Marquis de Sade while at the same time supporting an elaborate set of beliefs, as in *Antigone*. Here, for instance, is Clemence of Barking's description of the martyrdom of the fifty philosophers who are converted by Catherine's arguments for the immortality of Christ and thrown on a fire by the furious emperor Maxence:

> Un miracle vus voil mustrer
> que Deus deignad pur els ovrer.
> Cil ki furent geté el feu
> e lunges i ourent geu
> unkes ne furent entamé
> ne de [la] flambe devuré,
> ne lur bele culur plaissie,
> ne lur vesture atuchie.
> Un sul chevoil blesmé ne fu,
> si les guari le bon Jhesu.
> Tant par iert bele lur culur,
> que de lur mort oussiez errur.
> (1171–82)

I wish to recount to you a miracle that God graciously performed for them. Those who were thrown on the fire and had lain there for a long time were not in the slightest degree damaged or consumed by the flame, nor was their fine color spoiled nor their clothing affected. Not a single hair was harmed, so well did Jesus protect them. Their color was so extremely fine that you would not have taken them for dead.

The martyred philosophers have sublime bodies through which the violence addressed to them might be indefinitely prolonged. They could apparently remain in their perfect state forever, but they also "body forth" their belief in an immortality against which mere physical violence is powerless; their sublime body both expresses and resists the destructive urge to which it is subject. In further exploring how the sublime body of the martyr is used both to support the enjoyment of violence and to sublimate it, I will concentrate on the *Eulalia*, the Occitan *Faith*, Wace's *Margaret*, the anonymous *Life of St. Lawrence*, Clemence of Barking's *Catherine*, and Simund de Freine's *George*.

That there might be "two deaths" in hagiography can be seen as integral to its basic organizing principle, which is to articulate everything in a double perspective. For saints' lives explore, as Chapters 1 and 2 have already shown, the fundamental contrariety between the human and the divine orders. When saints are martyred, their death in human terms becomes the means to eternal life, a perception formulated, for instance, in Clemence's *St. Catherine*:

> Par mort les apelad a vie;
> bien la venquirent par sa aie.
> Par mort lur estuet vie querre.
> (1225–27)

Through death he called them to life, with his help they overcame it. Through death they were to seek life.

The dual perspective on death articulated in this passage is realized in the desires of the tyrant and the martyr, respectively. For although pagan rulers are seized with hatred toward Christians and with the urge to inflict ever greater torments upon them, so as to eradicate them from the face of the earth, their desires are anticipated and outstripped by the intending martyrs who, for their part, want nothing better than to die and suffer for their faith. This coincidence between the desire to murder and the desire to die emerges particularly clearly in the counterbalancing speeches pronounced, when they first meet, by Olibrius and Margaret in Wace's *Life of St. Margaret*:

> Li provos dist ireement:
> "[. . .] Se nos dex ne veus aorer,
> jo te ferai forment pener,
> en torment morir te ferai,
> en fu ardant ton cors metrai.
> Le tien Dé guerpis et ta loi,
> richement remanras od moi,
> riche feme de toi ferai

> et en mon lit te meterai."
> La virge dist, "ce n'est noient.
> Mon cors lairai metre a torment
> por ce que m'ame soit salvee
> et o les virges soit posee.
> De Deu ne voil jo departir,
> del tot me voil a li tenir;
> bien li tendrai ceste promese,
> ne m'en tenra por menteresse;
> bien doit on por celui morir
> qui por nos tos vout mort soffrir."
> (*A* text, 153–72³)

The provost said angrily, "[. . .] Unless you are willing to worship our gods, I shall inflict great pain on you and make you die in torment and put your body onto a burning fire. Give up your God and his law and you will live with me splendidly and I'll make you a wife of great splendor." The virgin said, "That is nothing. I shall let my body be tortured in order for my soul to be saved and placed with the virgins. I do not want to leave God but to hold to him utterly. I shall keep my promise to him; he will not find I break it. One should indeed die for the one who was willing to suffer death on behalf of us all."

Although they misrecognize their relationship, Margaret and Olibrius are in fact the ideal couple. They are made for each other, not for love but for death: the perfect cast for the snuff video that is about to unfold.

There are, then, two quite different attitudes to death played out in the martyr's text: on the side of the saint, a determination to exit from a world which is despised and, on the side of the tyrant, a determination to punish and utterly eradicate a recalcitrant and rebellious presence. Margaret is typical in the way she courts her death from the outset. In the Occitan *Life of St. Faith*, similarly, the narrator's initial description of his protagonist consigns her to death before the plot has even started:

> Honor qe d'aqest segle ag
> atretant non prezed detz brac;
> en Deu de Cel lo quors li jag,
> el seus servizis molt li plag.
> Non pausara ja, czo m'adag,

>   entro eiss Deu de ssa mort pag;
>   czo mes Diable en esmag.
>   (85–91)

> She didn't value worldly estate as highly as if it were so much mud.
> Her heart lay with God in Heaven and his service pleased her greatly.
> She will not rest, I think,[4] until she pays God himself with her death;
> this plunged the Devil into dismay.[5]

In the late twelfth century, the saints become increasingly aggressive in their search for martyrdom. Catherine and George do not wait for persecution to come to them but instead seek out conflict with the pagan authorities by challenging their injunctions to worship idols. When Maxence threatens Catherine with death, she replies: "iço desir, iço demant" (1396, "this is what I desire, this is what I want"). Such forwardness in the virgin martyrs outraged one English critic: "They address their persecutors in studiously offensive language," he splutters, "and seem intent on securing the crown of martyrdom at whatever cost of courtesy or good manners" (Wilson, *Early Middle English Literature*, 118). Eager to reiterate the sacrifice of the crucifixion, these saints ask for nothing better than to rush headlong into the embrace of death, confident that it will reverse into its contrary and enfold them in the eternal bliss of the life beyond. The tyrant may seek to impose on them the second death of utter annihilation but, for them, this death merely releases them into another sublime state which will endure throughout eternity (cf. Lacan, *Ethics*, 295). In this way, the contradictions of saintly sublimation are intimately meshed with the clash between the human and divine spheres staged throughout the genre.

Martyrs have from the outset, then, mentally and spiritually given up the world. Death is both acceptable and welcomed; and they all quickly meet with what should, under "natural" conditions, put an end to their bodily existence.[6] This is the point where, from there being two different desires regarding death, we can, following Lacan, speak of a separation between the two deaths. For although this initial "death" of the saint is enacted and embraced, it fails to "take" and the saint lives on in what, using Lacan's term, I will call the "zone between the two deaths." Eulalia is thrown on a fire but does not burn. Faith is also put on a pyre, but an angel puts it out. In Margaret's case, a *cheval-fust* (a contraption on which the saint is seated in the middle of a fire) features in the second torture scene; again the fire is extinguished by an angel. St. Lawrence lies for a long time on his gridiron, as relaxed as if it were a sunbed, taunting his executioners with the fact that, though he may be half-cooked, he is still alive:

> "Ohi, chetif maleuré
> de desverie forsené!
> Et n'avés vos dunc entendu
> que nule ardor n'ai d'icest fu?
> Ne jeo nel sent n'en char, n'en os,
> ains m'est frigerie et repos." [. . .]
> Dunc dist saint Lorenz en riant
> o simple vult, o bel semblant: [. . .]
> "Chaitif, l'altre part car tornez;
> mangez deça, quit est assez!"
> (880–96)

"Oh wretched and unhappy ones, crazed with madness! Haven't you understood that I am not being burned at all by this fire? That I can't feel it, in my flesh or in my bones? On the contrary, I see it as leisure and repose." [. . .] Then Saint Lawrence said with a smile, a straightforward look and a cheerful manner, "[. . .] Wretches, turn me the other way, eat from this side, it is well cooked!"

This motif of death by fire invokes at once the pagan's burning anger and the cleansing fire of the spirit, as suggested in this passage from the *Catherine*. It thus encapsulates the contrariety in the sublime body between exposure to unendurable violence and eternal resistance to its effects because, although the tyrant is consumed by metaphorical fire, the saint is not burned even by a real one:

> Li tyrant l'ot, mult s'en aire. [. . .]
> Mult par fu plein de marrement;
> de grant ire sun cuer esprent.
> Du[n]c cumande a faire un grant ré.
> [. . . *Catherine says to them:*]
> "El sanc Deu estes tuit lavé
> e par sa mort regeneré.
> Par la flame que ci veez,
> le seint espirt recevrez."
> (1109–13, 1143–46)

The tyrant hears it and is very angry. [. . .] He was overwhelmed with distress, his heart catches fire with wrath. Then he commands a great fire to be lit. [. . . Catherine says to them:] "You are all washed in God's blood and regenerate through his death. Through the flame you see here you will receive the Holy Spirit."

As the century advances, there is an escalation in the kinds of torment inflicted and the technological sophistication they require. Catherine is threatened with a wheel set with steel blades, but an angel dashes it to pieces. George in particular is subjected to a long series of ingenious forms of execution, which I will detail below; he actually does die—three times—but springs back to life. Between the time of first exposure to the longed-for death they seek and might, symbolically and naturalistically, have been allowed, and the death finally reserved for them at the end of each of their texts, the martyrs are positioned between two deaths.

The second death recorded in martyrology is not the ultimate destruction of which the tyrant dreams, but it is nonetheless a definitive release from earthly existence, which comes about less through his agency than by God's will (Vitz, *Medieval Narrative*, 183–84). The way God delays the arrival of his second death, however, allows more space to the murderous desires of the persecutors and so creates a disturbing collusion between the obscenity of pagan violence and its miraculous prolongation by God's power. For all the individual pagan tyrants are consumed with hatred toward the Christians: they feel outraged at their noncompliance with the rule of law, offended by their disdain for their religion, and disgraced and frustrated by their victims' refusal to yield to either persuasion or force. The later the text, the more frustrating the tyrant's experiences and the angrier he gets. In Clemence's *Catherine*, Maxence gets progressively more furious as not only do his attempts to browbeat and then kill Catherine fail, but onlookers keep converting and have to be martyred too: the fifty philosophers, two hundred knights, his wife, his best friend Porphyry. And the *St. George* unfolds what approximates to a Tom and Jerry plot, in which the pagan ruler Dacien alternates between trying to win George over to his service and trying to kill him for good, with no success on either score, and consequent mounting irritation.

Dacien's first move is to make George sit on a razor-sharp plank, with weights attached to his feet, and a fire lit around him, but George "feels no ill effects whatever" (446, "mal ne senti tant ne quant"). Beating and foot piercing prove no more effective: God enables George to actually find it quite pleasant (467–68). So Dacien has him crushed under a wheel with big spikes sticking out of it. George dies (517) and his bones are thrown into a deep well, but God and St. Michael come down and restore him to life. George explains to baffled Dacien that God the Father overcomes his evil (565–68). Dacien wants revenge. He finds a magician who brews an unspeakable poison for George, but when George drinks it, "God saves him by a miracle" (633, "Deu le garit par miracle"). Now Dacien gets really angry. He has sixty nails hammered into George's head, but again, love of Christ turns George's pain into joy (657–59) and God heals his head up so there are no signs of injury. Dacien is growing apoplectic:

> Dacïen esteit engrés,
> fol fu ainz e fol après.
> Pais a Deu ne vout granter,
> mès seint George vout danter.
> (668–71)

Dacien was wild; he was crazy before and crazy afterward. He had no intention of making a truce with God, but he did want to get the upper hand over George.

Dacien's solution is to have George sawn in half and the pieces boiled in pitch until they all dissolve, then have the liquor thrown away. But St. Michael gathers his remains together and George revives (695). Spitefully, Dacien sends George to live in a widow's hovel, where he performs a series of miracles. After more efforts of seduction on Dacien's part, more teasing resistance on George's, George causes the ground to swallow up all the pagan idols. Dacien is now beside himself. He pronounces a long speech raving at George for his magic tricks and concludes, "I'll make you die a vile death" (1121, "Mult vilment vus frai murir"). George is burned to death by candles placed on his back (1124 ff.) so that his body liquefies, and all the fat in it runs out. He dies again—this the third time. Whatever is left of him is transported onto a hillside to be eaten by ravens. Dacien is determined there should be no potential for resuscitation left (1152–53). But God raises George up for the third time. Dacien calls up wild beasts and they all do George homage. . . . Intermittently throughout these goings-on, various other characters convert, are martyred, and in some cases are resurrected before dying again. No doubt the sublime body of the martyr is being coopted to support the doctrine of resurrection,[7] but it is impossible not to see it also as an opportunity for the enjoyment of violence, as Dacien's destructive impulses—which outdo even those of the Marquis de Sade—are given full rein. Indeed, the two impulses of enjoying violence and sublimating it as ideology are found side by side in George's constant reminders of how joyful his torments are.

The sexual dimension of torture, the possibility that the enjoyment has an erotic charge, is rarely exploited in texts dedicated to male martyrs; though note that the initial torture of George, seated astride a sharp blade with heavy weights attached to his feet, is pretty explicitly sexual. But torturers eroticize their relation to their female victims, offering them feminine adornments and often marriage; the texts suggest an equation between virginity and Christianity on the one hand, and between idolatry and lust on the other. Thus worldly offers of marriage are firmly declined by martyrs whose sights are set on the heavenly Bridegroom in the sky. St. Faith, for example, rejects Dacien with the words

> Deus, nostre Donz, lo glorios [. . .]
> Aqel volri'aver espos,
> qualque plaid m'en fezess ab vos,
> q'el si m'es belz & amoros.
>   (301, 311–13)

God, our Lord, the glorious one [. . .] Him I want as my Bridegroom, whatever dealings you may undertake with me, for to me he is so handsome and full of love.

The body of the female martyr establishes itself early as the metaphor of her spiritual state. Already in the *Eulalia*, when the saint is brought before Maximian, he summons her to give up the name of Christian but, the text continues:

> melz sostendreiet les empedementz
> qu'elle perdesse sa virginitét
> por os furet morte a grand honestét.
>   (16–18)

she would rather endure obstacles [*empedementz*: tortures? persecutions?] than lose her virginity; for that she died most honorably.

No one in the text has threatened her with loss of physical virginity; *virginitet* seems rather to indicate "purity of heart" or "steadfastness of intent"—something, that is, which she would lose by abandoning the "name of Christian." The body as a metaphor for spiritual meaning will become increasingly graphic and more "physical" in later texts.

Wace's *Margaret* opens with the horrid Roman prefect Olibrius trying to seduce Margaret, a fifteen-year-old shepherdess tending her sheep. The *pastorela* framework makes this instantly recognizable as a rape plot; the saint's resistance to physical rape will be equated with her stand against idolatry. In the event, there is more rape than theology here. Margaret's rebuffs are met with tortures that directly assault her modesty (she is stripped, hanged in midair, and beaten; then roasted astride the *cheval-fust*); and in between, she is almost devoured by a *dragon* ("serpent") in what is unmistakably another attempt at rape, this time by the devil in disguise. Although the devil/dragon attempts to swallow her, to take her body into its own, its attack on her is seen as a threat of penetration. Making the sign of the cross, Margaret bursts out of its body and rebukes its exploded remains with the words:

> Ne t'entremetes tu jamais
> de tolir ma virginité.
> Jo sui espouse Damedé.
> (380–32)[8]

Do not ever again attempt to take my virginity. I am the bride of God.

With a change of sexual metaphor, her deliverance from inside the dragon is also read as a birth, in consequence of which the *Life* is enjoined to be read to women in labor.

Margaret's brush with the dragon is also a metaphor of resurrection, a theme we have already seen in the *George*. This is made clear when she invokes Christ's harrowing of Hell in her prayer to escape from its belly:

> "Dex," dist ele, "qui pués garder
> et ciel et terre et air et mer
> [. . .]

> Infer brisas, Sathan lias,
> pri toi que oies m'orison
> que puisse vaincre cest felon
> que il mal ne me puisse faire
> ne a sa fosse avoc lui traire."
> (319–28, *A* only)

"Oh God," she said, "who hast the power to watch over heaven and earth and air and sea, [. . .] who broke Inferus and bound Satan, I beg you to hear my prayer so that I may overcome this villain and he may do me no harm nor drag me to his lair."

Thus we find on the one hand eroticized torments of the body and on the other its ideologization as an image of the soul. Not only is death the true life, but, more shockingly perhaps, the sexual is the true expression of the spiritual. In relying on this metaphor, the text is drawn to the very carnality whose threat to salvation it seeks to avert and conveys the enjoyment which it reprobates. Margaret may resist actual rape but, like George again, she embraces her violent treatment as the means to eventual bliss:

> Se mes cors est en paine mis,
> m'ame sera en Paradis;
> por les paines que ont li cors,
> m'ame sera de paine fors.
> (215–18^9)

If my body is made to suffer, my soul will go to heaven; on account of the sufferings of the body my soul will be released from suffering.

The antithesis—and equation—between bodily suffering and spiritual salvation is insistent. Margaret "between the two deaths" is an object of obscene violence bizarrely sublimated as Christlike virginity.

In such stories we can see how the collusion between the desire to die and the desire to kill provides enjoyment in which violence is meshed with sexuality. This enjoyment centers on the creation of an indestructible sublime body with a powerful ideological remit. In imitating the crucified Christ, prototype and guarantor of their own ultimate immortality, the saints expect to be resurrected with him, and this belief, as well as being explicitly expressed, is enacted by their miraculous endurance in the zone between the two deaths. The sublime body of the martyr is a powerful meeting point of violence, imagination, and doctrine. It is to doctrine—the extraction of truth, its endorsement, and its imposition—that I now turn.

All these vernacular passion texts feature verbal confrontation between saint and pagan in which Christian beliefs are to some extent debated. In those from the second half of the twelfth century—*Lawrence, Catherine,* and *George*—this debate becomes more substantial, with the dual nature of Christ, his virgin birth, crucifixion, and resurrection, featuring largely in all three (see Chapter 3). Here is a further aspect of the double universe of hagiography: the fact that the saint has confidence in argument, whereas the pagan's best hope is violence. As Maxence says in *Catherine*:

> Jo li querai tels turmenz
> u poi valdrunt ses argumenz.
> (443–44)

I'll seek out tortures for her against which her arguments will be of little avail.

The typical hagiographic plot shows the martyr making mincemeat of the persecutor's arguments while the persecutor labors to demolish the martyr's body. Audiences are more likely to be persuaded that what the saint says is true when she (or he) endures such violence for the sake of it. The trope is a familiar one whereby the victim of violence is entitled to be heard. The blood of the innocents cries out, the victims' demand on our attention the greater as their sufferings are more graphically recorded, their innocence more insistently proclaimed. In Christian thought, this claim to righteousness and perpetuity on the part of the victim is enshrined in the foundational narrative of the guiltless crucified and subsequently resurrected, and in the doctrine of a truth revealed in the Scriptures where this narrative is set down. Indeed, by more or less explicitly echoing the life, sufferings, and death of Jesus, hagiographic texts lay claim to some of the authority of the Gospels. Scenes of the martyr before the pagan ruler recall Christ before Pilate; the protracted deaths are often accompanied by reminiscences of biblical times. St. Faith's execution, for example, is compared with that of John the Baptist (390). Although the resemblances between saints' lives can be exaggerated, there is truth in the claim that they all repeat a common model.[10]

The persecutors' show of force thus invokes a whole textual tradition whereby truth is oppressed only to reemerge triumphant. All this violence exerts a coercive pressure on its audience, disciplining us to fall into line. Furthermore, the saint's position is endorsed by his or her miraculous survival in the face of this violence; it is supported and glorified by that violence. One way or another, then, truth and violence are intricately interconnected in these texts. They are part of the same economy in which the greater the violence, the better and more enduring the truth, and the greater our obligation to believe in it.

It is striking that all of the saints' lives discussed here, except *St. Lawrence*, end with the martyr being beheaded. The final solution, for the persecutor, is to cut the saint through the throat, putting an end to the rebel voice which the text endorses as true. Only then does the sublime body of the martyr meet with its second death. But even this apparent success backfires: the very fact of silencing the voice endows it with permanence, and instead of being annihilated, it is incorporated into the texts in order to direct medieval audiences. Thus although Eulalia's life is ended by decapitation, "we" are enjoined to pray to her that she might intercede for "us" in Heaven. Her voice and those of the audience are the ones that prevail at the end of the *Sequence*. Just before her head is cut off, Margaret herself bequeaths her story to the women in labor who will come after her. In the Occitan *Faith*, Faith and Dacien confront one another in direct speech (lines 227–325, roughly a sixth of the text). Faith's part in this is to declare her faith, and to persist in so doing in the face of seductions and threats: that is, she speaks her nature, and her name. When, like the others, her head is cut off, she too is silenced only in the literal sense. The blood streams in a great torrent from her neck and the people, amazed at this supernatural occurrence, are afraid to bury her. Instead, they make a little hollow in the ground and leave her body exposed. It smells sweeter and sweeter while, from the blood, a painting of her head emerges. Later a marble tomb is made for her, sculpted with her likeness; when her remains are translated to Conques, her memory is witnessed in a written document. Faith cannot be silenced, and the martyr's voice survives in the various texts into which it is transmuted: painting, sculpture, document, and ultimately the Occitan *Life* itself.

The theme of the voice is even more prominent in *Catherine*. Catherine is a highly educated young woman, trained in dialectic (see Chapter 3).

She argues the pagan emperor Maxentius into the ground before going on to confound all the arguments of his philosophers and converting them all (and everyone else in sight), to Maxentius's great irritation. Finally she is decapitated and thus deprived of the organ of speech which made her such a troublesome presence. She gladly accepts this death, a heavenly voice having welcomed her through the pearly gates to the Bridegroom beyond. Milk rather than blood flows from her neck; and her body, we are told, has been a source of miracles from the time of her death until now. The self-same arguments about Christ's immortal nature with which Catherine had converted the philosophers are now assumed by the narrator (2653–55), and "we" are all asked to pray to Catherine to incline us to love God as she did. Clemence concludes with an epilogue saying she translated the work for love of Catherine and hopes its readers will pray for her. As in the *Faith*, a chain of transmission ensures that the voice of the Christian martyr will be available to medieval readers and its message imposed upon them. All these stories represent a transmutation of voice into text through the medium of torture. In each case the speech of martyrs is endowed with authority and permanence by their steadfastness in the face of suffering, and the sacrifice of their life for their religion. This making permanent is explicitly associated with the written form in which the texts themselves are enshrined.

The sublime body of the martyr is thus an object "raised to the dignity of the Thing." In the tortured but miraculously enduring body the enjoyment of violence is articulated with sacrificial desire, the endorsement of value, the enforcement of belief, and the production of vernacular texts. Even the second death which the texts so graphically describe, the martyr's release from life and the apparent fulfillment of the tyrant's destructive will, results in a further sublime state, an endless zone between deaths where there is no ultimate death but instead a perpetual demand on our adherence. The configuration of violence with belief and enjoyment will recur, though with modifications, in many of the courtly texts which flourished in the wake of the success of saints' lives such as these, and indeed contemporary with the later instances (*Lawrence, Catherine, George*). I will look next at the treatment of the sublime body in the secular universe of the *romans antiques* before turning to that model of "martyrdom" for love, Fenice in *Cligés*.

Sublime for all of history: the slaughtered warrior

The martyr's sublime body results from arresting the natural process of death at its very frontier. Although subjected to lethal violence, the saint is suspended in a miraculous state of indestructibility. The more intense the tortures, the more serene their victim until the blessed release of the second death arrives, eternity is embraced, and the martyr's text is born. In the *Roman d'Eneas* and the *Roman de Troie*, the body of the warrior is also elevated to the sublime but, in these texts, the zone between the two deaths occurs not just before, but just after, literal death. The slain body of a hero is pulled back from the process of corruption, restored to a semblance of life, adorned, addressed, embalmed, and entombed so as to endure for all of history. Inscriptions contained within the tombs reiterate the link between death, the body, and the text found in hagiography but endow it with a different significance. I will concentrate on the sublime bodies of Pallas and Camilla from the *Eneas* and Hector from the *Troie*, contrasting them with the treatment meted out in the latter romance to the body of Achilles. Consonant with the preoccupations of these texts, the treatment of the sublime is more rational and secular than it is in hagiography; it forms part of the genre's careful attention to continuity and discontinuity in the *translatio studii*, enabling its audiences to further negotiate the paradoxes and moral dilemmas posed by the antique past.

Both the *Roman d'Eneas* and the *Roman de Troie* alternate descriptions of battles with periods of truce in which the bodies of the dead are buried. This rhythm is particularly relentless in the *Troie*, where twenty-three battles precede the final capture of the city by the besieging Greeks (Levenson, "Narrative Format," 63–64). The battle scenes in both romances lead to wholesale slaughter, and again this is especially emphatic in the *Troie*. Death takes place here on a horrific scale: its stench is all-pervasive. One of the most horrific descriptions occurs after the seventh battle:

> i ot des morz si grant merveille
> que tote la terre vermeille:
> les eves e li flueve grant
> corent de sanc trestuit sanglant;
> des charoignes ist la flairor
> e li airs est pleins de puör
> des cors qui sont, piece a, ocis,

Hagiography, the *romans antiques*, and *Cligés* 233

> qui ne sont ars n'en terre mis;
> et por l'olor, que si est male,
> en gisent mil envers e pale,
> gros e enflé.   (12805–15)

There was such an astonishing number of dead that all the ground is reddened; streams and even big rivers flow bloody with gore; the smell rises from the corpses and the air is full of the stench of the bodies of those recently slain who have not been cremated nor buried. And because of the smell, which is so dreadful, thousands lie on their backs, pale, swollen, and distended.

This passage is echoed after the eighth battle (14555–65), as corpses lie unburied in the field. Levenson comments powerfully on this tide of destruction: "As the battles continue, the encompassing chaos relentlessly swallows up moments of personal bravery; lamentation swells again and again over the deaths of great warriors; passion, incessant, warps mind and spirit" ("Narrative Format," 64). In the *Eneas*, after the first battle, an emissary from Turnus's army asks for a truce in which to dispose of the dead (6043–46). This is the battle in which Pallas, son of King Evander, Eneas's first contact and ally in Italy, is killed by Turnus. Both sides collect their corpses by the wagon load—ten thousand dead on Turnus's side alone—burn them, and bury the remains (6081–92).

Pallas's body is treated differently from that of all the others in this first battle. For them, in Lacan's terms, there is no distinction between the first and the second death: mown down on the battlefield, they are eliminated at once from material existence and from historical record; neither their deaths nor their graves are individualized. Pallas after death, however, is given the life he never had and never could have had: the second death, that of annihilation, is held at bay. I will take the account of his death and obsequies as a model, comparing them with the very similar ones accorded to Camilla and Hector (for more detail, see Baumgartner, "Tombeaux").

Pallas is a young warrior, only just armed a knight. As soon as he is killed, he starts to discolor (6383; cf. Camilla, *Eneas*, 7218–21, and Hector, *Troie*, 16230). He, and Camilla likewise, are mourned as flowers cut down in their beauty (cf. *Eneas*, 6147, 6193–96, 7400), while Hecuba mourns the signs of death in Hector's body (*Troie*, 16440–42). Death brings calls for vengeance. Eneas promises to avenge Pallas (*Eneas*, 5855–56, cf. *Troie*,

16391–96), and Camilla's slayer is killed in revenge (*Eneas*, 7211–12). Pallas is lamented by Eneas as if he were his lover: Eneas gives to him clothing presented to him by Dido and a blanket he received as a wedding present from Priam, so the corpse is adorned with mementos of his past sexual partners.[11] Turnus's grief for Camilla is likewise amorous in tone (e.g., *Eneas*, 7383–84), while Hector is lamented by his wife and a series of family members. The dead hero is thus the object of intense anger, love, and grief. And in the devout attention to the corpse which ensues, the course of death seems to be halted and even reversed.

The obsequies of the warrior fall into three main parts: exhibition of the body on a bier, its preparation for burial, and its subsequent entombment in a splendid tomb. Pallas's corpse is brought on a fabulously valuable bier to his father Evander; at this point, he is decked out in Eneas's love gifts. Then he is washed in wine, his hair is cut, he is perfumed and embalmed; he is dressed again in fine clothes as a knight (with spurs, 6397) and a king (with a ring, the crown, and his father's stole, 6399–404). The ring replaces the one stolen from his body by Turnus and thus restores him to how he was at the moment when he was killed. Similarly, the spurs remind us that Pallas was only recently knighted; they return him to the shape in which he set out for his first and final battle. But the royal regalia endow him with an ideal body image that he had never had. The text is clear that he is given not *a* but *the* crown, as well as the king's *escharpe* ("stole"). Rather than reversing into the past, these tokens project Pallas into a future that should have been his. The preparations for Pallas's entombment act as a fantasmatic prolongation of his life and as an attempted restoration of the proper order whereby sons outlive their fathers. As his father says,

> . . . trop ai vescu,
> quant ai ne tens ne jor veü
> que tu es morz e ge sui vis.
> (6301–3)

I have lived too long, when I have seen the day that you are dead while I am alive.

To underline this tragic reversal of the natural order, Pallas is then laid in a sarcophagus and placed in a vaulted tomb that had been intended for his father (6415–16).

Not only does Pallas in death receive the body of his own future life, but that body is made to resist all further change. First he is embalmed during his laying out

> por ce que pas ne porresist
> ne male odor de lui n'isist.
> (6389–90)

so that it would not putrefy or evil smells issue from it.

Then in the tomb he is rigged up to a permanent embalming system which operates through the nasal cavities to seal up the body (6467–74). Both sarcophagus and vault are likewise sealed so that the body will never be corrupted (6481–84). The body within is treated as though it were not dead: it is given a lamp by which to see and which we are assured will never go out:

> Il ne remest pas sans veüe:
> une lampe ot desor pandue. [. . .]
> ja puis estointe ne sera.
> (6509–17)

He was not left without the means of seeing: a lamp was hung above [. . .] which will never be extinguished.

An epitaph narrating the circumstances of his death is set on the lid of the sarcophagus—made of a single enormous amethyst—which is then placed in the vault. This vault, meanwhile, inaugurates the series of sumptuous edifices that become more and more elaborate with the tombs of succeeding heroes. A wealth of artistry and precious materials has gone into its construction. Finally, it is sealed up like a time capsule, insulating the body against any future interference (6527–28).

The obsequies of Camilla and Hector follow similar lines, except that both are washed, dressed, and laid out before being placed on the bier, and then dressed again for entombment. (On Hector's death, see Sullivan, "Translation.") Unlike the corpse of Pallas, the embalmed corpse of Camilla has to be displayed on the bier for three months while a tomb is built for her; its marvelous construction will be considered below. She too is entombed with royal regalia, a permanent embalming kit, an inscription, and a lamp which will never go out and which is protected by an ingenious automaton that acts as a burglar alarm. Her coffin is then sealed in the highest chamber of a tomb constructed on three floors, making her completely invisible as well as inaccessible. In Hector's case, the purpose of the laying out is made explicit:

> E quant il li orent vestue
> semblant vos fust que toz fut vis.
> (16526–27)

And when they had dressed him in it [a fabulously splendid garment of gold cloth] you would have thought he was alive.

Unlike the *Eneas* heroes, Hector is disemboweled prior to embalming so that the body can be embalmed inside and out (16512–17). I take this detail as confirming the sublime character of the preserved body: relieved of the abject interior, with its susceptibility to rapid liquefaction and putrefaction, the corpse becomes pure formal outline, the shape of an ideal body.[12] When made ready for the tomb, Hector is seated on a throne with his feet in vats of embalming fluids in order to preserve this formal perfection for all time; the tomb is surmounted by a statue of Hector himself, upright and seemingly calling for vengeance. As with the other heroes, perpetual light is provided along with an inscription. The main difference from the *Eneas* heroes is that Hector's body is not described as being sealed up. It is left enthroned in the magnificent inner chamber of a temple attended by a religious community, or "convent." On the anniversary of his death, relatives and sightseers flock in to find it still perfectly preserved (17489 ff.).

The perpetuating of all three warrior heroes in an ideal body form corresponding to how they would have been in maturity, had they attained it, offers a secular parallel to the Christian concept of individual bodily resurrection witnessed to by hagiography. Canonically, the resurrected body is aged thirty-three regardless of the age at which one dies; it perpetuates an ideal identity as opposed to a fleshly reality, the distinction between the body and the flesh being particularly important to twelfth- and thirteenth-century Christian thought (see Boureau, "Sacrality"). The preservation of the sublime body of the warrior supports this distinction from the standpoint of secular history rather than God's eternity. The hero's funereal body assumes a formal perfection that underwrites and preserves his or her identity at an ideal point while being immune to the corruption of the flesh.

The body which, from the point of view of the "first death," is a victim of the violence of death and of the changes wrought by time becomes a sublime object, a means of resisting their lethal effects so long as the "second death" of annihilation is kept at bay.[13]

Thus whereas the sublime body of the martyr is infused with the immortality of eternity, the sublime body of the warrior is set to endure throughout historical time ("until Judgment Day," *Troie*, 17509). The marvelous tombs in which all three heroes are buried image their capacity to remain perennially beautiful and incomparably valuable, regardless of the ravages of time. All are exquisite architecturally, laden with precious stones and beautified with intricate carvings. In each case the exceptional character of the tomb expresses the extraordinary qualities of its occupant. Pallas, who should have lived to be a king, is buried in a royal tomb. Camilla, who died because she exposed herself to attack when trying to take a fabulous golden helmet from a corpse, is preserved after her death by the fabulous riches of her tomb which are, moreover, guaranteed against theft by the antiburglary device. Hector's tomb is surmounted by a golden statue of its occupant as a warrior. The tomb, then, is not just a container but also the external expression of the enduring presence within. Indeed, as each description passes from the tragic preservation of the sublime body to the eternally gorgeous riches of the tomb, there is a distinct slippage from one to the other. It is, after all, easier to believe in the permanence of a building than in that of a body, however resourcefully Rube Goldberg the embalming arrangements. Whereas in hagiography the body of the saint is the primary focus of the sublime, in the *romans antiques*, it falls to human artifacts to serve as the fantasmatic support of sublimation. As Žižek says of people in the commodity-dominated modern world, "They no longer believe, *but the things themselves believe for them*" (*Sublime Object*, 34, Žižek's emphasis).

These marvelous constructions can also be read, of course, as images of the romances themselves, or more precisely of the artfulness and splendor to which they aspire. Camilla's tomb, the most astonishing of the two funerary monuments erected in the *Eneas*, is a case in point. The warrior-virgin's coffin is placed in the top floor of a construction something like an upside-down wedding cake balanced on the top of a pillar, which in turn stands on the junction of two intersecting arches, the four feet of which are supported on blocks carved in the shape of lions. The three tiers of this wedding cake are circular, and each projects further outward and is higher than the one below. It seems that at least one of the two lower tiers is surmounted by a vault, so that the tier above is balanced, like the bottommost one which stands on the column, on a relatively minuscule point.[14] Camilla's tomb places the medieval text in a relation to antiquity of the same kind as the *Eneas* itself holds in relation to modern readers. It is a metaphor of the enduring and commemorative value of the narrative of which it forms a part, with its foundations in antiquity, but enlarged and developed heavenward by the long tradition of commentary to which these foundations gave rise. Control over time is accentuated, and imaged, by the mind-boggling control over space effected by this construction.

Although fantastic edifices such as this form an artistic link with the historical past, and as such serve as metaphors of the *translatio* effected by the authors of the *romans antiques*, it is striking that they also enclose, and so seal off from future readers, the epitaphs of their heroes. In Arthurian romances, epitaphs and memorials are placed in full view and are often read and commented on by the characters. But in the entombing of Pallas and Camilla, inscriptions are described as placed *within* the tomb. In Pallas's case, two couplets are written on a band around his coffin lid recording his name, parentage, and death at the hands of Turnus (6491–94). The coffin is then placed in a vault which is entirely sealed with pitch, although it does contain just one small window (6422). Is it possible that, by the eternal light within, passers by could make out the inscription? It seems unlikely. Camilla's coffin likewise has an inscription on a band around it (7659–68). Because the coffin is on the third floor of the gravity-defying building, with no means of access whatever, the inscription will presumably remain unread. Although her head is propped up on a cushion, Camilla is unlikely to read it herself through her heavy coffin lid of precious stones mixed in a mortar made with dragon's blood. Thus although it is implied that both tombs survive to this day we have no means of ever seeing the writings they enclose.[15] The inscription over the body of Hector is represented differently, but it is still placed beyond our reach. It trumps both of those in the *Eneas* by requiring "more than seven golden bands" to contain its lettering (*Troie*, 16809). Presumably those who attend the anniversary of Hector's death could read it, though they are not said to do so. The tomb itself is lost to us now, however, as a result of the destruction of the city. Thus although

Hector's body could have lasted until Judgment Day, history dictated otherwise (17509–10).

David Rollo comments that Benoît creates a parallel between the gold bands bearing the inscription and the golden garment in which Hector's body is clothed: "Thus, as Benoît implies by bringing *escriture* and *sepouture* into eloquent rhyme at a later stage of the description (16637–38), the corpse of Hector is preserved in writing" (*Historical Fabrication*, 212). Just as in the hagiographic texts discussed above the violence inflicted on the body of the saint imprints itself in a text, so too response to the deaths of these warrior heroes involves recording them in writing. But it is striking how differently this translation from body into text is handled in the two genres. Whereas narratives commemorating the lives of the saints are enforced upon "us" "now," it is clear that the epitaphs of the antique warriors consign their dedicatees to oblivion as much as they immortalize them. There is a hiatus between the inscriptions made to last as long as history and the texts offered to medieval readers because the epitaphs are explicitly stated to be inaccessible. This hiatus can only be bridged by the say-so of the vernacular authors: all we can know of the epitaphs is what they tell us. It is striking that we find the identical disposition of elements miniaturized in the *lai* of "Laüstic." There too the dead body (of the nightingale) is accompanied by an inscription (the embroidered cloth) which is then sealed up in a precious container (the casket). The link with the past is preserved only in such a way as to place it beyond our knowledge: it is a link which is, to all practical purposes, a breach. This constitution of the medieval text as displacing and replacing its own source is perhaps conceded by the account of Hector's inscription in the *Troie*. Benoît records it in indirect discourse and thus conflates it with own text, unlike the *Eneas* epitaphs which are cited verbatim (cf. Rollo, *Historical Fabrication*, 213). In this regard, the *romans antiques* reiterate the "as if" stance which we have already discerned in them in other contexts: they record the *translatio* of body into text as though it were an enduring historical truth, while at the same time conceding that we can have no evidence that it was so: it is up to us whether we believe in it or not.

The letter of the inscription is, in these circumstances, a dead letter.[16] So in place of the living sublime body of the martyr and the immediately relevant text of their life, we find in the *romans antiques* an awareness instead of the intimate bond between art and death. However gorgeous and majestic the tombs may be, however lavish their splendors and however wondrous the enjoyment of looking at them, they enclose within them dead bodies and inert texts whose presence they overlay and conceal with their own self-display. In so doing, although they may resist death as a process of corruption, they also admit its lifelessness, its petrifaction, into their very nature. This is notable in the case of Hector, where the tomb contains the hero's body but is surmounted by a statue of him: the sculpture may be eternally upstanding, but it is so by virtue of never having been a body. Its commemoration of a death, and its defiance of the changes wrought by death, is also a capitulation to the absence of life. (One of the columns of his tomb, interestingly, is made from a stone which in turn is made from a petrified fruit, marking this same transition from life into enduring but inanimate art.) The will to define a limit to death, to arrest its course and halt its corruption, contrasts with the will to utter destruction attested elsewhere in the narratives of these poems. Art is elevated precisely to define a limit of such destruction: in the tombs erected between the moment of loss of life and the effacement (by a second death) of the dead from the world. In this way creativity preserves its debt to death as much as it denies it. The tombs which enact sublimation on the audience's behalf betray the necessarily conflictual nature of the object as it oscillates between presence and nothingness, between radiance and horror. Their beauty witnesses to the deathly undertow of the signifier as it drives toward the *jouissance* of annihilation.

This intimacy of art and destruction is borne out by the narrative in the *Troie* of the death and entombing of Achilles. Achilles does not have a sublime body in the way that these other warriors do. From the moment he first sees the Trojan princess Polyxena at the anniversary of Hector's funeral, we know he has fallen in love with his own death (17535–44), and soon Achilles recognizes it too:

> Narcisus sui, ço sai e vei,
> qui tant ama l'ombre de sei
> qu'il en morut sor la fontaine.
> Iceste angoisse, iceste peine
> sai que jo sent: jo raim mon ombre,
> jo aim ma mort e mon encombre.
> (17691–96)

I am Narcissus, this I know and see, who so much loved his reflection
that he died for it at the spring. I know that I feel this selfsame anguish
and pain: I too love my reflection, I love my death and my destruction.

First he refuses to fight in hopes of winning Polyxena as a gift in exchange
for the securing of peace; then, when he is sucked back into the war, he
foolishly goes to a secret rendezvous in Troy, half believing she will be given
to him yet also aware that he is rushing to his doom:

> Que nule rien plus ne desire
> qu'aler al doloros martire
> e a sa pesme destinee.
> (22133–35)

For he desires nothing so much as to go to painful martyrdom[17] and
his baleful fate.

With Paris waiting in ambush to destroy him, the unarmed Achilles is
overwhelmed and hacked to pieces that are then thrown out for the wild
beasts to devour. He dies for love, but without the sublime body of the
martyr. Nor does he get the sublime body of a warrior. Although subsequently handed back to the Greeks, the mutilated state of his body defeats
even the expert morticians of the *romans antiques*. With no hope of preserving the corpse from corruption, all that can be done is to burn it
(22465–69).[18] No body then; and no inscription either: Achilles has only a
tomb. Surmounting it, as though in answer to Hector's vengeful statue, is
a life-size replica of the anguished Polyxena (22439–40), the description of
which is interrupted for the narrator to interpolate his account of the real
Polyxena's grief. The message is clear that this text transforms the will to
destruction into art: it has ceased even to glorify it as sublime. Perhaps only
inanimate things, such as buildings, can still "believe" in the sublime.

How sublime?—And for how long?
Fenice in Cligés

Achilles's fate as a martyr for love anticipates that of Fenice in Chrétien's
Cligés, a romance probably composed within a decade of the *Troie*. Its protagonists for the most part lack the chilling coherence of the sublime. Far

from being endowed with larger-than-life aesthetic or moral force, they strike us as being less-than-convincing fictions, their outlines blurred by the throng of fictional doubles that overlay them. Sometimes these ghostly doubles belong earlier in the same text (as Cligés's behavior may be foreshadowed by his father's, for example; see Haidu, *Aesthetic Distance*, 64–70). Sometimes they belong in other texts, acknowledged (as when Fenice schemes to avoid Isolt's fate[19]) or not (as in the innumerable echoes of the *romans antiques*). At other times, the insubstantiality of the characters results from their own deceitful intentions, as when first Alixandre and then Cligés stage the illusion of their own death and set out temporarily disguised as one of the enemy, or when Cligés fragments his identity by pretending to be four different, contrastingly colored knights at the Oxford tournament. And at other times again, their presence as representations is knowingly undermined by their narrator who opposes his debunking reflections to their beliefs and thoughts, suggesting that his characters deceive themselves as much as they do other people (Polak, *Cligés*, 86–87). The narrator himself, meanwhile, is stalked by his own *louche* doubles: a devil-working witch from Thessaly, an ingenious slave of a builder, and three horrible doctors from Salerno, all of whom offer derisive perspectives on his vaunted *clergie*.[20] As a result of his ironies, we readers start looking out for doubles of ourselves—for people less clever than we are who may fail to grasp his subtleties. The romance, then, is not a propitious setting for the sublime. Far from acquiring miraculous endurance and awesome beauty, its protagonists are merely a fine tissue of allusion and illusion. Among these allusions, however, is a narrative recalling the sublime bodies of martyrology and the *romans antiques*.

Fenice is married to the Byzantine emperor Alis: unfortunately, because she is in love with his nephew Cligés, and also unlawfully, because Alis had promised not to compromise Cligés's future as his heir by marrying. She decides to fake her own death and thus escape her husband forever by means of a medicine which will render her unconscious. A coffin containing an illusory body will be buried while her real one will live happily ever after concealed in a tower, permanently available for enjoyment with her lover. Fenice wants to be like the heroes of the *romans antiques* who, immured within a fabulous and hermetically sealed edifice, elude the historical process—except that, crucially, she plans to omit the step of actually dying first. And she is like the martyrs of hagiography in that she undergoes Christlike sufferings as she "dies" in the cause of a supreme love—except that she has no prior intention of suffering, let alone dying, for the sake of her beloved. Unfortunately, the plot backfires and Fenice does almost get killed. Her imitation of her literary models, the saints and heroes of earlier texts, gets out of hand as she appears actually to die while still being, amazingly, alive, and may thus find herself, if only fleetingly, halted between two deaths.

Fenice's false death is intertwined with an important earlier part of the plot which also revolves around the use of drugs to create an illusory body image; again, her husband is the butt of her deception. Under the influence of a spiked drink, Alis hallucinates having sexual relations with Fenice, although in reality he is fast asleep and dreaming; she, meanwhile, retains her virginity for Cligés, whom she already loves. Peggy McCracken (*Romance of Adultery*, 42–51) has pointed out how both of these illusory double narratives present similarities with the medieval belief in the king's "two bodies" famously expounded by the historian Ernst H. Kantorowicz. The king has both a "natural" and "divine" body; the "divine" one bears his kingly nature and is passed, undying, from one "natural" king to his successor so that the support of royalty never dies (Kantorowicz, *King's Two Bodies*, 42–61). (Here is another manifestation of belief in a "sublime" body opposed to the corruptible and changeful flesh.) McCracken argues that Fenice likewise attempts a separation between the natural body dedicated to the reproduction of royal heirs and a queenly essence which could be abstracted from dynastic and temporal claims. In McCracken's view, Fenice's efforts founder, however, and her failure "to create a distinction between the corporeal, sexual body and the symbolic, royal body [. . .] demonstrates that this is an impossible distinction for a queen: [. . .] the queen consort's political role in the medieval court was located entirely in her physical body" (42–43). The reason why McCracken thinks that Fenice failed to successfully create two bodies in the case of the "false death" plot is that her "queenly" reputation is undermined by the public disgrace which follows from the lovers being discovered. Because this is precisely what Fenice was trying to avoid, saying that she failed is fair enough. In political and dynastic terms, Fenice does not have the sublime body of a queen. So far as the love plot is concerned, however, McCracken's case is less secure.

In defense of her view that Fenice is confined to her physical body, Mc-Cracken cites a well-known passage describing how the deluded emperor, thinking he is with his wife, in fact fondles and embraces nothingness:

> Tenir la cuide, n'en tient mie,
> mais de neent est a grant ese,
> neent enbrace et neent baise,
> neent tient et neent acole,
> neent voit, a neent parole,
> a neent tence, a neent luite.
> Molt fu bien la poisons confite
> qui si le travaille et demaine.
> De neent est en si grant poine. . . .
> (3312–20)

He imagines that he holds her, and yet he doesn't at all, but he is full of pleasure with nothing, embraces nothing and kisses nothing, clasps nothing and hugs nothing, sees nothing, speaks to nothing, quarrels with nothing, struggles with nothing. The potion was well put together which treats him and makes him behave in this way. He is put to so much effort on account of nothing. . . .

McCracken contends that the "nothing" embraced by the emperor "questions the nature of its absent model" and "puts into the question the nature of the original" (46). But the word *neent* is used consistently in *Cligés* to dismiss error or stupidity (e.g., 2049 and 2065–69, 2589, 2630–31, 4061, 4338–39, etc.); Alis's embrace of "nothing" is more likely to reflect negatively on him than on Fenice. Indeed, Fenice might be judged to be uncannily successful in off-loading all the sexual and dynastic duties of a wife onto this imaginary body, which is nonexistent. By so doing, she is already following the path blazed by the virgin martyrs who likewise (though of course in a different register) elude the sexual obligations of the world so as to preserve their virginity for the Bridegroom of their choice. Just as the martyrs' service of God places them in conflict with secular powers, so Fenice's love overrides the expectations of marriage and dynasty in the service of a "higher" power. And just as the secular powers in hagiography are "wrongful," so likewise in *Cligés* Alis's sexual and dynastic aspirations are themselves transgressive of his original promise not to marry. Analogously to the martyrs (though by quite different means), Fenice is able to occupy a body which is subject to the Law of Love while eluding the punishments of human law. In other words, if we refer back to the model of the king's two bodies, Fenice is successful in retaining a transcendent body while the natural body, the one obliged to pay the marital debt, dissolves into illusion. She creates for herself a body which, if not sublime, is at least virginal and undivided; a body dedicated to "true Love" which will, if things go according to plan and Cligés eventually takes Alis's place, also continue to be that of "queen."

Among the many instances of the word *neent* in *Cligés*, the following is of particular interest. The narrator contends that love and fear are inseparable and declares that he will pulverize any opposition to this view:

> einsint le vueil a nient metre,
> que la o crieme s'en desoivre
> ne fait amors a rementoivre.
> (3846–48)

And in this way I intend to reduce [a hypothetical opponent or view] to nothing, for love is not worthy of mention where fear is divorced from it.

The context of this attack is a (probably tongue-in-cheek) denunciation of those who fail to perceive the mysterious consistency of love. Love, it is asserted, has its nature defined by fear as does fire by heat, daylight by the sun, a honeycomb by honey, and so on (3841–45). All these definitions are self-evident, apart from the first which they are adduced to support. The contention that the nature of love is to be fearful, by contrast, could be seen as a contradiction in terms; and it certainly contradicts the famous biblical declaration that "perfect love casts out fear" (I John 4:18). The narrator is saying that the man who does not understand that the contradictory nature of love is precisely where its consistency lies, understands "nothing."

I will return to the significance of this passage later. What I want to point out now is that the term *neent* is connected here with reflections on the contradictions of love and with the humor of approaching those contradictions armed with the intellectual machinery of dialectical debate. These connections replay the intermeshing of the concept of "nothing" with contradiction and dialectic in the riddle poems analyzed in Chapter 4. Alis's happy nights in the enjoyment of "nothing" can also be read as a move in the riddle of love and "nothing" as it is explored in *Cligés*, because Alis's pleasures—the only sexual activity described in this romance about love—are a "nothing" at the end of a chain of contradictoriness.[21] By looking more closely at this chain we will better understand the implications of Fenice's imaginary body double, both in the "false love" plot and in its development into the plot of the "false death." In this way, if there is a sublime body in *Cligés*, its links with the workings of contradiction elsewhere in the text will be revealed.

The passage where Fenice describes her love symptoms to her nurse Thessala can be contrasted with the equivalent passage in the *Eneas* where Lavinia is instructed by her mother (see Chapter 1). In the *Eneas* the few contraries which are invoked are carefully marshaled in temporal alternation (first pain, then joy, etc.). Fenice is, by contrast, a virtuoso of contrariety, systematically accumulating opposing terms in a manner reminiscent of Giraut de Bornelh's riddling "Un sonet fatz." Her speech concludes:

> mes tant ai d'ese en mon voloir
> que doucement me fait doloir,
> et tant de joi en mon anui
> que doucement malades sui.
> (3035–38)

But I feel so much pleasure in my desire that it makes me suffer sweetly and I have so much joy in my torment that I feel pleasurably ill.

Thessala immediately goes to the heart of the riddle because she recognizes the structure of Fenice's love-discourse (*sa parole*, 3051) and knows

> que d'amor est ce qui l'afole.
> Por ce que douz l'apele et claime
> est certeine chose qu'ele aime,
> car tuit autre mal son amer
> fors solement celui d'amer,
> mais cist seus torne s'amertume
> en douçor et en soatume,
> et sovent retorne a contraire.
> (3052–59)

that what is destroying her comes from love. Because she calls it and complains of it as sweet, it is an open-and-shut case that she is in love, for all other sources of harm are bitter except for loving, but this one alone transforms its bitterness into sweetness and pleasure, and often reverts back to being adverse [or: to its contrary].

On the practical level, Thessala's solution is the hallucinogenic potion that will protect Fenice from having to have sex with her new husband and so preserve her virginity for the man she loves. The description of her making the potion, however, also proposes a solution to the riddle of love, because it resolves precisely this opposition which she has just formulated (and which is likewise found in the Occitan *devinalhs*) of sweetness and bitterness:

> Espices i met a foison
> por adoucir et atemprer.
> Bien la fist batre e destremper
> et coler tant que toute est clere
> et qu'ele n'est n'aigre n'enmere,
> car les espices qui i sont
> douce et de boenne odor la font.
>   (3206–12)

She put plenty of spices in it in order to sweeten and temper it; she had it whipped up, infused, and filtered until it was completely clear, and neither sour nor bitter, for the spices in it make it sweet and pleasant-smelling.

This philter "rationalizes" the contrariety of love, eliminating the bitter and leaving only the sweet. When Alis drinks it, the oppositions of the riddle world return because he—like the protagonists of Guilhem de Peitieu's and Jaufré Rudel's riddles—confuses sleep and wakefulness: "an dormant cuidera veillier" (3282, "he will imagine, sleeping, that he is awake"), "et veillier cuide quant il dort" (5181, "and he imagines he is awake when he is asleep"). The *neent* of Alis's nighttime embraces thus recalls the dreamlike contradictions of the troubadour *devinalh*, most obviously the vacuity of an absent or nonexistent love evoked by Guilhem. Yet the way his delusion is manufactured suggests that the reason for this absence is precisely the misconception that you can have love without contradiction. The learned pseudoclerk Thessala, by rationalizing away its contraries in her concoctions, has reduced "true Love" to "nothing."

Where does that leave Fenice? Far from suggesting that the contrarieties of her emotions are reduced to "nothing," the narrator "proves" to us that Love is an inverted order of reality, where the prevailing logic of the world is suspended. Why does Cligés, a man who is so bold, tremble before so weak a creature as a girl, he asks, in terms that anticipate Raimbaut de Vaqueiras's "Las frevols venson lo plus fort" (3795–97)? Cligés's behavior belongs, he says, in a world upside down, where a lamb hunts the wolf and a dove the eagle (3798–806). This passage leads on to the argument about the consistency of love that first led me to compare Cligés with the *devinalhs*: love comprises fear like fire does heat and daylight the sun, and so love is an inconsistency which possesses its own consistency. True love overturns the natural, logical order because it is the natural, logical order of love to be reversed. If you don't subscribe to this view, then you understand "nothing" of love. The "nothingness" experienced by Alis is in the last resort a failure to grasp the supreme (or risible) something that eludes Aristotelian dialectic: the point where contraries *do* coincide. To return, then, to McCracken's idea of the queen's two bodies, the amorous body which Fenice preserves for Cligés is one consecrated to the transcendent order of Love, while the body Alis believes he holds is, literally, nonexistent (*neent*). The logic of love's *devinalh* in *Cligés* opens up a space for a sublime body located on some higher plane of reality than the mundanely logical and literal: one where contraries are mysteriously synthesized.

Postulating such a plane is, as we have seen, characteristic of certain registers of religious thought. On a par with Fenice's sublime cultivation of contrariety, then, we should consider the suggestions found throughout the romance—irreverent or unconvincing as they may be—that love is a quasi-mystical experience. An example is the passage elaborating on the perception and union of hearts, a phenomenon which the narrator affects not to understand (2800–1).[22] Are these pointers to Love's belonging on a level of experience beyond the rational? Another motif which points flickeringly in the direction of a possibly sublime register, a sublime body beyond the flesh, is the aura of radiance which intermittently surrounds Fenice, as it does Mary in Adgar's miracles. She is, the narrator claims, indescribable (unlike Cligés, who is treated to a relentlessly efficient *descriptio*, 2716 ff.). She is a "miracle and marvel" (2688) of beauty who lights up the palace like the medieval equivalent of halogen bulbs:

> et la luors de sa beauté
> rent el palés si grant clarté
> com feïssent .iiii. escharbocle.
> (2703–5)

And the glow of her beauty sheds as much brightness on the palace as four carbuncles would do.

Her radiance combines with Cligés's beauty to form a single beam of light which makes the entire building gleam as though in warm sunlight (2709–14).

The status of this sublimity is, however, contested by the constant reassertion of mundane reality. The narrator's disquisition on the inverted nature of love is soon undercut by his admission that is fear of his uncle, rather than of his lady, which keeps Cligés quiet (3859). This reference to political circumstance is just one of innumerable reminders that the love plot is orchestrated in an intricate counterpoint against real dynastic interest. For if Fenice wants to create a sublime body, it is partly to dedicate herself to an ideal love but also to avoid conceiving an heir who would disinherit Cligés; sublimity for her may be an expression of love's mystery, but it is also a form of birth control. Whatever the rights and wrongs of Cligés's claims to heirship and Alis's claims on his wife, it is clear that what we have so far been willing to describe as "transcendent" could also be seen as "transgressive" or "subversive." We ought properly to hesitate before endorsing Love's rule. Do we really want it to turn us from wise men into fools (1633–34)? The romance stages a conflict between the claims of the rational, everyday, historical world and those of a transcendent world of Love. More is at stake than hesitation over which tradition of thinking about contradiction to embrace. This conflict intensifies with the plot of the "false death" to which I now turn.

Once Cligés and Fenice have overcome their fears and declared their love to one another, Fenice becomes determined to dedicate her life to a single beloved who will be everything to her. She rejects Cligés's lame idea that he should abscond with her like Paris did with Helen (5231–35) as being too like the Tristan story (!), making a public display of enjoyment, and consequently being bad for her reputation (5244–50). Her countersuggestion takes St. Paul as its authority. But Fenice is misleading us: Paul said it was better to marry than burn (I Cor. 7:9), not—as she asserts—better to avoid scandal than incur it. Besides, as events unfold, she will actually reverse Paul's sentence, finding it better to be burned than stay married (and she will lose her reputation too; cf. D. W. Robertson Jr., "Chrétien's *Cligés*," 40). Another textual parallel, the story of the wife of Solomon who likewise faked death to escape her husband,[23] seems unknown to Fenice but is immediately spotted by the clever Salernitan doctors, who recognize her deception only to be defenestrated for their pains. The other sources of Fenice's scheme are not acknowledged. They include Alixandre from the first part of the romance (cf. 1632, 5293–94), the Gospel story of the crucifixion,[24] her own name of "phoenix" (a traditional image of Christ's death and resurrection), and the saints' lives and *romans antiques* discussed earlier in this chapter.

The secret tower room in the house built by Cligés's slave, Johan, resembles the tombs of the *romans antiques*.[25] The house itself is an architectural marvel, full of elaborate artwork, and elevated on several floors (like the tombs of Camilla and Achilles). The secret room is a beautiful vault (like the tombs of Pallas, Camilla, and Hector: *Eneas*, 6419, 7643, and *Troie*, 16766), apparently inaccessible to human entry (like all the tombs except for Hector's), and with a spiral staircase (like the tomb of Achilles, *Troie*, 22431). A great place to hide your girlfriend, says Johan incongruously, after showing off the plumbing (5552–55). Fenice meanwhile elicits from Thessala a promise to brew a drug which will make her pass for dead, her phraseology recalling the descriptions of corpses in the *romans antiques*:

> descoloree et pale et roide
> et sanz parole et sanz aleinne.
> (5394–95)

Discolored and pale and stiff, speechless and not breathing.

Fenice throws herself dramatically into the role of invalid, Cligès complicitously feigns unhappiness while inwardly rejoicing (5616–17), and Thessala befriends a dying woman in order to obtain corroboratory urine samples (5646 ff.). When this woman dies, the last stage of the deception swings into action. The ghastly-looking urine is shown to Fenice's doctors, they declare she won't live past noon, Thessala administers the drug which at once makes Fenice appear lifeless, she is declared dead, and the whole city collapses in pious laments. Everything is poised, then, for a burlesque of the sublime body of the antique warrior heroes to unfold its black humor. We expect Fenice's body to be restored to the form it had before she "died," and the "dead" person to be given the life she could have aspired to but was prevented from living in the "real" world—in her case the life not of a king, but of a consort and future queen—sealed up in the fabulous "tomb."

By now, reminiscences of saints' lives have also begun to impinge on the narrative. For instance, Fenice is mourned as "la meillor chose et la plus sainte" (5720, "the best and most saintly of creatures"). But she does not start seriously looking like a saint until the three learned doctors get to work on her.[26] These doctors have the role of pagan tormentors in female martyrology, performing sexually charged tortures on their victim and eventually paying for their cruelty with their lives. Theirs is the real enjoyment of inflicting pain. The sufferings they inflict on Fenice, which recall those of Christ, are also very like those of St. Margaret in Wace's *Life*: they flagellate her until she bleeds (5904–14) and then threaten to roast her over a fire, this latter torture also, of course, invoking St. Lawrence:

> Ja la voloient en feu metre
> por rostir et por greïllier.
> (5936–37)

Now they were on the point of putting her over the fire to roast her and grill her.

For a queasy moment, the plot backfires, the nothing of illusion is transformed into something deadly serious, and the death intended to be borne by the carefully contrived fictional body looks like impacting on the real one. Even though Fenice is rescued from the fire by her ladies, she is referred to as having undergone martyrdom (5945, 5976) and as a saint (6016). We are warned that the doctors' "treatment" may indeed have killed her:

> Car il crient molt, e si a droit,
> qu'afolee o morte ne soit.
> (5979–80)

For he [Cligés] is very afraid, and rightly so, that she is dead and destroyed.

When Fenice is then buried, the two narrative models of saint and warrior converge. Amid general grief, her body is placed in a sarcophagus with a quilt under her (like the cushions placed under the heads of Camilla and Pallas), and the tomb is sealed up (6078, like Christ's, but also like the tombs in the *romans antiques*). Death has lurched alarmingly from the wife's illusory body (which Fenice planned to bury), to the lover/queen's transcendent real body (which she was intending to keep). As she pauses on the frontiers of her death, the flickerings of the sublime from earlier in the text may momentarily come together. We may fear that Fenice has succumbed to the appalling violence of the so-called healers, that the power of Love has caused deception to reverse into truth as the death intended for the illusory body has been accepted by the real one; time may mark a pause as Fenice's body is "raised to the dignity of the Thing." If this is the case, then the zone between two deaths differs here from the way it features in either of the groups of texts previously examined. Fenice's first death comes (like that of martyrs or heroes) with the horrific onslaught which we have seen her undergo—and which should, by rights, have made an end of her. But her second death takes the form of the "death of death": the shocked realization (or relief) that she didn't die but instead survived her "martyrdom" literally in this world, not in eternity or the perenneity of the tomb, and can thus resume her scheme to live in comfort in the well-appointed *garçonniere* (6188 ff.).[27]

Of course, we need not respond to this moment as sublime but as an instance of hilarious comedy, black humor, intertextual play, or blasphemy. Its complexity, as in the earlier and related plot of the wifely body double, is bound up with the structures of contradiction in the text. We saw that the "nothing" embraced by Alis is the end point in a series of contraries and results as much from Thessala's "clerkly" rationalizations of Fenice's love rhetoric as from her response to the practical requirements of her situation. Similarly, the sublime body of Fenice's false death is led up to by the literal, rational reduction of the conceits of her "true Love" by the various doubles of the narrator who crowd in on this episode: Thessala again, Johan the speculative builder, and the three overeducated doctors.

Thessala's contribution, as with her first potion, is to separate out the contraries that characterize love. Love is sweet suffering and a pleasant disease (3036–38), but the illness feigned by Fenice lacks any element of suffering at all (5588–89, 5619–20) and, when Thessala administers her potion, it accentuates this collapse in love's traditional contrariety. Fenice, we are told, could be flayed alive without responding (5704–5): unconscious, she won't feel a thing. Johan also brings about a rational, real-world simplification of Fenice's cult of contrariety. She has declared that, once "entombed," she will have Cligés as both servant and master and will be his lady only if he is her lord (5283–88); this passage picks up the metaphors of lordship and serfdom from her earlier monologue reflecting on the meaning of Cligés's words when he left for Britain (4438 ff.), and will be revived at the end of the romance when Cligés makes her his "amie," "femme," and "dame" (6671–72). The "rubber logic" of this metaphorical love hierarchy, where subordinates can be superior and vice versa, is countered by the literalism of Cligés's offer to free Johan and his family from serfdom and Johan's willingness to do anything in his power to gain that freedom (5425–43). Finally, the Salernitan physicians arrive as the answer from hell to Fenice's declaration that one doctor alone has the power of life and death over her:

> qu'ele dit que ja n'i avra
> mire fors .i. qui li savra
> legierement doner santé
> quant lui vendra a volenté.
> Cil la face morir ou vivre,
> en celui se met a delivre
> de sa santé et de sa vie.
> (5627–33)

For she said that she would never have any doctor except for one who will know how to restore her easily to health when he so wishes. Let him cause her to die or to live, she freely places her health and her life in his hands.

This speech is taken by those who hear it to refer to God; it is intended by Fenice to express her love for Cligés, but it may be understood by us in retrospect as an ironic forecast of the "more-clerical-than-thou" misogynists who rightly suspect the worst of her and do their best to "cause her to die" in their efforts to prove she is alive.

I have argued that Fenice does achieve a separation between the "queen's two bodies" in the love plot because she is able to separate a wifely, dynastic, sexual body, which is delusory, from her real body as Cligés's intended lover and queen. The reason the wifely body is delusory is due, on the literal level, to hallucinogenic drugs, but on the rhetorical level, its *neent* marks the end point in a riddle of contraries, like those of the midcentury Occitan *devinalh*, and results from their rationalization. Having carefully fabricated this illusory body, Fenice then plans to kill it off and bury it, thus putting an end forever to her wifely duties and leaving her only with her real-life lover's body. The complexity of the false death plot, however, causes this scheme to founder, not just because the reputation she has tried so hard to maintain is destroyed. Rather, when the pseudo- or ultralearned doubles of the clerical narrator intervene, their leaden-witted ingenuity causes the metaphorical order of "true Love" to collapse, and with it the distance separating the rhetorical (but real) body from the natural (but illusory) one. The transcendent, symbolic body (which, thanks to Fenice's determination, is also the real body of flesh and blood) merges with the illusory one that has so far been required to bear all the fleshly problems of sex and death. This convergence of the two may strike us simply as funny or as another clever reversal of Love's rule which, we know, reverses everything. But it may also sound an awesome or uncanny note, because its effect is to put the real body (= the transcendent one) in front of sex and death (ingeniously consigned hitherto to the illusory body) and thus "raise it to the dignity of the Thing." Caught out for real in what promised to be only a trick, the lifeless Fenice may actually—momentarily—be a sublime body.

The constant sense of meditating upon contrivance which is the experience of reading this romance means that, unlike in the saints' lives and the *romans antiques* discussed above, there is no demarcation between "body" and "text" in *Cligés*. On the contrary, I have argued that Fenice's real body (at the level of the plot) is precisely a rhetorical body, separated from the illusory one by its anti-Aristotelian acceptance of contrariety. The violence done to the rhetorical body by the clerical doctors is intellectual as well as physical: the learned will not accept the higher reality of "true Love." But if Fenice was prepared to suffer for such love, perhaps we should be willing to believe in it too? Is not the law of Love a law to which, with her as its "martyr," we should submit? Or knowing that, being drugged, she could not resist, should we just smile at her insensibility? Such dilemmas provide us with a textual enjoyment of our own which is refracted through the romance's myriad ironies. As members of the audience, we are flattered into thinking that *we* are privileged to share the narrator's cleverness, although of course there will be other listeners who are left behind; that *we* are privileged to follow the twists and turns of contradictoriness and to condescend to the naiveties of others. As we savor the text's ingenuities, its ironic disinvestment from its various causes, we may also allow ourselves to be split on its equivocations, its appeal to law and counterlaw. Whereas the *romans antiques* encourage us to let artifacts support belief in the sublime on our behalf, *Cligés* allows us to imagine there are less astute readers than ourselves who will believe in it for us. We say to ourselves, that is, "*I* know very well she didn't really die as a martyr for Love, but even so [I can believe at one remove that she did because] other people no doubt do."[28]

Our attitude to the various levels of law in this text may also be equivocal. Although we distance ourselves from the Salernitan doctors, do we altogether avoid obscene complicity with them as they pour molten lead through their patients' hands in execution of their understanding of morality? Finding Fenice's procedures distasteful, might we think they served her right? Lured into believing in the mundane reality of the dynastic, the political, the rational, might we momentarily yield to their destructive *jouissance*? But if we do not, do we instead find gratification in Alis's being cruelly deprived of his marital rights? Is anyone prepared to rejoice that the man who planned to disinherit his own nephew should be reduced to "nothing"? And if we don't enjoy these things ourselves, do we imagine—as I am doing here—that someone else will do so for us?

Fenice between the two deaths may or may not be sublime, but our very hesitation on this score arouses anxieties about belief and enjoyment.

∽

This chapter has examined three sets of vernacular texts in the light of Lacan's concept of the sublime, according to which that which is ideologically valued (for instance, as miraculous, edifying, or beautiful) can be seen to result from the "sublimation" of the drive to destroy or to be destroyed: that is, from the setting up in the path of that drive of a sublime object which serves both as object of the drive and as its disguise. Enjoyment (*jouissance*) is half hidden, half visible, behind the values which the sublime object upholds, and which derive from its subordination to a symbolic rule—whether that of Christianity, heroism, or Love.

In hagiography the martyr's resolve precipitates the first death (which is consented to but not fulfilled) and the tyrant's the second—although it turns out, from the Christian perspective we are invited to believe in, not to be the annihilation which the tyrant was hoping for. The zone between the two deaths, where appalling violence is both indulged and denied, is the space of the sublime in which, while the miraculous is manifested and doctrine propounded, at the same time the thrill of enjoyment is elicited. The more rational, pagan-derived narratives of the *romans antiques* locate the zone between the two deaths immediately following the natural death of the body. The first death is the inevitable effect of war, which achieves a sickening violence in the *Roman de Troie* especially; yet in the corpse of the warrior-hero, its destructiveness is fantastically reversed, and an ideal body-form is generated which will last throughout historical time. When a second death will supervene is not specified in the *Eneas*, although it is in the *Troie* (when the city is destroyed). As though conceding the difficulty in believing in the "eternal life" of such sublime bodies, the texts assimilate them to the gorgeous tombs to which they are committed. Through such monuments, the enduring values of antique culture are transmitted to us in an unalterable, fabulous form; the entrusting of this culture to stone sepulchers implies, however, that its death is underlined as much as it is denied, just as its memory (in the form of inscriptions) is both transmitted and lost. Finally, the heroine of *Cligés* may or may not present an instance of the sublime body. She is certainly subjected to horrendous violence. We are made to fear that her efforts to create an illusory body which can safely "die" may have been foiled, in such a way that she appears to die for real (the first death). Our hearts—or Cligés's heart at least—miss a beat while we wait to discover whether this death has taken place. Has she truly transcended her scheming ways to achieve authentic martyrdom, supported by the quasi-divine power of Love? Or has that "death" in effect "died," leaving a shocking moment of emptiness before releasing Fenice to pursue her deception?

These twelfth-century texts resemble the sublime texts of Sophocles and Sade discussed by Lacan because, like them, they exploit a fantasy of unrestrained violence against an indestructible object.[29] Widely separate from them in time, they illustrate how the real of human destructiveness can be given a specific historical cast through the imaginary and symbolic dimensions of its representation. The awful tortures of the saints are imprinted with the Christian ideology the texts are composed to endorse, and the saints' resistance provides a sublime foretaste of the resurrected body to which their audiences are enjoined to aspire. Similar patterns inform the admiration for the cultural achievements of antiquity promoted in the *romans antiques* (*translatio studii*). Yet here, the cultural differences separating us from antiquity tend to ossify the past and to present our relation to it in terms of discontinuity as much as of continuity; buildings rather than people become a frozen repository of edification, literally a mausoleum of the past. In *Cligés*, finally, Fenice's martyrdom for Love may likewise recommend its cult to us, although we are likely to approach it gingerly, aware of the relativity with which the text presents all discourses and intellectual systems, treating them with as much derision as respect. In the last resort, it is the ability to respond to these discourses which is valued in *Cligés* over either bodies or things. Like many great works of courtly literature, of which ironic distance is an inevitable constituent, *Cligés* appeals to the existence of some imaginary other, less sophisticated than oneself, to fail to unravel its complexity and unquestioningly subscribe to belief in the sublime.

In each section of this chapter, I have brought out the way the construction of the sublime interacts with the way contradictoriness is treated in the genre concerned. Sublimation is itself inherently contradictory because, like all forms of object formation (see Chapter 5), it is an imaginary operation in the face of the absence/presence in the symbolic order of the Thing behind it. But it interacts differently with the preoccupations of different kinds of text. In hagiography the sublime body receives miraculous resistance from the clash of the divine order with the earthly one; the first death only intensifies the martyr's strength, and the texts which result from the second are vital and powerful. In the *romans antiques*, with their sober evaluation of the complex relations between our own world and that of antiquity, the sublime body is presented in more realistic guise as the product of wonderfully expert morticians and tomb designers, as much dead (in short) as alive. But in Chrétien's *Cligés*, the whole gamut of approaches to contradiction seems to have been rolled together. Fenice's promotion of simultaneous contraries is endorsed by the narrator in what seems like parodic mode, but then it is dismissed by a series of pseudo- or ultraclerical doubles of the narrator. We are left struggling in a mesh of irony which is so entangling that we can't make out the edges of the net.

Cligés, of course, predates the latest of the saints' lives discussed here. In light of it, we should reexamine the torments depicted in the *Lawrence* and the *George*. Are they not portrayed with the same gruesome humor as are those of the learned doctors from Salerno?[30] Similarly, what of the impact of courtly love literature on hagiography? If Fenice can be presented as martyred for Love under the influence of hagiography, the discourse of the heroines of hagiography is also informed by the rise of courtly literature, perhaps from as early as Wace's *Margaret*.[31] By the end of the century, this interaction between "religious" and "secular" sacrifice is patent so that, for example, the similarities between Clemence of Barking's *Life of St. Catherine* and the Thomas *Tristan* have been widely remarked upon.[32] Female martyrs, like Fenice, die for love, even if their love is of a different order. Maybe there is more scope for irony, and less for the sublime, in late hagiographic texts than my reading has allowed.

The way the saints, like Fenice, subordinate themselves to a Law, derive their enjoyment from its rule, and encourage the destructive impulse unfurling everywhere around them, may mark hagiography (like *Cligés*) as turning from the sublime toward the perverse.[33] I have deliberately alluded to the perverse structures of fetishism (in this case, in the sense of delegating beliefs to objects or other people) in my discussion of audience response to the *romans antiques* and *Cligés*. These latest considerations suggest that the way belief is enforced may not differ fundamentally between hagiography and romance. It also exposes the precariousness of the distinction between the sublime and the perverse, which is the subject of the next chapter.

CHAPTER 7

Sublime and perverse objects: love and its contradictions in *Yvain* and *Partonopeu de Blois*

One of the arguments which runs through Lacan's *Ethics of Psychoanalysis* is that courtly love played a foundational role in the development of the modern psyche. That is why, in his Seminar addressed to trainee analysts, Lacan devotes so much time to the troubadours. Žižek endorses Lacan's view: "The impression that courtly love is out of date, long superseded by modern manners, is a lure blinding us to how the logic of courtly love still defines the parameters within which the two sexes relate to each other" (*Metastases*, 89). What, then, are these structures of enduring significance, handed down to us in medieval poetry?

At one point, in what seems an uncharacteristically straightforward statement, Lacan says: "Courtly love is, in effect, an exemplary form, a paradigm, of sublimation. [. . .] [W]e still feel today the ethical ramifications" (*Ethics*, 128). Traditionally in psychoanalysis, sublimation involves a sacrifice of immediate sexual satisfaction in favor of behavior which is socially and morally approved. As such, it is the mainstay of human ethical and cultural aspiration (cf. Chapter 6). Lacan seems to be saying that when the troubadours celebrated the self-denial of courtly love, they gave a lasting shape to this endeavor. But things are not so simple. Žižek opens his dissection of Lacan's views on courtly love with this warning: "The first trap to be avoided apropos of courtly love is the erroneous notion of the lady as the sublime object: as a rule, one evokes here the process of spiritualization, the shift from raw sensual coveting to elevated spiritual longing" (*Metastases*, 89). A few paragraphs later, Žižek writes: "We are dealing with a strict fictional formula, with a social game of 'as if,' where a man pretends that his sweetheart is the inaccessible Lady. And it is precisely this feature which enables us to establish a link between courtly love and a phenomenon which, at first, seems to have nothing whatever to do with it: namely, masochism, as a specific form of perversion" (91). So courtly love, says Žižek, is not sublime; on the contrary, it lays the foundations of perversion which, broadly defined, is the release of sexual desire in activities not geared to sexual reproduction: activities, that is, such as masochism, sadism, fetishism, voyeurism, or exhibitionism, which are often subject to social censure and ethical condemnation (though not, of course, by analysts). In expounding Lacan's account of courtly love, Žižek seems to have come up with its diametrical opposite.

This polarity of sublime and perverse is the theme of this chapter. I will explain how these terms are interconnected in Lacan's teaching, so much so that they constitute the two ends of the same structure.[1] Then I will illustrate their significance for courtly literature by comparing two romances from the late twelfth century, both of which can be credited with transmitting medieval conceptions of love in an enduring form given that they inspired imitations and adaptations into many languages: Chrétien's *Le Chevalier au lion*, also known as *Yvain*, and *Partonopeu de Blois*.[2] The "twist" of structure whereby the sublime shifts into the perverse can be observed in both of these texts and has major consequences for the nature of the object. This twist is furthermore enabled by the complexity of contradictoriness in these late twelfth-century texts (or alternatively, one could say that the complexity of contradictoriness is its formal correlate). This chapter thus links the psychoanalytic understanding of love, the cultivation of contradiction by medieval texts, and the development of the literary object in the later twelfth century.

Sublime and perverse

I start, then, with the observation that the identical analysis of courtly love is presented by Lacan as sublime and by Žižek as perverse. In his seminar on *The Ethics of Psychoanalysis*, and the critical essay "Kant avec Sade" written at about the same time, Lacan too uses the concepts of sublimation and perversion in ways that are initially surprising. The *Ethics* continually refer to Kant's *Critique of Practical Reason* as a landmark text in the history of ethical thought. The categorical imperative adduced by Kant as the fundamental moral law, "So act that the maxim of your will could always hold at the same time as a principle in a giving of universal laws" (*Critique of Practical Reason*, 28), with its sacrifice of individual whim to universal necessity, is a paradigm of our subordination to the inflexible Thing, and thus it is the very prototype of sublimation.[3] More controversially, Lacan also sees the Marquis de Sade as a major ethical thinker. But contrary to what we might expect, in the *Ethics* Lacan represents Sade—who after all gave his name to one of the most notorious of perversions—as a sublime thinker along with Kant, whereas in the essay "Kant avec Sade," he treats Kant as a perverse thinker (or at least, as a precursor of perverse thought) along with Sade. Thus both the *Ethics* Seminar and "Kant avec Sade" are more interested in the similarities than the differences between the two eighteenth-century writers, and these similarities are ascribed in one text to the sublime and in the other to the perverse. To understand these apparent contradictions, we need to look more closely at these two key terms.

In the *Ethics*, Lacan reinvigorates the concept of the sublime through a brilliant rapprochement between the Freudian notion of sublimation, which involves the redirection of libido into socially acceptable activities, and the way the term is used by Kant, for whom it serves as a kind of bridge between the aesthetic and the moral.[4] The Kantian sublime has a stark nobility, and an undercurrent of awe, which Kant contrasts with the much tamer concept of the beautiful. As a result of Kant's influence, Lacan's concept of sublimation takes on aesthetic as well as moral value; and the starkness and awesomeness of the Kantian sublime are harnessed to Lacan's view that the drive which is sublimated is not just our friendly old sex urge but the far more alarming death drive. The death drive is much more fundamental and horrific than the sexual one; it is what precipitates us into life-destroying activities of all kinds, whether of our own or other peoples' lives. That there is in all of us "that which in life would prefer death" (*Ethics*, 104) is a major part of Lacan's concept of the real.

Throughout this Seminar, Lacan uses the term "the Thing" to refer to the point where the pressure of this real is felt; it is something to which we cannot give expression, because it marks the very limit of what language can conceive. Sublimation, then, takes on a much more precise, if abstract, meaning: it involves putting an object in the place where we sense the

Thing, in such a way as to seek to block it out, and so dam up the real of the drives, in particular the death drive, behind it. "Thus the most general formula that I can give you of sublimation is the following: it raises an object [. . .] to the dignity of the Thing" (*Ethics*, 112). Sublime objects, objects which are so placed, will appear imbued with a kind of eternal value precisely because they are invoked to block out the impulse toward death, and it is this "eternal" quality which makes them seem aesthetically or morally uplifting. But because they are put up to mask the Thing, they also become shot through with some of the horror that lies behind it. We have seen examples of this in the motif of the "sublime body" in Chapter 6.

Now, Lacan argues, elevating an object in this way is precisely what the Marquis de Sade does. The victims of "sadism" appear perennially beautiful, whatever the torments to which they are exposed, and this is precisely what shows them to be "sublime," that is, to result from sublimating a death drive to which Sade's writings, in their horrific violence, give eloquent testimony. "The victims are always adorned not only with all kinds of beauty, but also with grace, which is beauty's finest flower" (*Ethics*, 261). At the same time, Kant's concept of the sublime as stark and awesome meshes surprisingly well with the grim beauties of Sade's tortures. Sade turns out to be the exponent of the Kantian sublime because he shows us how the sublime is a fantasy invoked in the place of the Thing and which, precisely because it is aligned with the Thing, participates in its horror.

But if Sade is sublime, why is Kant perverse? To grasp Lacan's thinking here, we need to look more closely at the way the Thing stands at the juncture between the real and the symbolic. On the side of the real, it stands in the abyss of the unrepresentable, what Lacan calls "the first outside" (*Ethics*, 52). But because we are human, speaking subjects, we can only sense the real from the perspective of language, as a kind of hole on the edge of language or, more frighteningly, as the traumatic otherness of language itself, as a terrible machine imposed upon us by outside: an outside, in this case, that is right inside us, because without language in our minds, we couldn't conceive even of our own existence. The language in which Lacan evokes this machinelike Otherness is entirely Kantian: "In the end, it is conceivable that it is as a pure signifying system, as a *universal maxim*, as that which is most lacking in a relationship to the individual, that the features of *Das Ding* [the Thing] must be presented. It is here that, along with Kant, we must see the focal point, aim and convergence, according to which an action that we will qualify as moral will present itself" (*Ethics*, 55).[5]

It is just such a maxim that Sade proposes: the universal right to absolute enjoyment in which individual inclination is sacrificed. "Anyone can say to me, I have the right to enjoyment of your body, and I shall exercise that right without any limit to put a stop to whatever capricious demands I may feel inclined to satisfy" ("Kant avec Sade," 768–69).[6] Any person, all people, may claim this right to derive enjoyment from the speaker. The way Lacan proceeds to analyze Sade's writings in both the *Ethics* and in "Kant avec Sade" places this maxim as a kind of revelation of the Thing. Sade is understood to have unmasked the real of the drives as inhabiting a universal rule, an inexorable and mechanical structure over which no individual has any control but which instead controls us all.

The crucial point for Lacan, however, is not just that Sade shows more nakedly than Kant how we are subject to the real of the drives. It has to do more with the *position* of the subject under this regime than with the nature of his subjection. In his analysis of the Sadean sublime in the *Ethics*, Lacan implies that the victim of sadism fulfills the function of sublime object, elevated to the dignity of the Thing. In "Kant avec Sade," however, a different analysis is advanced.[7] In fantasy, the sadist occupies a role which Lacan defines as that of object-instrument; his role is to serve as a support or cause for the imagined enjoyment of the other. What is sick, in other words, about the pervert, is that he actually represents himself as staging the act for the benefit of the "victim." He is not himself the subject of this scene; instead, he is there in the role of the third person. By means of such objectification, the pervert succeeds in being both involved in, and oddly distanced from, the scene. "Lanval," examined in Chapter 5, provides an example of perverse thinking where the subject positions himself as object: Lanval identifies himself as that which the *fée* might be thought to lack, a lack the text both underlines and denies by means of the "logic of the veil." The end of Chapter 6 also drew attention to perverse structures in later hagiographic texts. The saints, in a way similar to Fenice in *Cligés*, can be seen as objectifying themselves when they encourage the enjoyment of others—God, Love, torturers—at their own expense. Audiences of the *romans antiques* and *Cligés* are also encouraged to desubjectivize themselves by passing responsibility for belief onto others.

Sade comes out of this analysis as a pervert. But so, at least in anticipation, does Kant. Sade's thinking, Lacan is saying, is altogether Kantian in his recognition of the need to subordinate oneself to a universal maxim. All Sade does, according to Lacan, is to take further the tendencies of Kant's teaching. Kant thought that the objects of the moral law were the values it produced: the good, the object of the law, does not precede that law but follows from it, according to Kant (*Critique of Pratical Reason*, 50–51). His perception of the object as elusive is appropriated by Lacan for comparison with the always secondary, imaginary status of the object in psychoanalysis ("Kant avec Sade," 780–81, also 768). But, Lacan goes on, Kant failed to envisage that the subject could identify *itself* as the object and agent of law—the perspective opened up by Sade (772). Kant also saw desire as belonging in the realm of individual affect (what he calls "pathology"), which he thought needed to be subordinated to a public law, analogous to the law of the state; Sade, however, like Lacan, recognizes that desire and law are inseparable, because desire inhabits the very signifying system that serves at once to inhibit and provokes that desire.[8] But for these two factors, Lacan implies, Kant would have been a full-fledged pervert. So it is that, as Žižek has put it, "Lacan conceives Sade as the truth of Kant" (*Sublime Object*, 81).[9]

Lacan pursues the imbrication of the sublime and perverse to the point of contending that they are reverse forms of the same structure. Following one sequence, the subject cultivates a sublime object; following the reverse sequence, the pervert as object supports the enjoyment of a sublime subject. In the first order, the sublime object is placed up against the Thing, both masking it with beauty and calling attention to its awesome dangers; in the second, it is the other subject which is exposed to the rigors and inhumanity of the Thing as it suffuses the symbolic order with deathly enjoyment. An element which acts as a hinge allowing the two sides to change places is the superego which, in the case of sublimation, induces the subject to take up *objects* which it has approved and, in the case of perversion, requires the subject to position *itself as an object* supporting the unfurling of law and drive. Lacan sees the superego as an inner agency which may ultimately derive from external social approval but which is independent of external verification: that is, we do as it says whether it has society behind it or not. When the superego calls upon the perverse subject to abstract and objectify itself as a pervert, it imposes on it a sacrifice very much like that involved in sublimation: the subject gives up its own immediate enjoyment for that of the Other. Both sublimation and perversion, then, are potentially beautiful, or obscene, or both as the current of the superego is switched this way or that: the difference between sublime and perverse is not a moral one; it is simply the formal one of the location of the subject. Lacan says this quite plainly in *The Four Fundamental Concepts of Psycho-Analysis*: "what defines perversion is precisely the way in which the subject is placed in it" (182); "[the structure of perversion] is an inverted effect of the phantasy. It is the subject who determines himself as object, in his encounter with the division in subjectivity" (185). In Lacanian algebra, the pivot between the two terms of subject and object is the $\lozenge$, which in "Kant avec Sade" Lacan glosses as "le désir de."[10] The formula of sublimation is $\$ \lozenge a$ and that of perversion is $a \lozenge \$$. The apparently divergent structures are thus two ways of conceiving a single relationship between the barred subject (the subject of desire and the unconscious, $\$$) and *objet a*.

That said, do we indeed find sublime and perverse structures reversing one into the other in courtly love texts? Was Žižek right to read what Lacan identifies as the sublimation embodied in courtly love poetry as no more than a manifestation of its incipient perversity? These are the questions which I bring first to the opening scenes of *Yvain* and *Partonopeu*, where the protagonists fall in love.

The sublime, the gaze, and voyeurism in Yvain

The scenes where Yvain has pursued the fountain knight back to his castle and then proceeds to fall in love with his widow (discussed at the end of Chapter 4) unfold in a frenzy which results from the way various narrative strands involving violence are interwoven with asymmetries in the visual field. Yvain still wants revenge on the fountain knight and on Kay; the fountain knight's people are consumed with grief at his death and want to punish his killer; and his widow in her distress ravages her own body as well as calling for revenge; everything is made more complex by the fact that Yvain is invisible, so he can see others but they can't see him.

The Lady first appears like a vision of preternatural beauty against the violence of the surrounding scene:

> vint une des plus beles dames
> c'onques veïst riens terrïenne.
> De si tres bele crestïenne
> ne fu onques plait ne parole.
>
> (1146–49)

there came in one of the most beautiful ladies that any earthly creature ever saw. Never was there word nor talk of so lovely a Christian.

Although she contrasts with the destructiveness around her, she is also a prey to it, the intensity of her distress only increasing her appeal for Yvain:

> Grant duel ai de ses biax chevax
> qui fin or passent, tant reluisent;
> d'ire m'esprennent et aguisent
> quant je li voi rompre et tranchier
> n'onques ne poent estanchier
> les larmes qui des iex li chïent.
> Toutes ches choses me dessïent.
> Atout che qu'ils sont plain de lermes,
> si que che n'est ne fins ne termes,
> ne furent onques si bel oeil, etc.
>
> (1466–75)

I am filled with distress over her lovely hair which shines more brightly than gold; it spurs me and burns me with anguish when I see her tear and cut at it; nor can the tears that fall from her eyes ever be staunched; all these things dismay me. Yet even if they are full of tears without end or limit, never were any eyes so beautiful, etc.

Throughout this long speech Yvain is torn between admiring the Lady's beauty *in spite of* her grief, and *because of* it. Each of her magnificent features takes on a new radiance from the very violence to which it is subjected. The brightness of her hair is lit by the fire of her distress, her eyes supremely beautiful when full of tears, the bright colors of her face emphasized when she tears at it, her throat glistening white against the violence she does it, and so on.

The destructiveness which her beauty both contrasts with and embodies is one respect in which the Lady is sublime; her unattainability is another. As Yvain looks at her,

> . . . il ne puet quidier ne croire
> que ses voloirs puisse avenir;
> puis dist, "Pour fol me doi tenir
> quant je veul chou que ja n'arai.
> Son seigneur a mort li navrai,
> et je quit a li pais avoir!"
> (1430–35)

. . . he could not imagine nor believe that he might have his desire; then he said, "I should think myself a fool for wanting what I shall never have. I wounded her husband so that he died, and I imagine I can make peace with her!"

The impossibility of his possessing the Lady, as Yvain sees it, is causally connected with the violence permeating the scene. His expression in line 1433, "je veul chou que ja n'arai," recalls Calogrenant's earlier description of himself as "uns chevaliers / qui quier che que trouver ne puis" (356–57). "Love," like "adventure," requires a sacrifice of satisfaction in order to uphold the ideal. In the manuscript which forms the basis of Hult's edition of *Le Chevalier au lion*, as indeed in the majority of manuscripts of the romance, the Lady is not named, and this underlines the extent to which she is abstracted from social reality.[11] Throughout this scene, furthermore, she is ogled by Yvain without herself being able to see him, and so she is also removed from the erotic potential of the situation, which exists only in his imagination. She will not see him in the flesh until she has already resolved to take him as her next champion. She is thus so far located solely as the object of Yvain's and the narrator's admiration.

This lack of reciprocity in the visual field is due to the ring of invisibility given to Yvain by Lunete. With it, Yvain can see but not be seen. The imbalance persists when the funeral procession leaves the room and he watches its progress from a position behind a window. The fountain knight's followers are still in the room; they hunt everywhere for their lord's killer, and their inability to see him makes them appear blind. The way they rush round ineffectually striking everything in sight while he sits peacefully invisible has a comic verve comparable to the *fabliaux* (1136–43). This comedy of those who want to see but cannot is contrasted with the beauty of the Lady of the fountain which, although registered by the eye, possesses a grace beyond the visible. In the passage where she first appears, quoted above, the rhymes *terrïenne* and *crestïenne* present her as an otherworldly, quasispiritual presence. She appears to Yvain to have been made by God himself (1502–10) and thereby endowed with a perfection which is not only aesthetic, but moral and spiritual.

The Lady and her followers thus transmute violence into the contrasting registers of the ridiculous and the sublime, in the form, respectively, of the failure of inquiring eyes and the triumph of invisible worth. In another register again, violence is transposed into the uncanny as the dead knight's wounds drip fresh blood in their assailant's presence. Thus, while those who can see appear blind and beauty depends on the invisible, the only one actually to "see" Yvain is the corpse, whose wound turns out to be a "seeing eye":

> Car li sans touz chaus e vermaus
> rissi au mort par mi la plaie;
> et che fu prouvanche bien vraie
> qu'encor iert chil laiens sans faille
> qui avoit faite la bataille
> et qui l'avoit mort e conquis.
>
> (1180–85)

For the hot red blood issued out once more through the dead man's wound. And this was certain proof that the man who had fought the battle and killed and defeated him was still in there without a doubt.

This silent accusation by the dead body seems to possess a supernatural dimension; the Lady's followers declare it to be *merveilles* and *diablie* ("wonders" and "devilry," 1202), the spiritual contrary of the Lady's miraculous and God-given charms. And whereas the sublimation effected by the Lady invokes moral worth, the oozing flesh is a grim reminder of human wrongdoing. Indeed, it is precisely Yvain's vengefulness that the corpse signals, given that the expression *prouvanche vraie* (1182) recalls Yvain's determination to obtain evidential proof, *enseignes vraies* (897),[12] of his victory in order to confound Kay. Just as Yvain's invisibility made the dead lord's followers blind, so the seeing wounds confer on him a measure of visibility. As his pursuers surge around the room a second time, some of their blows now reach their mark (1192–93), and a measure of Yvain's own violence is returned against him.

This "marvel" of the dead man's blood which "sees" Yvain's guilt is an example of what, in *The Four Fundamental Concepts*, Lacan calls "the gaze." By the gaze, Lacan does not mean what the subject sees, but rather his exposure to being seen by the Other; the gaze is contrasted with the seeing eye. It is thus marked at the outset by asymmetry: the point from which I may be gazed at is neither the point at which I look nor the point from which I see. This triadic structure recalls that of interpellation (see Chapter 4) in which the subject responds to the invocation of the Other in relation to an object or third person.[13] Indeed, "voice" and "gaze" are similar objects—in film theory, for instance, but also, as we will see, in *Yvain* and *Partonopeu*.

When presenting his theory of the gaze, Lacan stresses from the outset that it appears as a traumatic disturbance. It disarms and distresses us because, out of the blue, it impresses on us the sense of meeting with our own incompleteness, or as he puts it, our "castration." This meeting with the gaze is thus an encounter with the failure of the symbolic to take account of the real:

> The gaze is presented to us only in the form of a strange contingency, symbolic of what we find on the horizon, as the thrust of our experience, namely, the lack that constitutes castration anxiety. (*Four Fundamental Concepts*, 72–73)

This vocabulary of "horizon" and "lack" alerts us to the similarity between the gaze and the Thing, and like the Thing, the lack which the gaze manifests is also the real of the drives, except that the drive in question is the scopic drive (the urge to see). The gaze is thus situated both outside and at the heart of the subject, and the Other from which it stems is the unconscious (*Four Fundamental Concepts*, 75). Consciousness, by contrast, deludes us that what we see is the whole picture. If we are aware of the gaze in our waking state, it is as something uncanny, an intrusion that catches us off guard. Insofar as we sense the gaze and try to relate to it, or even to control it, it is an object. As such, in addition to its real and symbolic features, it has an imaginary dimension which Lacan invokes as follows: "The gaze I encounter [. . .] is not a seen gaze but a gaze imagined by me in the field of the Other" (*Four Fundamental Concepts*, 84).

An example Lacan offers of a gaze imagined in this way is the skull in the foreground of Holbein's famous painting of "The Ambassadors" in the National Gallery (London, UK). The skull is distorted by the process known as "anamorphosis" so as to lie in a quite different plane from the principal subject of the painting, a plane which is only legible from a perspective from which the rest of the painting retreats into a blur. Because the distorted skull has a vaguely phallic shape, Lacan sees it as representing the symbolic framework of castration as the place of lack; the eyes of the skull look out at the viewer of the painting with the gaze that presents, in the form of an imaginary object, the real of death which is beyond representation and so provokes that lack. Like a sublime object, then, the gaze both disguises and transmits the real behind it. The effect of meeting the gaze is both to present the viewer with a fantasy object and to challenge our dependence on such objects, because the gaze reminds us of the extent to which subjectivity is riven by repression and lack:

> For the secret of this picture [. . .] is given at the moment when, moving slightly away, little by little, to the left, then turning around, we see what the magical floating object signifies. It reflects our own nothingness in the figure of the death's head. It is a use, therefore, of the geometrical dimension of vision in order to capture the subject, an obvious relation with desire which, nevertheless, remains enigmatic. (*Four Fundamental Concepts*, 92)[14]

Lacan also discusses Holbein's painting in Seminar VII, reading the anamorphosis in relation to what he there calls "the Thing" (*Ethics*, 135). The coexistence of incompatible systems of perspective in the same painting shows up the constructedness, and consequent limitations, of its represented "reality." By drawing attention to the shortfall in representation, the clash of perspectives points toward the disturbing, real "Thing" behind it. In the same way the supernatural qualities attributed to the courtly lady act as an anamorphosis in courtly love poetry, her sublime facade unmasks its own construction as a fantasy while at the same time pointing to the rigor of the inhuman "Thing" beyond (*Ethics*, 139–54). The effect of the gaze, that is, is to manifest the structure of fantasy, $\$ \lozenge a$, which is also the formula of sublimation, because it underlines the flimsiness of the $\$$ (the fact that it is split by lack and the Thing) and its dependence on its fantasy support, *objet a*.

Like Holbein's anamorphosis, Chrétien's introduction in *Yvain* of a corpse that bleeds in the presence of its killer introduces an abrupt and disruptive change in narrative perspective. The corpse localizes the gaze as its wounds stare accusingly at Yvain; like the visual anamorphosis it forms, of course, a part of the imaginary–symbolic fabric of the larger work, and yet the uncanny character of the event invokes, like the death's head in "The Ambassadors," the alarming irruption of the real of human destructiveness. Indeed, Lacan frequently uses the term "stain," as in "bloodstain," to refer to this presence of the gaze, a term remarkably appropriate to the medieval text, where the gush of blood "gazes" at Yvain's guilt (cf. the miracle of the stained altar cloth discussed in Chapter 5). Consequently, the whole scene possesses a triadic structure whereby Yvain is "seen" from a position quite different from the one from which he looks: dumbstruck by the beauties of the Lady, he sees her with the eyes of his desire, but the dead man's gaze on him is a reminder of the Thing which, precisely, causes men to look for objects to uplift them and make them "whole." The gaze of the bleeding corpse, in other words, lays bare the structure of the fantasy $ $\lozenge$ a whereby Yvain finds the Lady to be sublime.

So far I have shown how, in these opening scenes of *Yvain*, the various strands of violence and the layered imbalances in the field of vision are interconnected. The violence amid which the Lady first appears is sublimated in the supernatural beauty she seems to possess; she is positioned both as the object of Yvain's desiring look and as possessing qualities beyond the visible. Her followers, whose sight proves no use to them, exercise violence fruitlessly and ridiculously. Although Yvain is invisible to them, however, he is "seen" and denounced by the results of his own violence in his victim's body. The relations of similarity and inversion between the uncanny and the sublime underline how sublimation itself can act as an anamorphosis of the violence which underlies it. The weakness of the subject and it dependence on the fantasy are exposed.

But does this whole structure flip over, in such a way as to turn Yvain into the object, disavow the violence, and expose instead deficiencies in the other subjects, notably the Lady? To put the question another way, how literally should we take Hult's characterization of Yvain's behavior as "a moment of voyeurism doubly underlined given that the hero himself is invisible" (Hult, Introduction, 10)?

It is clear that Yvain is not a voyeur in the clinical sense described, for instance, in Seminar IV: a man who spies on women in public toilets to see what they haven't got (*Relation d'objet*, 89–91). The scenes which Yvain observes turn on grief and violence, the erotic element is only secondary. True, he is, as Lacan says of the sadist, the object-instrument of this pain. But what is most obvious about his voyeurism, underlined by Hult, is Yvain's dissimulation of his own presence in the scene. Although I have alluded to the effects of this, I have yet to consider it closely.

The ring which Lunete gives Yvain contains a stone which, when turned toward the palm of the hand, makes the wearer invisible. Its mechanism works the opposite way from Chrétien's most likely source here, the ring of invisibility given by Medea to Jason to help him win the golden fleece in the opening episode of the *Troie*, which works by turning the stone *outward*.[15] Medea's ring works by a law of contraries: by displaying (the stone) one conceals (oneself), whereas Lunete's works by attraction: by concealing a little, one conceals all. It is as if the stone, withdrawn into the palm of the hand, were able to draw into its own invisibility the whole body by which it is borne. This triumph of interiority over the externally visible is consonant with the valuing of the inner over the outer which I spoke of earlier in relation to the invisible beauties of the sublime. But it goes further by (as it were) sucking the outside into nothing at all: an apparent emptiness. Yvain's vanishing act adds another supernatural element to these scenes, one more akin to the uncanny of the bleeding corpse than to the divine merits of the Lady and, like it, attributed to devilry (1130–31). I have argued that the "seeing wounds" are an instance of the Lacanian gaze, and my comments on Yvain's invisibility also draw on Lacan's discussion of voyeurism in relation to the gaze.

Lacan insists that what is important about the voyeur is not that he is an agent of seeing. His purpose as a pervert is not to exercise his own agency by seeing this thing or that, but to sustain the activity of vision; and so he situates himself not as the subject of the urge to see, but as the empty place of the real (or of the Thing, in the language of the *Ethics* Seminar) which shapes and sustains that urge and around which the scopic drive moves. In short, says Lacan, the voyeur situates himself in the scene as a hidden gaze, as the empty space imagined as the place from which the real would see if it could:

> What occurs in voyeurism? At the moment of the act of the voyeur, where is the subject, where is the object? I have told you that the subject is not there in the sense of seeing, at the level of the scopic drive. He is there as pervert, and he is situated only at the culmination of the loop [formed by the drive]. As for the object [. . .]—the loop turns around itself, it is a missile, and it is with it [i.e. the completion of the loop], in perversion, that the target is reached.
>
> The object, here, is the gaze—the gaze that is the subject, which attains it, which hits the bull's eye [. . .]. [T]he other surprises him, the subject, as entirely hidden gaze. (*Four Fundamental Concepts*, 182)

Although these remarks are obscure, they are nonetheless suggestive for *Yvain*. In order not to bring an end to the spectacle of grief (for example, by letting himself be captured), Yvain vanishes into nothing, and the empty space which he then occupies provokes the spectacle to continue turning around it as its absent center. Chrétien's own imagery suggests that Yvain has taken over the role of the corpse as "gaze," but one which is entirely hidden from view. For as Yvain falls in love with the Lady, he is described as himself becoming like the wounds of the corpse that previously gazed at him; Love

> . . . par les iex el cuer le fiert,
> et cist cols a plus grant duree
> que cols de lanche ne d'espee.
> Colz d'espee garist et saine
> mout tost, des que mires y paine;
> et la plaie d'Amours empire
> quant ele est plus pres de son mire.
> Chele playe a mesire Yvains
> dont il ne sera jammais sains.
>
> (1372–80)

. . . strikes him through the eyes in the heart, and this blow lasts longer than a lance or sword stroke. A sword blow heals and gets better quickly, as soon as a doctor sees to it; yet the wound of Love gets worse the closer it is to its doctor. My lord Yvain has this wound, of which he will never be healed.

And so, from the metaphorical wounds in his invisible body, he watches the lady and finds her to be—as Sade's sadist found his victims—sublime.

Could we not say that the formula is indeed reversed here, and that Yvain has assumed in imagination the pervert's position of the gaze as object-instrument? The subjects he serves include the audience of the romance, for it is not just the enjoyment of other characters which is fueled by his position as "hidden gaze" but ours too as, privileged by his invisibility, we too can gaze at the scene (see Spearing, *Medieval Poet*, 76).

The narrator, for his part, does not hesitate to cast Yvain in the role of object. For now the romance takes on an entirely new perspective as we realize the expediency of the Lady marrying her husband's killer and so securing a proven champion for her lands. Initially, the whole plot has been run through the eyes of male fantasy. The romance opens with Calogrenant telling the embarrassing story of his adventures; some parts have to be told twice because the queen joins the audience partway through and insists he start again. When Yvain decides to attempt the same quest, he anticipates its course in his imagination (719). His actual experience of the early parts of the adventure is thus the second or third rerun. Like someone on a well-trodden tourist trail, he tours from the hideous herdsman to the hospitable vavassor; it is only when he defeats the fountain knight that his models run out and he is forced to improvise. The one-sidedness of the male perspective at once begins to show. Now we see the Lady resituate Yvain's desire in terms of her own concerns. In this playful reversal, we see him as occupying the space of the object upon which designs are made and being assigned a space in *her* fantasy as she rehearses in her own mind the form her eventual meeting with him might take (1757–80). The skillful manipulations of Lunete contribute further to the "objectification" of Yvain, who throughout acts under her direction.

As the romance advances, the tone also changes. Previously we have seen elements of slapstick, and perhaps also of black humor with the bleeding corpse, but the more Yvain falls in love, the more whimsical and ironic the narrative style becomes. Principally the irony centers on the contrasts and similarities between Yvain's situation as a lover and his political reality as virtual prisoner. The narrator goes to enormous lengths to stress how indiscriminate Love is before finally conceding that in Yvain, she found a worthy abode. It is also hinted that Yvain's love is in no small part a response to the burial of his victim and the consequent problem of confounding Kay with the evidence of his victory—a problem to which displaying the Lady as his trophy would provide a neat solution. Imbalances multiply as we are repeatedly invited to see Yvain from a position from which he doesn't see us: so far as the fiction is concerned, we too are a hidden gaze licensed to expose the credibility gap in the sublime.

In Chapter 4 I contrasted *Yvain* with the *romans antiques* whose narratives it redeploys while omitting their foundation in interpellation. We can now see that in these opening scenes of Chrétien's romance, the role of the voice has been taken over by that of the gaze. Both voice and gaze position protagonists in asymmetric relations to death and love and can cast them in the object role as well as in that of subject. This asymmetry in *Yvain* is maximized by the way love and death are superimposed. Yvain looks at the Lady with eyes of love while she looks at her dead husband with eyes of mourning, and the dead husband completes the triangle by "looking" at Yvain with a call for revenge. Of the three parties to the scene, one is dead and another invisible; the invisible man loves the lady because of her grief for the dead one, and she will love him in return because, having killed her husband, he is qualified to replace him! The Otherness of death acts as the middle term to create the framework within which these "lovers" can come together. All the same, the perverse absence of Yvain from the scene of his own desire makes the Lady its sublime, unique, and indeed altogether extraordinary subject. The episode seems calculated to flesh out an apothegm of Lacan's which could serve as the theme of this whole chapter:

> When, in love, I solicit a look, what is profoundly unsatisfying and always missing is that—*You never look at me from the place from which I see you.*
> Conversely, *what I look at is never what I want to see.* (*Four Fundamental Concepts*, 103, original emphasis)

I will show later how this asymmetry is bound up with the structure of contradiction in the romance. But first, I want to examine the similar but even more bizarre love plot that opens *Partonopeu de Blois*.

Anamorphosis and the gaze in Partonopeu de Blois

The love affair in this romance begins, like Yvain's, with the hero pursuing his quarry into unknown territory. Partonopeu, thirteen-year-old nephew of King Clovis, is hunting in the Ardennes when he chases after a boar, strays from the hunting party, and becomes lost. He boards an empty boat, which puts to sea and takes him to a mysterious empty city. Here he wanders, bewildered, deciding finally to rest in the most splendid of its many palaces; that night, the Lady Melior, whose magic powers he will later learn have brought him there, joins him in bed. The ensuing love affair between them forms the romance's main plot.

There are indications that this empty city is the realm of the dead. Its name, we later learn, is Chef d'Oire, so called because it is situated on the estuary of the river Oire (1767–68). But the words also mean "journey's end" which, given the familiar metaphors of a river as life and a journey as life, could also be a euphemism for death. We are repeatedly told that Partonopeu cannot see any living thing here (774, 896, 978, 1178, 1610, 1698). Even the animal forms, contrasting with the wild animals of the hunt earlier, are lifeless sculptures made of gold and mounted on the rooftops (841–46). The city has the sumptuous beauty of the marvelous edifices of the *romans antiques*. Its palaces are built in great checkers of red and white marble, gleaming with light that brightens up the night sky, and filled with gorgeous furnishings in the best courtly-literature-cum-lifestyle-magazine tradition. A rich feast is laid out, the absence of living people underlined by the enumeration of all who aren't there ("neither emperor nor king, nor clerk, knight or burgher, lady nor damsel," 899 ff.). Silence reigns. Partonopeu is dumbstruck, but hunger draws him to the laden tables. And now, the objects take on a life of their own. Two water bowls ("one drinks wine from less splendid vessels," 976) wait upon him, one pouring water into the other; a towel dances up to dry his hands. At table, the serving dishes whiz about, providing him with food, drink, and more water to wash with. Then a candle lights him to a bedroom, whereupon his spurs come off of their own accord (1111–12). When he pulls up the coverlet (trimmed with exotic scented white ibex skin), the candle discreetly withdraws from the room.

An anecdote told by Lacan will exemplify how these lifeless objects in Chef d'Oire might be interpreted as "gazing" at Partonopeu. As a young man, Lacan went out with some local fisherman in their boat. One of them sees an empty sardine tin gleaming as it bobs on the water and says to him: *"You see that can? Do you see it? Well, it doesn't see you!"* (*Four Fun-

damental Concepts, 95, original emphasis). The fisherman thinks it is a tremendous joke, but Lacan finds it discomfiting and later reflects that, as an intellectual among working men, the very possibility of the sardine can "gazing" at him did indeed expose him as "rather out of place in the picture" (96). Similarly, Partonopeu initially feels confused and out of place amid the splendor that "gazes" upon him:

> Tant voit li enfes grans biautés
> que molt cuide estre mesalés.
> (807–8)

The boy sees such great beauties that he imagines he has gone very astray.

He quickly protects himself against such exposure, however, by recourse to disavowal: that is, he contrives to believe both that he is in a world of enchantment (which he randomly labels *faerie*, 809, *paradis*, 874, *fantosme*, 880, and "fable et ovragne de dïable," 983–84—devil's work and inventions), and that he is the victim of some delusion or trick (905–10). If the latter, he reflects,

> quant il i doit este engigniés,
> qu'el cief de tote la cité
> et el palais plus haut levé
> el principal et el plus mestre,
> soit engigniés s'il le doit estre.
> (926–30)

that if he is to be deceived here, then it would be better for him to be so at the chief position in the entire citadel, in its loftiest, principal, and most important palace, if deceived he must be.

If all these luxuries are a delusion, at least let him exploit them "as if" they were real! Eventually seated at table and served with wine from the most splendid cup in sight, Partonopeu is convinced he is somehow the guest of honor at this people-less banquet:

> Molt i entent quant il le voit
> et par la cope li est vis
> qu'il est molt richement assis.
> (1038–40)

He is very intent upon it when he sees it and, because of the cup, it is borne in upon him that he is most splendidly seated.

The uncanny "gaze" of these objects, lifeless and yet alive, is thus parried and eventually harnessed as an imaginary support to Partonopeu's own self-regard.

As the story progresses and we learn more about Chef d'Oire, the sense increases that it and France are situated in inverse perspective relative to one another: Partonopeu is invisible to the people of Chef d'Oire and they to him.[16] The only things which can pass from one field of vision to the other are occasional animals, like the boar hunted by Partonopeu in the darkness of Ardennes, and which lures him to Melior. When Partonopeu first goes back to France, the boatmen who convey him are invisible (1967–68). He cannot see "any living thing" (1979), a phrase which recalls the apparently total absence of life in Chef d'Oire and suggests that it takes a while to adjust to the new visual plane: all he can see are the horse and hounds he brought with him (1980–81). Then Melior sends him packhorses laden with gold which materialize just outside Blois (1991–95).[17] On his return journey, Melior's knight who accompanies him materializes on the riverbank, the boatmen again are invisible, and the horse and hounds flicker in and out of sight, like an anamorphotic stain:

> El batel entre volentiers;
> son cheval lait et ses levriers.
> Li batiaus vait et il repose;
> oïr poés repuse cose:
> il voit les avirons nagier
> et ne voit pas son chevalier,
> ne ses levriers, ne son cheval,
> ne ciaus qui nagent contreval.
> Et quant est a sa nef venus,
> iluec a ses levriers veüs;
> ses chevaus i estoit tos cois
> qu'il laissa al gravier sos Blois.
> (4135–47)

He gladly enters the little boat, leaving his horse and hounds. The boat moves off and he reclines. Now let me tell you a secret: he can see the oars rowing, but he can't see his knight, hounds, horse, or the men rowing down there. And when he has reached the ship, he saw the hounds on it; his horse was standing there quietly, which he had left on the shore below Blois.

As this passage shows, Partonopeu here sails from Blois, although initially he arrived in Chef d'Oire from the Ardennes: journeys between Chef d'Oire and France can reach or leave France from widely separate places. The pun on *oirre* ("journey")–Loire (4123–24) underlines the homonymy Loire–l'Oire and suggests that the mysterious world is not so much separate from our own as the familiar world of the Loire valley seen from a different perspective.

Why is there this strange curvature of space between Blois and Chef d'Oire such that each is invisible to the other—a difference which will disappear later in the romance when Partonopeu breaks Melior's taboo and shatters her magic powers? The hints of death in Chef d'Oire certainly make it uncanny. They may even be coherent enough to constitute it as sublime, although audiences may prefer to model their response on Partonopeu's, deriving what pleasure they can from contrivances in which they do not wholly believe. The luxury items with a "life" of their own are probably too domestic to support the sublimity of the magnificent buildings. More like the work of a high-class poltergeist, these objects invoke a lack more comic than guilty, more symbolic than real, more suggestive of the phallus than of death. And this accords with the reason which the romance gives for the mutual invisibility of the two worlds, that of safeguarding erotic desire. Melior does not want Partonopeu to be seen by her court because (unlike the artifacts, which show him honor) they would scorn him as a mere boy (1495–96). And they must remain invisible to him so he can't speak to any of them until their marriage can be announced (in two and a half years' time). Until then, their sexual relationship is to remain utterly private:

> Et moi avrés cascune nuit
> por acomplir l'autre deduit. [. . .]
> Home ne feme n'i verrés
> ne a nului n'i parlerés
> desci que li jors iert venus
> que li conciles iert tenus.
>
> (1465–72)

And you will have me every night to fulfill the other pleasure. [. . .] You will see neither man nor woman there, nor speak to anyone until the day comes for the council to be held.

So far we see that anamorphosis and the gaze are treated differently in *Partonopeu* than in *Yvain*. The mutual invisibility of Partonopeu and the inhabitants of Chef d'Oire is symmetrical, whereas in *Yvain* the protagonist could see the inhabitants of the castle but they could not see him. The role of third party on this visual stage, occupied in *Yvain* by the "seeing" corpse, passes in *Partonopeu* to some rather obsequious items of tableware. These changes lead to a shift in accent from sublimity to disavowal and from the deathly to the erotic between the two texts. But although disavowal may be a first stage on the road to perversion, and although the flying objects in *Partonopeu* may have phallic connotations, nothing we have so far seen qualifies as perverse. (Strictly, fetishism is a fixing of the structure of disavowal in an object: "I know that my mother has not got a phallus, but I still believe that this is the object that is it.") This changes, however, when we come to consider the erotic relation between Partonopeu and Melior.

This relation is strikingly asymmetrical. Initially it is the reverse of that in *Yvain* because Melior can see Partonopeu (indeed, she chose him for his beauty), whereas he is forbidden to attempt to look at her until the moment comes for their love to be made public. To her, he is spectacle; to him, she is voice, and a threatening one at that. When she first climbs into bed with him, she appears furious to find him there. Partonopeu, terrified she will eject him (as he imagines) to his death, throws himself on her mercy, but it is a long time before she agrees to let him stay. Eventually, in a scene whose clumsy violence is quite disturbing, he forces her to have sex with him. Only then do we learn that she has stage-managed everything about his presence in Chef d'Oire, from the hunt onward, perhaps even including this "forcible seduction."[18] Then, in an arrangement reminiscent of "Lanval," she tells him that he can enjoy all the sex, wealth, and luxuries he likes, but must not attempt to see her until she is ready to present him to her council. The taboo, backed with threats, is repeated several times:

> Se vos ensi partés de moi
> et del deffens ne portés foi,
> dont m'arés vos asés ochise.
> (4229–31)

> Mais la mors est de moi veïr,
> ce saciés vos, sans moi garir.
> (4275-76)

If you leave me in this way and do not obey my injunction, then you will have slain me.

But it is death to see me, you can be sure, and will not bring me any health.

Melior's treatment of Partonopeu has a perverse ring to it because, through her reduction to invisibility and voice, she both controls the scene and yet appears absent from it: she poses as the object for Partonopeu as (her) subject. The refusal to let him see her literally effaces her from the scene, while her words convince Partonopeu it is all for his benefit: Chef d'Oire was created as a playground to amuse him in the daytime (1737–42); at night, after sex, she regales him with wonderful storytelling (1863–70). Melior exults in being an illusionist; she can make a hundred thousand men all invisible to one another (4654–57), as she has done in Partonopeu's case. She has the pervert's certainty that everything is staged for her partner's enjoyment and that she is the object-instrument of his *jouissance*. Through her magic, she effects on the scale of an entire city the pedophile's whispered words, "Let this be our little secret." (Whether or not the age of thirteen is too young for such a seduction in the world of the audience,[19] Melior is clearly using her magic to conceal a relationship perceived as transgressive in the world of the romance, as is shown when the taboo is broken; see below.) Her invisibility is the condition around which their sexual enjoyment will turn, and it directly translates the imbalance of power between them. Partonopeu is forced to accept her terms "voluntarily," and indeed promises eagerly to respect them (1779–82). Melior maintains her invisibility by force of command, not magic—when Partonopeu later rebels, all it takes to see her is a lantern.

Like Yvain, then, Melior is an entirely hidden gaze, but unlike him, she enjoys control over her lover (Yvain will, after all become subject to his Lady's injunction to return within the term she specifies—an injunction I will compare with that in *Partonopeu* later.) Thus relations between Partonopeu and Melior manifest to an even greater extent than those in *Yvain* Lacan's apothegm on the asymmetry of love: Partonopeu is *forbidden* to look at Melior from the place from which she sees him. And it does indeed turn out that, to paraphrase Lacan, "what he looks at is not what he wants to see" (*Four Fundamental Concepts*, 103, quoted above), as we will see in the episode where he breaks her taboo.

This taboo is another instance of the logic of the veil (see Chapter 5): it persuades us that behind the screen there is something to be seen, and it so provokes its own transgression. Partonopeu's mother is horrified when she learns of the taboo's existence. Her determination that he should break it forms part of a series of parallels and contrasts between Melior and herself, as though each were the anamorphotic distortion of the other; for example, each sees the other's influence over Partonopeu as diabolical (3936, 3946, 4192).[20] Determined to break her son's entanglement, the mother first tries drugging him and luring him into sexual involvement with another girl. Partonopeu condemns this trick as deception and folly (4174–75), although it could equally be seen as an anamorphotic distortion of Melior's enchantment and seduction of him. Foiled, the mother provides Partonopeu with an inextinguishable lantern and prevails on him straightforwardly to disobey Melior's command. The bishop, co-conspirator with the mother, warns Partonopeu that he may be horrified at what the lantern discloses, "por ço que lais est li maufés" (4476, "because the evil one is ugly"). Mother and bishop are already voyeurs, speculating on the terrors that Partonopeu will unmask. We in the audience may be implicated too.

The moment of truth arrives, and it is predictably anticlimactic:

> Quant Parthonopeus l'a sentue
> et set qu'ele est trestote nue,
> le covertoir a loing jeté,
> si l'a veüe o la clarté
> de la lanterne qu'il tenoit.
> A descovert nue le voit;
> mirer le puet et veïr bien
> c'onques ne vit si bele rien.
>
> (4523–30)

When Partonopeu felt her and knew her to be completely naked he threw the blanket right back and looked at her by the light of the lantern he was holding. He saw her nakedness revealed; he can gaze upon her and truly see that he never saw such a beautiful creature.

This outcome is absolutely unremarkable. After all, Partonopeu has been sharing Melior's bed for years: he must know she is not monstrous and that there is, in a sense, "nothing to see." On the other hand, this "nothing" turns out to be catastrophic and traumatic. Partonopeu is confronted with the shame of his suspicions and his broken promise; Melior reproaches him bitterly and grieves at the loss of her magic powers, the full extent of which is only revealed now that they are lost forever; Partonopeu is threatened with death at the hands of her knights; and, at daybreak, he meets with dreadful embarrassment now that he is suddenly visible to all Melior's attendants and they to him. So long as she was unseen, Melior, like the stone in Yvain's ring, can draw all those around her into magical invisibility alongside her; but once she is seen, and seen to have nothing magical about her, then her surroundings collapse back into everyday visibility, and her realm becomes just another kingdom like that of France.

There is a complex and eerie logic to this sequence; probing it will suggest that the character of Partonopeu too has a perverse relation to the gaze. At first, we are invited to see the fairy as "castrated"; that is, when Partonopeu looks at her, he finds there is "nothing" monstrous about her. Simultaneously, however, we are led to believe that she really *did* have something remarkable (her "magic"), but now, thanks to his looking, she has lost it. What she has lost, however, is not just her powers, but her boy toy: exposed to public censure, Partonopeu has to leave, and she grieves for him as much as for her shattered magic. The successive equations of absence of anything to see = absence of magic = absence of lover indicate that Partonopeu is, at some level, identified as the originary absence which Lacan calls "the phallus."

In fetishism, as we saw in Chapter 5, the fetishist's relation to the (maternal) phallus is one of identification. Lacan's Seminar IV, *La Relation d'objet*, explains the root of all the perversions in the way the child uses the maternal phallus as guarantor and support of his own imaginary self. The gradual realization that this magical object does not exist precipitates perverse reactions (192–93). Partonopeu's role as Melior's lover, considered in this framework, is to give her the phallus, already fantasized as hers, in the form of himself: all the magic she has woven around him makes him the manifestation of her omnipotence.[21] That is why, when "gazed at" by the magic objects, he is not discomfited but fortified: they are so many images of his magical worth whose dancing attendance invokes the phallus's fragile balance of presence and absence. "The point is to see where it is and where it isn't. It's never really present where it is, it's never really entirely absent from where it isn't" (*Relation d'objet*, 193).

An uncanny mixture of presence and absence also marks the scene of Partonopeu as voyeur, in which Partonopeu is located not just as phallus but also as gaze. Unlike Yvain's spying on the Lady of the fountain, Partonopeu's gaze is explicitly transgressive. Caught in the act, he switches from being the magic one who spies out his own (non-)existence to being the object of a public outcry, vilified and denounced (4841–44). The whole scene corresponds remarkably closely with Lacan's account of voyeurism:

> The gaze is this object lost and suddenly refound in the conflagration of shame, by the introduction of the other. Up to that point, what is the subject trying to see? He is trying to see, make no mistake, the object as absence. [. . .] What [the voyeur] is looking for is not, as one says, the phallus—but precisely its absence, hence the pre-eminence of certain forms as objects of his search. (*Four Fundamental Concepts*, 182; cf. *Relation d'objet*, 271–72)

In a further reversal, at the end of this scene, Partonopeu magically resumes the phallic role, becoming the object which captivates all the women's attention as they cluster round, goggling at his beauty and eventually enraptured by it (4863–69).

The triangular structure described here, whereby Melior is distraught and deprived of her powers by Partonopeu's gaze, Partonopeu is mortified and then flattered by the gaze upon him of her attendants, and the attendants are seduced by his looks, situates Partonopeu at the center of the scopic field, a perverse, fetishistic presence involved at once in prying and display, and showing up, in his own contradictions, the deficiencies in the other (female) subjects.[22]

The love of Partonopeu and Melior may occasionally be sublime. Melior is magnificent in her sorrows, and several of her speeches enforcing her prohibition, with the threat of death behind it, are remarkably fine. But despite the similarities between this love narrative and that of *Yvain*, *Partonopeu* tips further toward perversity than *Yvain* does. Both sublimity and perversion, however, involve asymmetry and contradiction. The next section observes how these are further emphasized by the way these two romances handle their lovers' separation and reconciliation.

Injunction and reconciliation in Yvain *and* Partonopeu

If the love born in the first part of these two romances does not flourish, this is not because it is asymmetrical; on the contrary, their conclusions suggest that the problem was rather that it was not asymmetrical enough.

In each romance, the lady places a single prohibition on her lover. Partonopeu, as we have seen, is forbidden to look at Melior; Yvain is given leave to depart by his Lady on condition he return by a stipulated date. When both lovers infringe the only condition which was placed in the way of their living happily ever after, they both go mad with distress and seek death in the wilderness, like men who have lost what is dearer to them than life itself. This suggests that these injunctions serve the function of the obstacle in courtly lyric, that of *"external hindrances that thwart our access to the object [. . .] precisely to create the illusion that without them, the object would be directly accessible"* (Žižek, *Metastases of Enjoyment*, 94, in italics in the original). The prohibition, that is, exemplifies the logic of the veil. It wills us to believe in the existence of an object behind it (a love which, but for the obstacles placed in its path, could be happy and harmonious). At the same time, it appeals to our knowledge of a literary tradition in which (as in "Lanval") such prohibitions are inevitably broken, alerting us to the impossibility of "the happily ever after." We know very well that the couples are going to be divided, but all the same we may be induced to believe that, if they hadn't been, they might have enjoyed perfect bliss. . . .

The breakdown of both relationships might be thought to draw attention to the inadequacies of the lost love which, in both romances, had seemed all too easily achieved: in *Yvain* through the hasty marriage of the widow to her husband's killer and in *Partonopeu* less ceremoniously still because love begins with consummation and only afterward progresses to those stages of courtship which usually come first.[23] But as in "Lanval," the conclusion to the sequence prohibition–infringement–reinstatement is a renewal of love which repeats in exaggerated form the structure of the one which it replaces. In both *Yvain* and *Partonopeu*, it is established on even more cursory and arbitrary grounds, with even greater asymmetry between the partners, than was at first the case.

When the injunctions are first broken, as in the heroes' first encounters with the land of the lady, there are gestures toward sublimity reinforced by religious allusion. The remorseful destitution of the two disobedient men, living crazed and naked in the wilderness, is particularly reminiscent of the story of Mary the Egyptian (and see also Hanning, "Audience," 24–27, on the religious resonance of Yvain's discovery by the damsels). In terms that anticipate Sade's distinction between the first and second deaths, Partonopeu longs not just to die but to die twice, as one death will not be enough to eradicate his guilty existence.

> Ki est vers s'amie revoiz,
> ne doit morir a une foiz;
> ne doit morir qu'il ne remuire.
> Ensi le doit la mors destruire:
> sovent soit vis et sovent mors.
> Molt ait dolors et pou confors!
> Ses cuers [l']ocie en ramembrant
> sa trahison et son dul grant.
>
> (5249–56)

The man who is convicted of a crime against his Lady should not die once; he should not die without dying a second time. Death should destroy him in this way: he should alternate between life and death. He should have much pain and little comfort. His heart should slay him by reminding him of his treachery and great grief.

When restored to health by magic ointment, Yvain continues the redemptive process by repeating in his behavior the love which he is apparently unable to remember by dedicating himself to the service of other ladies[24]; it is not until a couple of hundred lines from the end of the romance that he seeks reunion with his own. In *Partonopeu*, by contrast, the plot to reunite Partonopeu with Melior is mounted from the moment Uraque, Melior's sister, finds Partonopeu in the forest and begins to weave around him a tissue of lies. She persuades him to return with her by falsely reassuring him that Melior has forgiven him; she even writes forged letters to substantiate her deceit. Meanwhile, she goads Melior to remorse by falsely reporting that Partonopeu has gone completely mad and is as good as dead.

Thanks to her lies, the "truth" of each of the lovers is conveyed to the other. Uraque falsely convinces Partonopeu that Melior still loves him, which, as a result of her lies to Melior, eventually becomes the truth: Melior repents having dismissed Partonopeu and longs to be reunited with him. Had this lie not become true, then Uraque's lie to Melior that Partonopeu has died for love of her would have been the one which was true, for he would certainly have died without Uraque's help. Through Uraque, the two lovers receive their own message back in an inverted form.

In both *Yvain* and *Partonopeu*, the reconciliation relies on asymmetry because each lady is obliged to "choose" again the lover she had previously rejected. In both, too, asymmetry moves from the strictly visual field to that of language, from gaze to voice. Both men have embraced the social invisibility of incognito. The Lady of the fountain in *Yvain* is induced by Lunete to swear to reconcile the Knight of the lion with his lady, unaware that she is it and the Knight her repudiated husband. In *Partonopeu*, Melior promises her barons to marry the prizewinner of the three-day tournament which she hosts in the hope that the victor will be Partonopeu (cf. the similar plot in *Ipomedon*, discussed in Chapter 2), but the complexities of Partonopeu's incognito, imprisonment, and release on parole mean that initially not even her scheming sister Uraque knows whether he attends it. Midway through the fighting, Partonopeu reveals his presence. Suspense is prolonged, and it is only relieved when the African kings who act as tournament judges pick out Partonopeu as being handsomer than the other contenders. Melior thus is forcibly reunited with a man chosen for her in what can only be described as a gay beauty contest, a most bizarre ending to this constantly surprising romance.

Each lady, then, has her desire externalized (alienated) in the mechanisms of the plot and the desires of others. Each hero, through his incognito, is the hidden support of these mechanisms and desires. Although each hero contributes to the final reconciliation with his lady, the primary agent of this in both cases is a third party (Lunete in *Yvain* and Uraque and others in *Partonopeu*). The social invisibility conferred by incognito licenses the deceits and misrepresentations perpetrated on their behalf by their supporters with their ladies, who are presented with verbal distortions or anamorphoses that put in question any notion of a "true" perspective. Just as each hero was previously a hidden gaze supporting the scopic field, so now each is the concealed object around which the desire of his lady is obliged to turn, each lady being assured that "it is what she really wants." Indeed, there is a punitive edge to both plots, especially that of *Partonopeu*, whereby the manipulations to which the lady is subject are felt to be justly deserved (e.g., 9045–126 and cf. the self-castigation of La Fiere in *Ipomedon*). The move from sublimity to perversion, which I discerned in the episodes in which each couple "falls in love," is thus reenacted in their reconciliation. Again the balance between the two inclines more toward the perverse in *Partonopeu*, which might be read as suggesting that a man can get away with anything provided he is prepared to lie about it, and the woman, far from being entitled to impose conditions, should be grateful to have him. The truth of love is not equality and communication but imbalance and deceit. Lacan's aphorism was based on asymmetry in the visual field:

> When, in love, I solicit a look, what is profoundly unsatisfying and always missing is that—*You never look at me from the place from which I see you.*
>
> Conversely, *what I look at is never what I want to see.* (*Four Fundamental Concepts*, 103, original emphasis)

When sight is replaced by language, things only get worse.

Loving your enemy: the rhetoric of contradiction

To what extent do the contradictions of love in these romances correspond to their stylistic manipulation of contradictoriness? I conclude this chapter by considering how the balance between contradiction and resolution in the two romances illuminates the balancing act which they perform between the sublime and the perverse.

Yvain is famous for its ironic refinement and playful dialectic, and the style of *Partonopeu*, although the object of far fewer studies, is also a showcase of contradictoriness. Both romances translate into wordplay on the contraries "friend–enemy" and "love–hate" the fundamentally conflictual and asymmetric nature of the love relationship (or absence of relationship) which they depict. Given that a friend is by definition the one you love and an enemy the one you hate, what is one to make of a situation in which one finds oneself hating one's beloved, or loving the person who appears to be one's enemy?

In *Yvain*, this passage occurs when the hero is falling in love with the woman whose husband he has just killed. With every reason to hate him, even though he loves her, is she likely to become his *amie*? Would it be better for him *not* to love her? Reaching for dialectic's artful aids, Yvain argues through to a resolution:

> anchois amerai m'anemie,
> que je ne le doi pas haïr,
> se je ne veul Amours traïr:
> che qu'ele veut doi jë amer.
> Et me doit ele ami clamer?
> Oïl voir, pour che que je l'aim.
> Et je m'anemie le claim
> qu'ele me het, si n'a pas tort,
> car che qu'ele amoit li ai mort.
> Et dont sui je ses anemis?
> Nenil, chertes, mais ses amis,
> c'onques mais tant amer ne vaux.
> (1454–65)

Rather, I shall love my enemy for I ought not to hate her unless I mean to betray Love. That which Love wishes me to love, I should love. Yet should she call me her lover? Yes, truly, because I love her. Yet I call her my enemy, for she hates me, and she's not wrong to do so, because I have killed what she loved. And so am I her enemy? No, certainly not, but her lover, for I never desired to love anything so much.

The biblical reminiscence of the two opening lines ("Love thine enemy") crunches contraries together into paradox. Echoing the elements of the sublime in the depiction of the Lady as a spiritual beloved, these lines sweep erotic love up into divine love; Love is substituted for Christ as author of the commandment (1457). As one who loves her, subject to Love, Yvain is entitled to the name "lover." With a switch of perspective, however, he demonstrates that he is equally correct to call her his enemy (1460): what from one point of view may seem a lover (because of being in love) from another may seem an enemy (the perpetrator of a hostile act). The sufferings of lovers separated as a result of their being on different sides in hostilities is a common theme in romances (the *Roman de Troie*,

13725–26, exhibits the same wordplay). By specifying different contexts for the opposing terms, Yvain is able to tease apart, by the end of this passage, the paradoxical clash with which it began. Instead of loving his enemy, he will pursue the rational path of loving his beloved by subordinating one context (political enmity) to another (erotic love). (Such a desire to restore the orthodox in the teeth of the paradoxical lies at the heart of Aristotle's and Boethius's *Topics*; see Introduction.)

In *Partonopeu*, an analogous passage occurs in the discussion between Melior and her sister Uraque after Melior has dismissed Partonopeu. Melior, still in love with him, has submitted her fate to the outcome of the tournament. Uraque, sympathetic to the banished Partonopeu, makes a great deal of cruel capital out of Melior's desperate situation and states her own preference for retaining control of her own choices. The questions, where does choice lie? and to what extent can one have rational control? are thus part of the fabric of the episode (6769–73). Uraque, as yet innocent of love, protests that one should direct its effects, whereas Melior insists that is impossible:

> "Cant Deu plaira, ju amerai,
> mais ja mon ami ne harrai."
> Fait Melior: "Ce puet bien estre,
> mais cant amors avreis a mestre,
> ne de l'amer ne del haïr
> ne vos laira vostre plaisir."
> El li respont, si s'umilie:
> "Dont n'ai je soing de sa maistrie.
> S'amors fair haïr son ami,
> donc face amer son enemi."
> (6701–10)

"When God wills, I shall fall in love, but I shall never hate my lover." "That may be," Melior replies, "but when Love is your master, it will not allow you the choice between loving and hating." Uraque replies with a bow, "Then I don't care for its rule. If love makes one hate one's lover, then let it make one love one's enemy."

Uraque's preference is for consistency. Unlike Melior, she will love her lover and not hate him. As for Melior, Uraque argues, if Love is so nonsensical that it can make her hate her lover, then let it at least convince her that she is in love with the person she imagines she hates. By pitting one paradox against another and reversing the terms across the oppositions, one could at least end up with a semblance of rationality. The separation of levels achieved by Yvain's speech is not possible here because Partonopeu's contrary identities as friend and foe are both defined with respect to love (he is beloved because Melior loves him, and he is her enemy because, by breaking her injunction, he forfeited her love). For Uraque, then, the whole messy situation is a problem internal to love. Her argument works toward the biblical paradox likewise invoked by Yvain, but in a way that evinces disrespect for Love's mastery (6708); her overall contention is that contrariety is unreasonable, irrational, and should be done away with. Melior, however, disagrees: Love, she protests between Uraque's clever speeches, is not amenable to topical argument. You submit to the feelings it dictates, and that is it. It is beyond individual rational control.

The *Partonopeu* passage is thus very different from the one in *Yvain*. *Yvain* works toward a rational solution, whereas *Partonopeu* concludes that no such solution is possible. To the determination to reconcile contraries espoused by Yvain and Uraque is opposed the realization, on Melior's part, that she has no choice but to live with them. This is not because failing to resolve opposites is "illogical" but because logic is not at issue here; personal experience exceeds its dictates. Dialectic has met its limit and encountered its outside. One could say, of course, that the pervasive irony of *Yvain* also suggests an outside of dialectic. One senses that Chrétien finds it absurd to apply the machinery of one of the most prestigious intellectual disciplines of his day to the maunderings of a lovestruck knight. But the characters' and narrator's displays of dialectic float on a sea of unexpressed reservation; what lies beyond is a gap, an unsaid which relativizes that what is said (like the amputated lion's tail, the sliced-off horse, and the generally inadequate symbols which litter this text; see Haidu, *Lion-queue-coupée*). *Partonopeu*, by contrast, adopts the course of crowding the text with a whole series of incompatible responses to contradictoriness and is more similar in this respect to what we found in *Cligés*.

The prologue of *Partonopeu* exhibits with remarkable distinctness the plait of contradictoriness (to invoke the metaphor of Chapter 1) because it starts by interweaving strands which self-evidently stem from the lyric tradition on the one hand and the *romans antiques* on the other. It lurches from the oriole's lyric effusions, in which love's contrary states are (parodically?) superimposed:

> et chante de lointaine amor,
> et ramentoit douce dolor . . .
> Ceste chançon aim jo et has,
> car anui me fait et solas:
> solas de m'amor [r]amenbrer,
> anui quant pens del consirer,
> (53–60)

and sings of distant love, remembering sweet pain. I love this song and hate it, for it brings me torment and pleasure: pleasure at being reminded of love, torment when I am weighed down by longing,

to (likewise parodic?) enunciations of the principle of discriminating opposites:

> En nul escrit n'a nule rien
> ne senefit u mal u bien;
> li max i est que on l'eschiut,
> li biens que on en bien l'aliut.
> Mal et bien i doit on trover
> por conoistre et por deviser.
> (107–12)

There is nothing in any text which does not signify either good or bad. The bad is there to be shunned, the good to be welcomed. One should find good and bad there, in order to recognize and distinguish them.

In a third strand, we are enjoined to transform the bad into the good by following the example of the bee which can draw honey from nettles. This third strand differs from the other two by implying intellectual movement between contraries, the dynamic of arguing from one to another (119–34). The reader is exhorted to draw the wise out from the foolish (125–28), as there will be both bad and good in the story that follows (130)—it is up to us to turn one into the other. The prologue thus advances three ways in which we might approach contradictoriness and leaves us to puzzle over their mutual incompatibility.

These are also instanced in the narrator himself, who frequently interjects into the narrative. Sometimes he asks us to observe the difference between his own situation or behavior as a lover and those of his protagonists (and so "divide good from bad"; see, e.g., 1871–86, 4048–52, 4543–48, 7611–16). At other times, he betrays his own lack of control over precisely such distinctions:

> Segnor, ne vos anuit por Deu,
> se jo relais Parthonopeu
> et paroil de ce dont plus pens,
> car o soit o folie o sens,
> u as dolor, la est tes dois;
> u as amor, cele part vois;
> le main met on a la dolor,
> et les iex u on a amor.
> (3441–48)

Sirs, in God's name don't be annoyed if I leave Partonopeu again and speak of that which most preoccupies me, for whether it be wise or foolish, your finger is where the pain is and you look in the direction that you love. Everyone puts his hand to pain and his eyes to where he feels love.

The narrator doesn't say he cannot distinguish sense from folly, but he makes it clear that it doesn't help a lover to be able to do so. In another passage, although at first he insists on separating beauty from chastity, which he treats as contraries (beautiful women should not be chaste and chaste women should not be beautiful), he then admits that his own lady combines both qualities (6257–96; cf. *Troie*, 13479). He likewise praises the fact that men are always deluded as to their ladies' merit and fail to distinguish between contrary qualities, because otherwise they would all fall in love with the same woman (only he, he says with tongue firmly in cheek, loves an "objectively" worthy object):

> Por cest m'est vis qu'il est molt mielz
> qu'on [s]oit[25] al choisir engeigniez
> et qu'on les aint en tos parages,
> beles, laides, foles et saiges.
> (9239–42)

For this reason it seems to me preferable to be deceived in one's choice and to love women of all conditions, beautiful, ugly, foolish, and wise.

Elsewhere again the narrator invokes a dynamic interaction between opposites, as when he speaks of the transformations wrought by love on men's worth; for this reason, women are under a moral obligation to love (3424–48). His position on the separation of contraries is thus itself subject to contrariety: sometimes they should be distinguished, sometimes they can't be, sometimes they oughtn't to be, sometimes they interact. As a result, the narrative is constantly being interrupted and commented upon by a voice which continues the plait of contradictoriness initiated in its prologue.

In addition to their internal inconsistency, the narrator's interventions are also marked by their self-interest: whatever line he takes on contradictoriness, we may be sure it will serve to promote his own worth as the most ill-treated, adoring, and deserving of lovers. That the whole romance is being narrated to further his courtship of his own lady emerges at the end when he decides to break off at this point, having exerted himself in vain, announcing that he will only pick up the story again if his lady winks at him (10607–24). (The existence of a continuation may or may not suggest that she did so.) The earliest interventions are mainly geared to comparisons between the narrator and Partonopeu: he is superior to, but less fortunate than, his protagonist. The images the narrator gives of passion overriding sense and folly ("putting one's hand to the pain and looking at what one loves," 3445–46, cited above) are clearly chosen to echo Partonopeu's first touching Melior's resisting body and then violating the taboo on looking at her. (Conversely, the narrator's difficulties in applying the categories of *sens* and *folie* are echoed by Partonopeu; see 1426, 4175 ff., etc.; although Melior admits to the same problem, 4705, 4716–17.) As the romance progresses, however, these narratorial interjections increasingly aim to police women's behavior, enjoin their docility toward men, and incline Melior to relent. From being the butt of unfavorable comparisons, Partonopeu is now a figure whose interests the narrator actively pursues in tandem with his own, out of masculine solidarity and dislike for women who refuse men (see especially 6257–96, 8015–68, 8436–54).

Within the narration of events, as opposed to the interventions of the narrator, it is striking how effects of contradictoriness are clustered around

Melior rather than Partonopeu. She gives contradictory accounts of Partonopeu's presence in Chef d'Oire, claiming first to be outraged by it, then admitting she lured him there. Her taboo has a paradoxical ring reminiscent of the work of the very early troubadours: it is by not seeing her that Partonopeu will prove his love for her (4255–58), and his subsequent declaration, "Une dame aim c'onques ne vi" (4449, "I love a lady that I never saw"), quotes from the riddle poems of Guilhem de Peitieu and Jaufré Rudel (see Chapter 4). Like the characters in *Cligés*, Partonopeu is called upon to solve love's riddle, but in his case the answer seems to be, "woman as a nexus of contradiction."

Melior is the occasion of a number of "set piece" passages which revolve around contradiction. When Partonopeu infringes her prohibition, Melior complains at length of her reversal from bliss to woe (4735–66; Partonopeu's lament occupies a mere two lines, 4815–16). The separation of contraries is here assured by their temporal succession (*first* good, *then* bad); there is no concern with synthesis, no harmony of opposites. As the balance of power shifts in Partonopeu's favor, however, Melior is driven to admit the simultaneous experience of contraries. An example of this is the *ami–anemi* speech analyzed above where, despite Uraque's arguments for rational resolution, Melior remains subject to inner division. Whereas the conflation of contraries can serve the narrator's purpose (he can praise his lady for being both beautiful and chaste, for instance), its effect on Melior is to place her, as we saw, "beyond the edge" of reason (to invoke the theme of Chapter 3). Later again, when she is afraid that Partonopeu is not going to be awarded the prize at the tournament, another passage exposes contrariety as symptomatic of her *mal*: a word that means "illness," "suffering," "hurt," but also the "bad" we were enjoined to distinguish from the "good" and consequently shun (107–112):

> El cuer li tient li malz pennoz,
> li malz humles, li orguilloz,
> li frans, li fel, li haz, li baz,
> crüex et pius et liez et laz,
> et drois et tors, ciux et voians,
> muz et parlans, sorz et oians,
> amers et dolz, et bons et malz,
> grans et petits, lenz et isnelz.
> Ses mals est et delz et delis,

> travalz, repoz, perte, profiz,
> honte et honor, sens et folie,
> afaitemens et vilonie.
> Bien duet li cuers estre pennez
> qui de tel mal est affolez;
> bien doit en soi estre divers
> qui mals est si tor[s] et travers.
> (9201–17)

> The tormenting pain fastens on her heart: biddable, arrogant, noble, treacherous, high, low, vicious and upright and merry and weary, straight and crooked, blind and sighted, dumb and speaking, deaf and able to hear, bitter and sweet, good and bad, bold, cowardly, true and false, intimate and stranger, ugly and beautiful, large and small, slow and fast. Her pain is grief and delight, effort and rest, loss and gain, refinement and coarseness. A heart should indeed suffer which is destroyed by such pain; it should indeed be divided inwardly when its pain is so twisted and crossed.

This systematic and cruel accumulation of antitheses with which Melior's *mal* is described recalls (or, given the uncertain date of *Partonopeu*, anticipates) late troubadours such as Raimbaut de Vaqueiras and Peire Vidal. Far from rewarding with exaltation, as does the contrariety of the troubadours of the 1160s and 1170s, it instead punishes with mental anguish and the degeneration of reason.

What inferences can be drawn from this survey of contradictoriness in *Partonopeu*? A gamut of attitudes toward it is deployed humorously and self-servingly by the narrator, who derives as many benefits as he can from their potential for separation, conflation, or progression. But the same gamut is also used punitively against the central figure of the Lady, to imply that she suffers deservedly from deficiency and inner divisions. Contradictions do not "hurt" the narrator who is as though "filled" by their variety. However, the same contradictions are used to torture Melior and to mark her inner emptiness and division. They resonate with the earlier theme of her "castration" to mark her as a divided self, a representation of the barred subject $\cancel{S}$, stripped of content and reduced to an aching structure. Melior comes off worse than the narrator even though she, unlike him, is united with her loved one.

The narrator does admit to the potential of inner division. His own Lady is a source of anxiety. What does she want of him? How is he to gratify her? But he manages to find grounds for reassurance, parrying and covering over the threat. He seems to be saying, "I know that I am this hopelessly split ('castrated') creature and that the I which speaks is spoken by the language of the Other which both overwhelms me and yet also deprives me, refusing to take account of something about me; but I am going to cling on to that something which is left out and show you that it really *is* something, so that I am not hopelessly split after all!" (cf. Introduction, 33). The fabulous object—*objet a* in Lacanian terminology—which makes him so complacent is the romance in which he displays himself as author and as lover: he seeks to persuade his Lady that he and it are the objects of her desire. In manipulating his fantasy in this gratifying way, he struts seductively before his wider audience as well.

Within the fantasy itself, the role of leftover object, the *objet a*, is the position most closely approximated to by Partonopeu. As we have seen, Partonopeu always contrives to be both there and not there, included and excluded, invisible, exiled, incognito, and yet loved, mourned, desired. Comparison with him serves to bolster the narrator's self-satisfaction while at the same time his role shows women (in the person of Melior) what they are missing, and what they deserve. By identifying with these objects— Partonopeu and his story—the narrator and his audience become object-instruments for the gratification and punishment of women. They serve as a pretext for the enjoyment of satisfaction (on the part of the narrator's Lady) and for the even greater enjoyment of withholding satisfaction (from Melior, though she too will be gratified at the end). As Žižek puts it when explaining the position of the pervert in Lacan's "Kant avec Sade":

> by means of occupying himself in the place of the object—of making himself the agent-executor of the Other's will—he avoids the division constitutive of the subject and transposes his division upon his other. (*Everything*, 234).

The analysis of contradictoriness in *Partonopeu*, in other words, supports a reading of the text as structured both according to the formula of fantasy $ \$ \lozenge a $, and as perversely structured, because it shows both how the contradictions of the romance as object can "plug" the divisions in the subject, and conversely how that object, in particular its protagonist, can expose those same divisions in the subject of the Lady. To refer a final time to Lacan's aphorism, the romance invites "us" to look at her in a way quite different from the way it invites her to look at "us."

The inclination toward perversity is less marked in *Yvain*. Here divisions within the subject are not exposed to the same extent; instead, a rhetoric of resolution floats uneasily on a sea of irony. Are we persuaded of the wholeness of the fantasy? Is Yvain a sublime object of chivalry, plugging any subjective anxieties we may have? Or does a desire to punish the Lady of the fountain for her rejection of him inform the conclusion of the narrative, making her appear as the divided subject, with Yvain as object-instrument of both her come-uppance and our enjoyment? And what of the self-effacing narrator around whose alienation from his narrative our own enjoyment turns? The romance maintains a tantalizing balance between options, as the divergent readings of generations of critics attests.

⁓

This chapter began by citing the link which Lacan and, following him, Žižek have discerned between the psychic structures of courtly texts and those of today. This link, for them, consists in the damaging effect of a superego which obliges us to sublimate our drives under the impetus of "law," and then invites us to find enjoyment in the very act of sacrificing enjoyment. The first part of this process results in the generation of sublime objects. A sublime object captures for us in an imaginary form (one with which we can identify), the uncanny of the real enjoyment beyond it, but it does so with the support of a symbolic mandate, what Lacan calls "law." The effect of the sublime object is to reinforce the law by commandeering belief. The second leg of the process involves perversion, which is an extreme form of alienation. It involves abstracting oneself from the possibility of being the subject of enjoyment by positioning oneself as an object which does not exist (*objet a*).

In the *Ethics* Seminar and in "Kant avec Sade," Kant is represented as a key figure in the development of both sublimation and perversion. Kant's ethical imperative obliges us to accord immense value to it and to find satisfaction in subjecting ourselves to it, even though its effect is to deprive us of personal satisfaction. Medieval poets, according to Lacan, anticipated this double move. Although Lacan chooses a striking example to comment on—Arnaut Daniel's *sirventes* about whether or not a true lover should perform cunnilingus—what he seems to have in mind here is a very widespread understanding of courtly love as deferment and frustration: a kind of Lumpen-courtly love, the "have and have not" of Spitzer's famous formula, in which adulation of the Lady goes hand in hand with self-punishment and self-denial.

In this chapter, I have deliberately chosen mainstream courtly texts which, through their treatment of contradictoriness, tug in different ways at the interconnecting structure of perversion and sublimity. The presence of discourses of awe, spirituality, guilt, exaltation, and the backdrop of violence and death, ensure a foothold for the sublime in both *Yvain* and *Partonopeu*. But I think Lacan may be right that the position of subject of enjoyment is not their preferred option. Rather, the position which protagonists and readers are encouraged to adopt is that of object, and specifically the place of a hole or lack: a fetish, a gaze, an absent presence around which other things move. Yvain is less passive than Partonopeu; but in neither romance is it clear that agency is rewarded, whereas in both, enjoyment is held at bay by taboos and punishments. Texts such as these realize the trends which I have discerned in previous chapters. I have talked about fetishism or incipient fetishism in "Lanval," the *romans antiques*, and *Cligés*; and about abstraction and objectification in the path of the law in later hagiography and *Cligés*. The bizarre representation of love in *Yvain* and *Partonopeu*, texts which were imitated and translated across Europe, confirms the existence, in the last third of the twelfth century, of courtly (or contradictory) literature in a form that would persist for centuries.

Conclusion

This book has described the operations of contradiction in three interrelated genres of twelfth-century literature from the perspectives of medieval thought and of Lacanian psychoanalysis. It has suggested ways in which the emergence of mainstream courtly texts reflects the intellectual climate of the twelfth century, and it has also suggested how the structures contained in these texts correspond with some of those discerned by Lacan. In this way, it seeks to illumine not only the invention of a literature deploying courtly themes and intended as a form of courtly diversion, but also the conditions of its success and continued survival. Although these two approaches, medieval and modern, present similarities, they also differ. The fact that mechanisms of opposition (contrariety, relation, privation, and negation) inhere in language makes it inevitable that Lacan's address to contradiction will share some features with that of medieval philosophy, but Lacan is too obviously a post-Hegelian thinker for his approach to be reducible to pre-Hegelian terms, notably in his tolerance of self-contradiction within the framework of rational inquiry. The literary texts in this study occupy the role of "piggy in the middle," receptive to two different analytical systems which are not, themselves, wholly reconcilable. The first part of this conclusion reflects on how this convergence between medieval and modern patterns of contradictoriness is realized in courtly texts. The effect of this convergence, I have been arguing, is that through the medium of courtly literature, the contradictoriness of twelfth-century thinking is worked upon in such a way as to make it capable not only of attracting medieval audiences, but also of exerting a continuing influence today. Accordingly, the second part of this conclusion picks out the major themes of this book from the point of view of a retroactive history: what features of continuing significance has this study of contradictoriness highlighted in medieval literature? As a first step, I will summarize the argument which successive chapters have unfolded.

The mutual attraction exercised by about 1170 between the two secular genres of lyric and romance conduces to the emergence of a prestigious "courtly literature" whose procedures gradually influence hagiography. From the perspective of medieval thought, what characterizes this courtly poetry is the way it has absorbed the procedures of its predecessors and, in particular, found a means of combining what seem characteristically religious patterns of thought together with what looks like enjoyment of argument for its own sake. Although the influence of secular logic does not follow a simple progression, it is felt on all genres by the end of the twelfth century. We see an increasing tendency toward negativity manifested in the way that texts deny, or imply that they deny, their own apparent content. This makes for an uneasy balance between earnestness and irreverence which is at odds with the spirit of medieval philosophy, but remains explicable as the playful exploitation of its techniques (Chapter 1). The trope of "high" and "low" allows practices of contradictoriness to migrate across genres, permuting through modes of exaltation, pessimism, cynicism, comedy, hilarity, and even rationalism. Again, religious and nonreligious texts interact together in a shared inheritance, even though the very similarities between them can also underline their divergence; once more, the forging of a kind of coalition between the secular genres of lyric and romance emerges as historically significant (Chapter 2). Interrelations between religious and secular traditions also emerge when one tries to capture moments of transition in different genres' treatment of contradiction. In different ways, all use the tensions between contradiction and resolution to expose the limits of rationalism, with effects ranging from the earnest to the frivolous (Chapter 3).

The pressure exercised by courtly texts on the limits of reason draws our attention to dangerous areas of experience: the riddles of creativity, sexuality, incest, and death. From Chapter 4 onward, I have leaned increasingly on the teachings of Lacan, because his own riddling language both parallels that of medieval poetry and deals with these same issues. Lacan's analysis also enables us to analyze the mechanisms whereby these riddles are geared to the production of objects, both within the texts and in the form of the texts themselves. All of the various psychic structures discussed by Lacan in the volumes of the Seminar on which I have drawn consist in some form of dependency by the subject on the object. An imaginary construct which both conceals an underlying absence and parries an underlying threat, the object is thrown up between the subject and the Other in such a way as falsely to reassure as to the solidity and meaningfulness of both; hence Lacan's comment, quoted in the Introduction, that "man thinks with his object" (*Four Fundamental Concepts*, 62). The analyses presented in Chapters 4 to 7 converge in attributing a major role in literary texts to the object in this sense; that is, they present medieval authors and audiences as likewise "thinking with their object." The object with which the narrator thinks in *Partonopeu*—his romance—actually displays within its fiction the precedence accorded to the object in supporting the divisions of the subject.

I have discerned two principal ways of describing the object in religious texts: as phobic (in miracles of the Virgin; Chapter 5) and as sublime (in hagiography; Chapter 6). In both cases, the object is defensive. The phobic object holds the threat of castration at bay by means of a dense symbolic covering; the sublime object is held up to block, but also to meet, the destructive drive. By its proximity to the real which it wards off, the sublime object presents itself as momentous, awesome, and enlightening: as a key to meaning and value. In the courtly texts which can be seen as secular parallels of (or developments from) these religious works, the work of sublimation—and thus the production of sublime objects—can certainly be discerned. Indeed, some courtly texts (the riddle poems examined in Chapter 4; *Yvain* in Chapter 7) lay bare the mechanisms of sublimation. However, there is also a shift toward perversity. The phobic relation can tip into fetishism ("the perversion of perversions" [Lacan, *Relation d'objet*, 194]), as I argued in the case of Marie de France's *Lais* (Chapter 5). In *Cligés* (Chapter 6), and in *Yvain* and *Partonopeu* (Chapter 7), it is rather the sublime which shifts over into the perverse. The sublime in religious texts may also be drawn into a degree of perversity (Chapter 6). These various object structures are also characterized by contradictoriness, as comparison between medieval texts and Lacan's paradoxical prose amply demonstrates (Chapter 4).

How can two such different discourses as those of medieval philosophy and Lacanian analysis be successfully applied to medieval literature? How, that is, does medieval literature mediate between the two different ways of plotting contradiction, medieval and modern, which prevail in the first and second parts of this study respectively? Let me start by saying that, despite the formulation in that last sentence, this is a not a book of two halves. One theme which runs all through this book is that of the literary enigma or riddle, found in *Ipomedon* (Chapter 2), the riddles of Chapter 4, *Cligés*, and *Partonopeu*. Chapters 4 to 7 deal with many of the same texts as those discussed in Chapters 1 to 3. Throughout these later chapters, I have cited practices of contradictoriness which are the same as those found in the texts treated earlier. *Cligés* and *Partonopeu* especially emerge as display cases for a range of medieval approaches. Conversely, the earlier chapters (1, 2, and 4) draw attention to the way literature comes to constitute itself, by the end of the century, as its own object: as a set of traditions to be played with, undermined, or denied. The way the tropes of religious writing are adapted by secular authors (Chapters 1 and 2) would lend itself to an analysis similar to that conducted in Chapters 5 and 6. The similarities between *Partonopeu* and *Ipomedon* are especially striking. Not only does Ipomedon, like Partonopeu, exploit the use of incognito to abstract himself from social visibility and to expose his beloved to reproach and torment, he also positions himself as an object of admiration/ridicule/desire for the whole of the romance's cast of characters. If Alexis (in *L*) is sublime, Ipomedon is surely perverse, while the ambiguity attaching to Lancelot in the *Charrete* could be read as poising him equivocally, like Yvain, between the two structures.

There are several features of courtly texts that dispose them to serve as a meeting ground between medieval and Lacanian accounts of contradiction. First, the self-consciousness with which the medieval texts display their debts to multiple traditions of thought marks their "thematization" of contradiction in a way similar to that found in Lacan. Second, the combining of different approaches to contradiction in these texts anticipates

Lacan's concentration on the object as the point where the various potential forms of contradiction envisaged by his teaching coalesce. In particular, the way romances accumulate different kinds of contradictoriness provides them with an abundance of resonance (they resume several traditions of thought as well as other genres); but at the same time, it risks evacuating meaning through the clash of incompatible discourses. This alternation between "fullness" and "emptiness" chimes with Lacan's focus on the object as both presence and absence, fullness and lack, reality and lure. Finally, in my analyses of *Cligés* and *Partonopeu* in particular, I show how the fantasy structure (analyzed from a Lacanian perspective) of the romance is paralleled and picked out by the patterns of contradiction (analyzed from a medieval perspective). Both point to the positioning of the object as an ideal space around which law and the drives revolve.

Some readers may protest that I myself am simply constructing my objects retrospectively in conformity with my own theories; in my Introduction, I quoted a warning to this effect from Stanley Fish. According to this objection, psychoanalysis would inevitably find an application in medieval texts because it would reconstitute them according to its own expectations. If that were so, would I then also have redesigned the medieval thinkers I have read and the learned discussions by other scholars which I have drawn upon, in conformity with the same (or a different) model? Although from one perspective the irreducible differences between Lacanian analysis and medieval philosophical reflection create a gap in my argument, from another they sustain a sense of alterity and a potential for dialogue between past and present. It is this possibility of dialogue which opens up the potential for courtly literature to have been an agent of change. Žižek insists that rather than *constructing* the past, we *construe* it retroactively (how else?), positing our present as the cause of the effects delineated in it: "The anatomy of man offers the key to the anatomy of the ape, as Marx put it" (*Metastases*, 89).

Reviewing the arguments advanced in this book from this retroactive perspective, three elements stand out as historically important: the interrelation between religious and secular works and the ambiguity of the resultant culture; the emphasis on the object rather than the subject as the center of cultural and psychic operations; and the nature of enjoyment. I will end this conclusion by commenting briefly on all three.

In my Introduction, I invoked Bezzola's account of how courtly literature arises from the interaction of secular and clerical influences within court life to justify including hagiography among the genres covered. Bezzola's research, more detailed than that of any of his predecessors', shows this interaction to be not one of simple collaboration between clerks and knights, but one admixed with tensions and rivalries; social historians since have confirmed and fleshed out this view. Neither group, moreover, was homogeneous. Knights ranged from magnates to hired muscle, from seniors with families and estates to unmarried juniors with no prospects. Clerical culture ranged from delight in antique learning to exploration of theological doctrine and provided courtly society with personnel from menial clerks, to administrators and priests, to diplomats and prelates. With their differing levels of education, these court clerics would feel all manner of conflicting loyalties: some to the liberal arts, others to the Church as an institution, some to their Christian beliefs, and others to their secular employers. Court life, then, offered infinite possibilities for alliance, factionalism, dissimulation, disagreement, and negotiation. At any point, a courtier might be obedient to one loyalty or obligation only at the cost of flouting another. The multiple and conflicting systems of law represented in many courtly texts—from the political impasse in which supporters of Eteocles and Polinices find themselves (in the *Thebes*), to the debacle between Arthur's law and the rule of the *fée* (in "Lanval"), to the complex stacking of one rule on another which it transgresses (in *Cligés*)—are also surely a reflection of this complex courtly reality. The various different ways of constructing hierarchy—spiritual, moral, social, material—permit slippage and equivocation between what may seem to be primarily clerical, and primarily secular, systems of value (Chapter 2). No wonder courtly culture is ambiguous, enabling modern-day critics to draw contrary conclusions from it: for example, both that courtliness is a strategy on the part of the clergy to tame and confine the ill-regulated behavior of a warrior aristocracy,[1] and that it is a strategy on the part of a traditional aristocracy to evade the increasing control of the clergy.[2]

Twelfth-century vernacular literature, addressed to both groups and composed by members of both, exploits the complexity of this social mix. Courtly romance and lyric texts insert human protagonists and their loves in narrative or rhetorical frames evocative of mystical or other religious writings. These same texts deploy dialectic to elaborate on and sometimes ridicule the result. These texts are "humanist" in their attraction toward antique stories and skills; in their pleasure in the exercise of human intellect; in their placing of lover and Lady in literary structures elsewhere occupied by God or his saints. The slight adjustments of structure between miracles and *lais* (Chapter 5) or between hagiography and romance (Chapter 6) demonstrate the proximity and overlap between what we traditionally call "religious" and "secular" works. Courtly texts which thereby enfold secular concerns within clerical structures might seem to some audiences to be inclusive of both clerical and nonclerical elements in the court. To some, they might seem to incline to the side of secular interest over clerical values by the apparent complacency with which they calque secular practices, like love and chivalry, on religious models. But to yet others, they might seem to point to the discrepancy between religious models and the secular uses to which they are put, and thereby to ironize the limitations of merely human aspirations and the failure of the unenlightened intellect to grapple with ethical issues. Irony, indeed, provides a flexible framework for this ongoing negotiation between clerical and profane interest, permitting the apparently simultaneous commitment and disengagement so typical of medieval courtly texts.

Conversely, "religious" texts are increasingly overtaken by secular preoccupations. We have seen how they become more rationalist, more attentive to the concerns of secular existence, and more open to irony; how they may even be drawn toward perverse enjoyment. In the late twelfth-century *Life of St. Eustace*, the first vernacular version of this saint's life to survive, romance influence is manifest in the story of a knight exiled from home and identity who is then marvelously recognized and restored to favor. In the thirteenth century, the influence of secular literature on hagiography increases. The literature of medieval courts, then, encourages a gradual erosion of the categories of "religious" and "secular," even though such erosion encounters periodic resistance. (The dispute between Henry II and Thomas Becket, reflected in the two *Lives of Becket* discussed in Chapter 1, exemplifies this double process.) The result has been the gradual humanization and secularization of culture: two separate but linked processes which have proceeded unevenly ever since the Middle Ages.

The multiple overlapping and conflicting values and rules of court life, the overlapping and conflicting possibilities of self-identification, inevitably result in contradictory subject positions and incompatible demands on the object. The rise of the "object" in these circumstances is another instance in which this study furnishes a retroactive history. Feminist critics have argued that when—as is most usual—the subject of this process is a man, then the most likely object and major casualty is women. When I began this study, I expected to find that the contradictory makeup and objectification of the courtly text would coincide with those of the courtly Lady. A telling model for this coincidence is described by Teresa Brennan in *History after Lacan*, in the process which she terms "passification": a strategy whereby men exercise control simultaneously over women, goods, and the symbolic order.

According to Brennan's account, when a male lover addresses idealized love objects and fantasizes control over them, he embarks on a double move whereby, on the one hand, "the ego desires to make the other into a thing; and arrogates to itself the right to form or shape it, to objectify it, to make it passive" (*History*, 55) and, on the other, so as to anticipate and forestall a return of this treatment upon itself, sets out to appease and pacify the other by adopting itself a passive and objectlike stance. Brennan explains Lacan's analysis of how, in this situation, "woman is the symptom of man": she is made into a contradictory object in order to bear the burden of male subjectivity (to be, in other terms, the object with which he thinks). The woman is exalted and meshed into the discourse of the ideal; but she is also denigrated, policed, reprehended, and generally "passified" (62). The payoff is, then, that this contradiction, embodied in the woman, effects a link between the imaginary and symbolic orders and gives man the fantasy that, if he controls the one, he controls the other (56–75). This fantasy is characteristic of what Brennan calls "the ego's era": an epoch which she identifies as stretching from the early modern period to the present day, but which, if extended back to the Middle Ages, would provide another continuity for our retroactive history.[3]

In order to explain why it should be the woman that gets saddled with this ungrateful role of object, Brennan locates Lacan's "fundamental fantasy" within what she calls the "foundational fantasy." This she delineates in the first instance by identifying a different object—the commodity—as its symptom (*History*, 90 ff.). The features of this fantasy are the desire for instant gratification, the preference for visual and "object"-oriented thinking this entails, the desire to be waited upon, the envious desire to imitate the original, the desire to control the mother, and to devour, poison and dismember her, and to obtain knowledge by this process. (Brennan, *History*, 101)

Of interest here is the combination of three things: the widespread reduction of objects to the status of things (commodities) which are both cultivated and abused; the association between such objects and the mother; and the sense that control over objects is, at the same time, control over knowledge. The commodity too, on this analysis, yokes together imaginary and symbolic orders, offering the illusion that we, as controlling agents, control our material environment—that the world is under our mastery. Thus Brennan argues that, from the psychical fantasy of woman, man proceeds to a more general, psychotic relation to the environment.

Lacan himself traces this obsessive, controlling view of the object back to medieval love:

> It may seem to you that it's a curious and unusual detour to resort to a medieval theory of love in order to introduce the question of psychosis. It is, however, impossible to conceive the nature of madness otherwise. (*Psychoses*, 253)

And support for reading twelfth-century texts along the lines that Brennan suggests is forthcoming from the works studied here. For example, the plots of "Lanval" and *Partonopeu* can certainly be seen as betraying a desire for instant gratification; as overvaluing the visual field (its value emphasized by its partial withdrawal in *Partonopeu*); as indulging the fantasy of being waited upon (in *Partonopeu* especially); as manipulating a figure of the mother (in the characters of the *fée*/Guenevere and the mother/Melior), both adoring and punishing her. Envy, tale-bearing, and a general atmosphere of paranoia do indeed seem to form part of the climate of twelfth-century courtly texts; "Lanval" again is a good example. And it may be the case that the relationships these texts describe do indeed fuel psychotic developments.

There are a number of reasons, however, why I have not followed Brennan's lead. Her analysis derives its account of the "fundamental fantasy" from Lacan's Seminar XX (*Encore*). In this seminar, Lacan again appeals to courtly love: this time, in order to explore the role of woman as other to man and to illustrate his contention that the sexual relation does not exist (e.g., *Encore*, 44). The Lady is defined by her difference from the man—that is, her sexual difference: "The Other, in my terminology, can only be the Other sex" (*Encore*, 40, my translation). This is a very different analysis from that advanced in *The Ethics of Psychoanalysis*. In the *Ethics*, Lacan emphasizes that the Lady in courtly love is not the object because she is a woman; rather, the woman appears to be the Lady because she occupies the position of the object. Her "femininity" is largely without content: what confers on her the power, mystery, value, of Lady is her relation to the Thing:

> If the incredible idea of situating woman in the place of Being managed to surface, that has nothing to do with her as a woman, but as an object of desire. (*Ethics*, 214)

Of course, the two accounts differ only in emphasis; it would be foolish to deny that sexual difference is crucial to courtly texts. Nevertheless, the analysis in the *Ethics* strikes me as more persuasive than the later one in *Encore*.

One reason for this is the discovery which has surprised me in the course of writing this book—namely, that gender may arise as a secondary phenomenon in which the Lady's importance derives not from her being other to the man, but from her being positioned against the real of death which is his first and most significant Other. This is especially the case when she occupies the position of sublime object. For Lacan, the sublime is by definition related to the death drive; I have found no lack of examples where his account is appropriate to medieval texts. In the *romans antiques*, we also saw the object woman being interpellated—or interpellating—against the background of death. Of course, in the case of fetishism and voyeurism, the problematic of sexual difference and the threat of "castration" are what motivate the perverse structure. But even here death is at issue: written into the narrative of the gaze in *Yvain*, stalking the protagonist as a distant threat in "Lanval" and *Partonopeu*, courted and played with by the heroine of *Cligés*.[4]

Another reason for not seeing femininity as defining the object is that there are cases where the privileged object is not the Lady at all. Chapter 6 included among its sublime objects the bodies of male saints and warriors. Chapters 5 and 7 went further, suggesting that the object may be the protagonist. To say "man thinks with his object" does not exclude the possibility that it is the subject which is represented in the object: quite the reverse. When in *The Four Fundamental Concepts* Lacan discusses the child's game of *fort-da* with the cotton reel, he states that the reel which the child throws away and hauls back, thereby coming to terms with his mother's disappearances and returns, does not, as one might think, represent *her* movements. Rather, its opposition of absence and presence is to be conceived as applying to a small part of *himself*, as *objet a*: "it is in the object to which the opposition is applied in act that we must designate the subject" (Lacan, *Four Fundamental Concepts*, 62). Indeed, for Lacan, the ego is an object: a product of the subject's alienation in the Other. Thus interpellation, as we saw in Chapter 4, involves cultivating as object a certain ideologically desirable form of the ego, as well as fostering the subject's reliance on fantasy objects.

The practical consequence of this objectification–alienation of the subject is that the object in the courtly texts is very commonly not feminine at all, but masculine. Male protagonists, and the author, are offered up as objects for our desire. In texts where the male figure adopts the stance of pervert, the role of subject passes to the Lady; the split within her is that of her own castration, to which he may provide an answer, or which he may exploit to humiliate her further in her weakness. The promotion of masculine objects results in the queer ambiance of several of these late twelfth-century texts. Intense, homoerotic male friendships are (as Burgwinkle, "Knighting," shows) depicted within the plot of the *Eneas*, but they are solicited between narrator and character, audience and character, and between narrator and audience, in such texts as *Partonopeu* and *Ipomedon*. This may represent another path to the "ego's era" as described by Brennan, but it is the path not of psychosis but of the perversions: fetishism, voyeurism, homosexuality.[5]

By looking at the literary texts themselves as "objects" in one or another of these various structures (phobic, sublime, perverse), we can explain why they should engage the drives of their audiences, and hence their enjoyment. For Lacan, the drives are not a biological reality but already a part of the signifying system. It is understandable that texts which work upon their audience at the level of the drives should be capable of exerting a continuing influence on people's sensibility because "[the drive] embodies a historical dimension" which "is to be noted in the insistence that characterizes its appearances; it refers back to something memorable because it was remembered" (*Ethics*, 209). Cultural products like literature are a way of transmitting this signifying capacity of the drives in a memorable form.

In the ordinary functioning of desire, we are protected from awareness of the drives which underlie it by the profusion of distracting objects. By these means, Jason is kept happy, his mind diverted by the fleece, Medea, and all her many gifts to him, from the deathly course on which he is set (Chapter 4). Desire's job is to keep us on the move, according to the pleasure principle:

> The function of the pleasure principle is, in effect, to lead the subject from signifier to signifier, by generating as many signifiers as are required to maintain at as low a level as possible the tension that regulates the whole functioning of the psychic apparatus. (Lacan, *Ethics*, 119)

The domain "beyond the pleasure principle" (in the words of Freud's famous title) is that of the real. Lacan's interest in courtly love in the *Ethics* Seminar stems from the fact that he sees it as transgressing the pleasure principle, and as pointing beyond it. Medieval love poetry, he thinks, exposes the limitations of the way the pleasure principle meshes together desire and law. From the point of view of the symbolic order, we desire things by virtue of their being withheld from us, and the reason why the object is withheld is that it is prohibited. Desire is thus the inseparable consequence of law, its transgressive underside. But when medieval poets emphasize how truly unobtainable the love object is, they admit the impossibility of filling the space of the object of desire with anything other than an illusion. This admission makes the gap in the symbolic which desire seeks to fill—the place of the Thing—stand out as such (*Ethics*, 152). As a result, the law is seen in a new light: as a fiction whereby we pass off what is impossible as what is prohibited. The gap in the symbolic order is the place of the real, which, in its inhuman, alien monstrosity, infuses the symbolic with the rigor of the deathly, implacable drives. In portraying the lover as subject to an inflexible code of conduct and an intransigent and capricious Lady, "an inhuman partner" (*Ethics*, 150), love poetry draws attention to the rule of the drives beyond the law of desire. Love poetry thus obligingly performs the analysis Lacan himself is promoting, because it demystifies law and desire in favor of what lies beyond the pleasure principle. And this analysis is one which meets with support from medievalists. Lacan's formulations, "The object involved [in courtly love], the feminine object, is introduced oddly enough through the door of privation or of inaccessibility" (*Ethics*, 149), and "What man demands, what he cannot help but demand, is to be deprived of something real" (150), are strikingly similar to Scaglione's, that courtly texts reiterate "poem after poem, poet after poet, indeed, from country to country, generation after generation, a message that was familiar before it was restated. It amounted to saying: 'I want what I cannot get, I need what I will lack, I ask what I must be denied'" (*Knights*, 101).

One can of course find medieval examples of love's (or the Lady's) monstrous rule, but I myself am not persuaded that it is a common characteristic of courtly literature; the Ladies in the texts considered here all accord their lovers what they want in some way or other. The treatment meted out to the notion of law in the texts I have studied has rather served to expose, on the one hand, its deathly underside, and on the other, its fictionality. In the *romans antiques*, where the woman-as-object and the self-as-object are produced within structures of interpellation, in the context, that is, of a powerful symbolic mandate which brings death or strife or incest in its wake, this mandate is nonetheless usually issued by pagan deities or mythological beings (Apollo, the oracle, the sphinx, the goddesses in the Judgment of Paris, the sorceress Medea): it is up to us to decide whether to believe in its symbolic force. Although the law may be similarly—though in different ways—invoked as a threat of death (Chapters 5–7), it is also pastiched (in "Lanval"), or fragmented into competing and incompatible obligations (in *Cligés*). Interpellation is *not* found in Christian texts such as *Yvain* (Chapter 4); taboos in the *matière de Bretagne* seem to be pronounced only in order that they may be flouted (in "Lanval," *Yvain*, and *Partonopeu*). These texts, in short, demystify law in favor of the underlying drive.

When a person derives satisfaction not through pursuing the will-o'-the-wisp of desire but instead through adherence to the law, by milking its underside in the real, he makes of the law itself his means of access to *jouissance*. Thematizing the law, then, is a potential source of *jouissance* for the audience. Both sublime and perverse structures involve giving up the immediate satisfaction of desire in favor of adherence to law and to the drives that fuel it. The pivot between sublime and perverse provided by courtly literature is what constitutes for Lacan in the *Ethics* seminar and, following him, Žižek, the link between medieval and modern subjectivities. Lacan bases his own conclusions primarily on the lyric; Žižek glosses Lacan's material and applies it to film. By concentrating, in my later chapters, on narrative texts, I have suggested a wider range of forms of perversity than they. Their focus is on the enjoyment of self-denial: the *jouissance* of circling around the Thing, knowing that no object whatever can fill its space. Such a focus is valuable for looking at narratives which involve punishment, prohibition, and taboo—narratives that includes saints' lives as well as the *matière de Bretagne* such as *Partonopeu*—but I have drawn attention to the existence also of narratives centering on fetishism and voyeurism. The undercurrent of male homoeroticism to which this conclusion has drawn attention is another perverse element in courtly literature. The alternation between sublime and perverse structures brings with it an equivocation between commitment and disengagement. This corresponds in turn with the effects which result from the late twelfth-century courtly treatment of contradictoriness, whereby "full" meanings can be both affirmed and negated.

The narratives which I have described as potentially perverse have two things in common. On one hand, they exhibit the movement of the drive and its relation to law. For example, *Yvain* carefully stages the scopic drive in relation to relationships of power and justice; *Cligés* contrives the scene of Fenice's death in relation to the violence of the physicians, their exercise of "morality," and her own adherence to Love's law. By actually displaying the drive in this way these narratives communicate its *jouissance* to their audiences in a memorable form. At the same time they provide—as a point of identification and delectation for the audience—the figure of the pervert: objectified, passive, rapturous but unruffled. Taken together, then, these two features mean that the texts offer their audiences both danger and safety, *jouissance* and calm.

Guiette has written powerfully about the "vanity" imputed to courtly literature by its medieval critics.[6] Asserting that "Chrétien's art is founded in the interest of ambiguity" ("*Li conte,*" 9), he goes on to describe it in these terms:

> Too worldly, too secular, too imaginary, too mysterious, too futile, too frivolous, the work drives readers to the extravagance of its heroes, makes them dream blissful and disturbing things [voluptueuses et troubles]. This ambiguity justifies the epithet "vain."

> Commentators seek to reconstruct the not given.[. . .] The work's vanity/emptiness stems from this indeterminacy. ("*Li conte*," 10)

Guiette's words well evoke the combination in late twelfth-century courtly literature of intellectual play—the playful exposure of "law"—and its more troubling underside of something more blissful and disturbing which I am calling *jouissance*. It is not surprising that literary critical and analytical perceptions should coincide in these texts. Thinking with our object, we all depend on fantasies as our only means of engaging what we call "reality." As Lacan puts it, "The structural necessity borne along by any expression of truth is precisely a structure which is the same as that of fiction. Truth, if I may say so, has the structure of fiction" (*Relation d'objet*, 253). Courtly texts were successful and influential because their contradictory fictions contain what we can retrospectively designate as truths.

APPENDIX

Approximate chronology of works or authors discussed

DATE	LOGIC	HAGIOGRAPHY	LYRIC	ROMANCE
Before 1100	Old Logical texts transmitted by Boethius: Aristotle, *Categories, De interpretationes*; Porphyry, *Isagoge*; Boethius, *De topicis differentiis*	*Life of Saint Leger* (second half of 10th c.) *Life of Faith* (1170?)		
Before 1120		*Life of Saint Alexis* (*L* text) (but could be late 11th c.)	Guilhem de Peitieu (d. 1126)	
1120–1150	*Abbreviatio Montana* (? just prior to the New Logic) "New Logic" (1120s and 1130s); includes: Aristotle, *Topics* (available to John of Salisbury); *Sophistici elenchi* trans. James of Venice (ca. 1125–1150) Adam of Balsham	Wace, *Life of St. Margaret* (1130–40)	Jaufré Rudel (...1125–1148...) Marcabru (...1130–1149...) Cercamon (...1137–1149...) Alegret (...1145...)	Alberic of Pisançon, *Alexander* (first third of 12th c.)
1150–1160	John of Salisbury *Metalogicon* (1159)		Bernart Marti (mid 12th c.) Peire d'Alvernha (...1145–68...)	*Apollonius* (1150–60) *romans antiques*: (1) *Thebes* (1156) (2) *Eneas* (1160?)

(continued)

DATE	LOGIC	HAGIOGRAPHY	LYRIC	ROMANCE
1160–1170		*Life of Saint Gregory* (second half of 12th c.) Adgar, *Gracial* (second half of 12th c.) (both of these may belong futher below)	Bernart de Ventadorn (…1147–1170…) Raimbaut d'Aurenga (…1147–1173) Azalais de Porcairagues (…1173…) Giraut de Bornelh (…1162–99…) (so career extends below)	(3) *Troie* (1160–65?)
1170–1180		Guernes de Pont Sainte-Maxence, *Life of Becket* (1174) *Life of Saint Lawrence* (post 1170) Clemence of Barking, *Life of Saint Catherine* (after 1170, and perhaps after 1180) *Life of Saint Evroul* (1165–1180, and before 1214, so could belong below)	Peire Rogier (last third of 12th c.) (might belong further below)	Marie de France, *Lais* (impossible to date, could be either earlier or later) Thomas of Britain, *Tristan* (? early 1170s, and before *Cligés*) Chrétien de Troyes, *Cligés* (1176?), *Charrete* (1177–79?), *Yvain* (1177–79?)
1180–1200 or later	First surviving treatise on *insolubilia*	*Life of Saint Alexis* (*S* version) (before 1187?) Beneit, *Life of Becket* (between 1183 and 1189) Simund de Freine, *Life of Saint George* (maybe as late as early 13th c.)	Raimbaut de Vaquieres (…1180–1205…) Peire Vidal (…1183–1204…) Peirol (…1188–1222…) Arnaut de Maruelh (…1195…)	Hue de la Rotelande, *Ipomedon* (1180–88) Partonopeu de Blois (?end 12th c., but could be much earlier, ca. 1170)

Reference Matter

Notes

INTRODUCTION

1. This generalization calls for qualification. The best critical writing on medieval texts has always shown awareness of the contradictions which sustained it. A signal experiment in thinking about contradiction, though one which seems to have enjoyed little influence, is Gallais's *Dialectique*, which applies the Greimasian square, expanded into a hexagon in the light of Roger Blanché's study *Structures intellectuelles*, to Chrétien's romances. The centrality of contradiction, and the importance of distinguishing different manifestations of it, are promoted by writers in the semiotic tradition generally. Notable medievalists to have written in this tradition include Donald Maddox and Peter Haidu; for theoretical exposition, see the latter's "Considérations." An explicit reflection on contradiction has been at the center of a number of other works which have particularly influenced this study: Hunt's studies on the influence of dialectic on romance; Vance, *From Topic to Tale*; and Bruckner, *Shaping Romance*. Another work to which I am indebted, although it deals only glancingly with the Middle Ages, is Colie's *Paradoxica Epidemica*. My hope is that this book should combine what is best in these two last works: Bruckner's sensitive application of modern critical thinking to medieval texts and Colie's vigorous dissection of the implications of their intellectual background. Examples of such writing will be considered below.

2. See my "Contradictions of Courtly Love," 212–19.

3. Citations from troubadour songs are given in this form: number in the edition indicated in the Works Cited (in Roman numerals), then line numbers (in Arabic numerals).

4. Bec's term "incantatoire" here is a reminiscence of the founder of formalist interpretation of medieval lyric, Guiette: see Guiette's *D'une poésie for-*

melle, 34, where the phrase "Le langage doit être utilisé pour sa valeur incantatoire" follows on from "c'est l'oeuvre formelle, elle-même, qui est le sujet."

5. There is a risk, too, of the application of Greimas appearing arbitrary. Are "ecstasy" and "death" really contrary terms?

6. Köhler, "'Can vei la lauzeta mover,'" 463: "Sie [this poetry] feiert, transponiert auf die Ebene des 'paradoxe amoureux' zugleich sozialen Aufstieg als verdienten Lohn und Bereitschaft zum Verzicht als Ausweis edler Gesittung." This article is a complement to Köhler's foundational "Observations."

7. Köhler describes his own methodology in "Principes historico-sociologiques." Useful theoretical appraisals of Köhler's work are Krauff, "Historisch-dialektische Literaturwissenschaft" and Thoma, "Pour une science historico-sociologique."

8. E.g. *L'Amour discourtois*, 100: "Sur le corps de la femme—comme jadis sur le corps de la mère—l'homme ne cesse de voir, à la place évidente du pénis manquant à sa place, la blessure qui autorise son désir et lui rend précieux l'organe sauvegardé, mais en son souvenir toujours menacé, et qui le condamne à une jouissance interdisant tout 'rapport' avec la femme." This corresponds with some of Lacan's comments on courtly love: "L'amour courtois [....] C'est une façon tout à fait raffinée de suppléer à l'absence de rapport sexuel, en feignant que c'est nous qui y faisons obstacle. [...] c'est pour l'homme, dont la dame était entièrement, au sens le plus servile, la sujette, la seule façon de se tirer avec élégance de l'absence du rapport sexuel" (*Encore*, 65). Huchet explains his approach to the text in *Littérature médiévale*, especially 5–28, 101–2, 106–10. He insists that he is not seeking to "apply" theory to literature; just as there is no sexual relation, there is no real meeting of "theory" and "literature," and his work sets out to record this *rendez-vous manqué*.

9. Disavowal is the psychic double take whereby one both maintains a belief that something is the case and also acknowledges that it isn't: "je sais bien, mais quand même...." Its first association is with relation to the mother. The male child prefers to believe that she has, or has lost, a penis like his own, rather than acknowledge the reality of sexual difference, thus giving rise to the phenomenon known as fetishism. For further definition of this (and other) psychoanalytical terms, see Evans, *Introductory Dictionary*.

10. Psychoanalytic criticism can also focus on paired contraries (for example, the simultaneous love and hatred which constitute the phenomenon of ambivalence), but the critic who has approached the troubadours from this perspective—Cholakian—doesn't write on Bernart.

11. In the *Charrete*, which Chrétien must have undertaken (Köhler thinks) *à contre-coeur*, contradictions are felt with such intensity that they can only be

mediated by religious ecstasy, religion being already instituted in medieval society as guaranteeing of the validity of conditions that were already riven with insoluble contradictions (*L'Aventure chevaleresque*, 191). The abandon of reason and self-determination may provide Lancelot with an ethical alibi but does not square with the aspiration to autonomy embraced elsewhere by Chrétien (and the "ideal" of knighthood he serves to translate); the "ideal" of the knight wholly subject to love transforms itself into a representation of folly. The text of the *Charrette* thus represents in an extreme form the dialectic of ideal and reality, which implodes upon itself, undermining its own representation of the ideal: "La relation entre idéal et réalité s'épuise moins que jamais en une simple opposition, c'est bien plus la réalité une fois donnée qui—dans la mesure où elle devient incertaine—produit ses idéaux et une modification de la réalité au cours de l'histoire entraîne une modification des idéaux, les différencie ou les accule à une unilatéralité où ils deviennent insupportables et résistent à toute légitimation par la réalité. Dans le *Chevalier à la Charrette*, l'image idéale de l'homme chevaleresque est poussée jusqu'à ces limites, où l'idéal, hostile à la réalité, commande sa propre négation" (195). In the end, Chrétien abandons love as a means of mediation because it becomes so fraught with the very contradictions it is invoked to handle (207).

12. Compare Bruckner's footnote to this sentence, and her introduction (4), with Kristeva's "Le texte clos," 55–62.

13. I have advanced similar arguments about responses to the clash of religious and erotic elements in Giraut de Bornelh's *alba* ("Text(s) and Meaning(s)") and in the *Romance of the Rose* (*Romance of the Rose*, especially 88–89).

14. Thereby of course contributing to its prestige, e.g., Patterson, *Negotiating the Past*, chapter 1.

15. For a consummate dismantling of this approach, see Haidu, *Lion-queue-coupée*.

16. Jacobi, "Logic," 234.

17. Dod, "Aristoteles Latinus," 54; Jacobi, "Logic," 236; Marenbon, *Later Medieval Philosophy*, 35–36.

18. Tweedale, "Logic," 196; cf. Marenbon, *Early Medieval Philosophy*, 20: "Problems of logic fascinated the ablest minds, and logical distinctions influenced a host of other areas of knowledge—theology, rhetoric, poetic theory, grammar—in a way which has surprised, and sometimes appalled, later times"; and Marenbon, *Early Medieval Philosophy*, 113–18, on the flourishing Parisian schools.

19. References to Aristotle's works are given in the form: section and line numbers in the Greek text/book (in Roman numerals) and chapter (in Arabic

numerals), or other division of the text (§)/page number in the Oxford translation cited in the Works Cited.

20. 1005b11 ff., quoted from the translation by Dancy, *Sense and Contradiction*, 156.

21. Dod, "Aristoteles Latinus," 46.

22. Greimas represents the square repeatedly, with minor variations, in his different writings; the example I am referring to here is in *Du Sens* I, 137. The square depicts the ways in which significance is generated by relations of contradiction. The strongest form of contradiction, contrariety, is mapped onto the upper horizontal axis (s_1 and s_2, e.g., "black" versus "white"). The negation of it appears on the lower horizontal axis ($-s_2$ and $-s_1$, e.g., "not-white" versus "not-black"). Greimas's usage involves relations between single terms, whereas in the dialectical tradition, the relations mapped are usually those between propositions.

23. See Gersh, *Concord in Discourse*, for more on the medieval tradition of the "square of opposition."

24. For a property to change, it must be what is called an "accident," rather than defining of the substance to which it belongs (a *differentia* or *proprium*). The heat in fire, for example, cannot change into its contrary because you cannot have fire which is cold.

25. For twelfth-century teaching by William of Champeaux on the "middle term," see the *Metalogicon* of John of Salisbury, III, 9/187. Quotations from the *Metalogicon* take the following form: book (in Roman numerals), chapter (in Arabic numerals)/page reference in McGarry's translation. For Boethius, "differentiae" which index the points of division in a taxonomy serve as "intermediate" or "third" terms: see Stump's edition of *De topicis*, 195–99, 204–7.

26. References to the *De topicis* are to section number/book (in Roman numerals)/page number in Stump's translation.

27. In her edition of Boethius's *De topicis*, Stump (159–204) discusses the nature of topical argument in both Boethius and Aristotle. In Aristotle, a topic seems to be sometimes a principle commanding general assent (e.g., "what is nearer to the good is better and more worthy of choice and also what is more like the good," *Topics*, 117b, 10–11/III, 2/197) and at others an argumentative strategy (e.g., "[You must see] if the genus and the species are not in the same [category], but one is a substance and the other a quality," *Topics*, 120b, 36–37/IV, 1/202) (Stump, 166–67). In Stump's view, the strategic aspect predominates in Aristotle, but strategies are classified according to a taxonomy of predicables. What is important for Boethius is the reasoning process, again follow-

ing a taxonomy, but one which is based on uncontested relations between propositions, e.g., where one follows from another "by definition."

28. See also 1191B–1192A/II/56 ff., and 1197B ff./III/66–67. For twelfth-century advocacy of this concentration on ethical questions, see the *Metalogicon*, II, 11/100–1.

29. The format of quotations from the *Metalogicon* is explained in note 25 above.

30. These elementary dialectical works were taught in close relation with rhetoric and grammar: see Jacobi, "Logic," 239, and, for defense of this interrelation between grammar, rhetoric, and dialectic, the *Metalogicon*, Book I passim.

31. *Si est homo, est animal.* See, for example, Aristotle's *Categories*, 1b, 14–15/§3/4 and 2a, 35–36/§5/5, etc., and *Prior Analytics*, 25a, 11–12/I, 2/40.

32. Elsewhere, John deplores the hijacking by profane texts of music associated with the church. See Bezzola, *Origines*, III, 1, 28.

33. 2 Cor. 6:1–10, Rom. 8:35–37, 15:3.

34. Boethius, *Philosophiae Consolationis Libri Quinque*, IV.

35. See Evans, *Language and Logic of the Bible*, 2–3.

36. Evans, *Language and Logic of the Bible*, 133–39; Brown, *Contrary Things*, 83–90.

37. Reference is to book (in Roman numerals) and chapter (in Arabic numerals)/page number in the translation cited.

38. Spitzer, *L'Amour lointain*, 2. Other influential pioneers of this rapprochement between the contradictions of medieval love and those of religious writing are Denomy, "*Jois* among the Early Troubadours" and Frappier, "Sur un procès fait à l'amour courtois," 86–88.

39. Marnette shows how closely the dimensions and content of narrators' interventions in courtly texts mirror those of religious ones. See *Narrateur et points de vue*, 249, fig. 12, and discussion 92–95.

40. See Sirat, "Jewish Philosophy," and on Eriugena, Gersh, *Concord in Discourse*.

41. Priest, *Beyond the Limits of Thought*, 63. This argument is not the same as the famous ontological argument (Anselm of Canterbury, *Proslogion*, §§2–3/94) but a development from it.

42. For example, Anselm of Canterbury, "Meditation on Human Redemption," 137: "What strength can there be in such weakness, what majesty in such humiliation, what worthy of reverence in such contempt?"

43. For a provocative study of Anselm's different ways of dealing with contradiction and their implications, see Bencivenga, *Logic and Other Nonsense*.

44. See Ferry and Renaut, *La Pensée '68*, 51–53.

45. Fish, *Is There a Text in this Class?*, 327.

46. Although the main expression of Lacan's interest is in the *Ethics* and later in *Encore*, there are references to courtly love (and less frequently to chivalry) throughout the volumes of the Seminar I have read. See also Kristeva, *Tales of Love*, especially 281–96, and Žižek, *Metastases of Enjoyment*, 89–112.

47. Lacan, *Ethics*, 152–53.

48. For a commentary on Lacan's view of contradiction in terms similar to these, see Žižek, *Sublime Object of Ideology*, 171–72.

49. See Bowie, *Lacan*, 165 ff., and Žižek, *Metastases*, 177–81.

50. In Lacan's *Ethics*, an analogous exploration is conducted relative to what Lacan at this point calls the Thing, which is, broadly speaking, an earlier incarnation of *objet a*, although one which is situated on the side of the real; cf. also Žižek, *Metastases of Enjoyment*, 181.

51. Lacan reiterates here the Jewish joke about misleading one's interlocutor, which was also cited in *Psychoses*; see above.

52. The alienations effected by the imaginary and symbolic orders were described above, in relation to schema L.

53. See the helpful exposition by Dolar, "Cogito."

54. John's grumpy denunciation of the decline of logic into mumbo jumbo is rebutted by Jacobi, "Logic."

55. See, among others, Bezzola, *Origines et formation*; Bumke, *Courtly Culture*; Jaeger, *Origins of Courtliness*; Scaglione, *Knights at Court*.

56. Classically stated by Faral, *Recherches*, 195: "le chevalier amoureux est une invention littéraire du clerc."

57. Though see the reservations expressed by Hanning, "Audience," 5–6, on the role of women. Jaeger has argued for the German origins of courtliness, but as Scaglione points out, his resistance to seeing courtly literature and courtly love as other than an impediment to our understanding of courtliness prevents his account having much to say about these (Scaglione, *Knights at Court*, 61). Although Scaglione allows that Jaeger "does succeed brilliantly in locating an important background element of that literary phenomenon in the earlier curial ethos of imperial Germany," similar courtly conditions obtained elsewhere than in Germany (68), in Flanders, Normandy, and Anjou: regions which appear to have a more direct bearing on the development of courtly literature.

58. Bezzola, *Origines*, II, 1, 3. Confirmation of Bezzola's view of the geographical and origins of courtliness is found in Bond, *Loving Subject*. The landmarks Bond discerns in the evolution of the loving subject—a subject who plays at, or impersonates, a man in love—are the Bayeux tapestry, Bau-

dri of Bourgueil and Marbod of Angers, Guilhem de Peitieu, and Adela of Blois. Bond's chronological frame opens between 1066 and 1082 (the period within which the tapestry was commissioned), antedating Bezzola's by a couple of decades.

59. See my "Contradictions of Courtly Love" and "Courts, Clerks, and Courtly Love."

60. Scaglione, *Knights at Court*, 71.

CHAPTER I

1. Opposition, according to dialecticians, takes four forms: relative (father-son), privative (sick-well), contrary (just-unjust), and negative (so-not so). See Introduction, 14–15, for more details.

2. A Latin play with vernacular insertions on the parable of the wise and foolish virgins. The Marian texts are in the edition of the "*Sponsus*," 196–200.

3. See Meyer, "Anciennes poésies," for further examples.

4. Altman, "Two Types." Strictly there are four types of hagiographic text, *passiones* and *vitae* being the most common. The others are *miracula* (recounting miracles) and *translationes* (recounting the transfer of relics), but these are often integrated to the major genres.

5. Hahn, "Speaking."

6. See Uitti, "Old Provençal Song," Work, "Eleventh-Century Song," Leupin, *Fiction et incarnation*, 128–29; and cf. Uitti, "*Alexis*."

7. Dates of known activity of troubadours are taken from de Riquer, *Trovadores*, unless otherwise indicated. The dates with ellipsis dots before or after them indicate the earliest and last known date, respectively, of a poet's activity.

8. Cf. Benoît de Sainte Maure, *Roman de Troie*, 1–16.

9. On dating the *romans antiques*, see Petit, *Naissances du roman*, I, 12–14 and notes. On the period of composition (mid-1150s to late 1160s) of the *Troie*, see also Rollo, *Historical Fabrication*, 167. On the dating of all romance texts, I have consulted the *Grundriss*, IV.2.

10. See my "Contradictions," appendix I, sections A, B, C, and E for instances of various forms of good being bad, suffering joyous, and folly wise. On the topos that the lover's folly is wisdom, see also Akehurst, "Folie," and Topsfield, "'Natural Fool.'" For examples from later troubadours, see, e.g., Raimbaut de Vaqueiras, IX, or Peire Vidal, XL, stanza ii, where the density of oxymora echoes Natura's definition of love in the *De planctu*.

11. Like John, the authors of the *romans antiques* also locate dialectic firmly within the *trivium*: see *Thebes*, 4991; *Eneas*, 2209; *Roman de Troie*, 9–10.

12. See line 6162, and Walberg, "Introduction," iv–v. Guernes was probably patronized, even commissioned, by Becket's sister Marie, abbess of the Benedictine convent at Barking 1173–1175, a convent which witnessed extensive hagiographic activity, notably by Clemence of Barking; see Robertson, "Writing in the Textual Community." Adgar's *Gracial*, which seems to have been dedicated to another abbess of Barking, Henry II's natural daughter Maud, is discussed in Chapter 5.

13. Robertson, *Medieval Saints' Lives*, 184.

14. "De l'iglise prent il la corone e les leis" (Guernes, *Vie de Thomas Becket*, 59).

15. See Hunt, *Chrétien de Troyes: Yvain*, 94–95; Topsfield, *Chrétien de Troyes*, 50–51, 68–69, 106, 124, etc.; Kay, "Who was Chrétien de Troyes?"; Meneghetti, *Pubblico*, 101 ff.; Rossi, "Chrétien de Troyes."

16. Marie's debt to the Occitan lyric is yet to be fully explored, but see Huot, "Troubadour Lyric."

17. On Thomas's "isolating" use of opposition as compared with Gottfried's "synthesizing" one, see Dijsterhuis, cited by Hunt, "Aristotle," 120 and note 86.

18. Cf. also Sneyd[1], 238–50, where beneficial qualities are swallowed up by their opposites. On Tristan's incapacity for change, see Delcourt, *L'Éthique*, chapter 2.

19. Cf. Vance's point, *From Topic to Tale*, 60, that Chrétien exploits the narrative potential of logical antecedence and consequence.

20. For the influence of dialectic on these troubadours, see Paterson, *Troubadours and Eloquence*. On stanza order, Van Vleck, *Memory and Recreation*, chapter 4 and appendix A. Although Giraut de Bornelh composed relatively few songs with a fixed stanza order, they are transmitted with very little variation of order, perhaps because of his preference for long stanzas (80).

21. Nolting-Hauff, *Liebeskasuistik*, ascribes the momentum in romance "casuistry" to the influence of lyric (primarily the tension it displays between social norm and individual affect [15]), to the interplay between interior and external plots (both of which likewise display tension between social and individual expectation, e.g., 9–10), and the prevalence of gradualism, whereby oppositions are never resolvable on one plane but are passed on to the next level up (11–12). For an explicit instance of gradualism, see the discussion below of the *Life of Saint Evroul*.

22. On the Gregorian Reform as background to disparagement of the lay state, see Vauchez, "Lay People's Sanctity": "Some authors go so far as to asso-

ciate the laity solely with the flesh and clerics with the spirit, consequently arguing that clerics should control laymen" (23).

23. By 1254, according to Marshall ("Dialogues of the Dead," 41), "both pieces were current and were thought to be related."

24. In line 42, Peirol says that Bernart has made a fool of him. In his note to this line, Marshall ("Dialogues of the Dead," 49) glosses this as an admission by Peirol that Bernart "has turned the tables on him by his cynical argument in st. v." But surely, in citing the fable, Peirol is marking his disagreement with Bernart's cynicism. I think that when he says Bernart has made a fool of him, it is to counter his previous statement, in line 22, that Bernart has won him around to his point of view. If Peirol concurs with Bernart in line 22, now, in line 42, he thinks he has been made a fool of. This would be an example of contrariety. But it is also possible, and I think likely, that in lines 22–24, Peirol's agreement with Bernart is sarcastic, because as late as line 47, he still refers to "ma bona fe," presumably his fidelity in love. Agreeing with Bernart in lines 22–24 may then be tantamount to not agreeing with him, a step made explicit in line 42. His meaning in lines 22–24 would thus be in contradiction with what he actually says. For more on contradiction in this song, see below.

25. See, e.g., the second stanza of the *tenso* between Raimbaut de Vaqueiras and the Genoesa (Song III).

26. The *partimen* seems to emerge with the troubadours of Ussel, who debate with one another and a circle of other people, including Gaucelm Faidit. According to de Riquer, Gui d'Ussel's activity is attested 1195–1196.

27. This tradition starts with the exchange between Elias d'Ussel and a certain Aimeric and includes the raunchy *tenso* between Montan and his lady. See Neumeister, *Das Spiel*, appendixes, for the topics debated in *partimens*.

28. The date adopted by the *Grundriss*, 1182–1185, is that put forward by Fourrier, *Courant réaliste*. Bruckner, "Intertextuality," extends the time frame to 1182–1196. The case for a date in the early 1170s is made by Simons and Eley, "Prologue," and again in "*Partonopeus de Blois*." Harf-Lancner, however, argues for an even later date "probably at the end of the twelfth century" (*Fées*, 317). I myself find persuasive Harf-Lancner's argument that *Partonopeu* may be later than *Florimont* (1188).

29. The editor of the *Life of Saint Evroul* thinks the vernacular text was probably composed 1165–1180 (753) and in any case not later than 1214, but it is based on Orderic Vitalis's earlier *Ecclesiastical History* (completed in 1141), VI, 9. Its author was a Norman (766) who translated the life for the observance of Evroul's feast day (cf. lines 29–31).

30. In the *S* version of the *Alexis* (which is in *laisses*), Alexis is a courtier before the projected marriage precipitates his escape. See Pindar, "Intertextuality."

31. The ladder image is not in Orderic; on *Evroul*'s expansions of its source, see Pindar, "Intertextuality," 15.

32. Old French *contredire* standardly means "to argue against someone, gainsay, rebut." This passage follows Orderic's Latin closely.

CHAPTER 2

1. The *L* redaction is preserved in the St. Alban's Psalter made for Christine of Markyate, probably ca. 1120; see Camille, "Philological Iconoclasm." On the date of composition, see Mölk, "*Chanson de saint Alexis*," 342.

2. For the debate over *A*, see Elliott's edition of *S*, 15 and note 10, and Hemming's of *A*, xv–xxvii.

3. The same insistence is found in *A*, 214, 227, 242, 247, 332, 341.

4. On the diffusion of Latin *Alexis* texts in the twelfth century, see Mölk, "*Chanson de saint Alexis*," 345–53.

5. "Tristan as martyr of love may play Saint Alexis under the staircase but he does not project a view of joyous union in Paradise, nor does Thomas's narrative suggest any such extrapolation beyond death"(Bruckner, *Shaping Romance*, 50).

6. Cf. Crane, *Insular Romance*, 109–15, who compares versions of *Guy of Warwick* and the Middle English *Alexis* to show their differing views of religious and secular duties.

7. This reading is uncertain because of damage to the opening stanza.

8. Other similarities between Marcabru and Thomas exceed my purpose in this chapter but are worth briefly noting. Marcabru may be one of the very earliest commentators on the Tristan story (XI, 62–64) and persistently condemns precisely the kind of lover Tristan has become in the Douce fragment: a married man pursuing an affair with another man's wife. Marcabru's call to resist the pervasiveness of deceit similarly strikes a chord with a reading of the Douce fragment, which begins with Brengain's vengeful manipulation of King Mark and ends with Isolt's lie about the color of the sails. (For an account of Thomas as a moralist condemning the deceits of love and calling on reason to withstand them, see also Hunt, "Significance," 46–49.) The opposition which Marcabru works hardest to maintain, but simultaneously finds most labile, is that between good love (*fin' amor*) and bad love (*amar*). The latter term, which can be an adjective ("bitter"), noun ("loving," "bitterness"), or infinitive ("to love"), predominates to such an extent that is hard to identify passages in Marcabru's poetry unambiguously praising any love as good; and the word *amor*

often collapses into synonymy with *amar*, rather than being differentiated from it. Exactly the same wordplay occurs in the recently discovered Carlisle fragment of Thomas's *Tristan*, 40–70.

9. Although the leprosy motif has no parallel in the *Alexis*, its source in Thomas may be hagiographic given that the figures of lover and leper are likewise combined in the legend of *Ami and Amiles*, which also features the recognition of the leper by a cup (cf. Douce, 551).

10. Brown, *Contrary Things*, 25. The house represents the higher unity of its diverse parts.

11. Hult's edition reads *cors*, "body," but the reading *chas* of manuscript *H* accords better with the next line.

12. Topsfield, *Chrétien de Troyes*, chapter 4, especially 145–46, 156–57, 162, 166–73.

13. See the discussion of Azalais in my *Subjectivity*, 104–7, and the references there to Sakari. Giraut de Bornelh's debate with the King of Aragon on the suitability of the *ric ome* as lover is Giraut's Song LVIII. See also Guilhem de Sant Leidier III and Peire Rogier VIII.

14. Paterson, *Troubadours and Eloquence*, 178–85. The motif of dearness/dearth is taken up in Chretien's lyric "D'Amors qui m'a tolu a moi," 37–45, and cf. Haidu, "Text and History."

15. Paterson, *Troubadours and Eloquence*, refers to "Giraut's learned background" (90) and says the *leu* style "was too pedestrian for educated poets such as Peire [d'Alvernhe] and Raimbaut [d'Aurenga]" (133). Chrétien's "D'Amors" is thought to form part of a poetic dialogue with Raimbaut and Bernart de Ventadorn (see Chapter 1, note 15).

16. Giraut's allusion to having been made *contal* by his lady ("Si·m sentis," 90) is referred to in the *tenso* with Raimbaut d'Aurenga (Sharman, LIX, 56), in which Giraut also speaks of the *captal* ("capital") associated with song (LIX, 28; cf. "Si·m sentis," 55). This means that "Si·m sentis" must date from before Raimbaut's death in 1173, and before 1168 or 1170 if this is when the *tenso* was composed (see Pattison's edition of Raimbaut, XXXI). "Si·m sentis" survives in 14 manuscripts and is quoted by Dante in the *De vulgare eloquentia* as being an exemplary composition on the subject of love.

17. I use Sharman's text but have also consulted Paterson, *Troubadours and Eloquence*, 125–32.

18. Sharman thinks that Giraut is punning on *fizels* meaning both "faithful" and "genuine"; he is faithful but not a "genuine" lover because his love is not reciprocated. For Sharman, that is, one needs to reach lines 27–33 before being in a position to resolve the opening contradiction; see her introduction,

39. For Kolsen, Giraut's previous editor, the "fidelity" of the lover dates only to when he began to love well (9), and is for that reason not well established.

19. Literally, "to which now I give shelter": the lover admits these humiliating conditions in the sense that he gives them house room.

20. Sharman translates this as: "finds his reward insofar as love is equal on both sides, and is an excellent lover"; Paterson has: "receives according to how true love is to itself and the lover excellent."

21. I follow Paterson's (and Kolsen's) punctuation here; Sharman omits the question mark, construing lines 34–39 as a single sentence.

22. The term *l'os* is translated by Kolsen as "im Innersten."

23. Love is "for sale" because the lady extorts service from the lover without giving anything in return.

24. On the problematic of mercy and justice transposed from theology to the love lyric, see Scheludko, "Religiöse Elemente," 415–21.

25. In "Giraut de Bornhelh," 63–69, Sharman presents Giraut's poetry in general as synthesizing the previous generation of troubadours' debates between passion and moderation, eros and ethics.

26. Hue's relation to Chrétien has been much discussed. Calin ("Exaltation," note 1) provides a useful supplement to the bibliography in Holden's edition. Crane, *Insular Romance*, chapter 4, reads *Ipomedon* alongside Thomas's *Tristan*. The three-day tournament also features in *Partonopeu*; see below, Chapter 7.

27. Calin emphasizes how the hero's trickery and deceit exposes the limitations of other, especially women, characters ("Exaltation," 120–21).

28. The motif of a despised knight turning out to be a close relative of a noted household member is also found in *Li Biaus Desconneüs*.

29. Krueger, *Women Readers*, 73–82. Holden had also identified antifeminism as the romance's principal thrust; see his introduction, 55.

30. In this he resembles Erec in Chrétien's *Erec et Enide* who is censured for not going to tournaments and so rebuilds his reputation precisely by never going to any.

31. See Evans, *Introductory Dictionary*, s.v. "acting out." For other examples of behavior retroactively legitimizing the message to which they respond, see Žižek, *Metastases*, 93–94. Hanning, "Engin," 99, makes a similar point when he says that Ipomedon "dramatizes his alienation from himself." Hanning's discussion of *Ipomedon* in *Individual*, 123–36, concentrates especially on this tournament episode.

32. Calin ("Exaltation") and Eley ("Anti-Romance") have also seen an excessive, crazy logic as the driving force of comedy in *Ipomedon*.

33. The terminus of 1187 was suggested by Gaston Paris because *S* refers (line 341) to a journey to Jerusalem without mentioning that Jerusalem fell in that year—an argument which doesn't carry a great deal of weight. The *chansons de geste* with which Elliott compares *S* stem from ca. 1160 onward, but of course *chansons de geste* are also notoriously hard to date.

CHAPTER 3

1. See Colie, *Paradoxica Epidemica*, "Introduction."
2. Stewart, *Nonsense*, chapter 1.
3. "Rational" is a *differentia* on the Porphyrian tree serving to demarcate human beings (and pagan gods) from other species of animals which are "irrational." See Stump's edition of Boethius's *De topicis*, 241, and also note 21 below.
4. Sullivan, "Medieval Automata." See also Baumgartner, "Le temps des automates," "Peinture et écriture," and "Tombeaux pour guerriers"; Patterson, *Negotiating the Past*, 181; and Rollo, *Historical Fabrication*, 210–13.
5. On the death of Hector, see Sullivan, "Translation and Adaptation."
6. This description is imitated in *Partonopeu*, 4624–60, when Melior recounts her magical skills. She too is a mounter of courtly spectacle, her *chef d'oeuvre* being her own performance in conjuring Partonopeu to be with her.
7. Baumgartner, "Le temps des automates," 172; for Sullivan ("Medieval Automata," 11–12), the alabaster screen defines the "social barrier" between aristocracy and nonnobles.
8. For Aristotle, contraries are differentiated by two universals and contradictories by only one; this makes the relationship between contraries stronger and more capable of generating argument.
9. Cf. Gersh's suggestion that Alan of Lille's emphasis on the large X formed by Nature's headbands and on the contradictory positioning of phenomena invoke the square of opposition in the *De planctu*. Nature's "square" is presented as proportional to the square of the heavens; likewise, I will argue that Benoît's square of art is proportional to the square of history which lies outside it. See Gersh, *Concord*, 167–70.
10. Hector's tomb (*Troie*, 16653 ff.) is also a square of contraries on a smaller scale. Automata simpler than those of the Alabaster Chamber are placed at its four corners, two young men and two older ones, each supporting a pillar made of a different stone. See also Chapter 6.
11. The original study of the romance as structured by the love relationships is Lumiansky, "Structural Unity." Petit, *Naissances*, 463 ff., presents the story of the war as overlaid by that of four love affairs which become progressively more integrated to the martial theme (483). Nolan, *Chaucer*, sees the dif-

ferences between them as opposing "Ovidian foolish as opposed to legitimate married love" (96).

12. Lumiansky, Petit, Nolan, and others omit Esiona and instead take Jason and Medea as the first relationship, but I see the Medea story as a preface much as Penelope is an afterword, their stories symmetrically opposing a faithless husband and a faithful wife in a framing outer pair of contraries.

13. On the overwhelming of rationality by destructiveness, see Levenson's excellent "Narrative Format."

14. Though for a more optimistic interpretation see Baumgartner, "Le temps des automates," 172–75.

15. Polak, "Two Caves," 58–59, cites the corresponding passage from the *Saga* on which her argument is based. Similarities with Benoît's Chamber include the use of automata which are rigged to an ingenious air-freshening device, the possible influence of Neoplatonist cosmology, and the association with death (Thomas's cavern may be an ancient tomb). The statue of Iseut is said to stand "under the middle of the vault"; could this suggest that it is placed at the intersection of a great X formed by the arches that uphold the structure of the cavern? See my note 9, above.

16. This text has chiefly been studied on account of the "sin" Charlemagne confesses, the horror of which is never revealed.

17. Duncan Robertson, *Medieval Saints' Lives*, 39–71; his "Writing in the Textual Community" stresses the Marian material common to all three; cf. Clemence 1750–51 and *St. Lawrence* 480–83 (although these are in fact commonplaces; see Chapter 5). Lawrence, like Catherine, stresses the need to distinguish the Christian God as creator from pagan gods as created (*Lawrence*, 447–53, *Catherine*, 263–96); God made everything from nothing (*Lawrence*, 462–63, *Catherine*, 829–32); the incarnation was an effect of his power and not of his nature (*Lawrence*, 475–79, *Catherine*, 837–38).

18. See the works cited by Duncan Robertson; MacBain, "Five Old French Renderings"; Batt, "Clemence of Barking's Transformations"; and the introduction by Wogan-Browne and Burgess to their English translation, xxix–xxxv.

19. The fragmentary Manchester version, by contrast, focuses on action and confrontation. It is true that the part of the text which contained the dispute with the philosophers is lost. However, what survives lacks the lengthy speeches which, in Clemence's version, Catherine exchanges with Porphyry and the queen. Instead it proceeds at a brisk pace through the successive acts of torture: the martyrdom of the queen, the wheel, the death of Porphyry and two hundred knights, and the beheading of Catherine herself, all in ca. 200 lines.

20. The Latin *Passio* dates from the mid-eleventh century: see d'Ardenne

and Dobson, "Introduction," xv-xvi. The text followed by Clemence is the one known as the Vulgate because of its wide diffusion. Referring to a different text, MacBain mistakenly concludes that Clemence mistranslated her source at lines 901 and 807–8 (introduction to his edition, xiv). Comparison with d'Ardenne and Dobson's text shows that Clemence's translation of these passages is impeccable.

21. Maxence's argument, in other words, appeals to a conceptual arrangement such as that of the Porphyrian tree. Porphyry's *Isagoge* was the standard introduction to Aristotle's *Categories* used in the twelfth century; see John of Salisbury, *Metalogicon*, II, 16/110–11. Porphyry takes each of Aristotle's ten categories as the root of a tree, which is then developed via a series of branches, each of which represents a binary opposition. The tree would, if completely worked out, represent a taxonomy of everything there is. In the tree of "substance" (i.e., the first category), the distinction "mortal–immortal" is one such node, its terms subdividing the category of "rational" (as opposed to "irrational") animal. Man is a mortal, rational animal, whereas the pagan gods are immortal, rational ones.

22. "si s'esmerveille" (*Catherine*, 305); *stupens* (*Passio*, 154, line 203).

23. E.g., 162–63, lines 355–59.

24. 163, lines 362–73.

25. 163, lines 369–73: "who . . . since he was invisible God, assumed flesh from a virgin through which he might appear visible, and displayed himself to us, by means of which [. . .] it was evident to us that he was true man and God."

26. 165, lines 400–2: "Since assuredly, although it might be conceded in some fashion that one might be predicated either as god or as man, it is certain that he could be made one or the other, but could not be both at the same time." This is translated by Clemence as "I can allow that he is either God or man, but I don't see any justification for both. He must be one or the other, for he couldn't be both one and the other" (801–4).

27. The Latin is less explicit about the logical point being made. The text runs: "As I see it, this is the subtlety of your argument: that in that which you cannot believe you accept a part but undermine the whole, suggesting that, when he is a god, he cannot be a man, as though this were impossible to an omnipotent God" (165, lines 403–6).

28. Note Catherine's return to the distinction between creature and created made earlier to Maxence, 267–304.

29. See, e.g., Marenbon, "Gilbert of Poitiers."

30. For helpful progress on this road, see Batt, "Clemence of Barking's

Transformations," Duncan Robertson, "Writing in the Textual Community," and notes to the English translation by Wogan-Browne and Burgess at lines 785–804, 961–64. In his introduction to Clemence's text, xi–xii, MacBain refers to a series of articles from the 1920s on the background to the Greek *Catherine*, suggesting that it derives from second-century apologetic material relating to the Euhermerist position, so named after the Greek philosopher Euhemerus, who maintained that the gods were only dead men glorified. I am convinced that we should look instead to Clemence's more immediate intellectual environment.

31. "If the three persons in God are only one thing (*res*)—and are not three things, each one [existing] separately in itself (as do three angels or three souls) and yet [existing] in such way that they are wholly the same in will and in power—then the Father and the Holy Spirit were incarnate with the Son" (9). This is identical to the objection raised by Dacien in the *George*.

32. "For example, how will someone who does not yet understand how several men are one man in species be able to comprehend how, in that highest and most mysterious Nature, several persons—each one of whom, distinctly, is perfect God—are one God?" (13).

33. I simplify; for detailed analysis, see Hopkins, "Anselmian Theory of Universals."

34. Cited from Wogan-Browne and Burgess's note to these lines in their English translation (70).

35. See Gruber, *Dialektik*, appendix (266–68), in which he classifies the various practices of appropriation following, approximately, the categories of amplification, and other tropes. Gruber distinguishes three fields of "sublation," words, music, and theme, but his treatment of theme (195–98) is cursory.

36. Gruber, *Dialektik*, 120; in 138–42, Gruber considers the relations between this song and Marcabru Songs XXXIV, XXXVI, and XLII; see also Arnaut Daniel Songs IX and VII.

37. In II, 13–14, Cercamon professes indifference as to whether his Lady lies or not; in VI, 19, it is other troubadours whose words hover between truth and lies.

38. Contrast the transformations effected by love in Guilhem de Peitieu, IX, 25–30, which involve health, wisdom, looks, and rank, but not Cercamon's compromising truth/lies opposition.

39. According to Spade, a lost treatise on "insolubles" is referred to in the anonymous *Dialectica Monacensis*, and Alexander Neckham in *De naturis rerum* refers to the liar paradox as an example of the vanities of dialectic ("Five Early Theories," 25–27).

40. Although I base my translation on Beggiato's text, I have also drawn on the edition, translation, and commentary of this song in Gaunt, *Troubadours*, 92–96, 188. This passage is quoted by Tortoreto among other parallels between Cercamon and Bernart Marti (edition of Cercamon, 261–65).

41. Other references to lying in Bernart Marti are II, 13–18 (the success of lying courtiers), and V, 43–48 (the need to separate truth from lies, an attack on Peire d'Alvernha).

42. Spade, "Origin," 303–5.

43. Lambert of Auxerre and Robert Grosseteste; see Spade, *Medieval Liar*, XLV and LIX.

44. Cf. the second solution of Anonymous XX in Spade, *Medieval Liar* (early thirteenth century): the verb of the insoluble refers to some prior time.

45. "Insolubles do not fit very well the pattern of the fallacy *secundum quid et simpliciter*, so that such approaches were always strained" (Spade, "Insolubilia," 247).

46. Cf. Cercamon, III, 31–32: "Plas es lo vers, vauc l'afinan / ses mot vila, *fals*, apostitz," ("the verse is smooth/polished, and I set about refining/purifying it, without any rustic, *false* or inappropriate word/thought"); IV, 23: "de dig ver" ("for true speech").

47. Shared motifs include the impossibility of speaking of, or approaching, the Lady: cf. Cercamon I, 15–18; III, 15–16, 21–24 and Arnaut I, 6–16; III, 1–3; V, 8–14; IX, 15–21; XIV, 5–7, 26–28; XX, 9–16; desire to see the Lady naked or share her bed: cf. Cercamon I, 23–24; II, 40–41; IV, 45–49, and Arnaut VIII, 35–38; IX, 29–35; X, 18–21; XI, 53–55; XVI, 29–35 (some of these take the form of dreams and so have more in common with Jaufré Rudel than with Cercamon); the lover as mad, cf. Cercamon I, 37–38; III, 21; IV, 26 and Arnaut I, 19; XIII, 18–20; XX, 27; XXIII, 38–40; XXIV, 25–29.

48. In his edition of Arnaut de Maruelh, Johnston translates: "Rien ne put jamais me défendre contre Amour," taking *poc* as third person, but this really strains the meaning ascribed to *contradire*.

49. In the last lines of this stanza, [I shall never win her unless] "per fin' Amors [. . .] / lo sieu ric cor per forssa non languis," Johnston's admission of *languis* as a transitive usage of *languir* is surely indefensible (edition of Arnaut de Maruelh); we could read *l'anguis*, from *angoisar* (Raynouard, *Lexique Roman*, II, 88) "affliger," "if true love [. . .] does not constrain her powerful heart by force," or else adopt the variant *lanquis* (i.e., *l'anquis*) from *I*, "if true love [. . .] does not seek out her powerful heart by force," thus again bringing power and language together.

50. The motif of lying truthfully or in a good cause also appears in Ar-

naut's V, 6; VIII, 13; XII, 15–21 (discussed in my *Subjectivity*, 21–23); and XVI, 40–42.

51. Arnaut is translating into dialectical terms a concept of Love which was discerned as early as the poetry of Guilhem de Peitieu by Scheludko, "Religöse Elemente," 34: "Love becomes conceived as the supreme good, the highest moral principle, and established as judge of men's moral conduct."

52. Spade, *Medieval Liar*, Anonymous IX.

53. "A term does not stand in for the utterance of which it is a part," Spade, *Medieval Liar*, Anonymous XX. Lacan's resolution of the liar paradox, which essentially consists in separating that which speaks (the Other) from that which is referred to (the self), could also be seen as an example of "restriction": the utterance "I am lying" is analyzed as "I that am the self produced by language say truthfully that the Other is lying through me." See Introduction, 33.

CHAPTER 4

1. Taylor, *Literary Riddle*, 1–3.
2. Sadly, fewer than fifty lines of this romance survive. But the fact of its existence in the vernacular at this date testifies to the importance of the riddle of incest in the generation of vernacular culture. Other texts, apart from the *Thebes*, to share this preoccupation are the *Life of Saint Gregory* and miracles of the Virgin Mary (see Chapter 5). The surviving Old French fragment contains Apollonius's answer to the riddle which Antiochus poses to all his daughter's potential suitors; as with the riddle of the sphinx, if they cannot answer it, they die. In the Latin *Historia*, §4, the riddle runs, "I am borne on crime; I eat my mother's flesh; I seek my brother, my mother's husband, my wife's son; I do not find him." Apollonius's answer in the Old French solves the riddle by identifying Antiochus as an incestuous father.
3. The imaginary is a key constant of fantasy and ideology, which obviously change over time. An important exposition of this area of Lacan's thought can be found in Brennan, *History*; cf. also my "Contradictions."
4. See Lacan, *Ethics*, 213: "Without the signifier at the beginning, it is impossible for the drive to be articulated as historical."
5. The extrahistorical cast of the real is made explicit by Žižek, *Plague of Fantasies*, 48–54.
6. The following texts (listed here in approximate chronological order) have been considered as *devinalhs* by different critics: Guilhem de Peitieu, "Farai un vers de dreit nien" (IV); Jaufré Rudel, "Non sap chantar" (I); Cer-

camon, "Quant l'aura doussa" (I; see Chapter 3); Raimbaut d'Aurenga, "Escotatz, mas no say que s'es" (XXIV); Giraut de Bornelh, "Un sonet fatz malvatz e bo" (LIV); Guillem de Berguedà and (?) Peire de Galceran, "En Gauseran, gardats"; Guilhem Ademar, "Ieu ai ja vista manhta rey" (XVI); Raimbaut de Vaqueiras, "Savis e fols" (XI) and "Las frevols venson lo plus fort" (XXVI); Aimeric de Peguilhan and Albertet de Sisteron, "Amics Albertz tensos sove" (VI); Peire Cardenal, "Una ciutatz fo, no sai cals" (LXXX); and anon., "Sui e no suy." This last is rubricated *devinalh* in the MS (*C*), the only occurrence of the term as a generic label in Occitan. Köhler, "Rätselgedicht," 151–56, stresses the difficulty of defining the corpus. Overviews are provided by Pasero, "*Devinalh*"; Rieger, "'Lop es nomnat lo pes'" (who proposes later additions to the corpus, 498); and Holmes, "Unriddling the *Devinalh*." Taylor, *Literary Riddle*, does not include Occitan texts in his survey, but many of his observations about the role of contradiction and obscenity in literary riddles are relevant to the Occitan tradition.

7. I omit Jaufré Rudel I (whose relationship with the *vers de dreit nien* has been thoroughly explored; see most recently Meneghetti, "Intertextuality," 187–88), Cercamon I (discussed in Chapter 3), and Raimbaut de Vaqueiras XI (because only the first stanza is riddling, as Köhler, "Rätselgedicht," points out).

8. Most recently Ménard, "Sens, contre-sens, nonsens," reviews existing scholarship. For a more pungent résumé of the dilemma over "nothing," see Gaunt, *Troubadours and Irony*, 27–29. The critic most inclined to take Guilhem's nothingness as expressing a mysterious something, the negative "beyond" of our possible thoughts, is Köhler, "No sai qui s'es." Lawner, "Notes," considers that the parade of paradoxes in fact resolves itself in a very concrete love object.

9. The wording in this line is problematic, and de Riquer, *Trovadores*, edits with the third-person plural form *cudan*; see Corcoran, "Song 53," 320, note 3.

10. The *tornada* summarizes the oppositions rehearsed in the song:

36 Per frevols son vencut li fort,
37 e potz d'agre doussor gitar,
38 e caut e freyt entremesclar,
39 e niens met son don a mort,
40 et el mort a trop gran ricor,
41 e tres perdon si per honor
42 que fan, e deu lur escazer.

The mighty are overwhelmed by the weak, sweetness can issue from sourness, heat and cold can mingle together, nothing can kill its lord, and the dead man is very wealthy, and thereby they utterly lose the honor they do, and so it must be.

(Linskill, in his edition of *The Poems of the Troubadour Raimbaut de Vaqueiras*, following the poem's first editor, Tobler, emends *tres perdon* to *ric perdon*.) If my ordering is adopted, we find that line 36 corresponds to lines 1–7, 37 to 8–12, 38 to 13–14 (reprised in 29–32), 39 to 15–21, 40 to 22–28, and 41–42 to 33–35. The logic of the song is that the struggle between strong and weak, bitter and sweet, hot and cold, leads to nothingness and death, but also to wealth or its loss. Raimbaut likewise concludes his multilingual descort with a systematic *tornada* which resumes all the languages used, in the right order, in successive couplets; and compare the programmatic opening stanza of "Savis e fols" (XI), which announces oppositions in the order in which they will be treated in subsequent stanzas. Both Tobler's edition and his solutions to the riddle are taken over by Linskill. They are: stanza i, weak women often get the better of a strong man; stanza ii (their stanza iii), the maturing of wine; stanza iii (their stanza ii), reputation and honor; stanza iv, seed corn; stanza v, the mouth and "You will be rich so long as you have money to spend."

11. See his edition of this Song, 267. Lawner ("Riddle," 32) suggests a possible influence of Plato's discussion of the reciprocal generation of contraries in the *Phaedo*, translation into Latin of which began in 1156. It is striking that Plato's ordering (weak–strong, sour–sweet, cold–heat, death–life) is the same as Raimbaut's, especially with my suggested interversion of the stanza order.

12. This stanza is a systematic amplification of line 24 of Raimbaut d'Aurenga's "Escotatz."

13. Fassbinder ("Trobador," 190) had earlier pointed out that the purpose of the antitheses seemed no more than a game to see how many words could be made to revolve around nothing, but her views are dismissed by Linskill and others (see his edition, 267, and references).

14. E.g., in XVIII where Amors separates honey from wax (32) and slays men without recourse to the sword (44) or XLIV, where the whore ruins and betrays the man who trusts her (5–8) because she is first sweet and then bitter (9–12).

15. Paul Lehmann, *Parodie im Mittelalter*, 244. For "nobody" jokes, see 235, 240–45, and for "nothing" jokes, 245–46.

16. Dejeanne's text reads: "D'aiqi nais l'avols barata, / ric cui mortz e Dieus descresca," lacking the allusion to the living dead which is so illuminating for Raimbaut's riddle.

17. Cf. the Swedish riddle cited from Taylor at the start of this chapter.

18. See Rieger, "*Vers de dreyt nien*," for a solution offering a numerological and astrological reading of the author's life.

19. Köhler, "No sai qui s'es," 352–54, also stresses the centering of this song on its subject (*qui s'es*), by contrast with the shift to the object (*que s'es*) in Raimbaut d'Aurenga.

20. On the real, see Lacan's *Relation d'objet*, 31–35, 43–46, where it is defined (1) as psychic mechanisms or drives and (2) as that which is lacking in the symbolic; see also Introduction, 31–32.

21. On obscenity in the riddle tradition, see Taylor, *Literary Riddle*, 7, and de Filippis, *Literary Riddle in Italy*, 13: "one of the most pronounced characteristics of Italian riddles is their obscenity."

22. I agree here with Milone, "Il 'ver de dreit nien,'" who argues against Pasero's view ("*Devinalh*," 116) of this passage as marking as resolution. Milone sees the opposition *sai–non sai* of lines 35 and 37 as further instance of the parodic use of opposition.

23. A self-denial central to Lacan's analysis of courtly love (*Ethics*, 149, 151) and confirmed by Žižek, *Metastases*, 96: "The Object of desire coincides with· the force that prevents its attainment." See also my "Desire and Subjectivity."

24. Rieger's list of examples ("'Lop es nomnat,'" 500–1) of troubadour references to a "burden" is convincing evidence of the erotic charge of Guillem de Berguedà's *coblas*. If additionally *pes* means "pitch," its corrupting force is increased, for who can touch pitch and not be defiled?

25. A skepticism shared by Köhler, "Rätselgedicht," 156.

26. Althusser, "Ideology"; cf. Butler, *Theories*, 106–31.

27. For a psychoanalytical critique of Althusser on interpellation, see Žižek, *Sublime Object of Ideology*, 43–44, 120–21, and *Metastases*, 59–62.

28. *Psychoses*, 299–300, and especially pithily 101, and 273, cited below, 172. On the nonexistence of the third person and the fact that ultimately the Other does not exist, see 278, 301.

29. Poirion, "Edyppus," 297, note 3. Poirion also discusses the introductory episodes of both the *Thebes* and the *Eneas* in chapter 3 of his *Résurgences*.

30. For discussion of the text of this riddle and its relation to the Occitan *devinalh* tradition, see Rieger, "'Aufgehobene' Genera," 82–83.

31. Many of the oldest riddles are actually pronounced in the first person, taking the form, "If I am all these contradictory or impossible things, what am I?" It is noteworthy that this is how Antiochus's riddle in the *Apollonius* romance is framed; see note 2 above.

32. Poirion ("Edyppus," 294–95) suggests that the riddle carries sexual connotations from the association of walking with sexual potency.

33. Althusser, "Ideology," 163, and Butler, *Theories*, 107 onward, on guilt. Note that Oedipus is called to recognize himself as incestuous, unlike Apollonius, who identifies incest in another. Zink (*Roman*, 25–26) interprets the *Apollonius* riddle as deriving from the Oedipal scenario.

34. Baswell, *Virgil*, 10, 96–97, 130, 154.

35. Nolan, "Judgement," argues that the narrative in *Eneas* could have been taken from contemporary marginal glosses on the *Aeneid* and is close to that of the first Vatican mythographer. Other explanations are those of Faral that the *Eneas*-poet was drawing on Donatus, an account discussed by Huchet, *Le Roman médiéval*, 40–41 (see Faral, "Récit"), or from the *Excidium Trojae* (see Baumgartner, "Sur quelques versions," 221).

36. Gaunt, "From Epic to Romance," 1–27; though for a reading which marginalizes the homophobic sentiment in the poem and foregrounds male friendship, see Burgwinkle, "Knighting."

37. According to Nolan (*Chaucer*, 99 and notes), Benoît's main sources are *Heroides* XII and *Metamorphoses* VII.

38. See also Žižek, *Looking Awry*, 44.

39. Desbordes, *Argonautica*, discusses the contradictions involved in the voyage of the Argonauts.

40. These marvels wrought by Medea, like those ascribed to the sorceress by Dido (*Eneas*, 1908–26), recall the miracles of hagiography.

41. "In true speech the Other is that before which you make yourself recognized. But you can make yourself recognized by it only because it is recognized first. It has to be recognized for you to be able to make yourself recognized" (Lacan, *Psychoses*, 51). This is an instance of the subject receiving its own message ("I recognize you") from the Other in inverted form.

42. "*Thou art the one who will follow me* presupposes [. . .] the imaginary assembly of those who are the supports of the discourse, the presence of witnesses, indeed, of the tribunal before which the subject receives the warning or the opinion that he is called upon to reply to" (Lacan, *Psychoses*, 301).

43. *Thebes*, 2921–36. The riddle is posed by a devil in the guise of an old woman, and Thideus's answer adopts the generic "man" rather than the first person singular assumed by Oedipus, starting: "when a man is old . . ." etc.

44. A subsequent episode in heaven represents the gods as a dysfunctional family similar to that of Thebes; here Juno, quarrelling with Jupiter, declares:

>   je sui ta seur et sui t'epouse.
>   (9459, cf. 9475)

I am your sister and your wife.

But the authenticity of this episode is in doubt and with it the question of whether incest extends to the immortals as well as to the doomed house of Thebes (see editor's introduction, xxxiii).

45. Cf. *Apollonius* where Antiochus kills those who solve the riddle as well as those who fail to!

46. Seducing a mortal to a world of enchantment by means of a visual lure, as in *Erec* and *Partonopeu*, does not involve the voice and so cannot constitute an interpellation.

47. Burgwinkle ("Knighting," 14, 19, 32–33) suggests that the *Eneas* reacts to troubadour codification and exaltation of heterosexual love.

48. Although the greatest similarity of the *Thebes* riddle is with "Sui et no suy," according to Rieger, "'Aufgehobene' Genera."

49. As attested in Taylor, *Literary Riddle*.

CHAPTER 5

1. The earliest is the *Passion* of Clermont-Ferrand (tenth century), the role of Mary in which is discussed by Nichols, *Romanesque Signs*, 117–26. References to Mary in hagiographic texts dedicated to other saints include the *Life of Saint Alexis*, where the speaking statue at Edessa is a statue of the Virgin. The legends of Theophilus and Mary the Egyptian can be included in Mary miracle collections or treated as self-standing saints' lives. There are evidently lost vernacular texts of both of these, because in the *Gracial* Adgar refers to a previous translation of a Theophilus text and states that he is summarizing the familiar story of Mary the Egyptian. An overview of the textual tradition of lives of Mary the Egyptian, and a twelfth-century *Life* of her, can be found in Dembowski's edition.

2. See also *Deuxième collection* and *Treize miracles*. An overview of vernacular Mary miracles is provided by Ebel, *Altromanische Mirakel*.

3. E.g., (in 1912) Chaytor, *Troubadours*, 14–15: "If chivalry was the outcome of the Germanic theory of knighthood as modified by the influence of Christianity, it may be said that troubadour love is the outcome of the same theory under the influence of Mariolatry."

4. Cf. the title of Warner's famous study, *Alone of All Her Sex*.

5. Another famous title: Gold's feminist study (*Lady and the Virgin*) of the relation between Mary and the courtly Lady in medieval art and literature.

6. See, for example, Gay-Crosier, *Religious Elements*; Scheludko, "Religiöse Elemente."

7. For comparison between secular and religious "wonders," see Ebel, *Altromanische Mirakel*, 33 ff., and Gallais, "Remarques."

8. *La Relation d'objet* has not been translated into English and all translations are my own. Because the English translation of Kristeva is often unhelpful, I likewise use my own but provide page references to the published translation (given first) as well as to the original French (given second).

9. Brennan's summary (*History*, 100) is very clear: "Kristeva [. . .] makes 'abjection' the foundation of objectification. Abjection is the feeling that one has revolting (including excremental) substances within; objectification comes from the need to exclude these substances by depositing them in the other, which brings the other, as object, into being."

10. See Kunstmann's introductions to his editions of the *Gracial* (19 ff.) and the *Treize miracles* (3); also Gallais, "Remarques."

11. This is less true of the "tourist industry" cycles such as that of Rocamador, which provide a more "local doctor" treatment of injuries than "intensive care" for the soul in peril.

12. One has to have a foot operation (XXI), another suffers from a broken limb (XXXIX). There is a wider range of healing miracles in the Rocamador collection.

13. Cf. Chaucer's "Prioress's Tale," where the child killed by the Jews and thrown into the privy sings despite having his throat cut.

14. See Poncelet's index of Latin miracle texts, "Miraculorum Beatae," nos. 94, 109, 290, 385, 464, 631, 926, 964, and 1059. Mussafia (*Studien*, I, 943) also identifies them as a group ("Marienbräutigam"), initially with respect to a Latin version corresponding to Adgar XXXVI included in the collection he calls PEZ. For a survey of the relations between the Latin examples of this group and a selection of vernacular examples, see Wyrembek and Morawski, *Légendes*.

15. I have emended this line at the suggestion of Ian Short.

16. Compare, for example, the rivalry and fighting between the wife and the mistress over the man in Adgar XLIII.

17. Poncelet, "Miraculorum Beatae," nos. 47, 360, 242, 425, 450, 483, 625, 662, 950, 1001, 1010, 1090, 1267, 1300, 1406, 1559, 1588, 1590. Further examples are included in Tubach, *Index Exemplorum*, nos. 2730, 2735, 2736.

18. The text of this group of Occitan miracles closely follows that of the first thirteen in Vincent of Beauvais's *Speculum Historiale*. Vincent in turn cites as his authority the *Mariale Magnum*, also cited as the source of the miracle collection in B.L. Additional 15723, a twelfth-century manuscript which contains many of the same miracles as Vincent; see Ward, *Catalogue*, 2:627. In his *Treize Miracles*, Kunstmann (Introduction, 8) identifies the *Mariale Magnum* with B.N. lat. 3177, which is also a twelfth-century manuscript containing a

version of the mother-incest miracle (*incipit* the same as Poncelet, "Miraculorum Beatae," 843). The Occitan collection includes an example of the *sponsus marianus* miracle (IX: young man gives a ring to a statue of the Virgin).

19. Ebel, *Altromanische Mirakel*, 24, cites the Occitan collection as an example.

20. Poncelet, "Miraculorum Beatae," 483. Dahan (editor, "Un Miracle de Notre Dame," 108–9) lists the verse miracles in the collections from which his text is edited. In B.N. lat. 17491, the miracle (*incipit* "Erat Rome vir quidam nobilis") is the first of twelve; in B.N. lat. 2333A, it is the first of thirteen and is immediately followed by a version of Theophilus. The remainder of the collections is the same in both manuscripts.

21. See Breeze, "Virgin Mary." Breeze shows that the topos, contrary to previous opinion, predates Augustine, and he illustrates its widespread use in vernacular languages, including French.

22. Comparison between "Lanval" and this group of miracles goes back to Wyrembek and Morawski, *Légendes*, 15. Bloch (*Medieval Misogyny*, 139–42) compares "Lanval" to Gautier de Coinci's version of the miracle of Theophilus.

23. Žižek, *Metastases*, 90–92.

24. Harf-Lancner, *Fées*, 94–101, 102–9, 113, 211–12, 243–61; see also my discussion of *Partonopeu* in Chapter 7.

25. Emphasis on the purchase value of the *fée*'s accessories accords with Marx's application of the term "fetish" to the commodity.

26. The fetish is symbolic because veiling the object marks the possibility of conceiving it as alternatively absent or present, and the veil itself "symbolizes" the object behind. See Lacan, *Relation d'objet*, 56–57, 86, 228, and *pace* Dylan Evans, *Introductory Dictionary*, s.v. "fetishism" and "phobia."

27. Bloch, *Medieval Misogyny*, sees this contradiction as constitutive of "courtly love"; *Lanval* is among the texts he discusses. My reading differs from his in that he seems to believe that the love, if it remained veiled, would really exist.

28. Žižek, *Plague of Fantasies*, 103: "Crucial for the fetish object is that it emerges at the intersection of the two lacks: the subject's own lack as well as the lack of his big Other. [. . .] The fetish functions simultaneously as the representative of the Other's inaccessible depth *and* as its exact opposite, as the stand-in for that which the Other itself lacks ('mother's phallus'). At its most fundamental, the fetish is a screen concealing the liminal experience of the Other's impotence." Žižek's account situates the fetish as occupying the place of *objet a*, as described in my Introduction, 32–35.

29. An analogous procedure of "fetish-formation" occurs in "Guigemar,"

where the image of love as a wound is replaced by the belt and shirt: by covering up the "wound," they perpetuate its existence as a myth in which the characters can believe.

30. See Maréchal, "Le lai de Fresne," 136; and on the miracle of the sacristine, Guiette, *Légende*.

31. Maréchal argues that the plot of "Fresne" is geared to the avoidance of incest; cf. Poirion's comment (*Résurgences*, 105) that the story of a recognition of the child by the parents is the inverse of the Oedipus story. In the *lai* of "Les Deus Amanz," the *Apollonius* scenario of father–daughter incest is likewise conjured only to be evaded.

32. "Lanval" and "Yonec" occur on their own in B.L. Cott. Vesp. B XIV and B.N. fr. 24432, respectively. The excerpts of the *Gracial* found in Dulwich College MS 22 consist in a portion of "Theophilus" (XXVI), the prologue, and the beginning of the miracle of the sick monk "Wettinus" (XXXII). See below for discussion of the status of the miracle of the pregnant abbess (XLIX).

33. See Mussafia, *Marienstudien*, IV, 14. On the other hand, Adgar may be innovating when he relegates most of the miracles with female subjects to the end of his collection. This parallels the order adopted in estates satires, such as *Le Livre des Manières* by Adgar's contemporary Etiennes de Fougères.

34. Legge, *Anglo-Norman Literature*, 187–88, supported by Ebel, *Altromanische Mirakel*, 22.

35. See Sol's introduction to the edition of *La Vie du Pape Saint Gregoire*, xvii and note 26.

36. In recent years, "for" Marie as author of the *Lais* are the contributors to Maréchal, editor, *In Quest of Marie de France*. Essays in this volume do not engage with the contrary position, put by Baum, *Recherches*, and Masters, *Esthétique*. See most recently Griffin, "Gender," whose reflections on symbolic paternity in the *lai* are echoed below.

37. "William's style is almost incomparable with that of Adgar. His method is not one based on authorial intervention and he is not at all intrusive. As an author he takes a back seat, merely reporting the miracles. Of course there are odd remarks of the type 'nisi me fallit memoria' (104), and so on, but this is an utterly different type of interpolation from those of Adgar" (Dominic Selwood, personal communication recorded with thanks).

38. Kristeva's point (*Powers*, 45/56) about the homosexual coloration, although without commitment to a homosexual stance, of the phobic's fetishistic use of language is borne out in the *Gracial* by the general disgust toward heterosexual relations and by the cultivation of male friendship, both in

Adgar's addresses to his friend Gregory and in the narrative of Miracle XXXVII.

39. As maintained, for example, by Gallais, "Remarques."

40. "Par ço nus mustre apertement / ke quiqunke la sert bonement / la grace Deu avra pur veir / e la sue, matin e seir. / E Deu servir la nus duinst / e de nos pecchez nus esluinst!" (I, 109–14).

41. At the end of XLVII, the phrase "E Deu la nus duinst si tenir" definitely means "And may God grant to us to observe it [Candlemass]."

CHAPTER 6

1. It may also support the desire of the tortured, but this is not explored by Lacan. The death wish turned in upon the self, the drive toward one's own death, is recognized by Lacan in Antigone (see below).

2. For various studies of how the concept of "two deaths" underpins the sublime in a series of examples from popular culture, see Žižek, *Looking Awry*, chapters 1–6.

3. I quote from Francis's edition of the separate manuscript versions rather than Keller's synoptic edition. *A* is the only manuscript to transmit this passage, the others being lacunary.

4. Textual difficulty: see Thomas's note on possible ways of understanding *m'adag* in his edition of the *Life of Saint Faith*.

5. Cf. also *St. Lawrence*, 142–44.

6. The zone between the two deaths is more literally connected to physical death, then, than in the *Antigone* where the heroine is "shut up or suspended in the zone between life and death. Although she is not yet dead, she is eliminated from the world of the living" (Lacan, *Ethics*, 280).

7. The insistence on the number three may also reflect a Trinitarian impulse here. The treatment of the body between two deaths in *George* offers an interesting illustration of the distinction between the body and the flesh drawn by Boureau, "Sacrality."

8. These lines, cited from *A*, occur in all manuscripts.

9. Cf. also 164–65, also in *A* only, and 269–70, in *AM*.

10. As stressed, for example, by Heffernan, *Sacred Biography*.

11. On the homoerotic quality of Eneas's love for Pallas and the description of Pallas's death, see Burgwinkle, "Knighting," 31–33.

12. I thus disagree with Rollo (*Historical Fabrication*, 212), who sees this evisceration as emphasizing how lifeless Hector is in death, though his comparison between Hector's "empty" body and the "full" bodies of the martyrs is interesting.

13. This same contradiction is perceived, but from a different standpoint, by Patterson (*Negotiating the Past*, 170–83), who sees the *Eneas* as both flattening out the historical process and as admitting "a counterawareness of the human cost of historical life" (181).

14. On the *Eneas* tombs, see Poirion, "De l'*Enéide* à l'*Éneas*," especially 221–24; and Sullivan, who describes Camilla's tomb as "an extraordinary and architecturally implausible mausoleum shaped like an ice-cream cone balanced on two interlocking arches" ("Medieval Automata," 4).

15. *Eneas*, 7531 ff., speaks of Camilla's tomb still being one of the marvels of the world. The historic present used in the descriptions of the tomb of Pallas has the same effect.

16. Compare Lacan's remarks on primitive cave painting in *Ethics*, 139–40. Why paint where no one can see? Lacan suggests that the very invisibility of these paintings is a mark of what he calls "extimacy," of the fact that what seems most secret and internal to us (the Thing) is also that which most patently infuses the external symbolic fabric.

17. Although the word *martyre* is used throughout the *Troie* in the purely secular sense of "terrible suffering," the translation "martyrdom" here is justified by the accumulation of religious overtones to Achilles's passion and death: he is to be crucified (20769, 20776), while Polyxena's qualities are spiritual and angelic (20799–800).

18. Baumgartner, "Tombeaux," comments on this difference between the *Troie* and the *Eneas*. King Mennon and the Amazon queen Panthesilia in the *Troie* are likewise dismembered.

19. See the overview of the relationship of *Cligés* to the Tristan story in Polak, *Cligés*, chapter 4.

20. I do not contest Chrétien's debt to learning, amply documented by Haidu, *Aesthetic Distance*, Hunt, "Aristotle," and others. I take issue, though, with Freeman, who sees the figures of Thessala and Johan as endorsing Chrétien's *clergie*. See, e.g., Freeman, *Poetics*, 134, where "a strong analogy between *Cligés* as text and the *poisons*" is read as contributing to "the process of self celebration the fiction performs." Hanning (*Individual*, 114–18) goes to the other extreme in emphasizing the inadequacies of *engin*. The most critical view of Thessala I have met is that adopted by D. W. Robertson Jr., "Chrétien's *Cligés*," 38.

21. The fact that the "nothing" which is Alis's lot is precisely *not* the female genitals but their absence reinforces my skepticism toward interpreting Raimbaut de Vaqueiras's "nothing" as female genitalia in "Las frevols"; see Chapter 4.

22. On Chrétien's possible self-mockery here, see Polak, *Cligés*, 45–46. On

the mystical resonances of heart–eye imagery in *Cligés*, see Paoli, "La Relation oeil–coeur." On the image (699 ff.) of love's dart passing through Alixandre's eye without harming it, like light through glass—an image of the incarnation—see Gros, "*Semblance*"; there is a similar passage in Wace's *Conception*, 1035–41.

23. This tale, without biblical authority, was widely cited as an antifeminist *exemplum*.

24. Owen ("Profanity," 40–41) offers a detailed comparison between Fenice's "passion" and "resurrection" and those of Christ in Matt. 17–18; see also Hanning, "Audience," 22–23.

25. Freeman (*Poetics*, 164) describes Johan's building as "a sort of enchanted mausoleum which vies with a structure like Camilla's tomb for first place."

26. For previous discussions of Fenice's "martyrdom," see Haidu, *Aesthetic Distance*, 92.

27. The phrase "death of death" is adapted from Žižek, *Looking Awry*, 86, where he speaks of the "second death" of Madeleine in Hitchcock's *Vertigo* as the "loss of loss" when the hero's belief in her collapses.

28. The structure of disavowal, "I know very well . . . and yet," is the subject of Mannoni, "Je sais bien, mais quand même," who adduces impressive examples of our half-denying beliefs which we are happy to let other people hold on our behalf. Cf. Žižek, *Looking Awry*, 111–16, on the fantasmatic "other" audience of nostalgia movies. Most courtly literature, riven as it is by irony, depends on imaginary others, less sophisticated than oneself, as the fantasmatic support of its sublime elements.

29. Indeed, the doctors who torture Fenice are compared by Haidu to the *divin Marquis* (*Aesthetic Distance*, 94).

30. See Duncan Robertson, *Medieval Saints' Lives*, 50–51, who refers to the "cartoon-like unreality" of the *George* and concludes "the pathos of martyrdom has become transformed into an exercise of wit."

31. See Gravdal, *Ravishing Maidens*, 38–41.

32. See, for example, Duncan Robertson, "Writing in the Textual Community," 18–22; MacBain, "Five Old French Renderings," 57–63. The proximity of hagiography and romance in the thirteenth century is the subject of Cazelles, *The Lady as Saint*.

33. Cf. Lacan, *Ethics*, 322: "[The saint's] goal is, in effect, access to sublime desire and not at all his own desire, for the saint lives and pays for others."

CHAPTER 7

1. It is helpful to think of Lacanian theory as a vast cat's cradle in which one structure can be transformed into a quite different one by tweaking a par-

ticular point in the crisscrossing of a single string: a quick flip and the whole disposition of relations is transformed, even though the terms that constitute them remain the same.

2. On the success of *Partonopeu*, see Fourrier, *Courant réaliste*, 315–17. I pass over the example of the sublime-perverse chosen by Lacan and briefly discussed by Žižek—the obscene *sirventes* by Arnaut Daniel (XVIII)—because I have written elsewhere ("Desire and Subjectivity") on Lacan's writing on the troubadours.

3. Lacan, *Ethics*, 315–16 (cf. also 70): "The breakthrough is achieved by Kant when he posits that the moral imperative is not concerned with what may or may not be done. To the extent that it imposes the necessity of a practical reason, obligation affirms an unconditional 'Thou shalt.' The importance of this field derives from the void that the strict application of the Kantian definition leaves there."

4. Lacan, *Ethics*, 310: "We haven't yet extracted from the Kantian definition of the sublime all the substance we might. The conjunction of this term with that of sublimation is probably not simply an accident nor simply homophonic." In what follows, Lacan draws on Kant's *Critique of Judgment*.

5. See Žižek, *Sublime Object*, 131–33, on the relation of the death drive to the symbolic in different periods of Lacan's thought.

6. My translation. An English translation exists of this essay, but I have been unable to obtain it. The same passage is cited in abbreviated form, and consequently misleadingly, by Lacan, *Ethics*, 79: "Let us take as the universal maxim of our conduct the right to enjoy any other person whatsoever as the instrument of our pleasure." The important difference is that in "Kant avec Sade," the speaker of the maxim offers himself as object of the other's enjoyment, whereas in the abridged version of the *Ethics*, the speaker claims the other as object of his own.

7. This is implied too in Žižek, *Sublime Object*, where he speaks of the victim as sublime, though Lacan also speaks of her as a double of the subject (*Ethics*, 261). But there is not a contradiction here because, as the second graph in "Kant avec Sade" shows (778), the effect of Sade's sadistic law is to put a in the position on Schema L usually occupied by S, and to put $\$$ in the position usually occupied by a: in this way, the split ("sublime") subject occupies, for the pervert, the position of imaginary object. See Žižek, *Everything*, 219–23.

8. To illustrate the difference between himself and Kant, Lacan cites Kant's anecdote of the man threatened with being hanged if he has sex. Kant assumes that the death penalty will act as a universal deterrent; Lacan, however, observes that for some it might well act as a stimulus. What we desire to

do depends not on some external machinery of legislation but on the way the law of the signifier is installed within us.

9. See also Žižek, *For They Know Not*, 229–53, and most recently "Kant with (or against) Sade."

10. But see also my Introduction, 33–34.

11. Hult, introduction, 12, "la Dame est résolument dépersonnalisée par Chrétien."

12. Cf. the variant to line 1182 in *V: ensegne veraie*.

13. This rapprochement between the gaze and invocation is made in Lacan, *Four Fundamental Concepts*, 104: "At the scopic level we are no longer at the level of demand, but of desire, of the desire of the Other. It is the same at the level of the invocatory drive, which is the closest to the experience of the unconscious."

14. Cf. Lacan, *Four Fundamental Concepts*, 88–89: "Holbein makes visible for us here something that is simply the subject as annihilated—annihilated in the form, that is, strictly speaking, the imaged embodiment of the minus-phi ($-\phi$) of castration, which for us centers the whole organization of the desires through the framework of the fundamental drives."

15. Chrétien may, however, have also drawn on the story of Gyges, the shepherd who used a magic ring to spy on the wife of King Candaulus, and then killed him and took his place. This story is referred to by Cicero in his *On Duties*, III, 38/305, a work widely known in the twelfth century. In Cicero's account too, the stone is turned inward to make the wearer invisible.

16. Lacan, *Four Fundamental Concepts*, 87: "This is why it is so important to acknowledge the inverted use of perspective in the structure of anamorphosis."

17. Line 1995: "Trestot sont noir, mais molt sont bel." Does their dark color represent a minimal level of visibility?

18. The phrase "forcible seduction" is Krueger's ("Textuality," 59). The text is unclear whether Melior planned him to come to her bed or not. The text clings in a sentimental-cum-moral way to representing her as a modest maiden as well as an all-powerful magician, a disavowal on the part of the narrator as marked as those of Partonopeu himself; see, e.g., 1137 ff.

19. Childhood was standardly divided into the periods of *infantia* (birth to age 7), *pueritia* (7–12 for girls, 7–14 for boys), and *adolescentia* (12 or 15–20). At 13, Partonopeu is still a *puer* and not yet deemed capable of consenting to or refusing marriage. See Shahar, *Childhood*, 22, 24–26.

20. Antagonism between the *fée* and the mother is traditional in the folklore analogues (Harf-Lancner, *Fées*, 327). The Celtic tradition of fairy lovers often assigns a maternal-cum-tutorial role to the *fée* (Bruckner, *Shaping Romance*, 124).

21. "The phallus is fundamental as a signifier, fundamental to the mother's imaginary with which he seeks to ally himself, since the child's ego rests upon the mother's omnipotence" (Lacan, *Relation d'objet*, 193).

22. On the inversion of the usual depiction of gender, so that the plot proceeds through Partonopeu winning a series of beauty contests while Melior is virtually not described, see Bruckner, *Shaping Romance*, 117–33, especially 120.

23. See Bruckner, *Shaping Romance*, 129–30, 137.

24. Lacan, *Four Fundamental Concepts*, 129: "What cannot be remembered is repeated in behavior."

25. The edition reads *doit*.

CONCLUSION

1. Jaeger, *Origins*, summarized 234–35.

2. This is how Bezzola presents the creation of love by Guilhem de Peitieu, *Origines*, part II, vol. 2, 295 ff. It was also the view promoted earlier this century by Robert Briffault and has been taken up again recently by Kendrick (*Game of Love*, 15, 180–82).

3. Brennan's account influenced my "Contradictions" essay, whose conclusions I wish to modify in the light of the far more abundant and wide-ranging analysis conducted in this present study.

4. In any case, perverse structures are not the same as psychotic ones, so the importance of sexual difference for perversion does not of itself confirm the analysis proffered by Brennan on the basis of *Encore*.

5. Cf. Eley and Simons, "Male Beauty and Sexual Orientation in *Partonopeu de Blois*."

6. Guiette's title refers to a well-known passage from the beginning of Jean Bodel's *Les Saisnes*, according to which *romans antiques* are wise and instructive, Breton tales pleasing and vain, and *chansons de geste* truthful. Kelly, "Romance and the Vanity," is also dedicated to unpacking this passage, but Kelly's contention that romance achieves a synthesis of social meaning through a "fullness" of meaning on several levels is, to my mind, less persuasive than Guiette's.

Works cited

I. ANTIQUE AND MEDIEVAL WORKS

To facilitate consultation, all saints' lives are entered by the name of the saint concerned, including Saint Mary the Virgin. Similarly, all editions of troubadours are preceded by the troubadour's name spelled as elsewhere in this book (namely the orthography used by de Riquer, *Trovadores*). Where more than one edition of the same text or author is listed, the one marked * is the edition cited unless otherwise indicated.

Abbreviatio Montana. In *The Cambridge Translations of Medieval Philosophical Texts*, edited by Norman Kretzman and Eleonore Stump. Vol. 1, *Logic and the Philosophy of Language*, 39–78. Cambridge: Cambridge University Press, 1988.

Aimeric de Peguilhan. *The Poems of Aimeric de Peguilhan.* Edited by William P. Shepard and Frank M. Chambers. Evanston, Ill.: Northwestern University Press, 1950.

Alberic of Pisançon. *Alexander.* In *The Medieval French "Roman d'Alexandre."* Edited by Edward C. Armstrong. Vol. 3 prepared by Alfred Foulet. Elliott Monographs 38. Princeton, N.J.: Princeton University Press, 1949.

Albertet de Sisteron, *see* Aimeric de Peguilhan.

Alegret. *Jongleurs et troubadours gascons des XIIe et XIIIe siècles.* Edited by Alfred Jeanroy. Classiques Français du Moyen Âge 39. Paris: Champion, 1923.

Anselm of Canterbury. *Works.* Edited and translated by J. Hopkins and H. Richardson. 4 vols. London: Mellen, 1974–1976.

———. "The Incarnation of the Word." In *Works*, 3:9–37.

———. "A Meditation on Human Redemption." In *Works*, 1:137–44.

———. *Proslogion.* In *Works*, 1:87–112.

Apollonius of Tyre, Old French text:
Schulze, Alfred. "Ein Bruchstück des altfranzösischen *Apolloniusromanes*." *Zeitschrift für romanische Philologie* 33 (1909): 226–29.
Apollonius of Tyre, Latin text of the *Historia Apollonii regis Tyri*, with English translation:
Archibald, Elizabeth. *"Apollonius of Tyre": Medieval and Renaissance Themes and Variations*. Cambridge: Brewer, 1991.
Aristotle. *The Complete Works of Aristotle*. Revised Oxford Translation. Edited by Jonathan Barnes. 2 vols. Bollingen Series 71.2. Princeton, N.J.: Princeton University Press, 1984.
———. *Categories*. In *Complete Works*, 1:3–24.
———. *De interpretatione*. In *Complete Works*, 1:25–38.
———. *Prior Analytics*. In *Complete Works*, 1:39–113.
———. *Topics*. In *Complete Works*, 1:167–277.
———. *Sophistical Refutations*. In *Complete Works*, 1:278–314.
Arnaut Daniel. *Arnaut Daniel: Canzoni*. Edited by Gianluigi Toja. Florence: Sansoni, 1960.
Arnaut de Maruelh. *Les Poésies lyriques du troubadour Arnaut de Marueil*. Edited by Ronald C. Johnston. Paris: Droz, 1935.
Augustine. *Confessions*. Translated by Henry Chadwick. Oxford: Oxford University Press, 1991.
———. *De doctrina Christiana (On Christian Teaching)*. Translated and with an introduction and notes by R. P. H. Green. World's Classics. Oxford: Oxford University Press, 1997.
Azalais de Porcairagues. Angelica Rieger, *Trobairitz: Der Beitrag der Frau in der altokzitanischen höfischen Lyrik. Edition des Gesamtkorpus*, 480–504. Beihefte zur *Zeitschrift für romanische Philologie* 233. Tübingen: Niemeyer, 1991.
Benoît de Sainte Maure. *Le Roman de Troie*. Edited by Léopold Constans. Société des Anciens Textes Français. 6 vols. Paris: Firmin-Didot, 1904–1912.
Bernart Marti. *Il trovatore Bernart Marti*. Edited by Fabrizio Beggiato. Modena: Mucchi, 1984.
Bernart de Ventadorn. *Bernard de Ventadour, troubadour du xiie siècle. Chansons d'amour*. Edited by M. Lazar. Paris: Klincksieck, 1966.
Boethius. *De topicis differentiis*. Translated with notes and essays on the text by Eleonore Stump. Ithaca, N.Y.: Cornell University Press, 1978.
Boethius, *Philosophiae Consolationis Libri Quinque*. Edited by Walter Berschin and Walter Bulst. Heidelberg: Winter, 1977.
Cercamon. *Il Trovatore Cercamon*. Edited by Valeria Tortoreto. Modena: Mucchi, 1981.

Chrétien de Troyes. *Cligès*. Edited by Charles Méla and Olivier Collet. Lettres gothiques. Paris: Le livre de poche, 1994.
———. *Le Chevalier au lion*. Edited by David F. Hult. Lettres gothiques. Paris: Le livre de poche, 1994.
———. *Le Chevalier de la Charrette ou le roman de Lancelot*. Edited by Charles Méla. Lettres gothiques. Paris: Le livre de poche, 1992.
———. "D'Amors qui m'a tolu a moi." In *Cligès*, 460–62. Edited by Charles Méla and Olivier Collet. Lettres gothiques. Paris: Le livre de poche, 1994.
Cicero. *On Duties*. Translated by Walter Miller. Loeb Classical Library 30. Cambridge, Mass.: Harvard University Press, 1913.
Elias d'Ussel. *Les Poésies des quatre troubadours d'Ussel*. Edited by Jean Audiau. Paris: Delagrave, 1922.
Eneas. Roman du XII siècle. Edited by J.-J. Salverda de Grave. 2 vols. Classiques Français du Moyen Age 44, 62. Paris: Champion, 1925, 1929.
Geffrei Gaimar. *L'Estoire des Engleis*. Edited by Alexander Bell. Anglo-Norman Texts Society 14–16. Oxford: Blackwell, 1960.
Giraut de Bornelh. *The Cansos and Sirventes of the Troubadour Giraut de Borneil: A Critical Edition*. Edited by Ruth Verity Sharman. Cambridge: Cambridge University Press, 1989.
Sämtliche Lieder des trobadors Giraut de Bornelh. Edited by A. Kolsen. 2 vols. Halle: Niemeyer, 1910, 1935.
Gui d'Ussel, *see* Elias d'Ussel.
Guilhem Ademar. *Poésies du troubadour Guilhem Adémar*. Edited by Kurt Almqvist. Uppsala: Almqvist and Wiksell, 1951.
Guilhem de Peitieu. *Guglielmo IX d'Aquitania: Poesie*. Edited by Nicolò Pasero. Modena: Mucchi, 1973.
Guilhem de Sant Leidier. *Poésies du troubadour Guillem de Saint-Didier*. Edited by Aimo Sakari. Mémoires de la Société Néophilologique de Helsinki 19. Helsinki: Société Néophilologique, 1956.
Guillem de Berguedà and (?) Peire de Galceran. "En Gauseran, gardats." Edited by Dietmar Rieger, "'Lop es nomnat lo pes, e lop no es.' Un devinalh sans solution?" In *Mélanges de langue et de littérature occitanes en hommage à Pierre Bec*, 497–506. Poitiers, C.É.S.C.M., 1991.
Hue de la Rotelande. *Ipomedon*. Edited by A. J. Holden. Bibliothèque française et romane B17. Paris: Klincksieck, 1979.
Jaufré Rudel. *Il Canzoniere di Jaufre Rudel*. Edited by Giorgio Chiarini. Rome: L'Aquila, 1985.
John of Salisbury. *The "Metalogicon" of John of Salisbury: A Twelfth-Century Defense of the Verbal and Logical Arts of the Trivium*. Translated with an in-

troduction and notes by Daniel D. McGarry. Berkelely: University of California Press, 1955.

Marcabru. *Poésies complètes du troubadour Marcabru*. Edited by J.-M.-L. Dejeanne. Toulouse: Privat, 1909.

———. **The Poetry of the Troubadour Marcabru*. Edited by Simon Gaunt, Ruth Harvey, and Linda Paterson. Woodbridge, UK: Boydell and Brewer, 2000.

Marie de France. *Lais*. Edited by A. Ewert. Oxford: Blackwell, 1944.

Montan. *Burlesque et obscénité chez les troubadours. Le Contre-texte au moyen âge*. Edited by Pierre Bec, 161. Paris: Stock, 1984.

Orderic Vitalis. *Ecclesiastical History*. Edited by Marjorie Chibnall. 6 vols. Oxford: Oxford University Press, 1969–1980.

Partonopeu de Blois. Edited by Joseph Gildea, O.S.A. 2 vols. Villanova, Pa.: Villanova University Press, 1967–1970.

Passion. Gaston Paris, "*La Passion du Christ*, texte revu sur le ms. de Clermont-Ferrand." *Romania* 2 (1873): 295–314.

Peire Cardenal. *Poésies complètes du troubadour Peire Cardenal (1180–1278): Texte, traduction, commentaire, analyse des travaux antérieurs, lexique*. Edited by René Lavaud. Bibliothèque Méridionale 34. Toulouse: Privat, 1957.

Peire d'Alvernha. *Peire d'Alvernha: Liriche*. Edited by Alberto del Monte. Turin: Loescher-Chiantore, 1955.

(?) Peire de Galceran, *see* Guillem de Berguedà.

Peire Rogier. *The Poems of the Troubadour Peire Rogier*. Edited by Derek Nicholson. Manchester: Manchester University Press, 1976.

Peire Vidal. *Peire Vidal: Poesie*. Edited by D'Arco Silvio Avalle. 2 vols. Milan: Riccardo Ricciardi, 1960.

Peirol and fictional Bernart de Ventadorn. "Peirol, cum avetz tant estat?" Edited by John Marshall, "Dialogues of the Dead." In *The Troubadours and the Epic: Essays in Memory of W. Mary Hackett*, edited by Linda M. Paterson and Simon B. Gaunt, 37–58, at 45–49. Warwick: French Department, University of Warwick, 1987.

Raimbaut d'Aurenga. *The Life and Works of the Troubadour Raimbaut d'Orange*. Edited by Walter T. Pattison. Minneapolis: University of Minnesota Press, 1952.

Raimbaut de Vaqueiras. **The Poems of the Troubadour Raimbaut de Vaqueiras*. Edited by Joseph Linskill. Mouton: The Hague, 1964.

———. "Las frevols venson lo plus fort" (XXVI). Edited by Adolf Tobler. Report of a session held on February 14, 1882. *Archiv für das Studium der neueren Sprachen* 68 (1882): 84–85.

Saint Alexis, *L* version:
"*La Vie de saint Alexis:" Texte du manuscrit de Hildesheim (L)*. Edited by Christopher Storey. Geneva: Droz, 1968.
Saint Alexis, *A* version:
La Vie de saint Alexis: Texte du manuscrit A. Edited by T. D. Hemming. Exeter: Exeter University Press, 1994.
Saint Alexis, *S* version:
Elliott, Alison Goddard. *"La Vie de saint Alexis" in the Twelfth and Thirteenth Centuries: An Edition and Commentary*. North Carolina Studies in the Romance Languages and Literatures 221. Chapel Hill: University of North Carolina Press, 1983.
Saint Catherine. *The Life of St. Catherine by Clemence of Barking*. Edited by William MacBain. Anglo-Norman Texts Society 18. Oxford: Blackwell, 1964.
Saint Catherine, English translation:
Wogan-Browne, Jocelyn, and Glyn S. Burgess. *Virgin Lives and Holy Deaths: Two Exemplary Biographies for Anglo-Norman Women*. Everyman Library. London: Dent, 1996.
Saint Catherine, Manchester version:
Fawtier-Jones, E. C. "Les Vies de Sainte Catherine d'Alexandrie." *Romania* LVI (1930): 80–104.
Saint Catherine, Latin text of the *Passio S. Katerine*, "Vulgate" version:
d'Ardenne, S.R.T.O., and E. J. Dobson, editors. *Seinte Katerine Re-edited from MS Bodley 34 and the Other Manuscripts*, 132–203. Early English Text Society. Oxford: Oxford University Press, 1981.
Saint Eulalia. *The Sequence of St. Eulalia*. In *The French Language*, translated and edited by Alfred Ewert, 353–54. London: Faber, 1933.
Saint Eustace. "Das altfranzösische *Eustachiusleben*." Edited by Andreas C. Ott. *Romanische Forschungen* 32 (1913): 481–607.
Saint Evroul. Ferdinand Danne. "Das altfranzösische Ebrulfusleben. Eine Dichtung aus dem 12. Jahrhundert." *Romanische Forschungen* 32 (1913): 748–893.
Saint Faith. *La Chanson de Sainte Foi d'Agen*. Edited by Antoine Thomas. Classiques Français du Moyen Age 45. Paris: Champion, 1925.
Saint Genevieve. *La Vie de Sainte Geneviève de Paris*. Edited by Lennart Bohm. Uppsala: Almqvist and Wiksells, 1955.
Saint George. *La Vie de Saint Georges*. In *Les Oeuvres de Simund de Freine*, 61–117. Edited by John E. Matzke. Société des Anciens Textes Français. Paris: Firmin-Didot, 1909.
Saint Giles. *La Vie de Saint Gilles par Guillaume de Berneville. Poème du xii*

siècle. Edited by Gaston Paris and Alphonse Bos. Société des Anciens Textes Français. Paris: Firmin-Didot, 1881.

Saint Gregory. *La Vie du Pape Saint Gregoire. Huit versions françaises médiévales de la légende du bon pêcheur*. Edited by Hendrik Bastiaan Sol. Amsterdam: Rodopi, 1977.

Saint Lawrence. *La Vie de saint Laurent: An Anglo-Norman Poem of the Twelfth Century*. Edited by D. W. Russell. Anglo-Norman Texts Society 34. London: Anglo-Norman Texts Society, 1976.

Saint Lawrence, English translation:

Wogan-Browne, Jocelyn, and Glyn S. Burgess. *Virgin Lives and Holy Deaths: Two Exemplary Biographies for Anglo-Norman Women*. Everyman Library. London: Dent, 1996.

Saint Leger. *Saint Léger. Etude de la langue du manuscrit de Clermont-Ferrand suivie d'une édition critique du texte*. Edited by Joseph Linskill. Paris: Droz, 1937.

Saint Margaret. *Wace. La Vie de sainte Marguerite*. Edited by Elizabeth A. Francis. CFMA 71. Paris: Champion, 1932.

Wace. *La Vie de sainte Marguerite*. Edited and with an introduction and glossary by Hans-Erich Keller. Commentary and glosses on the illuminations of Manuscript Troyes 1905 by Margaret Alison Stones. Beihefte zu *Zeitschrift für romanische Philologie* 229. Tübingen: Niemeyer, 1990.

Saint Margaret, York version:

Spencer, Frederic. "The Legend of St Margaret. III. The York MS, *xvi, k, 13*." *Modern Language Notes* 5 (1890): 213–21.

Saint Mary the Egyptian. *La Vie de sainte Marie l'Egyptienne*. Edited by Peter F. Dembowski. Publications Romanes et Françaises 144. Geneva: Droz, 1977.

Saint Mary the Virgin, *see also Sponsus, Passion*.

The "Conception Nostre Dame" of Wace. Edited by William Ray Ashford. Menasha, Wis.: George Banta, 1933.

Saint Mary the Virgin, French and Anglo-Norman miracles:

Adgar. Le Gracial. Edited by Pierre Kunstmann. Ottawa Mediaeval Texts and Studies 17. Ottawa: Éditions de l'Université d'Ottawa, 1982.

Adgars Marienlegenden. Edited by Carl Neuhaus. Alfranzösische Bibliothek 9. Heilbron: Henninger, 1886.

Les Miracles de Nostre Dame par Gautier de Coinci. Edited by F. Koenig. 4 vols. Geneva: Droz, 1955–1970.

La Deuxième collection anglonormande des miracles de la sainte Vierge et son original Latin. Edited by H. Kjellmann. Uppsala: V. Ekmans Universitetsfond 27, 1922.

Treize miracles de Notre-Dame, tirés du Ms. B.N. fr. 2094. Edited by Pierre Kunstmann. Ottawa Mediaeval Texts and Studies 6. Ottawa: Editions de l'Université d'Ottawa, 1981.

Saint Mary the Virgin, Occitan miracles:
"Miracles de Notre Dame en Provençal." Edited by J. Ulrich. *Romania* 8 (1879): 12–28.

Saint Mary the Virgin, Latin miracles:
William of Malmesbury. *El libro "De Laudibus et miraculis sanctae Mariae" de Guillermo de Malmesbury O.S.B. († c. 1143): Estudio y texto*. Edited by José M. Canal. 2nd ed. Rome: Alma Roma Libreria Editrice, 1968.

"Un Miracle de Notre Dame: La Juive de Narbonne Convertie." Edited by Gilbert Dahan. In *Medieval Studies in Honour of Avrom Saltman*, 97–119. Ramat-Gan, Israel: Bar-Ilan University Press, 1995.

Les Miracles de Notre Dame de Roc Amadour au xiie siècle. Edited by E. Albe. Paris: Champion, 1907.

Saint Nicholas. *La Vie de Saint Nicolas par Wace. Poème religieux du xiie siècle*. Edited by Einar Ronsjö. Etudes Romanes de Lund 5. Lund: Ohlsson, 1942.

Saint Stephen. "Epître farcie de la Sainte Étienne." In *Chrestomathie Provençale*, edited by Karl Bartsch, 23–26. 6th ed. Marburg: Elwert, 1904.

Saint Thomas Becket. Guernes de Pont-Sainte-Maxence. *La Vie de Saint Thomas Becket*. Edited by Emmanuel Walberg. Classiques Français du Moyen Age 77. Paris: Champion, 1936.

La Vie de Thomas Becket par Beneit. Poème anglo-normand du xiie siècle. Edited by Börje Schlyter. Etudes Romanes de Lund 4. Lund: Ohlsson, 1941.

Le "Sponsus." Mystère des vierges sages et des vierges folles suivi des trois poèmes limousins et farcis. Edited by Lucien-Paul Thomas. Paris: Presses Universitaires de France, 1951.

"Sui e no suy." No. 42 in *Provenzalische Chrestomathie, mit Abriss der Formenlehre und Glossar*, edited by Carl Appel. 6th ed. Leipzig: Reisland, 1930.

Thebes. *Le Roman de Thèbes*. Edited by Guy Raynaud de Lage. 2 vols. Classiques Français du Moyen Age 94, 96. Paris: Champion, 1966–1967.

Thomas. *Les Fragments du Roman de Tristan*. Edited by Bartina H. Wind. Geneva: Droz, 1960.

Thomas, Carlisle fragment:
Benskin, Michael, Tony Hunt, and Ian Short. "Un nouveau fragment du *Tristan* de Thomas." *Romania* 113 (1992–1995): 289–319.

Wace. *Le Roman de Rou de Wace*. Edited by A. J. Holden. 3 vols. Société des Anciens Textes Français. Paris: Picard, 1970–1973.

2. MODERN WORKS

Akehurst, F. R. P. "Les Étapes de l'amour chez Bernard de Ventadour." *Cahiers de Civilisation Médiévale* 16 (1973): 133–47.

———. "La Folie chez les troubadours." In *Mélanges de philologie romane offerts à Charles Camproux*, 19–28. Montpellier: Centre d'Études Occitanes, 1978.

Althusser, Louis. "Ideology and Ideological State Apparatuses (Notes towards an Investigation)." In *Lenin and Philosophy and Other Essays*, translated by Ben Brewster, 127–88. New York: Monthly Review Press, 1971.

Altman, Charles F. "Two Types of Opposition and the Structure of Latin Saints' Lives." *Medievalia et Humanistica*, n.s. 6 (1975): 1–11.

Baswell, Christopher. *Virgil in Medieval England: Figuring the Aeneid from the Twelfth Century to Chaucer*. Cambridge Studies in Medieval Literature 24. Cambridge: Cambridge University Press, 1995.

Batt, Catherine. "Clemence of Barking's Transformations of *courtoisie* in *La Vie de sainte Catherine d'Alexandrie*." In *Translation in the Middle Ages*, edited by Roger Ellis. *New Comparisons* 12 (1991): 102–33.

Baum, Richard. *Recherches sur les oeuvres attribuées à Marie de France*. Annales Universitatis Saraviensis, Philosophische Fakultät 9. Heidelberg: Winter, 1986.

Baumgartner, Emmanuèle. "Peinture et écriture: la description de la tente dans les romans antiques au xiie siècle." In *De l'Histoire de Troie au livre du Graal. Le temps, le récit*, 179–87. Orléans: Paradigme, 1994.

———. "Sur quelques versions du *Jugement de Pâris*." In *De l'Histoire de Troie au livre du Graal. Le temps, le récit*, 221–29. Orléans: Paradigme, 1994.

———. "Le temps des automates." In *De l'Histoire de Troie au livre du Graal. Le temps, le récit*, 171–77. Orléans: Paradigme, 1994.

———. "Tombeaux pour guerriers et amazones: sur un motif descriptif de l'*Eneas* et du *Roman de Troie*." In *De l'Histoire de Troie au livre du Graal. Le temps, le récit*, 189–202. Orléans: Paradigme, 1994.

Bec, Pierre. "L'Antithèse poétique chez Bernard de Ventadour." In *Mélanges de philologie romane dédiés à Jean Boutière*, 107–37. Liège: Soledi, 1971.

———. "Troubadours, trouvères et espace Plantagenêt." *Cahiers de Civilisation Médiévale* 29 (1986): 9–14.

Bencivenga, Ermanno. *Logic and Other Nonsense: The Case of Anselm and His God*. Princeton, N.J.: Princeton University Press, 1993.

Bezzola, Reto R. *Les Origines et la formation de la littérature courtoise en occident (500–1200)*, 3 parts in 5 vols. Bibliothèque de l'École des Hautes Etudes 286, 313, 319, 320. Paris: Champion, 1966–1968.

Bloch, R. Howard. *Etymologies and Genealogies: A Literary Anthropology of the French Middle Ages.* Chicago: University of Chicago Press, 1983.

———. *Medieval Misogyny and the Invention of Western Romantic Love.* Chicago: University of Chicago Press, 1991.

Bond, Gerald A. *The Loving Subject: Desire, Eloquence, and Power in Romanesque France.* University of Pennsylvania Press Middle Ages Series. Philadelphia: University of Pennsylvania Press, 1995.

Boureau, Alain. "The Sacrality of One's Own Body in the Middle Ages." In *Corps mystique, corps sacré*, edited by Françoise Jaouën and Benjamin Semple. *Yale French Studies* 86 (1994): 5–17.

Bowie, Malcolm. *Lacan.* London: Fontana, 1991.

Breeze, Andrew. "The Virgin Mary, Daughter of Her Son." *Études Celtiques* 17 (1990): 267–83.

Brennan, Teresa. *History after Lacan.* London: Routledge, 1993.

Brown, Catherine. *Contrary Things: Exegesis, Dialectic and the Poetics of Didacticism.* Stanford, Calif.: Stanford University Press, 1998.

Bruckner, Matilda Tomaryn. "Intertextuality." In *The Legacy of Chrétien de Troyes*, edited by Norris J. Lacy, Douglas Kelly, and Keith Busby, 2:223–65. Amsterdam: Rodopi, 1987, 1988.

———. *Shaping Romance: Interpretation, Truth and Closure in Twelfth-Century French Fictions.* University of Pennsylvania Press Middle Ages Series. Philadelphia: University of Pennsylvania Press, 1993.

Bumke, Joachim. *Courtly Culture: Literature and Society in the High Middle Ages.* Berkeley: University of California Press, 1991.

Burgwinkle, William. "Knighting the Classical Hero: Homo/Hetero Affectivity in *Eneas.*" *Exemplaria* 5 (1993): 1–43.

Butler, Judith. *Theories in Subjection: The Psychic Life of Power.* Stanford, Calif.: Stanford University Press, 1997.

Calin, William. "The Exaltation and Undermining of Romance: *Ipomedon.*" In *The Legacy of Chrétien de Troyes*, edited by Norris J. Lacy, Douglas Kelly, and Keith Busby, 2:111–24. Amsterdam: Rodopi, 1987, 1988.

Camille, Michael. "Philological Iconoclasm: Edition and Image in the *Vie de Saint Alexis.*" In *Medievalism and the Modernist Temper*, edited by R. Howard Bloch and Stephen G. Nichols, 371–401. Baltimore, Md.: Johns Hopkins University Press, 1996.

Carlson, David. "Losing Control in Bernart de Ventadorn's 'Can vei la lauzeta mover.'" *Romance Notes* 23 (1982–1983): 270–76.

Cazelles, Brigitte. "*Alexis* et *Tristan*: les effets de l'enlaidissement." *Stanford French Review* 5 (1981): 85–95.

———. *The Lady as Saint: A Collection of French Hagiographical Romances of the Thirteenth Century*. Middle Ages Series. Philadelphia: University of Pennsylvania Press, 1991.

Chaytor, Henry J. *The Troubadours*. Cambridge: Cambridge University Press, 1912.

Cherchi, Paolo. *Andreas and the Ambiguity of Courtly Love*. Toronto: University of Toronto Press, 1994.

Cholakian, Rouben C. *The Troubadours: A Psychocritical Reading*. Manchester: Manchester University Press, 1990.

Colie, Rosalie L. *Paradoxica Epidemica: The Renaissance Tradition of Paradox*. Princeton, N.J.: Princeton University Press, 1966.

Corbin, S. "Miracula Beatae Mariae semper Virginis." *Cahiers de Civilisation Médiévale* 10 (1967): 409–33.

Corcoran, M. C. "Song 53 of Giraut de Bornelh. Nonsense Rhyme or Lover's Lament?" *Neuphilologische Mitteilungen* 88 (1987): 320–30.

Crane, Susan. *Insular Romance: Politics, Faith, and Culture in Anglo-Norman and Middle English Literature*. Berkeley: University of California Press, 1986.

Dancy, R. M. *Sense and Contradiction: A Study in Aristotle*. Dordrecht: Reidel, 1975.

Delcourt, Denyse. *L'Éthique du changement dans le roman français du XIIe siècle*. Geneva: Droz, 1990.

Denomy, A. "*Jois* among the Early Troubadours: Its Meaning and Possible Source." *Medieval Studies* 13 (1951): 177–217.

Desbordes, Françoise. *Argonautica. Trois études de l'imitation dans la littérature antique*. Brussels: Latomus, 1969.

Di Girolamo, C. "'No say que s'es' e lo spazio lirico di Raimabut d'Aurenga." *Medioevo Romanzo* 12 (1987): 261–74.

Dod, Bernard G. "Aristoteles Latinus." In *The Cambridge History of Later Medieval Philosophy*, edited by Norman Kretzman, Anthony Kenny, and Jan Pinborg, 45–79. Cambridge: Cambridge University Press, 1982.

Dolar, Mladen. "Cogito as the Subject of the Unconscious." In *Cogito and the Unconscious*, edited by Slavoj Žižek, 11–40. Durham, N.C.: Duke University Press, 1998.

Dragonetti, Roger. *La Technique poétique des trouvères dans la chanson courtoise. Contribution à l'étude de la rhétorique médiévale*. Rijkuniversiteit te Gent. Werken uitgegeven door de Faculteit van de Letteren en Wijsbegeerte, 127. Bruges: De Tempel, 1960.

Dronke, Peter. *A History of Twelfth-Century Western Philosophy*. Cambridge: Cambridge University Press, 1988.

Ebel, Uda. *Das altromanische Mirakel. Ursprung und Geschichte einer literarischen Gattung.* Studia Romanica 8. Heidelberg: Winter, 1965.
Eley, Penny. "The Anti-Romance of *Ipomedon.*" Unpublished paper. (*See also* Penny Sullivan.)
———, and Penny Simons. "Male Beauty and Sexual Orientation in *Partonopeu de Blois.*" *Romance Studies* 17 (1999): 41–56.
———. "*Partonopeu de Blois* and Chrétien de Troyes: A Reassessment." *Romania* 117 (1999): 316–41.
Evans, Dylan. *An Introductory Dictionary of Lacanian Psychoanalysis.* London: Routledge, 1996.
Evans, G. R. *The Language and Logic of the Bible: The Earlier Middle Ages.* Cambridge: Cambridge University Press, 1984.
Faral, Edmond. *Recherches sur les sources latines des contes et romans courtois du moyen âge.* Paris: Champion, 1913.
———. "Le Récit du Jugement de Paris dans *l'Enéas* et ses sources," *Romania* 41 (1912): 100–102.
Fassbinder, Klara M. "Der Trobador Raimbaut von Vaqueiras." *Zeitschrift für romanische Philologie* 49 (1929): 129–90.
Ferry, Luc, and Alain Renaut. *La Pensée '68. Essai sur l'antihumanisme contemporain.* Paris: Gallimard, 1988.
Filippis, Michele de. *The Literary Riddle in Italy to the End of the Sixteenth Century.* Berkeley: University of California Press, 1948.
Fish, Stanley. *Is There a Text in This Class? The Authority of Interpretive Communities.* Cambridge, Mass.: Harvard University Press, 1980.
Fourrier, Anthime. *Le Courant réaliste dans le roman courtois en France au moyen âge. I: Les Débuts.* Paris: Nizet, 1960.
Fradenburg, Louise O. "Criticism, Anti-Semitism, and the Prioress's Tale." *Exemplaria* 1 (1989): 69–115.
Frappier, Jean. "Sur un procès fait à l'amour courtois." In *Amour Courtois et Table Ronde*, 61–96. Geneva: Droz, 1973. First published in *Romania* 93 (1972): 145–93.
Freeman, Michelle A. *The Poetics of "Translatio Studii" and "Conjointure" in Chrétien de Troyes's "Cligés."* French Forum Monographs 12. Lexington, Ky.: French Forum, 1979.
Freud, Sigmund. "Analysis of a Phobia in a Five-Year-Old Boy" (1909). In *Standard Edition of the Complete Psychological Works of Sigmund Freud*, edited by James Strachey, 10:5–149. London: Hogarth Press, 1953-1974.
Gallais, Pierre. *Dialectique du récit médiéval. (Chrétien de Troyes et l'hexagone logique).* Amsterdam: Rodopi, 1982.

———. "Remarques sur la structure des 'Miracles de Notre-Dame.'" In *Epopées, Légendes et Miracles. Cahiers d'Etudes Médiévales*, 1:117–34. Montréal: Institut d'études médiévales, Université de Montréal, 1974.
Gaunt, Simon. "From Epic to Romance: Gender and Sexuality in the *Roman d'Eneas*." *Romanic Review* 83 (1992): 1–27.
———. *Gender and Genre in Medieval French Literature*. Cambridge Studies in French 53. Cambridge: Cambridge University Press, 1995.
———. *Troubadours and Irony*. Cambridge Studies in Medieval Literature 3. Cambridge: Cambridge University Press, 1989.
Gay-Crosier, Raymond. *Religious Elements in the Secular Lyrics of the Troubadours*. Studies in the Romance Languages and Literatures 111. Chapel Hill: University of North Carolina Press, 1971.
Gersh, Stephen. *Concord in Discourse: Harmonics and Semiotics in Late Classical and Early Medieval Platonism*. Berlin: Mouton de Gruyter, 1996.
———. "(Pseudo-?) Bernard Silvestris and the Revival of Neoplatonic Virgilian Exegesis." In *Chercheurs de sagesse. Hommage à Jean Pépin*, 573–93. Paris: Institut d'Etudes Augustiniennes, 1992.
Gold, Penny Schine. *The Lady and the Virgin: Image, Attitude, and Experience in Twelfth-Century France*. Chicago: University of Chicago Press, 1985.
Gravdal, Kathryn. "Confessing Incests: Legal Erasures and Literary Celebrations in Medieval France." *Comparative Literature Studies* 32 (1995): 280–95.
———. *Ravishing Maidens: Writing Rape in Medieval French Literature and Law*. New Cultural Studies Series. Philadelphia: University of Pennsylvania Press, 1991.
———. *"Vilain" and "Courtois": Transgressive Parody in French Literature of the Twelfth and Thirteenth Centuries*. Lincoln: University of Nebraska Press, 1989.
Green, Denis. *Irony in Medieval Romance*. Cambridge: Cambridge University Press, 1979.
Greimas, Algirdas Julien. *Du Sens. Essais sémiotiques. I*. Paris: Seuil, 1970.
Griffin, Miranda. "Gender and Authority in the Medieval French *lai*." *Forum for Modern Language Studies* 35 (1999): 42–56.
Gros, Gérard. "La *Semblance* et la *verrine*. Description et interprétation d'une image mariale." *Le Moyen Age* 97 (1991): 217–57.
Gruber, Jörn. *Die Dialektik des Trobar. Untersuchungen zur Struktur und Entwicklung des occitanischen und französischen Minnesangs des 12. Jahrhunderts*. Beihefte zur *Zeitschrift für romanische Philologie* 194. Tübingen: Niemeyer, 1983.
Grundriss der romanischen Literaturen des Mittelalters. Fasc. 2 of vol. 4. *Le Ro-*

man jusquà la fin du XIIIe siècle. Directed by Reinhold R. Grimm. Heidelberg: Winter, 1984.

Guiette, Roger. "*Li conte de Bretaigne sont si vain et plaisant.*" *Romania* 88 (1967): 1–12.

———. *La Légende de la sacristine. Etude de littérature comparée*. Bibliothèque de la revue de littérature comparée 43. 1927. Reprint, Geneva: Slatkine, 1981.

———. *D'une poésie formelle en France au moyen âge*. Paris: Nizet, 1972.

Hahn, Cynthia. "Speaking without Tongues: The Martyr Romanus and Augustine's Theory of Language in Illustrations of Bern Burgerbibliothek Codex 264." In *Images of Sainthood in Medieval Europe*, edited by Renate Blumenfeld-Kosinski and Timea Szell, 161–80. Ithaca, N.Y.: Cornell University Press, 1991.

Haidu, Peter. *Aesthetic Distance in Chrétien de Troyes. Irony and Comedy in "Cligés" and "Perceval."* Geneva: Droz, 1968.

———. "Considérations théoriques sur la sémiotique socio-historique." In *Exigences et perspectives de la sémiotique: Recueil d'hommages pour A. J. Greimas*, edited by H. Parret and H. G. Ruprecht, 215–28. Amsterdam: Benjamin, 1985.

———. *Lion-queue-coupée. L'écart symbolique chez Chrétien de Troyes*. Histoire des idées et critique littéraire 123. Geneva: Droz, 1972.

———. "Text and History: The Semiosis of Twelfth-Century Lyric as Sociohistorical Phenomenon (Chrétien de Troyes: 'D'Amors qui m'a tolu')." *Semiotica* 33 (1981): 1–62.

Hanning, Robert W. "The Audience as Co-Creator of the First Chivalric Romances." *Yearbook of English Studies* 11 (1981): 1–28.

———. "*Engin* in Twelfth Century Romance: An Examination of the *Roman d'Énéas* and Hue de la Rotelande's *Ipomedon*." In *Approaches to Medieval Romance*, edited by Peter Haidu. *Yale French Studies* 51 (1974): 82–101.

———. *The Individual in Twelfth-Century Romance*. New Haven, Conn.: Yale University Press, 1977.

Harf-Lancner, Laurence. *Les Fées au moyen âge. Morgane et Mélusine. La naissance des fées*. Paris: Champion, 1984.

Heffernan, Thomas J. *Sacred Biography: Saints and Their Biographers in the Middle Ages*. New York: Oxford University Press, 1988.

Heidegger, Martin. "The Origin of the Work of Art." In *Poetry, Language, Thought*, translated and with an introduction by Albert Hofstadter, 5–87. New York: Harper and Row, 1975.

Holmes, Olivia. "Unriddling the *Devinalh.*" *Tenso* 9 (1993): 24–62.

Hopkins, Jasper. "The Anselmian Theory of Universals." In the *Works* of Anselm of Canterbury, 4:57–96. Toronto: Mellen, 1976.

Huchet, Jean-Charles. *L'Amour discourtois. La "fin' amors" chez les premiers troubadours.* Paris: Privat, 1987.

———. *Littérature médievale et psychanalyse. Pour une clinique littéraire.* Paris: Presses Universitaires de France, 1990.

———. *Le Roman médiéval.* Paris: Presses Universitaires de France, 1984.

Hult, David. "Author/Narrator/Speaker. The Voice of Authority in Chrétien's *Charrete*." In *Discourses of Authority in Medieval and Renaissance Literature*, edited by Kevin Brownlee and Walter Stephens, 76–96. Hanover, N.H.: University of New England Press, 1989.

Hunt, Tony. "Aristotle, Dialectic, and Courtly Literature." *Viator* 10 (1979): 95–129.

———. *Chrétien de Troyes: Yvain.* London: Grant and Cutler, 1986.

———. "The Dialectic of *Yvain*." *Modern Language Review* 72 (1977): 285–99.

———. "The Significance of Thomas's *Tristan*." *Reading Medieval Studies* 7 (1981): 41–61.

Huot, Sylvia. "Troubadour Lyric and Old French Narrative." In *The Troubadours: An Introduction*, edited by Simon Gaunt and Sarah Kay, 263–78. Cambridge: Cambridge University Press, 1999.

Jacobi, Klaus. "Logic (ii): The Later Twelfth Century." In *A History of Twelfth Century Philosophy*, edited by Peter Dronke, 227–51. Cambridge: Cambridge University Press, 1988.

Jaeger, C. Stephen. *The Origins of Courtliness: Civilizing Trends and the Formation of Courtly Ideals 939–1210.* University of Pennsylvania Press Middle Ages Series. Philadelphia: University of Pennsylvania Press, 1985.

Johnson, Phyllis, and Brigitte Cazelles. *Le Vain Siecle Guerpir: A Literary Approach to Old French Hagiography of the Twelfth Century.* North Carolina Studies in the Romance Languages and Literatures 205. Chapel Hill: University of North Carolina Press, 1979.

Kant, Immanuel. *Critique of Practical Reason.* Edited by Mary Gregor and introduction by Andrews Reath. Cambridge Texts in the History of Philosophy. Cambridge: Cambridge University Press, 1997.

———. "Observations on the Feeling of the Beautiful and the Sublime." Translated by J. T. Goldthwait. Berkeley: University of California Press, 1960.

Kantorowicz, Ernst H. *The King's Two Bodies: A Study in Medieval Political Theology.* Princeton, N.J.: Princeton University Press, 1957.

Kay, Sarah. "The Contradictions of Courtly Love and the Origins of Courtly

Poetry: The Evidence of the *Lauzengiers*." *Journal of Medieval and Early Modern Studies* 26 (1996): 209–53.
———. "Courts, Clerks, and Courtly Love." In *The Cambridge Companion to Romance*, edited by Roberta L. Krueger, 81–96. Cambridge: Cambridge University Press, 2000.
———. "Desire and Subjectivity." In *The Troubadours: An Introduction*, edited by Simon Gaunt and Sarah Kay, 212–27. Cambridge: Cambridge University Press, 1999.
———. *The Romance of the Rose*. Critical Guides to French Texts 110. London: Grant and Cutler, 1995.
———. *Subjectivity in Troubadour Poetry*. Cambridge Studies in French. Cambridge: Cambridge University Press, 1990.
———. "The Sublime Body of the Martyr: Violence in Early Romance Saints' Lives." In *Violence in Medieval Society*, edited by Richard W. Kaeuper, 3–20. Woodbridge, UK: Boydell and Brewer, 2000.
———. "Text(s) and Meaning(s) in the *Alba* of Giraut de Bornelh." In *The Art of Reading: Essays in Memory of Dorothy Gabe Coleman*, edited by Philip Ford and Gillian Jondorf, 2–10. Cambridge: Cambridge French Colloquia, 1998.
———. "Who Was Chrétien de Troyes?" *Arthurian Literature* 15 (1997): 1–35
Kelly, Douglas. "Romance and the Vanity of Chrétien de Troyes." In *Romance: Generic Transformations from Chrétien de Troyes to Cervantes*, edited by Kevin Brownlee and Marina Scordilis Brownlee, 74–90. Hanover, N.H.: University of New England Press, 1985.
Kendrick, Laura. *The Game of Love: Troubadour Wordplay*. Berkeley: University of California Press, 1988.
Köhler, Erich. *L'Aventure chevaleresque. Idéal et réalité dans le roman courtois. Etudes sur la forme des plus anciens poèmes d'Arthur et du Graal*. Translated by Eliane Kaufholz. Preface by Jacques Le Goff. Paris: Gallimard, 1974. First published as *Ideal und Wirklichkeit in der höfischen Epik*. 1956. Revised edition, Tübingen: Niemeyer, 1970.
———. "'Can vei la lauzeta mover': Überlegungen zum Verhältnis von phonischer Struktur und semantische Struktur." In *Semiotics and Dialectics: Ideology and the Text*, edited by Peter V. Zima, 445–68. Amsterdam: Benjamin, 1981.
———. "No sai qui s'es—No sai que s'es (Wilhelm von Poitiers und Raimbaut von Orange)." In *Mélanges [. . .] Delbouille*, 2:349–66. Gembloux: Duculot, 1964.
———. "Observations historiques et sociologiques sur la poésie des troubadours." *Cahiers de Civilisation Médiévale* 7 (1964): 27–51.

———. "Principes historico-sociologiques et science littéraire." *Travaux de l'Institut d'Etudes Latino-Américaines de l'Université des Sciences Humaines de Strasbourg* 13–14 (1973–1974): 3–10.

———. "Rätselgedicht." In *Grundriss der Romanischen Literaturen des Mittelalters*. Vol. 2, *Les Oeuvres lyriques*, part 1, fasc. 3. Directed by Erich Köhler. Heidelberg: Winter, 1987.

Krauff, Henning. "Historisch-dialektische Literaturwissenschaft. Zum Werk Erich Köhlers." In *Mittelalterstudien Erich Köhler zum Gedenken*, 9–13. Heidelberg: Winter, 1984.

Kristeva, Julia. *Powers of Horror: An Essay on Abjection*. Translated by Leon S. Roudiez. New York: Columbia University Press, 1982. First published as *Pouvoirs de l'horreur. Essai sur l'abjection*. Paris: Seuil, 1980.

———. *Tales of Love*. Translated by Leon S. Roudiez. New York: Columbia University Press, 1987. First published as *Histoires d'amour*. Paris: Denoël, 1983.

———. "Le texte clos." In *Semiotike: Recherches pour une sémanalyse*, 52–81. Paris: Seuil, 1969.

Krueger, R. L. "The Author's Voice: Narrators, Audiences, and the Problem of Interpretation." In *The Legacy of Chrétien de Troyes*, edited by Norris J. Lacy, Douglas Kelly, and Keith Busby, 1:115–40. Amsterdam: Rodopi, 1987, 1988.

———. "Textuality and Performance in *Partonopeu de Blois*." *Assays* 3 (1985): 57–72.

———. *Women Readers and the Ideology of Gender in Old French Verse Romance*. Cambridge Studies in French 43. Cambridge: Cambridge University Press, 1993.

Kruger, Steven F. *Dreaming in the Middle Ages*. Cambridge Studies in Medieval Literature 14. Cambridge: Cambridge University Press, 1992.

Lacan, Jacques. *The Seminar of Jacques Lacan*, edited by Jacques-Alain Miller.

———. *Book III. The Psychoses. 1955–56*. Translated with notes by Russell Grigg. London: Routledge, 1993. First published as *Les Psychoses*. Paris: Seuil, 1981.

———. *Livre IV. La Relation d'objet. 1956–7*. Paris: Seuil, 1994.

———. *Book VII. The Ethics of Psychoanalysis. 1959–60*. Translated and with notes by Dennis Porter. London: Routledge, 1992. First published as *L'Éthique de la psychanalyse*. Paris: Seuil, 1986.

———. [Book XI] *The Four Fundamental Concepts of Psycho-Analysis*. Translated by Alan Sheridan. Introduction by David Macey. London: Penguin, 1994. First published as *Les Quatre concepts fondamentaux de la psychanalyse*. Paris: Seuil, 1973.

———. *Livre XX. Encore*. Paris: Seuil, 1975.

———. "Kant avec Sade." In *Ecrits*, 765–90. Paris: Seuil, 1966.

Lawner, Lynne. "Notes towards an Interpretation of the *vers de dreit nien*." *Cultura Neolatina* 28 (1968): 147–64.

———. "The Riddle of the Dead Man (Raimbaut de Vaqueiras, 'Las frevols venson lo plus fort')." *Cultura Neolatina* 27 (1967): 30–39.

Lecoy, F. "Notes sur le troubadour Raimbaut de Vaqueyras." In *Etudes romanes dédiées à Mario Roques*, 23–38. Société des publications romanes et françaises. Paris: Droz, 1946.

Legge, Dominica. *Anglo-Norman Literature and Its Background*. Oxford: Clarendon Press, 1963.

Lehmann, Paul. *De Parodie im Mittelalter*. Munich: Drei Masken, 1922.

Lejeune, Rita. "Le Rôle littéraire d'Aliénor d'Aquitaine et de sa famille." *Cultura Neolatina* 14 (1954): 5–57.

Leupin, Alexandre. *Fiction et incarnation. Littérature et théologie au moyen âge*. Paris: Flammarion, 1993.

Levenson, J. L. "The Narrative Format of Benoît's *Roman de Troie*." *Romania* 100 (1979): 54–70.

Lewis, C. S. *The Allegory of Love: A Study in Medieval Tradition*. 1936. Reprint, Oxford: Oxford University Press, 1958.

Lumiansky, R. M. "Structural Unity in Benoît's *Roman de Troie*." *Romania* 79 (1958): 410–24.

MacBain, William. "Five Old French Renderings of the *Passio Sancte Katherine Virginis*." In *Medieval Translators and their Craft*, edited by Jeannette Beer, 41–65. Kalamazoo: Medieval Institute Publications, 1989.

McCracken, Peggy. *The Romance of Adultery: Queenship and Sexual Transgression in Old French Literature*. Philadelphia: University of Pennsylvania Press, 1998.

Mannoni, Octave. "Je sais bien, mais quand même." In *Clefs pour l'Imaginaire ou l'Autre Scène*, 9–33. Paris: Seuil, 1969.

Maréchal, Chantal. "Le lai de Fresne et la littérature édifiante du xiie siècle." *Cahiers de Civilisation Médiévale* 35 (1992): 131–41.

———, editor. *In Quest of Marie de France, a Twelfth-Century Poet*. Lewiston: Mellen, 1992.

Marenbon, John. *Early Medieval Philosophy (480–1150): An Introduction*. Rev. ed. London: Routledge, 1988.

———. "Gilbert of Poitiers." In *A History of Twelfth-Century Western Philosophy*, edited by Peter Dronke, 328–52. Cambridge: Cambridge University Press, 1988.

———. *Later Medieval Philosophy (1150–1350): An Introduction*. Rev. ed. London: Routledge, 1991.
Marnette, Sophie. *Narrateur et points de vue dans la littérature française médiévale. Une approche linguistique*. Bern: Lang, 1998.
Marshall, John. "Dialogues of the Dead." In *The Troubadours and the Epic: Essays in Memory of W. Mary Hackett*, edited by Linda M. Paterson and Simon B. Gaunt, 37–58. Warwick: French Department, University of Warwick, 1987.
Masters, Bernadette. *Esthétique et manuscripture. Le "moulin à paroles" au moyen âge*. Heidelberg: Winter, 1992.
Méla, Charles. *La Reine et le Graal. La "conjointure" dans les romans du Graal de Chrétien de Troyes au "Livre de Lancelot."* Paris: Seuil, 1984.
Ménard, Philippe. "Sens, contre-sens, nonsens, réflexions sur la pièce 'Farai un vers de dreyt nien' de Guillaume IX." In *Mélanges de langue et de littérature occitanes en hommage à Pierre Bec*, 339–48. Poitiers: C.É.S.C.M., 1991.
Meneghetti, Maria-Luisa. "Intertextuality and Dialogism." In *The Troubadours: An Introduction*, edited by Simon Gaunt and Sarah Kay, 181–96. Cambridge: Cambridge University Press, 1999.
———. *Il Pubblico dei trovatori*. 2d ed. Turin: Einaudi, 1992.
Meyer, Paul. "Anciennes poésies religieuses en Langue d'Oc." *Bibliothèque de l'Ecole des Chartes* 5e série 1 (1860): 481–33.
Milone, Luigi. "Il 'ver de dreit nien' et il paradosso dell'amore a distanza." *Cultura Neolatina* 40 (1980): 123–44.
Mölk, Ulrich. "La *Chanson de saint Alexis* et le culte du saint en France au XIe et XIIe siècles." *Cahiers de Civilisation Médiévale* 21 (1978): 339–55.
Morse, Ruth. *The Medieval Medea*. Woodbridge, UK: Brewer, 1996.
Mussafia, Adolf. *Studien zu den mittelalterlichen Marienlegenden* I–V, in *Sitzungsberichte der Philosophisch-historischen Classe der Kaiserlichen Akademie der Wissenschaften*. Vienna, 113 (1886), 917–94; 115 (1887), 5–92; 119 (1889), 1–66; 123 (1891), 1–85; 139, 8 (1898), 1–74.
Neumeister, Sebastian. *Das Spiel mit der höfischer Liebe*. Beihefte zu *Poetica* 5. Munich: Fink, 1969.
Nichols, Stephen G. "Amorous Imitation: Bakhtin, Augustine, and *Le Roman d'Enéas*." In *Romance: Generic Transformation from Chrétien de Troyes to Cervantes*, edited by Kevin Brownlee and Marina Scordilis Brownlee, 47–73. Hanover, N.H.: University Press of New England, 1985.
———. *Romanesque Signs: Early Medieval Narrative and Iconography*. New Haven, Conn.: Yale University Press, 1983.
Nolan, Barbara. *Chaucer and the Tradition of the Roman Antique*. Cambridge: Cambridge University Press, 1992.

———. "The Judgement of Paris in the *Roman d'Eneas*: A New Look at Sources and Significance." *Classical Bulletin* 56 (1980): 52–56.
Nolting-Hauff, Ilse. *Die Stellung der Liebeskasuistik im höfischen Roman*. Heidelberger Forschungen 6. Heidelberg: Winter, 1959.
Owen, D. D. R. "Profanity and Its Purpose in Chrétien's *Cligés* and *Lancelot*." *Forum for Modern Language Studies* 6 (1970): 37–48.
Paoli, Guy. "La Relation oeil–coeur. Recherches sur la mystique amoureuse de Chrétien de Troyes." In *Le "Cuer" au Moyen Age (Senefiance 30)*, 233–44. Aix-en-Provence: Publications du CUERMA, Université de Provence, 1991.
Pasero, Nicolo. "*Devinalh*, 'non-senso,' e 'interiorizzazione testuale': osservationi sui rapporti fra strutture formale e contenuta ideologica nella poesia provenzale." *Cultura Neolatina* 28 (1968): 113–46.
Paterson, Linda. *Troubadours and Eloquence*. Oxford: Oxford University Press, 1975.
Patterson, Lee. *Negotiating the Past: The Historical Understanding of Medieval Literature*. Madison: University of Wisconsin Press, 1987.
Petit, Aimé. *Naissances du roman. Les techniques littéraires des romans antiques au douzième siècle*. 2 vols. Geneva: Slatkine, 1985.
Pindar, Janice M. "The Intertextuality of Old French Saints' Lives: St Giles, St Evroul, and the Marriage of St Alexis." *Parergon* n.s. 6A (1988): 11–21.
Polak, Lucie. *Chrétien de Troyes. Cligés*. Critical Guides to French Texts 23. London: Grant and Cutler, 1982.
———. "The Two Caves of Love in the *Tristan* by Thomas." *Journal of the Warburg and Courtauld Institutes* 33 (1970): 52–69.
Poirion, Daniel. "De l'*Enéide* à l'*Éneas*: mythologie et moralisation." *Cahiers de Civilisation Médiévale* 19 (1976): 213–29.
———. "Edyppus et l'énigme du roman médiéval." In *L'Enfant au Moyen Age (Senefiance 9)*, 287–97. Aix en Provence and Paris: CUERMA and Champion, 1980.
———. *Résurgences. Mythe et littérature à l'âge du symbole (XIIe siècle)*. Paris: Presses Universitaires de France, 1986.
Poncelet, Albert. "Miraculorum Beatae Virginis Mariae quae saeculis vi–xv latine conscripta sunt. Index." *Analecta Bollandiana* 22 (1902): 241–360.
Poundstone, William. *Labyrinths of Reason: Paradox, Puzzles, and the Frailty of Knowledge*. 1988. Reprint, Harmondsworth: Penguin, 1991.
Priest, Graham. *Beyond the Limits of Thought*. Cambridge: Cambridge University Press, 1995.
Raynouard, François. *Lexique Roman, ou dictionnaire de la langue des troubadours*. 6 vols. Paris, 1838–1844.

Ribard, Jacques. *Chrétien de Troyes. Le Chevalier de la Charrette. Essai d'interprétantion symbolique.* Paris: Nizet, 1972.

Rieger, Dietmar. "'Aufgehobene' Genera. Gattungszitate und Gattungsinstrate im altfranzösischen *Thebenroman.*" *Vox Romanica* 48 (1987): 67–86.

———. "'Lop es nomnat lo pes, e lop no es.' Un devinalh sans solution?" In *Mélanges de langue et de littérature occitanes en hommage à Pierre Bec,* 497–506. Poitiers: C.É.S.C.M., 1991.

———. "Der *vers de dreyt nien* Wilhems IX von Aquitanien: Rätselhaftes Gedicht oder Rätselgedicht? Unterschung zu einem 'Schlüsselgedicht' der Trobadorlyrik." Sitzungsberichte der Heidelberger Akademie der Wissenschaften. Philosophisch-historische Klasse 1975. Heidelberg: Winter, 1975.

Riquer, Martín de. *Los Trovadores. Historia literaria y textos.* 3 vols. Barcelona: Ariel, 1976.

Robertson, Duncan. *The Medieval Saints' Lives: Spiritual Renewal and Old French Literature.* Lexington, Ky.: French Forum, 1995.

———. "Writing in the Textual Community: Clemence of Barking's *Life of St Catherine.*" *French Forum* 21 (1996): 5–28.

Robertson, D. W., Jr. "Chrétien's *Cligés* and the Ovidian Spirit." *Comparative Literature* 7 (1955): 32–42.

———. *A Preface to Chaucer: Studies in Medieval Perspectives.* Princeton, N.J.: Princeton University Press, 1963.

Rollo, David. *Historical Fabrication, Ethnic Fable and French Romance in Twelfth-Century England.* Edward C. Armstrong Monographs on Medieval Literature 9. Nicholasville, Ky.: French Forum, 1998.

Rossi, Luciano. "Chrétien de Troyes e i trovatori: Tristan, Linhaure, Carestia." *Vox Romanica* 46 (1987): 26–62.

Salvat, Joseph. "La Sainte Vierge dans la littérature occitance du Moyen Age." In *Mélanges de Linguistique et de Littérature romanes à la mémoire d'István Frank,* 614–56. Annales Universitatis Saravensis 6. Universität des Saarlandes, 1957.

Scaglione, Aldo. *Knights at Court: Courtliness, Chivalry, and Courtesy from Ottonian Germany to the Italian Renaissance.* Berkeley: University of California Press, 1991.

Scheludko, D. "Religiöse Elemente im Weltlichen Liebeslied der Trobadors. (Zu Form und Inhalt der Kanzone.)" *Zeitschrift für französische Sprache und Literatur* 59 (1935): 402–21 and 60 (1935): 18–35.

Secor, John R. "The *Planctus Mariae* in Provençal Literature: A Subtle Blend of Courtly and Religious Traditions." In *The Spirit of the Court,* edited by Glyn S. Burgess and Robert A. Taylor, 321–26. Woodbridge, UK: Brewer, 1985.

Shahar, Shulamith. *Childhood in the Middle Ages*. Translated by Chaya Galai. London: Routledge, 1990.

Sharman, Ruth Verity. "Giraut de Bornelh: *Maestre dels Trobadors*." *Medium Aevum* 52 (1983): 63–76.

Simons, Penny, and Penny Eley. "The Prologue to *Partonopeus de Blois*: Text, Context and Subtext." *French Studies* 49 (1995): 1–16.

Sirat, Colette. "Jewish Philosophy." In *Medieval Philosophy*. Vol. 3, *Routledge History of Philosophy*, edited by John Marenbon, 65–95. London: Routledge, 1998.

Southern, R. W. "The English Origins of the Miracles of the Virgin." *Medieval and Renaissance Studies* 4 (1958): 176–216.

Spade, Paul Vincent. "Five Early Theories in the *Insolubilia* Literature." *Vivarium* 25 (1987): 24–46.

———. "Insolubilia." In *The Cambridge History of Later Medieval Philosophy*, edited by Norman Kretzman, Anthony Kenny, and Jan Pinborg, 246–53. Cambridge: Cambridge University Press, 1982.

———. *The Medieval Liar: A Catalogue of the Insolubilia Literature*. Subsidia Mediaevalia 5. Toronto: Pontifical Institute of Medieval Studies, 1975.

———. "The Origin of the Mediaeval *Insolubilia* Literature." *Franciscan Studies* 33 (1973): 292–309.

Spearing, A. C. *The Medieval Poet as Voyeur: Looking and Listening in Medieval Love-Narratives*. Cambridge: Cambridge University Press, 1993.

Spence, Sarah. *Rhetorics of Reason and Desire: Vergil, Augustine, and the Troubadours*. Ithaca, N.Y.: Cornell University Press, 1988.

Spitzer, Leo. *L'Amour lointain de Jaufré Rudel et le sens de la poésie des troubadours*. University of North Carolina Studies in the Romance Languages and Literatures 5. Chapel Hill: University of North Carolina Press, 1944.

Stewart, Susan. *Nonsense: Aspects of Intertextuality in Folklore and Literature*. Baltimore, Md.: Johns Hopkins University Press, 1978.

Sullivan, Penny. "Medieval Automata: The 'Chambre de Beautés' in Benoît's *Roman de Troie*." *Romance Studies* 6 (1985): 1–20.

———. "Translation and Adaptation in the *Roman de Troie*." In *The Spirit of the Court: Selected Proceedings of the Fourth Congress of the International Courtly Literature Society (Toronto 1983)*, edited by Glyn S. Burgess and Robert A. Taylor, 350–59. Woodbridge, UK: Brewer, 1985.

Taylor, Archer. *The Literary Riddle before 1600*. Berkeley: University of California Press, 1948.

Thoma, Heinz. "Pour une science historico-sociologique de la littérature. Quelques remarques sur l'oeuvre d'Erich Köhler." *Littérature* 43 (1981): 100–15.

Topsfield, L. T. *Chrétien de Troyes: A Study of the Arthurian Romances.* Cambridge: Cambridge University Press, 1981.

———. "The 'Natural Fool' in Peire d'Alvernhe, Marcabru and Bernart de Ventadorn." In *Mélanges d'histoire littéraire, de linguistique et de philologie romane offerts à Charles Rostaing*, 1149–58. Liège: Association des Romanistes de Liège, 1974.

Tubach, Fredric C. *Index Exemplorum: A Handbook of Medieval Religious Tales.* Helsinki: Suomalainen Tiedeakatemia/Akademia Scientiarum Fennica, 1969.

Tweedale, Martin M. "Logic (i): From the Late Eleventh Century to the Time of Abelard." In *A History of Twelfth Century Philosophy*, edited by Peter Dronke, 196–226. Cambridge: Cambridge University Press, 1988.

Uitti, Karl. "*Alexis, Roland,* and French 'Poésie Nationale.'" *Comparative Literature Studies* 32 (1995): 131–50.

———. "The Old Provençal Song of Saint Fides and the Occitanian Concept of Poetic Space." *Esprit Créateur* 19 (1979): 17–36.

Van Vleck, Amelia E. *Memory and Recreation in Troubadour Lyric.* Berkeley: University of California Press, 1991.

Vance, Eugene. *From Topic to Tale: Logic and Narrativity in the Middle Ages.* Theory and History of Literature 47. Minneapolis: University of Minnesota Press, 1987.

Vauchez, André. "Lay People's Sanctity in Western Europe: Evolution of a Pattern (Twelfth and Thirteenth Centuries)." In *Images of Sainthood in Medieval Europe*, edited by Renate Blumenfeld-Kosinski and Timea Szell, 21–32. Ithaca, N.Y.: Cornell University Press, 1991.

Vitz, Evelyn Birge. *Medieval Narrative and Modern Narratology: Subjects and Objects of Desire.* New York: New York University Press, 1989.

Walberg, E. "Date et source de la Vie de Saint Thomas par Beneit, moine de Saint-Alban." *La Tradition hagiographique de Saint Thomas Becket avant la fin du XIIe siècle,* 9–33. Paris: Droz, 1929. First published in *Romania* 44 (1915–1917): 407–26.

Walters, Lori. "The Poet-Narrator's Address to His Lady as a Structural Device in *Partonopeu de Blois.*" *Medium Aevum* 61 (1992): 229–41.

Ward, H. D. *Catalogue of Romances in the Department of Manuscripts in the British Museum.* 2 vols. London: Trustees of the British Museum, 1883, 1893.

Warner, Marina. *Alone of All Her Sex: The Myth and Cult of the Virgin Mary.* London: Weidenfeld and Nicholson, 1976.

Wilde, Lawrence. *Marx and Contradiction.* Aldershot: Avebury, 1991.

Wilson, Richard Middlewood. *Early Middle English Literature*. London: Methuen, 1939.
Wogan-Browne, Jocelyn, and Glyn Burgess. *Virgin Lives and Holy Deaths: Two Exemplary Biographies of Anglo-Norman Women*. Everyman Library. London: Dent, 1996.
Work, Elizabeth P. "The Eleventh-Century Song of Saint Fides: An Experiment in Vernacular Eloquence." *Romance Philology* 36 (1982–1983): 366–85.
Wyrembek, Anna, and Josef Morawski. *Les Légendes du "Fiancé de la Vierge" dans la littérature médiévale. Essai de synthèse*. Poznanskie Towarzystwo Przyjaciól Nauk Prace Komisji Filologicznej VII zeszyt 3. Poznan, 1934.
Zink, Michel. *Le Roman d'Apollonius de Tyr*. Bibliothèque médiévale. Paris: 10.18, 1982.
Žižek, Slavoj. *For They Know Not What They Do: Enjoyment as a Political Factor*. London: Verso, 1991.
———. "Kant with (or against) Sade." In *The Žižek Reader*, edited by Elizabeth Wright and Edmund Wright, 283–301. Oxford: Blackwell, 1999.
———. *Looking Awry: An Introduction to Jacques Lacan through Popular Culture*. Cambridge, Mass.: MIT Press, 1992.
———. *The Metastases of Enjoyment: Six Essays on Woman and Causality*. London: Verso, 1994.
———. *The Plague of Fantasies*. London: Verso, 1997.
———. *The Sublime Object of Ideology*. London: Verso, 1989.
Žižek, Slavoj, editor. *Everything You Always Wanted to Know about Lacan (But Were Afraid to Ask Hitchcock)*. London: Verso, 1992.

Index

Abbreviatio Montana, 14, 16
Abelard, 14, 53, 127; *Sic et Non*, 20
abject, abjection 181–90, 213–14, 342 n. 9. *See also* object
Adam of Balsham (Adam of Petit Pont), 134, 141
Aimeric de Peguilhan, VI, 336–37 n. 6
Alan of Lille, *De planctu Naturae*, 21, 118, 331 n. 9
Alberic (teacher of John of Salisbury), 16–17
Alberic of Pisançon, *Roman d'Alexandre*, 44–45
Albertet de Sisteron, *see* Aimeric de Peguilhan
Aubri, source of Adgar's *Gracial*, 207–8
Alegret, I, 77–79, 88, 107–8
Alexander, see Alberic of Pisançon
Althusser, Louis, 160, 161, 164. *See also* interpellation
Anselm of Canterbury, 24, 127; "The Incarnation of the Word," 24, 127–30; *Meditations*, 24; *Proslogion*, 24, 130
Apollonius of Tyre (Old French verse fragment), 143, 197, 341 n. 45, 344 n. 31. *See also Historia Apollonii regis Tyri*
Apuleius, 13

Aristotle, 11–15, 17, 22, 23, 24, 39, 109–10, 146; *Categories*, 12, 14–15, 17, 18, 50; *De interpretatione*, 12–14, 18, 126; *Metaphysics*, 12; *Posterior Analytics*, 11; *Prior Analytics*, 11, 15; *Sophistici elenchi / Sophistical Refutations*, 12, 136–37, 140, 141; *Topics* 12, 15–16, 22
Arnaut Daniel, 66; II, 66; VII, 334 n. 36; VIII, 66; IX, 66, 334 n. 36; XV, 66; XVIII, 299
Arnaut de Maruelh, 66, 137–38, 335 n. 47, 335–36 n. 50; X, 66; XV, 131, 138–42; XVI, 66
Augustine, 10, 22, 24–5, 109–10, 114; *Confessions*, 19; *De doctrina Christiana*, 21, 24
Azalais de Porcairagues, 88

Bec, Pierre, 3–4, 5, 6, 7, 8, 47, 54
Benoît de Sainte Maure, *Le Roman de Troie*, 46, 48, 110–21, 143, 160, 161, 166–78, 232–41, 250, 256, 289–90, 311, 312
Bernardus Sylvestris, 20–21
Bernart de Ventadorn, 3–8, 57–62, 73, 151; II, 58; IV, 54; XIII, 47–48; XV, 48; XXVIII, 57–62; XXXVI, 4; XXXI, 4–7; XLII, 47

Bernart Marti, 44; IV, 131, 134–37, 140–41; VII, 135–36
Bezzola, Rheto R., 36–37, 305
Bible, The, 19–20, 21, 44, 245, 249–50, 347 n. 24
Bloch, R. Howard, 7–8, 180
Boethius, 12; *Commentary on Aristotle's Categories*, 14; *De consolatione Philosophiae*, 19; *De topicis differentiis*, 15–16, 52–53, 57, 290; translations of Aristotle, 11–12; translation of Porphyry, 12
Bond, Gerald A., 324–25 n. 58
Bourdieu, Pierre, 26
Brennan, Teresa, 307–8
Brown, Catherine, 19–20, 22
Bruckner, Mathilda Tomaryn, 8–9, 23

Carlson, David, 4–6, 7
Cercamon, 178, 335 nn. 46, 47, 336–37 n. 6; I, 131–35, 140–41
Chaucer, "The Prioress's Tale," 342 n. 13
Chrétien de Troyes, 22, 51–52, 53–54, 65; *Le Chevalier au lion* (*Yvain*), 18, 53–54, 73, 74, 85–86, 161, 176–78, 260, 265–75, 280–81, 284–91, 298–99, 302, 303, 309, 312, 313; *Le Chevalier de la Charrete* (*Lancelot*), 3, 8–11, 74, 81–95, 107–8, 303; *Cligès*, 49, 52, 63, 64, 73, 94, 95, 241–58, 263, 291, 299, 302, 303, 304, 305, 309, 312, 313; "D'Amors qui m'a tolu a moi," 329 n. 15; *Erec et Enide*, 22; hagiographic influence on 81–83, 88, 243, 248, 251–52, 286; lyric influence on, 54–55, 88–94. *See also* riddles
Cicero, 349 n. 15
contradiction, contradictoriness: in the cult of the Virgin Mary, 179–98; in Lacan, 26–36; in medieval thought, 11–22; the principle of noncontradiction, 13–14, 17, 19, 35, 41, 109; resolution of contradiction, 19–21, 68–70, 109–10, 122, 246–47, 252–53, 289–90. *See also* contrariety; contradictories; negative theology; object; paradox; privation; riddles; square of opposition
contrariety, 72–108; in Benoît de Sainte-Maure's *Roman de Troie*, 114–19, 169–70; in Clemence of Barking's *Life of Saint Catherine*, 126–27; in *Cligès*, 63, 246–47, 252–54; contraries versus contradictories, 12, 13–14, 40–41; in hagiography, 49–51, 55–57; in lyric, 47–48, 54–55, 57–62, 132–33, 147–52; in *Partonopeu de Blois*, 290–98; in romances in general, 63; in the *romans antiques* in general, 48–49; in Thomas's *Tristan*, 52–53; in *Yvain*, 53–54, 288–90
contradictories, negation, denial, 62–67, 69 in lyric, 60–63, 148; in romance, 63–66; in Thomas's *Tristan*, 119–21. *See also* contrariety
Colie, Rosalie L., 22–23
Corcoran, M. C., 156

Delcourt, Denise, 76
Derrida, Jacques, 26
"Desiré" (anonymous *lai*), 198
devinalh, *see* riddle
Dragonetti, Roger, 4

Eley, Penny, 98
Elias d'Ussel, 327 n. 27
Eneas, le Roman d', 46, 48–49, 63, 143, 160, 164–66, 174, 232–41, 246, 250, 256, 310, 312
Eriugena, 24
Etienne de Fougères, *Le Livre des manières*, 344 n. 33
Evans, Dylan, 218, 343 n. 26

fetishism, *see* object; perversion
Fish, Stanley, 25–26, 304
Florimont, 327 n. 28
Frappier, Jean, 8
Freud, Sigmund, 27, 28, 32, 154, 181

Geffrei Gaimar, *L'Estoire des Engleis*, 40
gender, 160–78, 307–10
Gilbert of Poitiers, 127
Giraut de Bornelh, 55, 88, 178; III, 89; IX, 89; XI, 89; XII 89; XXIII, 89; XXX, 89–94, 107–8; XXXVI, 89; LIV, 145, 147–48, 152, 155–57, 246; LIX, 329 n. 16
gradus amoris, 139
"Graelent" (anonymous *lai*), 198
Green, Denis, 10
Greimas, 4, 13, 23, 319 n. 1. See also square of opposition
Gruber, Jörn, 111, 130–31, 134, 141–42
Guernes de Pont-Sainte-Maxence, *see* Saint Thomas Becket
Gui d'Ussel, 327 n. 26
Guiette, Roger, 313–314
Guilhem Ademar: V, 63; XVI, 145, 152–53, 156, 337 n. 6
Guillem de Berguedà, "En Gauseran, gardatz," 145, 152–3, 156, 337 n. 6
Guilhem de Peitieu, 43–44, 178, 324–25 n. 58, 336 n. 6; II, 43; IV, 143, 145–47, 152, 155, 157–59, 295; V, 43; VII, 43, 131, 155; IX, 43; X, 43–44
Guilhem de Sant Leidier III, 88
"Guingamor" (anonymous *lai*), 198
Guy of Warwick, 328 n. 6

Hegel, Georg F. W., 39, 130–31, 300
Heidegger, Martin, 145, 153, 154, 159
Historia Apollonii regis Tyri, 336 n. 2
Huchet, Jean-Charles, 6–7
Hue de la Rotelande, *Ipomedon*, 63–64, 74, 94–105, 108, 288, 303, 310

Hugh of Saint Victor, 20
Hult, David, 10–11
Hunt, Tony, 17–18, 21, 53, 63

incest, *see* riddle
insolubilia, 111, 133–42
interpellation, 160–78
Ipomedon, *see* Hue de la Rotelande

Jaufré Rudel, 44, 47, 178; I, 131, 295, 336–37 n. 6, 337 n. 7
Jehan Bodel, *Les Saisnes*, 350 n. 6
John of Salisbury, *Metalogicon*, 12, 15, 16–19, 35, 48

Kant, Immanuel, 260–65, 298–99
Kantorowicz, Ernst H., 243
Köhler, Erich, 5–7, 8
Kristeva, Julia, 23, 26, 181–83, 188–90, 210, 213
Kruger, Steven, F. 21
Kunstmann, Pierre, 206, 208

Lacan, Jacques, 6, 39, 119, 144, 158, 161, 213, 216–18, 222, 233, 259–65, 283–84, 288, 298–99, 302–14; anamorphosis in, 269–71, 278–80; courtly love, 26–27, 38, 199, 259–60, 265, 308–9, 311–13; the formula of fantasy, 32–35, 265, 270–71, 297; the gaze 268–85, 287–88; historicism in, 26–27, 144, 157, 216; the logic of the veil, 201–05, 263, 282; *jouissance* (enjoyment), 218, 255–56, 258, 263, 298, 305, 310–14; *objet a*, 32–35, 37, 270, 297, 298, 310; real, 29–30, 31–32, 186, 217–18, 262, 270–71, 339 n. 20; "receiving one's message in inverted form," 30–31, 287, 340 n. 41; schema L, 27–29, 172, 348 n. 7; the Thing, 144, 153–59, 199, 216, 231, 252, 257, 261–63, 270, 324 n. 50, 346 n. 16. *See also* contradiction;

interpellation; object; perversion; riddle; sublimation; "zone between the two deaths"
Lawner, Lynne, 152, 156
Legge, Dominica, 206
Levenson, J. L., 233
Lewis, C. S., 9

Maimonides, 24
Mannoni, Octave, 347 n. 28
Marcabru, 44, 49, 54, 55, 79, 84, 88, 108, 150, 328–29 n. 8; VI, 47; VII, 79–81, 93; XI, 151; XVIII, 338 n. 14; XIX, 49; XXIV, 79; XXXI, 49, 79; XXXIV, 334 n. 36; XXXVI, 334 n. 36; XLII, 134; XLIV, 338 n. 14
Marie de France, *Lais*, 52, 180 198–215, 302; "Fresne," 198, 203–5; "Guigemar," 343–44 n. 29; "Lanval," 198–203, 263, 285, 299, 305, 308, 312; "Laüstic," 239; "Les Deus Amanz," 344 n. 31; "Milun," 209, 212; "Yonec," 208, 212–13
Marshall, John, 60–61
Matthew of Vendôme, 11
McCracken, Peggy, 243–45, 248
Méla, Charles, 8
middle term (in logic), 15, 101
Montan (et una domna), 327 n. 27

negative theology, 23–24, 31–32, 109
Neoplatonism, 19–22, 109, 114, 118, 332 n. 15
"New Logic" 11–12, 15, 35, 71, 110, 136
Nicodemus, Gospel of, 9

object, 180–83, 199, 257, 264, 302–03, 304, 307–11, 348 n. 6; in fantasy, 160–61, 174–76, 270; as fetish, 182–83, 200–205, 213–15, 302, 343 n. 26, 343 n. 28; "man thinks with his object," 32, 302, 309; as perverse

263–65, 274–75, 297–99, 302; as phobic, 181–98, 201–2, 213–15, 302; in schema L, 27–29; as sublime, 216–58, 261–62, 264–68, 273, 284, 297–99; versus subject in the *devinalh*, 152–59; versus subject in the *romans antiques*, 163–70. *See also* abject; Kristeva; Lacan; perversion; sublimation; voice
"Old Logic," 12. *See also* "New Logic"
Orderic Vitalis, *Ecclesiastical History*, 37, 327 n. 29
Owen, D. D. R., 9

paradox, 2–3, 16, 22–23, 40–46; in hagiography, 41–43, 75–76, 122–24; in the *romans antiques*, 45–46, 170; in troubadour lyric, 43–44, 146–47. *See also insolubilia*
paradoxe amoureux, le, *see* Spitzer, Leo
Partonopeu de Blois, 65, 73, 74, 260, 275–88, 290–99, 302, 303, 304, 308, 309, 310 312, 313, 331 n. 6
Pasero, Nicolò, 152
Passion of Clermont-Ferrand, 341 n. 1
Peire Cardenal, LXXX, 337 n. 6
Peire d'Alvernha, 44, 55
Peire de Galceran, *see* Guillem de Berguedà
Peire Rogier: VII, 62; VIII, 88
Peire Vidal, 108, 296; III, 88; XXIII, 66; XXVI, 66; XXXVII, 66, 102–3; XL, 325 n. 10; XLII, 66, 103–5; XLV, 62
Peirol, "Peirol, cum avetz tant estat?", 58–62
perversion, 258, 259–65, 280–85, 312–14; fetishism, 237–39, 242, 254–55, 280, 283–84, 320 n. 7, 347 n. 28; homoeroticism, 287, 310, 344–45 n. 38, 345 n. 11; voyeurism, 271–74, 282–84. *See also* object
Plato, *Phaedo*, 338 n. 11
Porphyry, *Isagoge*, 12, 18, 333 n. 21

Poundstone, William, 25
Priest, Graham, 24, 39
privation, 14, 50

Raimbaut d'Aurenga, 55, 88, 178; XXIV, 145, 147–48, 152, 155, 337 n. 6; XXXI, 329 n. 16
Raimbaut de Vaqueiras 296; III, 327 n. 25; VII, 62; IX, 325 n. 10, 333–37 n. 6; XXVI, 145, 148–52, 156–59, 248, 337 n. 6, 346 n. 21
Renaut de Beaujeu, *Li Biaus Desconneüs*, 65, 330 n. 28
Ribard, Jacques, 10
riddles, 142–78, 303; in *Ipomedon*, 100–102; in Lacan, 154–55, 170–75; in lyric (*devinalh*), 143, 145–52; in Mary miracles and saints' lives, 195–98; in the *romans antiques*, 162–63; incest as riddle, 197–98; presence of *devinalh* in romances, 178, 245–46, 247, 248, 254, 295, 339 n. 30
Rieger, Dietmar, 178
Robert of Melun, 17
Robertson, D. W. Jr., 9–10, 21
Rollo, David, 239

Sade, le Marquis de, 217–19, 226, 256, 260–65, 270
Saint Alexis, Life of, 52, 67, 73–108; *A* version, 74; *L* version, 74–77, 106–7, 303; Middle English version, 328 n. 6; *Saint Brendan, Life of,* 40; *S* version, 105–8, 328 n. 30
Saint Catherine: *Life of St Catherine* (by Clemence of Barking), 60, 110–11, 122–30, 142, 219–20, 222, 223–24, 229, 230–31, 258; *Life of St Catherine* (Manchester version), 332 n. 19; *Passio S. Katerine*, 124–30
Saint Edmund, Life of, (by Denis Piramus) 207

Saint Eulalia, Sequence of, 220, 222, 226–27
Saint Eustace, Life of, 306
Saint Evroul, Life of, 67–70
Saint Faith, Life of, 41, 220, 221–22, 226, 229, 230
Saint Genevieve, Life of, 67
Saint George, Life of (by Simund de Freine), 60, 122, 220, 222, 224–26, 229, 231, 258
Saint Giles, Life of, (by Guillaume de Berneville) 67, 122
Saint Gregory, Life of, 197, 206
Saint Lawrence, Life of, 60, 122, 220, 223, 229, 230, 231, 251, 258
Saint Leger, Life of, 41, 42–3, 49, 67
Saint Margaret: *Life of Saint Margaret* (by Wace), 220, 220–21, 222–23, 227–28, 251, 258
Saint Mary the Egyptian, Life of, 73, 286, 341 n. 1
Saint Mary the Virgin, 179–99; *Conception Nostre Dame* (by Wace), 179, 195, 347 n. 22; *De Laudibus* (by William of Malmesbury), 183, 205, 207–8; *Deuxième collection anglonormande*, 183; *Le Gracial* (by Adgar), 179, 183–93, 196–97, 203, 205–15; *Miracles de Nostre Dame* (by Gautier de Coinci), 179, 193, 197–98; Occitan miracles, 193–95; Occitan rhymed prayers, 179, 195; *Rocamador* cycle, 342 n. 11; *Treize miracles de Notre-Dame, tirés du Ms. B.N. fr. 2094*, 341 n.2, 342 nn. 10, 18; "Un Miracle de Notre Dame: La Juive de Narbonne Convertie," 194, 343 n. 20
Saint Nicholas, Life of (by Wace), 184
Saint Stephen, "Epître farcie," 41
Saint Thomas Becket: *Life of St Thomas Becket* (by Guernes de Pont-Sainte-

Maxence), 49–51, 55–57, 60, 306; *Life of St Thomas Becket* (by Beneit), 55–57, 60, 69, 306
Scaglione, Aldo, 312
sophistry, 100–102
Sophocles, *Antigone* 217–19, 256
Southern, Richard, 207
Spitzer, Leo, 2, 5, 21, 299
square of opposition, 13–14, 23, 110, 113–14; in relation to Lacan's schema L, 27–29; in relation to Benoit de Sainte Maure's *Troie* and Thomas's *Tristan*, 113–121
sublimation 154–155, 157–9, 216–265. See also Lacan: formula of fantasy; object; perversion
"Sui e no suy," 337 n. 6
Sullivan, Penny, 111

Taylor, Archer, 143–44
Thebes, Roman de, 45–46, 143, 160–64, 170–78, 197, 305, 312
Theophilus, 341 n. 1, 343 n. 20, 343 n. 22

Thomas, *Tristan*, 50, 51–53, 65, 74, 76–84, 108, 258, 328 n. 8
Thomas Becket, 12. See also Saint Thomas Becket, Lives of
Troie, Roman de, see Benoît de Sainte Maure

Vance, Eugene, 17–18, 21, 22
Vincent of Beauvais, *Speculum Historiale*, 342 n. 18
Virgin Mary, see Saint Mary the Virgin
voice, 269, 275, 281, 341 n. 46. See also Lacan: the gaze

Wace *Le Roman de Rou*, 183. See also Saint Margaret; Saint Mary the Virgin; Saint Nicolas

Žižek, 26, 33, 89, 216–19, 237, 259–60, 264, 285, 297, 304, 313–14; "*the things themselves believe for them*," 237
"zone between the two deaths," the 216–58, 286
Zumthor, Paul, 4

FIGURAE: READING MEDIEVAL CULTURE

Sarah Kay, *Courtly Contradictions: The Emergence of the Literary Object in the Twelfth Century*
Bruce Holsinger, *Music, Body, and Desire in Medieval Culture*
Rainer Warning, *The Ambivalences of Medieval Religious Drama*
Virginia Burrus, *'Begotten, Not Made': Conceiving Manhood in Late Antiquity*
Peter S. Hawkins, *Dante's Testaments: Essays in Scriptural Imagination*
Daniel Boyarin, *Dying for God: Martyrdom and the Making of Christianity and Judaism*
Catherine Brown, *Contrary Things: Exegesis, Dialectic, and the Poetics of Didacticism*
Paul Freedman, *The Image of the Medieval Peasant as Alien and Exemplary*
James F. Burke, *Desire Against the Law: The Juxtaposition of Contraries in Early Medieval Spanish Literature*
Armando Petrucci, translated by Michael Sullivan, *Writing the Dead: Death and Writing Strategies in the Western Tradition*
Renate Blumenfeld-Kosinski, *Reading Myth: Classical Mythology and Its Interpretations in Medieval French Literature*
Paul Saenger, *Space Between Words: The Origins of Silent Reading*
David Wallace, *Chaucerian Polity: Absolutist Lineages and Associational Forms in England and Italy*
Sylvia Huot, *Allegorical Play in the Old French Motet: The Sacred and the Profane in Thirteenth-Century Polyphony*
Ralph Hanna III, *Pursuing History: Middle English Manuscripts and Their Texts*
Theresa Tinkle, *Medieval Venuses and Cupids: Sexuality, Hermeneutics, and English Poetry*
Seth Lerer, ed., *Literary History and the Challenge of Philology: The Legacy of Erich Auerbach*

Martha G. Newman, *The Boundaries of Charity: Cistercian Culture and Ecclesiastical Reform, 1098–1180*

Brigitte Cazelles, *The Unholy Grail: A Social Reading of Chrétien de Troyes's 'Conte du Graal'*

John Kleiner, *Mismapping the Underworld: Daring and Error in Dante's 'Comedy'*

M. Victoria Guerin, *The Fall of Kings and Princes: Structure and Destruction in Arthurian Tragedy*